WASEDA University Academic Series —— **060**

Semantic Externalism and Cognitive Linguistics

Tomohiro Sakai

Waseda University Press

Semantic Externalism and Cognitive Linguistics

SAKAI Tomohiro, Ph.D, is Professor of linguistics at the Faculty of Letters, Arts and Sciences at Waseda University.

First published in 2024 by
Waseda University Press Co., Ltd.
1-9-12 Nishiwaseda
Shinjuku-ku, Tokyo 169-0051
www.waseda-up.co.jp

© 2024 by Tomohiro Sakai

All rights reserved. Except for short extracts used for academic purposes or book reviews, no part of this publication may be reproduced, stored in a retrieval system or transmitted in any form whatsoever—electronic, mechanical, photocopying or otherwise—without the prior and written permission of the publisher.

ISBN978-4-657-24701-8

Printed in Japan

Preface

Externalism is the philosophical thesis that meaning and mental content are partly dependent for their individuation on one's environment. If externalism is true, then two speakers who are molecule-for-molecule identical may nevertheless have different thoughts and mean different things by employing exactly the same word forms. Externalism and its implications have not received sufficient attention in the linguistics literature. The goal of this book is to investigate the relationships between externalism and cognitive linguistics.

Literally interpreted, this purpose would certainly be impossible for me (or perhaps for anyone, for that matter) to achieve in one book. A glance at the internalism/externalism debate reveals that "there is no shortage of differences even within the externalist camp" (McGeer 1994: 431). The statement applies equally to the internalist camp (cf. Katz 1972, 1978, 1997). Gottlob Frege once employed the funny phrase "my Pythagorean theorem" (*mein pythagoreischer Lehrsatz*) in order to emphasize that a thought (*Gedanke*), unlike an idea (*Vorstellung*), can be shared by several people and needs no particular bearer (Frege 1918-1919a: 68/1956: 301). Akeel Bilgrami uses – sincerely, in my opinion – the phrase "my externalism" (Bilgrami 1992: 4ff), suggesting that there is no externalism *tout court* embraced by all externalists. This book focuses on the relationships between Hilary Putnam's (1973, 1985) and Tyler Burge's (1979a/2007, 1982/2007, 1986a/2007) externalism on the one hand, and Ronald W. Langacker's cognitive linguistics on the other. Although the origins of externalism can and must be traced back to earlier authors (Rowland et al. 2020), Putnam and Burge are indisputably the initiators of the current debate on externalism. Although cognitive linguistics has no single founder, few would hesitate to count Langacker among its founders. I hope that comparing Putnam and Burge with Langacker will offer readers a perspective from which they can best apprehend the interface between analytic philosophy and linguistic semantics.

There is presumably no relation between Putnam and Burge on the one hand,

and Langacker on the other, if the word 'relation' is construed as 'historical relation'. To the best of my knowledge, Langacker has never cited Putnam or Burge, or vice versa. Therefore, this book explores the implications of Putnam's and Burge's externalist arguments on Langacker's cognitive linguistics, in total independence of what these authors (do not) say about this issue. The guiding principle behind my enterprise is that, as Boyd (2013: 217) puts it, "a researcher will need to participate in the inferential practices of more than one research community in order to address an important scientific question".

The title of this book is somewhat misleading in two respects. First, externalism discussed in this work is the view that not only semantic content but also mental content is externally determined. This view is called 'content externalism' (Rowland et al. 2020) or 'mental externalism' (Liu 2002: 388) as opposed to 'vehicle externalism', a thesis concerning the bearer of mental content (Rowland et al. 2020). Second, externalism is not the view that semantic content and mental content are outside the subject who entertains the content. At stake is how the content is to be individuated, rather than where the content is to be found. The externalist thesis thus construed would be better characterized by the term 'anti-individualism', as Burge calls it. For the sake of intelligibility, however, I chose the term 'semantic externalism' in place of '(content) externalism' or 'anti-individualism'.

I am heavily indebted to the participants in the lectures I delivered at the Tokyo Institute for Advanced Studies of Language in 2018, 2019, 2021, 2022 and 2023 among others, where some of the references cited in this book were put under close scrutiny. All remaining errors are, of course, mine.

I would also like to thank the Editorial Board of *Tokyo University Linguistic Papers* for permission to reproduce portions of the material for this book.

This work was supported by JSPS KAKENHI #18K00551 and #22K00540.

Tomohiro Sakai

Contents

Preface i

Chapter 1 The (Lack of) Impact of Externalism on Cognitive Linguistics 1

    1.1 The Internalist Turn in Linguistics 1

    1.2 Internalism in Philosophy 11

           1.2.1 Intension and Extension   11

           1.2.2 Sense and Reference   13

    1.3 Externalism 24

           1.3.1 Physical Externalism   24

           1.3.2 Social Externalism   30

           1.3.3 What Externalism Is Not (Necessarily)   36

           1.3.4 (Ir)relevance of Externalism to Linguistics   55

Chapter 2 Social Externalism and Prototype Semantics 79

    2.1 Partial Compatibility of Social Externalism and Cognitive Linguistics ... 79

    2.2 Social Externalism and Incomplete Understanding 80

    2.3 Incomplete Understanding of Concepts 81

    2.4 Sawyer's (2003) Objection to Wikforss (2001): 'sofa' 87

    2.5 Conceptual or Analytic Truth 94

           2.5.1 Incomplete Understanding and Conceptual Truth   94

           2.5.2 Overview of Quine's Criticism of the Analytic-Synthetic
                  Distinction   98

           2.5.3 One-Criterion Words, Nominal Kind Words and Cluster Words
                  104

    2.6 Prototypes and Incomplete Understanding 113

            2.6.1 A Forever Absolutely True Synthetic Statement   113

2.6.2 Prototype Semantics and Cognitive Linguistics   118

2.6.3 Conclusion and Qualification   125

Chapter 3 Incomplete Understanding and Construal 135

3.1 Twin Cases and Frege Cases 135

3.2 Prototype and Concept or Epistemology and Metaphysics.....................137

3.3 Conceptual Content vs. Construal 140

3.4 Construal and Frege's Sense 153

3.5 Frege's Constraint and Incomplete Understanding.....................165

3.6 Identity and Distinctness of Concepts 183

3.7 Minimal Semantic Competence.....................192

     3.7.1 General Characterization of Minimal Semantic Competence with General Terms   192

     3.7.2 One-criterion Terms   193

     3.7.3 Nominal Kind Terms   198

     3.7.4 Cluster Terms   200

3.8 Incomplete Understanding as a Basis of Construal.....................203

Chapter 4 Deferential Construal.....................211

4.1 Different Construals vs. Same Concept 211

4.2 Frege Cases and *De Jure* Coreference 214

4.3 Construal and Mutual Understanding 226

     4.3.1 Identity in Form   226

     4.3.2 One-to-Many Correspondence Between Form and Construal   229

     4.3.3 Similarity in Construal   239

4.4 Deference.....................246

     4.4.1 Division of Linguistic Labor   246

     4.4.2 Recanati's (1997) Deferential Operator   249

4.4.3 Deferential Construal   255

4.4.4 Deferential Construal and Identity of a Concept   267

Chapter 5 Physical Externalism and Polysemy 277

5.1 Social Externalism vs. Physical Externalism..277

5.2 Deference and Physical Externalism..284

5.3 The (Un)importance of the Putative Underlying Structure 290

5.3.1 Physical Externalist Metasemantics vs. Philosophy of Science   290

5.3.1.1 The Physical Externalist Metasemantics   290

5.3.1.2 The *Qua* Problem   294

5.3.1.3 The Vacuity of the Sameness Relation   297

5.3.2 Physical Externalist Semantics vs. Linguistic Semantics   307

5.3.2.1 Relevance of Interests   307

5.3.2.2 Linguistic Arguments for and against Essentialism   310

5.4 The Polysemy of 'water' 318

5.4.1 Partial Semantic Representation of 'Water'   318

5.4.2 Meaning Change and Theory Change   333

5.5 Cognitive Linguistics and Physical Externalist Intuition 338

5.5.1 Quintessentialism   338

5.5.2 Deference to Future Usage   342

5.5.3 Coherence Raising   348

Epilogue 355

References...357

Index (item / person name) 376

Chapter I

The (Lack of) Impact of Externalism on Cognitive Linguistics

This chapter explores why little has been written and much has been misunderstood by linguists about externalism and concludes that, although linguistics has generally opted for internalism or individualism, no decisive argument has been adduced to demonstrate that everything about externalism is irrelevant to linguistics.

1.1 The Internalist Turn in Linguistics[1]

'Bachelor' is one of the best-known words in the linguistics literature. 'Arthritis' is one of the most renowned terms in the philosophy literature. While the word 'bachelor' also figures prominently in philosophical debates (Quine 1960: §10ff, Hull 1965: 323, Devitt and Sterelney 1999: 189, 307, Brown 2004: 22, Chalmers 2012: 4-6, Haukioja 2015: 2144-2147, Valente 2019, to name a few), linguists are largely unfamiliar with 'arthritis'. There is good reason for this. Unfamiliarity with 'arthritis' is synonymous with unfamiliarity with externalism, whereas familiarity with 'bachelor' translates into familiarity with internalism. In the 1970s, analytic philosophy witnessed an externalist turn, where, as will be discussed below, the word 'arthritis' played a significant role (Burge 1979a). Prior to that period, the discipline had long been dominated by the internalist conception of meaning and concept. The synonymy between 'bachelor' and 'unmarried man', which fluent speakers of English are expected to know, was commonly assumed to substantiate the internalist conception. Conversely, linguistics witnessed an internalist turn in the 1950s (Chomsky 1957, 1965), which made 'bachelor' a canonical example of a lexical item whose meaning is internally represented in the minds of fluent speakers (Katz and Fodor 1963, Bolinger 1965). Internalism was so firmly entrenched

---

1) Section 1.1 elaborates on Sakai (2022a: Section 2).

in linguistics that 'arthritis' had scant opportunity to breach the boundary between the two scholarly territories. Further complicating the matter is that it was not externalism but a position called 'mechanism', stemming from American structuralism (Bloomfield 1933), which was overturned by the internalist conception of language (Harris 1993). Neither in mechanism nor in internalism has 'arthritis' had no distinctive role to play.

American structuralism repudiated nonphysical or mentalistic notions such as thought, concept, image or feeling, because, as Bloomfield (1933: 143) emphasized, "[t]he mental processes or internal bodily processes of other people are known to each one of us only from speech-utterances and other observable actions". Since detailed observations underline scientific investigation, the empirical study of language should begin with, or even focus on, observable actions including speech-utterances, and only by observing these actions can we construct an illuminating theory of language. It is thus gratuitous to base the theory of language on unobservable mental processes. Bloomfields's repudiation of mentalistic notions is evident in his review of Paul's *Principles*:

> [...] The other great weakness of Paul's *Principles* is his insistence upon "psychological" interpretation. He accompanies his statements about language with a paraphrase in terms of mental processes which the speakers are supposed to have undergone. The only evidence for these mental processes is the linguistic process; they add nothing to the discussion, but only obscure it. (Bloomfield 1933: 17)

For the structuralist, the science of language only becomes possible when one embraces the standpoint of mechanism (as opposed to mentalism), which considers human actions including speech production and understanding "part of cause-and-effect sequences exactly like those which we observe, say in the study of physics or chemistry" (Bloomfield 1933: 33). The mechanist maintains that "mental images, feelings, and the like are merely popular terms for various bodily movements" (ibid.: 142). Bloomfield's mechanism was fueled by behavioral psychology, founded by John B. Watson, according to which psychology is not the science of mind or consciousness but the science of human behavior (Harris 1993: 24-25). Behaviorism considers language to consist first and foremost of directly observable bodily movements through which strings of sound are produced for the purpose of communication. Language enables human societies to function and allows individuals to interact interpersonally:

> *Language enables one person to make a reaction (R) when another person has the stimulus (S).* (Bloomfield 1933: 24, italics in the original)

> *The division of labor, and, with it, the whole working of human society, is due to language.* (Bloomfield 1933: 24, italics in the original)

> *The gap between the bodies of the speaker and the hearer — the discontinuity of the two nervous systems — is bridged by the sound-wave.* (Bloomfield 1933: 27, italics in the original)

On the behaviorist construal, the meaning of a linguistic form is best characterized as "the situation in which the speaker utters it and the response which it calls forth in the hearer" (Bloomfield 1933: 139). According to Harris (1993: 26), "mentalism in psychology and linguistics went the way of vitalism in biology, phlogiston in chemistry, ether in physics", and other similar superseded theses. Bloomfield acknowledged that defining meanings along this line is an extremely difficult task and that "the linguist cannot define meanings, but must appeal for this to students of other sciences or to common knowledge" (ibid.: 145). He was pessimistic about the prospect of a scientific study of meaning being conducted within the confines of linguistics:

> The statement of meanings is therefore the weak point in language-study, and will remain so until human knowledge advances very far beyond its present state. In practice, we define the meaning of a linguistic form, wherever we can, in terms of some other science. (Bloomfield 1933: 140)

> Any utterance can be fully described in terms of lexical and grammatical forms; we must remember only that the meanings cannot be defined in terms of our science. (Bloomfield 1933: 167)

Skinner (1948/1957) made "the most extensive attempt to accommodate human behavior involving higher mental faculties within a strict behaviorist schema of the type that has attracted many linguists and philosophers, as well as psychologists" (Chomsky 1959: 28). Skinner (1948: 3) targeted structural linguistics when he complained that "[t]he linguist has not developed a central science of verbal behavior because his interests have lain elsewhere". Beginning with "the muscular behavior of the speaker", namely, "the only observable datum with which a descriptive science of verbal behavior can begin" (ibid.: 10), Skinner attempts to characterize verbal behavior in terms of behavioristic notions such as stimulus, response, generalization and reinforcement, "without setting up any principle or process not already established in the field of nonverbal behavior" (ibid.: 164). Thus, he claims that "the concept of meaning is less confusing when it is used in connection with the behavior of the listener" (ibid.: 128).

In the mid-twentieth century, the mechanist or behavioristic conception of language was overturned by generative linguistics. Chomsky's influential review of Skinner (1948/1957) contended that the use of behavioristic apparatus in the study of verbal behavior is "entirely pointless and empty", because verbal behavior is a product of "the grammar that each individual has somehow and in some form internalized" (Chomsky 1959: 56). Thus, for the generativist, the science of language aims to discover the mental reality that underlies human behavior:

> The problem for the linguist, as well as for the child learning the language, is to determine from the data of performance the underlying system of rules that has been mastered by the speaker-hearer and that he puts to use in actual performance. Hence, in the technical sense, linguistic theory is mentalistic, since it is concerned with discovering a mental reality underlying actual behavior. Observed use of language or hypothesized dispositions to respond, habits, and so on, may provide evidence as to the nature of this mental reality, but surely cannot constitute the actual subject matter of linguistics, if this is to be a serious discipline. (Chomsky 1965: 4)

In this perspective, society and communication disappear from the frame and are replaced by the mind and cognition. The primary object of linguistics in the mentalistic conception of language is the mind, or, more specifically, the language faculty, of competent language users. Chomsky (1986: 22ff, 1995: 13, 2000: 26) refers to a person's language faculty as 'I-language', where 'I' means 'internal', 'individual' and 'intensional'. As Chomsky (2003a: 270) makes clear, I-language was simply called 'grammar' in his earlier works, but he soon recognized that this usage of the word 'grammar' was confusing, because, like other terms denoting mental states, it referenced both the internal state of an individual's faculty of language and the

Chapter 1   The (Lack of) Impact of Externalism on Cognitive Linguistics

linguist's theory of that state. Therefore, Chomsky decided to restrict his use of 'grammar' to the linguist's theory and invented the term 'I-language' for the individual's internal state as described by the linguist. In Chomsky's (1986: 19-20) terms, what Bloomfield (1933) regarded as language is nothing but 'E-language' or externalized language. If E-language is the primary object of linguistic descriptions, as Bloomfield assumed, grammar becomes a "derivative notion" and "the linguist is free to select the grammar one way or another as long as it correctly identifies the E-language" (Chomsky 1986: 20). Therefore, generative grammar shifted the focus of attention "from the study of E-language to the study of I-language, from the study of language regarded as an externalized object to the study of the system of knowledge of language attained and internally represented in the mind/brain" (ibid.: 24). This shift was partly motivated by the fact that "there is nothing in the world selected by such terms as 'Chinese', or 'German', or even much narrower ones" (Chomsky 1995: 48-49, 2000: 155). Notions such as Chinese or German are ultimately defined based on national boundaries demarcated for reasons external to scientific inquiry. Chomsky's position must not be confused with the claim that grammar is completely disconnected from the social lives of speakers, which is "an absurd idea, advocated by no one" (Chomsky 1995: 49, 2000: 156). Rather, Chomsky claims that what is externalized in the social lives of speakers is systematically related to their inner states (Chomsky 2000: 164, 2003b: 259). Chomsky fully acknowledges that "language engages the world" (ibid.). He is merely skeptical of the view that the basic function of natural languages is mediating communication (Chomsky 2000: 30). It is questionable, Chomsky suggests, that any biological system has what can plausibly be referred to as a basic function, and, *a fortiori*, that communication occupies this privileged position (ibid.). Furthermore, there is a danger that the study of communication, which is "far too complex" (ibid.: 70), will lead to "the study of everything" (ibid.: 69). Such broad inquiries would presuppose findings about the inner states of individuals (ibid.: 164). Attention should therefore be focused on the I-language, which, according to Ludlow (2003a: 144), is "part of an agent's psychology, and ultimately part of the agent's biology".

Internalism or individualism has been a productive approach to syntax and phonology, each of which constitutes a computational system. As Wilson (2003: 261) remarks, "insofar as mental states were computational, broader considerations about the physical or social worlds in which an individual is located seem irrelevant to that individual's psychological nature"[2]. Burge, one of the most committed

5

proponents of externalism or anti-individualism, concedes that the Chomskyan approach to the study of syntax and phonology captures "part of individual psychology" (Burge 2007: 24):

> [Chomsky's] accounts of the relevance of syntax and phonology to unconscious psychological states, of the large role of innateness in language development, of the universality of many specific linguistic structures, and of the modular character of linguistic abilities – all these have helped provide a specific shape to our understanding of mind. (Burge 2003: 451; see also 467)

While syntactic and phonological systems can be characterized in internalist or individualistic terms, it remains uncertain whether internalism or individualism can accommodate the semantics of natural language (Burge 1982: 112-113/2007: 95-96, Burge 1989: 180-181/2007: 282-283, Fauconnier 1997: 5-6). Intuitively, meaning mediates an individual's interpersonal interactions and engagements with the world. There seems thus to be no *a priori* reason to assume that meaning can be studied without any allusion to aspects of the world surrounding an individual. This explains why, as Chomsky (1995: 41, 2000: 148) remarks, "the internalism-externalism issues arise [...] only for the theory of meaning, not for phonology". As will be discussed below, Chomsky explicitly denies the relevance of the internalism-externalism debate to the study of language he envisages. Further complicating the issue is that Chomsky is even skeptical of the existence of semantics as we commonly understand it:

> As for semantics, insofar as we understand language use, the argument for a reference-based semantics (apart from an internalist syntactic version) seems to me weak. It is possible that natural language has only syntax and pragmatics; it has a "semantics" only in the sense of "the study of how this instrument, whose formal structure and potentialities of expression are the subject of syntactic investigation, is actually put to use in a speech community", to quote the earliest formulation in generative grammar 40 years ago, influenced by Wittgenstein, Austin and others (Chomsky ([1975], Preface), and Chomsky

---

2) As against this, Ludlow (2003b) argues that the logical form of an utterance may plausibly be considered sensitive to the environment in which it is tokened. On this view, neither content nor form can be studied in total isolation from the physical or social worlds in which an individual is located.

(1957, pp. 102-3). (Chomsky 1995: 26-27, 2000: 132)

Given that, for Chomsky, natural language only encompasses syntax and pragmatics, communication should not be described in semantic terms:

> Successful communication between Peter and Mary does not entail the existence of shared meanings or shared pronunciations in a public language (or a common treasure of thoughts or articulations of them), any more than physical resemblance between Peter and Mary entails the existence of a public form that they share. (Chomsky 2000: 30)

As suggested by Ludlow (2003a), these statements have yielded the impression that Chomsky denies all talk of semantics:

> It is widely assumed that Noam Chomsky is hostile towards semantics, and at least in the oral tradition, it is supposed that this hostility carries over to virtually everything that goes by the name 'semantics,' including lexical semantics and model-theoretic semantics. This latter supposition is entirely mistaken, and it appears to reflect a confusion about precisely what kinds of semantic theories Chomsky objects to. (Ludlow 2003a: 140)

For our present purposes we need not go into the question Ludlow raises toward the end of the quoted passage, because, as stated earlier, Chomsky is uninterested in the internalist/externalist debate[3]. What is important at this stage is that the internalist turn in linguistics did not innovate the study of semantics as much as the study of syntax. As Harris (1993: 249) puts it, Chomsky "retains the general Bloomfieldian dogma that meaning will never be allowed in the driver's seat". In the 1970s, Putnam (1975: 131) praised the achievements of generative grammar but deplored that "[t]he dimension of language associated with the word 'meaning' is, in spite of the usual spate of heroic if misguided attempts, as much in the dark as it ever was". The title of Putnam's paper published in 1970, 'Is Semantics Possible?', reveals that pessimism dominated the domain even after the cognitive turn brought about by generative linguistics (cf. Chomsky 2000: 175/2003: 268).

---

3) However, Chomsky (1995, 2000) addresses some related issues, which will be discussed in Chapter 5.

Some might think that the situation improved drastically due to the subsequent development of cognitive linguistics, a framework consisting primarily of cognitive grammar and cognitive semantics (Fauconnier 1985/1994, 1997, Lakoff 1987, Langacker 1987, 2008, Sweetser 1990, among others). This paradigm originated in generative semantics (Lakoff 1976[1963]), a movement launched by some of Chomsky's colleagues and students against what Jackendoff (2002: 33) calls "syntacticocentrism", an assumption "preserved in every subsequent version of Chomskyan theory" (ibid.: 108). In fact, some attempts were made in the 1960s to develop an internalist semantic theory within the generative framework. Nevertheless, these excessively restrictive attempts strained against the intuitive notion of meaning. Thus, Katz and Fodor (1963: 173-174) imposed the condition stated in (1) on the proper subject matter of linguistic theory:

(1) If speakers possess an ability that enables them to apprehend the structure of any sentence in the infinite set of sentences of a language without reference to information about settings and without significant variation from speaker to speaker, then that ability is properly the subject matter of a synchronic theory in linguistics. (Katz and Fodor 1963: 173-174)

Given this condition, we must, Katz and Fodor claim, seek for "an ability of speakers which cannot be accounted for by grammar, which is semantic in a reasonable sense, and which enables speakers to apprehend the semantic structure of an infinite number of sentences without information about setting and independent of individual differences between speakers" (ibid.: 176). Whatever the plausibility of such an enterprise, it is clear enough that the notion of meaning assumed by Katz and Fodor in no way exhausts the intuitive notion of meaning, since a person receiving an utterance generally exploits information about the setting in which the utterance is made. In fact, Katz and Fodor were fully aware of the incompleteness of their theory in setting their goal as "describe[ing] and explain[ing] the interpretative ability of speakers by accounting for their performance in determining the number and content of the readings of a sentence, by detecting semantic anomalies, by deciding on paraphrase relations between sentences, and by marking every other semantic property or relation that plays a role in this ability" (ibid.: 176). Katz and Fodor's parsimonious approach to meaning was motivated by the fact that any account of the ways in which contextual settings contribute to the understanding of utterances would mandate the systematic representation of the

Chapter 1   The (Lack of) Impact of Externalism on Cognitive Linguistics

entire worldly knowledge of the speakers (ibid.: 178-181). For example, in normal settings, 'alligator shoes' (2a) is interpreted as 'shoes made from alligator skins', while 'horse shoes' in (2b) is understood as 'shoes for horses'.

(2)   a. Our store sells alligator shoes.
       b. Our store sells horse shoes. ((2a-b): Katz and Fodor 1963: 178)

The selection of these correct interpretations from all the potentially available ones would require us to represent the fact that horses, but not alligators, wear shoes, along with the fact that shoes for people are sometimes made from alligator skin but never from the skin of horses (ibid.: 178-179). Katz and Fodor cite several other examples and conclude that the systematization of the entire relevant knowledge is infeasible and that the alleged complete theory "is ipso facto not a serious model for semantics" (ibid.: 179). In short, "a COMPLETE theory of this kind is impossible" (ibid.: 179, emphasis in the original). According to Katz and Fodor, any internalist theory is essentially equivalent to a parsimonious theory, as far as semantics is concerned,.

Dissatisfied with such a restrictive conception of meaning, Lakoff (1976[1963]) set out to develop a comprehensive semantic theory disposing of rules that did not "entirely depend on syntax" or were even "free of syntax" (ibid.: 45). His efforts resulted in a framework called generative semantics. Lakoff (1987: 582) character- izes cognitive semantics as "an updated version of generative semantics", even though not all scholars subscribe to this description (Langacker 1987: 4)[4]. Cognitive linguistics diverges from the generative tradition, declaring that "[m]eaning is what language is all about" (Langacker 1987: 12). Any description of syntactic phenomena in isolation from semantic considerations is defective in principle, because "[g]rammar is simply the structuring and symbolization of semantic content" (ibid.). In addition, contrary to Katz and Fodor's (1963: 178)

---

4) Langacker takes a more cautious stance toward the relationship between generative semantics and cognitive grammar:

> Cognitive grammar is not in any significant sense an outgrowth of generative semantics, but it does share with that conception a concern for dealing explicitly with meaning, and for providing a unified account of grammar and lexicon [...] (Langacker 1987: 4)

Langacker was skeptic of the generative semantic assumption that semantic representations are universal even before he elaborated his theory of cognitive grammar, (Langacker 1976: 317, 330, 355).

9

assumption that "the readings that a speaker gives a sentence in a setting are a selection from those which it has in isolation", cognitive linguistics even denies that the relationships between meaning and context can be the proper subject matter of any empirical inquiry, for the simple reason that meaning can never be efficiently divorced from the setting, According to Fauconnier (1985/1994, 1997), "language theory suffers when it is restricted to language" (Fauconnier 1997: 8) and "[t]he meanings assigned to sentences in isolation […] are obtained in reality by building local, maximally simple contexts in which the sentences can operate (Fauconnier 1985/1994: xxi). Katz and Fodor's (1993: 178) assertion that "theory of semantic interpretation is logically prior to a theory of the selective effect of setting" is, for Fauconnier, akin to putting the cart before the horse.

Cognitive linguistics has certainly made a remarkable contribution to the elaboration of semantic descriptions of linguistic phenomena, but its impact is restrained in one crucial respect. To employ Stalnaker's (1997: 535) and Haukioja's (2017: 866) terminology, cognitive linguistics has not contributed as much to descriptive semantics as it has to foundational semantics. Descriptive semantics concerns what the meanings of linguistic expressions are, while foundational semantics, also known as metasemantics (Burgess and Sherman (eds.) 2014, Häggqvist and Wikforss 2015: 111), investigates the basis on which the meanings of linguistic expressions are determined (Haukioja 2017: 866). We can say that the development of cognitive linguistics was made possible not because it successfully surmounted Putnam's pessimism, but because it has never shared that pessimism. Put differently, it has never concerned itself directly with foundational semantics or metasemantics. Putnam (1973: 700, 1975: 139) asked the foundational question, "Are meanings in the head?". He answered the question in the negative and advanced the view now called externalism or anti-individualism. Langacker (2008: 27) posed precisely the same question thirty years later but adopted the internalist position without reference to Putnam's (1973, 1975) or any other externalist arguments:

> Our concern is with the meanings of linguistic expressions. Where are these meanings to be found? From a cognitive linguistic perspective, the answer is evident: meanings are in the minds of the speakers who produce and understand the expressions. It is hard to imagine where else they might be. Yet there are many scholars who resist or reject that answer. (Langacker 2008: 27)

Langacker seems to assume that meaning is supervenient on the intrinsic proper-ties of the speaker[5], in accordance with the internalist conception of meaning mooted by Haukioja (2017: 865) and Valente (2019: 314) among others. Internalism or individualism is one of the few concepts shared by cognitive lin-guistics and its rival, generative grammar, despite their other significant theoretical divergences. What must be noticed here is that cognitive linguistics did not inherit its commitment to semantic internalism from generative grammar. As previously stated, Chomsky adopts no firm stance on the internalist/externalist issues and, moreover, the semantic theory elaborated by Katz and Fodor (1963) presupposes a highly restrictive notion of meaning that is obviously incompatible with the cog-nitive linguistic conception of meaning. Arguably, cognitive linguistics inherited from its rival the internalist conception of language and applied it to the domain of semantics. The question of whether it is actually possible to apply internalism to semantics without falling into an undesirably restrictive conception of meaning remains unanswered. Langacker's (2008) afore-cited categorical comment cannot sufficiently establish that meanings are located in the minds of the speakers. What is needed is not an assertion but an argument.

1.2 Internalism in Philosophy[6]

1.2.1 Intension and Extension

Notwithstanding his official stance, Langacker's semantic internalism probably stemmed from the internalist tradition in philosophy. In philosophy, meaning has traditionally been considered to consist of intension and extension (Lewis 1970: 23, Schwartz 1977: 13, Poncinie 1985: 416, Abbott 1989: 287, n. 3, Burge 1993: 312/2007: 294, Heim and Kratzer 1998: 302), or to use Mill's (1843: Book I, Ch. VIII ff) terminology, connotation and denotation. The extension of a term is the set of entities denoted by the term and its intension is what determines its exten-sion. Meaning can often be defined exclusively in terms of extension. Thus, 'cat' and 'dog' are considered to have different meanings precisely because these words have different extensions. As long as no other term has the same extension as 'cat',

---

5) Supervenience is defined as follows:

States of type X supervene on states of type Y if and only if there is no difference among X states without a corresponding difference among Y states. (Fodor 1987: 30; see also Segal (2000: 8) and Brown (2004: 4))

6) Section 1.2 is based on Sakai (2017: Section 3) and Sakai (2022a: Section 3).

it is possible to define 'cat' purely extensionally, and the same holds for 'dog'. Intension is called for because there are cases in which two terms share the same extension without being synonymous. As Quine (1951: 21-22) points out, the expressions 'creature with a heart' and 'creature with a kidney' are alike in extension but unlike in meaning. If a creature has a heart, then it has a kidney, and vice versa, at least in the actual world. Intuitively, however, we understand different things when we hear these two terms. Arguably the same applies to 'Indian nickel' and 'buffalo nickel' (Quine 1960: §11-12). The notion of intension, of which the Aristotelian notion of essence was the forerunner (Quine 1951: 22), ensures the intuitive distinction between 'creature with a heart' and 'creature with a kidney' or between 'Indian nickel' and 'buffalo nickel'. In general, the fact that two terms have different intensions may reduce to the fact that the subject associates different concepts with the terms in her mind. The traditional notion of intension or concept can be considered an internalist one because, as Rey (1983: 238) states, it "associates with (most) concepts necessary and sufficient, 'defining' conditions that an agent must appreciate in order properly to have the concept". Such delineating conditions are commonly referred to as descriptions. The descriptions associated with the term 'square', for instance, are (i) a closed, plane figure, (ii) has four sides, (iii) all sides are equal in length and (iv) all interior angles are equal (Rey 1983: 239). These descriptions are singly necessary and jointly sufficient for something to be a square. Any person who fails to associate, even tacitly, these descriptions to the word 'square' cannot be considered to possess the concept of *square* (ibid.). Such internalist conceptions of meaning are known under the general heading of 'descriptivism' (Bird and Tobin 2023: 4.1). Putnam (1975: 134) remarked that "[m]ost traditional philosophers thought of concept as something *mental*" (emphasis in the original) and that "the doctrine that the meaning of a term (the meaning 'in the sense of intension', that is) is a concept carried the implication that meanings are mental entities". Descriptivism diffused into linguistics when some generativists undertook the task of elaborating an internalist semantic theory. From a linguistic point of view, Katz and Fodor (1963) classified descriptions associated with a lexical item into two groups: semantic markers and distinguishers. The distinction between semantic markers and distinguishers corresponds to "the distinction between that part of the meaning of a lexical item which is systematic for the language and that part which is not" (ibid.: 188). The senses of the word 'bachelor', for example, contain four semantic markers, namely (Animal), (Human), (Male), and (Young). The combination of these semantic markers with distinguishers, represented in square brackets, gives rise to four senses of the word (ibid.: 190):

(3) a. (Animal) + (Male) + (Young) + [fur seal when without a mate during the breeding]
   b. (Human) + [who has the first or lowest academic degree]
   c. (Human) + (Young) + [knight serving under the standard of another knight]
   d. (Human) + (Male) + [who has never married]

The distinction between semantic markers and distinguishers enables us to attain both "the greatest possible conceptual economy" and "the greatest possible explanatory and descriptive power" (ibid.: 190). What is important for our present purpose is that both semantic markers and distinguishers serve to decompose the meaning of a lexical item into its atomic concepts (ibid.: 185-186). Katz and Fodor's framework postulated that "the lexical information to be represented by markers and by distinguishers will be controlled by our evidence about the disambiguations which a fluent speaker can make". For instance, the sense illustrated in (3d) is justified by the intuition that (4a) is redundant and that (4b) is "'empty', 'tautological', 'vacuous', 'uninformative'" (ibid.: 200, cf. Katz 1972: 50):

(4) a. unmarried bachelor
   b. Bachelors are unmarried.

Katz and Fodor's (1963: 200) statement that "the theory is confirmed if speakers take the expression or sentence in the appropriate way, and is disconfirmed if they do not" indicates that the concepts posited in their theory are considered to constitute part of the speaker's mental representation of linguistic meaning, in conformity with the internalist conception of meaning[7].

1.2.2 Sense and Reference

There is another possible construal of intension or concept, deriving from

---

7) There is a consensus among cognitive linguists that Katz and Fodor's (1963) distinction between semantic markers and distinguishers results from an arbitrary dichotomy between meaning and context. Cognitive linguists generally accept Bolinger's (1965: 561) claim that "the marker-distinguisher dualism [...] does not appear to correspond to any clear division in natural language".

Frege's (1892a/1997) well-known distinction between sense ('*Sinn*') and reference ('*Bedeutung*'). According to Frege (1892a: 27/1997: 152), the reference, but not the sense, of 'the morning star' (Morgenstern, Phosphorus) and 'the evening star' (Abendstern, Hesperus) is the same[8]. By 'sense' Frege means, among others, a mode of presentation of the reference, or, in Burge's (1979: 402/1990: 216) words, "epistemic basis for determining the reference"[9]. Thus, the names 'the morning star (Morgenstern)' and 'the evening star (Abendstern)' present one and the same reference from different perspectives[10]. As McCulloch (1995: 191) states, while the study of reference concerns word-world relations, the study of sense highlights word-mind relations. There is an exegetical dispute about what exactly modes of presentation consist of. A common but controversial interpretation of Frege's view is that modes of presentation are definite descriptions associated with the relevant terms (Sainsbury and Tye 2012: 22-23). On this interpretation, 'the morning star' (or 'Phosphorus') is presented under the description, say, 'the planet seen at position y in the morning sky' and 'the evening sky' (or 'Hesperus') is presented under the description 'the planet seen at position x in the evening sky' (Sainsbury and Tye 2012: 3). Due to the apparent affinity between modes of presentation and descriptions, the term 'Fregean' is commonly employed interchangeably with 'descriptivist' (cf. Mellor 1977: 301, Abbott 1989: 269). In this construal, sense determines reference just as intension determines extension[11].

Frege emphasized that senses (and thoughts) are essentially public entities and can be grasped by several people (Katz 1972: 38):

The being of a thought may also be taken to lie in the possibility of different

---

8) „Es würde die Bedeutung von ,Abendstern' und ,Morgenstern' dieselbe sein, aber nicht der Sinn." (Frege 1892a: 27)

9) As Burge (1977: 356, 1990/2005: 242-243), Kripke (1980: 59), Salmon (1981: 11-13), Heck (2012: 172) and Grabarczyk (2016: 155) emphasize, Frege's notion of sense is multifaceted and fulfills different functions, of which the mode of presentation is just one.

10) Sainsbury and Tye (2011: 109) claim that 'Phosphorus' and 'the morning star' express distinct concepts on the grounds that, unlike the former, the latter corresponds to a non-atomic concept comprising the concepts *morning* and *star*, each of which differs in origin from the concept *Phosphorus*. However, I shall use 'Phosphorus' and 'the morning star' interchangeably in subsequent sections.

11) Bell (1984: 369) proposes to define sense as "the condition which anything must meet in order to be the reference", although, as he clarifies, "Frege nowhere states the matter in just this way".

thinkers' grasping the thought as one and the same thought. In that case the fact that a thought had no being would consist in several thinkers' each associating with the sentence a sense of his own; this sense would in that case be a content of his particular consciousness, so that there would be no common sense that could be grasped by several people. (Frege 1918-1919b: 146/1997: 349)[12]

By a thought I understand not the subjective performance of thinking but its objective content, which is capable of being the common property of several thinkers. (Frege 1892a/1997, n. 5/E)[13]

Also, notably, Frege distinguished senses (*Sinn*) differ from concepts (*Begriff*): a concept is the reference, not the sense, of a predicate (Dummett 1973: 173). The reference of a proper name is an object, while the reference of a predicate is a concept (Frege 1892b/1997). On this view, predicates which are not true of anything, such as 'round square', also have a reference (Wiggins 1995: 68). Neither senses nor concepts are inner images, which Frege labeled as 'ideas' (*Vorstellung*) (cf. Burge 1993: 321/2007: 302, n. 15). To understand the concept expressed by the expression 'round square' is to comprehend what it takes for something to be a round square. This condition imposed by 'round square' is in no way subjective and its contradictory character is manifest to every rational thinker.

Frege extended the distinction between sense and reference, originally introduced for names, to the semantics of sentences. Indeed, as Ducrot (1972: 27) stresses, Frege's paper sought, among other objectives, to establish the parallelism between singular terms (i.e. proper names, definite descriptions, demonstratives, personal pronouns, etc.) and sentences[14]. Underlying all of Frege's works is the idea that the semantic power of a linguistic expression consists in its association with an extralinguistic entity (Evans 1982: 8-9). Just as a singular term is

---

12) „Man kann unter dem Sein eines Gedankens auch verstehen, dass der Gedanke als derselbe von verschiedenen Denkenden gefasst werden könne. Dann würde das Nichtsein eines Gedankens darin bestehen, dass von mehreren Denkenden jeder seinen eigenen Sinn mit dem Satze verbände, der dann Inhalt seines besonderen Bewusstseins wäre, so dass es einen gemeinsamen Sinn des Satzes, der von mehreren gefasst werden könnte, nicht gäbe." (Frege 1918-1919b, 146)

13) „Ich verstehe unter Gedanken nicht das subjektive Tun des Denkens, sondern dessen objektiven Inhalt, der fähig ist, gemeinsames Eigentum von vielen zu sein." (Frege 1982a, n. 5)

meaningful insofar as it is associated with an object, a sentence is meaningful insofar as it possesses one of the truth values, the True and the False. Such extra-linguistic entities constitute references (*Bedeutung*) of singular terms and sentences[15]. The parallel between singular terms and sentences is further expanded. Just as a singular term designates an object via a certain sense (*Sinn*), a sentence designates a truth value via a certain sense. Frege (1892a: 32/1997: 156, 1918-1919a: 61/1956: 292) called the sense of a declarative sentence 'thought' (*Gedanke*)[16]. A thought is "something for which the question of truth arises" (Frege 1918-1919a: 60/1956: 292). Both singular terms and sentences are associated with certain modes of presenting extralinguistic entities. A question naturally arises as to whether we can talk about the sense of predicates or general terms which denote concepts or relations as opposed to objects. I shall address this issue in Section 3.4.

The discovery of the distinction between sense and reference allowed Frege to develop a five-layered model: what may intuitively be referred to as the 'meaning' of a linguistic expression comprises its idea (*Vorstellung*), tone (*Beleuchtung*, *Färbung*), presupposition (*Voraussetzung*), sense (*Sinn*) and reference (*Bedeutung*).

---

14) The term Frege uses for 'sentence' is 'Satz'. This German word can be translated in English as 'sentence", 'proposition', 'theorem' or 'clause' (Beaney, ed. 1997: xiv). Ducrot (1972) translates 'Satz' as 'proposition', a French word that corresponds to 'proposition' or 'clause' in English. In this chapter, I follow Evans (1982) and translate 'Satz' as 'sentence'.

15) Frege's 'Bedeutung' is sometimes translated as 'Meaning' with initial capitalization, rather than as 'reference' (Evans 1982: 7-8, n.2). In this chapter, I follow Dummett (1973) and use the term 'reference', which is much more common in linguistics (cf. Langacker 1987: 165, n.13).

16) It is not the case that the sense of every sentence is a thought. Frege (1918-1919a: 61-62/1956: 292-294) restricted the notion of thought to sentences for which the question of truth could arise, i.e. declarative (indicative) sentences and sentence-questions. Equally important is the fact that Frege divorced the sense/thought of a sentence from its assertive force. Frege (1918-1919a: 62/1956: 294) stated:

> An interrogative sentence and an indicative one contain the same thought; but the indicative contains something else as well, namely, the assertion. The interrogative sentence contains something more, too, namely a request."

> (Fragesatz und Behauptungssatz enthalten denselben Gedanken; aber der Behauptungssatz enthält noch etwas mehr, nämlich eben die Behauptung. Auch der Fragesatz enthält etwas mehr, nämlich eine Aufforderung.)

This distinction is made possible by the separation between the act of grasping a sense and of judging it (Frege 1918-1919b: 145/1997: 348). I will not go into this issue in the present book, even though it is highly relevant to modern pragmatics.

Chapter 1   The (Lack of) Impact of Externalism on Cognitive Linguistics

Sense, a notion fundamental to internalism, must not be confused with the other four. Frege (1892a) defined 'idea' (*Vorstellung*) negatively in relation to reference and sense:

> The reference and sense of a sign are to be distinguished from the associated idea. If the reference of a sign is an object perceivable by the senses[17], my idea of it is an internal image, arising from memories of sense impressions which I have had and acts, both internal and external, which I have performed. [...] The idea is subjective: one man's idea is not that of another. There result, as a matter of course, a variety of differences in the ideas associated with the same sense. A painter, a horseman, and a zoologist will probably connect different ideas with the name 'Bucephalus'. This constitutes an essential distinction between the idea and the sign's sense, which may be the common property of many and therefore is not a part or a mode of the individual mind. For one can hardly deny that mankind has a common store of thoughts which is transmitted from one generation to another. (Frege 1892a: 29/1997: 154)[18]

Unlike the sense and reference of an expression, the idea is always subjective and cannot be shared by more than one person. The use of the singular article 'a' in "A painter, a horseman, and a zoologist" is essential, because the use of the plural as in "Painters, horsemen and zoologists" would imply that the same idea can be shared among painters, horsemen and zoologists and contradict the very definition of the

---

17) The term 'sense' means 'sensory organ' in this context. It must not be read as the Fregean 'sense' mentioned in the first sentence of this cited extract.

18) „Von der Bedeutung und dem Sinne eines Zeichens ist die mit ihm verknüpfte Vorstellung zu unterscheiden. Wenn die Bedeutung eines Zeichens ein sinnlich wahrnehmbarer Gegenstand ist, so ist meine Vorstellung davon ein aus Erinnerungen von Sinneseindrücken, die ich gehabt habe, und von Tätigkeiten, inneren sowohl wie äußeren, die ich ausgeübt habe, entstandenes inneres Bild. [...] Die Vorstellung ist subjektiv: die Vorstellung des einen ist nicht die des anderen. Damit sind von selbst mannigfache Unterschiede der mit demselben Sinne verknüpften Vorstellungen gegeben. Ein Maler, ein Reiter, ein Zoo loge werden wahrscheinlich sehr verschiedene Vorstellungen mit dem Namen ‚Bucephalus' verbinden. Die Vorstellung unterscheidet sich dadurch wesentlich von dem Sinne eines Zeichens, welcher gemeinsames Eigentum von vielen sein kann und also nicht Teil oder Modus der Einzelseele ist; denn man wird wohl nicht leugnen können, dass die Menschheit einen gemeinsamen Schatz von Gedanken hat, den sie von einem Geschlechte auf das andere überträgt." (Frege 1892a: 29)

idea. Frege (1918-1919a/1956) examined the nature of ideas more in depth, roughly identifying ideas with the contents of one's consciousness, such as sense-impressions, creations of one's imagination, sensations, feelings, moods, inclinations and wishes (Frege 1918-1919a: 66/1956: 299)[19]. Ideas are distinguished from the objects in the external world in the following four aspects: (i) ideas cannot be perceived, (ii) ideas are had, (iii) ideas need a bearer, and (iv) every idea has only one bearer (Frege 1918-1919a: 67-68/1956: 299-300). Frege (1918-1919a: 72/1956: 306) maintained that the content of an individual's consciousness must be clearly distinguished from the object of the individual's thinking.

The tone (*Beleuchtung*, *Färbung*) is an apparently similar aspect of meaning to the idea[20]. Frege (1892a, 1918a, 1919b) applied the notion of tone to the meaning of 'although' (obgleich), 'but' (aber), 'yet' (doch), 'alas' (leider) and 'thank God' (gottlob):

> Subsidiary clauses beginning with 'although' also express complete thoughts. This conjunction actually has no sense and does not change the sense of the clause but only illuminates it in a peculiar fashion. We could indeed replace the concessive clause without harm to the truth of the whole by another of the same truth value; but the light in which the clause is placed by the conjunction might then easily appear unsuitable, as if a song with a sad subject were to be sung in a lively fashion*. *Note: Similarly in the case of 'but,' 'yet.' (Frege 1892a: 45/1997: 167)[21]

---

19) Frege explicitly omitted decisions from ideas without citing a reason. I suspect that Frege regarded decision-making as belonging to what Austin (1962/1975: 157) called 'commissives', i.e. illocutionary acts consisting in committing the speaker to a certain course of action. Such acts necessarily involve persons to whom the commitment is addressed and thus cannot be defined purely in terms of the contents of the speaker's consciousness.

20) I follow Dummett's (1973) terminology here:

> What I have here called 'tone' Frege refers to as 'lightning' [Beleuchtung] or 'colouring' [Färbung], but these are less natural metaphors in English, and we may stick to the term 'tone'. (Dummett 1973: 84)

21) „Auch in Nebensätzen mit ‚obgleich' werden vollständige Gedanken ausgedrückt. Dieses Fügewort hat eigentlich keinen Sinn und verändert auch den Sinn des Satzes nicht, sondern beleuchtet ihn nur in eigentümlicher Weise*. Wir könnten zwar unbeschadet der Wahrheit des Ganzen de Concessivsatz durch einen andern desselben Wahrheitswertes ersetzen; aber die Beleuchtung wurde dann leicht unpassend erscheinen, wie wenn man ein Lied traurigen Inhalts nach einer luftigen Weise singen wollte. *Ähnliches haben wir bei ‚aber', ‚doch'."

Words like 'alas [leider]' and 'thank God [gottlob]' belong here. Such constituents of sentences are more noticeably prominent in poetry, but are seldom wholly absent from prose." (Frege 1918-1919a: 63/1956: 295)[22]

The tone is distinct from the idea because the former is (or can be) objective and does not require a particular bearer. As Dummett (1973) stated that all competent speakers of English must know the meaning of 'but', which cannot be reduced to the contents of their individual consciousness. Thus, the tone, but not the idea, can be deemed an object appropriate for linguistic inquiry. Evidently, the Fregean tone corresponds to conventional implicature (Grice 1989: 25-26) or procedural meaning (Blakemore 2002: 78-79), a much-discussed topic in modern pragmatics. Indeed, Carston (2002: 217-218) attributes the distinction between truth-conditional meaning and non-truth-conditional meaning to Frege (1892a):

> It is worth noting that Frege (1892a: [45, 1997: 167]) made a clear distinction between what he called tonal elements, such as 'but', 'although', 'yet', and 'fortunately', on the one hand, which cannot affect the truth value of the sentence/ utterance, and subordinating conjunctions such as 'because', 'since', 'after' and 'before', which have what he calls 'sense', and so do have a truth-conditional effect. (Carston 2002: 217-218, n. 46)

Frege explicitly defined the meaning of 'but' in a later work[23], claiming that the difference in meaning between 'and' and 'but' is external to the thought expressed by the sentence in which 'but' occurs (Burge 2012: 59-60):

> The word "but" differs from "and" in that with it one intimates that what follows is in contrast with what would be expected from what preceded it. Such suggestions in speech make no difference to the thought. (Frege 1918-1919a: 64, 1956: 295-296)[24]

The same applies to the meaning of 'still' (noch) and 'already' (schon). According to

---

22) „Wörter wie ‚leider', ‚gottlob' gehören hierher. Solche Bestandteile des Satzes treten in der Dichtung stärker hervor, fehlen aber auch in der Prosa selten ganz." (Frege 1918-1919a: 63)

23) Everyone agrees that 'p but q' expresses a contrast between p and q (cf. Langacker 2008: 59). However, p and q are not always straightforwardly contrasted. See Ducrot (1972: 128-129).

Frege (1918-1919a: 64/1956: 295), the sentence in (5) states that Alfred has not appeared and hints that his arrival is expected:

(5)   Alfred ist noch nicht gekommen.
      (Alfred has still not come.)

The whole sentence remains true even when the anticipation turns out to be false. Frege's description of 'but' and 'still' aligns with the dominant view in modern pragmatics, as represented by Carston's (2002: 53) remark:

> The crucial element here [= e.g. Luke likes Sam {a. and / b. but} Hank loves Bob.] is the much discussed 'but', whose truth-conditional contribution seems to be identical to that of 'and', although its inherent meaning clearly incorporates another feature (of 'contrast', roughly speaking). (Carston 2002: 53)

The notion of tone is slightly problematic because Frege himself sometimes suggested that tones are subjective, contrary to his claims about the obviously public contrast between 'and' and 'but':

> Such colouring and shading are not objective, and must be evoked by each hearer or reader according to the hints of the poet or the speaker. Without some affinity in human ideas art would certainly be impossible; but it can never be exactly determined how far the intentions of the poet are realized. (Frege 1892a: 31/1997: 155)[25]

On this account, a tone would be nothing but an idea (*Vorstellung*) as previously delineated. However, Dummett (1973: 85) points out that, unlike an idea, a tone

---

24) „Das Wort ‚aber‘ unterscheidet sich von ‚und‘ dadurch, dass man mit ihm andeutet, das Folgende stehe zu dem, was nach dem Vorhergehenden zu erwarten war, in einem Gegensatze. Solche Winke in der Rede machen keinen Unterschied im Gedanken." (Frege 1918-1919a: 64)

25) „Diese Färbungen und Beleuchtungen sind nicht objektiv, sondern jeder Hörer und Leser muss sie sich selbst nach den Winken des Dichters oder Redners hinzuschaffen. Ohne eine Verwandtschaft des menschlichen Vorstellens wäre freilich die Kunst nicht möglich; wieweit aber den Absichten des Dichters entsprochen wird, kann nie genau ermittelt werden." (Frege 1892a: 31)

can be conveyed to another person by using the word in question. Accordingly, contrary to Frege's own remark, a sharp distinction must be drawn between idea and tone.

Yet another notion is similar but external to thought: presupposition (*Voraussetzung*). Frege (1892a: 39-41/1997: 162-164) introduced the notion of presupposition in connection with sentences such as the one illustrated in (6):

(6)　Der die elliptische Gestalt der Planetenbahnen entdeckte, starb im Elend.
(Whoever discovered the elliptic form of the planetary orbits died in misery.)

At first glance, (6) might appear to encompass two thoughts (or propositions): there is someone who discovered the elliptic form of the planetary orbits, and this person died in misery. If so, the sentence in (7), which negates the sentence in (6), would mean (8) because the negation of 'p and q' is generally equivalent to 'not p or not q':

(7)　Der die elliptische Gestalt der Planetenbahnen entdeckte, starb nicht im Elend.
(Whoever discovered the elliptic form of the planetary orbits did not die in misery.)

(8)　Either whoever discovered the elliptic form of the planetary orbits did not die in misery or there was nobody who discovered the elliptic form of the planetary orbits.

However, (8) cannot be understood as the negation of (7). The negation in (7) affects only the thought that the person who discovered the elliptic form of the planetary orbits died in misery; the fact that there is someone who discovered the elliptic form of the planetary orbits remains intact. Frege argued that this discrepancy can be accounted for by assuming that the thought expressed by (6) does not contain the latter proposition. Ducrot (1972: 30) asserts that the proposition in question that is not negated when the sentence is negated, is not affirmed when the sentence is affirmed[26]. The truth of the proposition is rather presupposed by (6), just as the statement 'Kepler died in misery' presupposes the existence of Kepler (Katz 1972: 129)[27] More generally, the use of a sentence presupposes that every expression occurring within it has a reference. Frege concluded that the presupposition is always external to the thought expressed by the sentence.   .

Senses and thoughts must be distinguished from ideas, tones, presuppositions and references. Senses and thoughts belong neither to the inner world nor to the outer world of material, perceptible things (Frege 1918-1919a: 69, 75/1956: 302, 308). Putnam (1973: 699, 1975: 134), Burge (1990: 33/2007: 111, 2012: 46-47) and Millikan (1997: 515), among others, have clarified that senses and thoughts

---

26) Ducrot (1972: 30-31) points out that Frege (1892a) employed the negation test only as the last resort. If all information contained in a sentence that resisted negation were regarded as a presupposition, then the information (ii) contained in (i) should also be considered a presupposition of (i), because the negation of (i), i.e., (iii), also contains the information in (ii).
(i) Napoleon, who recognized the danger to his right flank, himself led his guards against the enemy position.
[Napoleon, der die Gefahr für seine rechte Flanke erkannte, führte selbst seine Garden gegen die feindliche Stellung.] (Frege 1892a: 44/1997: 166)
(ii) Napoleon recognized the danger to his right back.
(iii) It is not the case that Napoleon, who recognized the danger to his right flank, himself led his guards against the enemy position.
Frege does not say, however, that (ii) is presupposed by (i). According to Ducrot, this is because it is harmless to include (ii) in the thought expressed by (i). (ii) can be replaced by another clause of the same truth value, for instance (iv), without affecting the reference, namely the truth value, of the whole sentence, as in (v).
(iv) Napoleon was born in Corsica.
(v) Napoleon, who was born in Corsica, himself led his guards against the enemy position.
If both (i) and (iv) are true, it follows that (v) is true. In contrast, a replacement of this kind may alter the reference of (1) in the text.
(vi) Whoever discovered the elliptic form of the planetary orbits died in misery. [= (1)]
Even when both (vi) and (vii) are true, it does not follow that (viii) is true.
(vii) There is someone who discovered penicillin.
(viii) Whoever discovered penicillin died in misery.
In the Fregean system, this fact would remain a mystery, if the information in (ix) were contained in (vi).
(ix) There is someone who discovered the elliptic form of the planetary orbits.
Ducrot argues that this is the real reason why Frege had to eliminate (ix) from the thought expressed by (vi) by adopting the notion of presupposition,.
27) The analogy between 'Der die elliptische Gestalt der Planetenbahnen entdeckte' and 'Kepler' should be taken with a grain of salt. Although Frege treated both expressions as singular terms, the important difference between definite descriptions and proper names is well-established (Kripke 1980). Intuitively, the meaningfulness of the first expression does not hinge on the existence of the object fulfilling the description, while we can assume the meaning of 'Kepler' to be exhausted by the object denoted by the name.

Chapter 1 The (Lack of) Impact of Externalism on Cognitive Linguistics

are not mental entities; rather, they are abstract entities found in what Frege called the "third realm (*drittes Reich*)" (cf. McCulloch 1995: 64, Komorjai 2006: 138):

> A third realm must be recognized. What belongs to this corresponds with ideas, in that it cannot be perceived by the senses, but with things, in that it needs no bearer to the contents of whose consciousness to belong. Thus the thought, for example, which we expressed in the Pythagorean theorem is timelessly true, true independently of whether anyone takes it to be true. It needs no bearer. It is not true for the first time when it is discovered, but is like a planet which, already before anyone has seen it, has been in interaction with other planets. (Frege 1918-1919a: 69/1956: 302)[28]

Fregean thoughts are not mental representations (Millikan 1997: 515) and "are ontologically and conceptually independent of language and human agents" (Burge 1979b: 405/1990: 219). De Brabanter and Leclercq (2019: 2) suggest that Frege's view departs somewhat from the internalist standpoint, which assimilates the intension or sense of a word as a mental representation entertained by the subject. Nevertheless, it is true that Frege held an internalist conception of meaning: as Putnam (1973: 700, 1975: 134) indicated, the grasp or apprehension (*fassen*) of a sense or thought is still considered an individual psychological act[29]:

> The apprehension of a thought presupposes someone who apprehends it, who thinks. He is the bearer of the thinking but not of the thought. Although the thought does not belong to the contents of the thinker's consciousness yet something in his consciousness must be aimed at the thought. (Frege 1918-1919a: 75/1956: 308)[30]

---

28) „Ein drittes Reich muss anerkannt werden. Was zu diesem gehört, stimmt mit den Vorstellungen darin überein, dass es nicht mit den Sinnen wahrgenommen werden kann, mit den Dingen aber darin, dass es keines Trägers bedarf, zu dessen Bewusstseinsinhalte es gehört. So ist z. B. der Gedanke, den wir im pythagoreischen Lehrsatz aussprachen, zeitlos wahr, unabhängig davon wahr, ob irgendjemand ihn für wahr hält. Er bedarf keines Trägers. Er ist wahr nicht erst, seitdem er entdeckt worden ist, wie ein Planet, schon bevor jemand ihn gesehen hat, mit andern Planeten in Wechselwirkung gewesen ist." (Frege 1918-1919a: 69)

29) Likewise, Millikan (1997: 513) states that "although senses were not supposed to be psychological entities, *graspings* of them surely are dated, psychological occurrences" (emphasis in the original). Frege warned that 'fassen' was just a metaphorical expression selected because of the limits imposed by the structure of natural language (Frege 1918-1919a/1956: n. 6).

Millikan (1997: 513) remarks that "this constitutes a substantial psychological claim". Given that "[a] particular mental capacity, the power of thought, must correspond the apprehension of thought" (Frege 1918-1919a: 74/1956: 307)[31], Frege would have no qualms about accepting the internalist idea that grasping or apprehending the sense of an expression is tantamount to being in a certain state of mind, and that that state of mind determines the reference of the expression. It is thus reasonable to consider Frege's viewpoint to be a version of descriptivism. Indeed, Putnam (1975: 134-135) specified that no philosophers working in the Fregean tradition have ever doubted that knowing the intension of an expression is a simple matter of being in a certain psychological state[32]. The internalist conception of meaning is so persistent that, as previously observed in Section 1.1, it is immanent even in cognitive grammar, a relatively new framework in theoretical linguistics that has not been directly influenced by the Fregean tradition.

1.3 Externalism

1.3.1 Physical Externalism[33]

Putnam (1973, 1975) famously challenged the internalist view presented in the previous section, claiming that what is in the mind can fail to determine the extension of a word. The trouble with the internalist conception of meaning is that intension or sense is expected to simultaneously accomplish too many tasks (Grabarczyk 2016: 155). First, internalism defines intension as a speaker's understanding of meaning. Second, intension is considered to determine extension. However, in numerous instances, these two functions are not simultaneously fulfilled because a speaker's understanding of a word is often insufficient in determining its extension. Putnam's (1973, 1975) argument "started off a whole new

---

30) „Das Fassen der Gedanken setzt einen Fassenden, einen Denkenden voraus. Dieser ist dann Träger des Denkens, nicht aber des Gedankens. Obgleich zum Bewusstseinsinhalte des Denkenden der Gedanke nicht gehört, muss doch in dem Bewusstsein etwas auf den Gedanken hinzielen." (Frege 1918-1919a: 75)

31) „Dem Fassen der Gedanken muss ein besonderes geistiges Vermögen, die Denkkraft entsprechen" (Frege 1918-1919a: 74).

32) Several philosophers including Burge have attempted to reconcile the Fregean view with externalism. Kimbrough (1998), Brown (2003, 2004) and Wikforss (2006) argue that such attempts necessarily fail. This problem will be addressed in Chapter 3.

33) Section 1.3.1 is based on Sakai (2022a: Section 3).

philosophical technique" (McCulloch 1995: 166). Putnam invited us to imagine a planet called Twin Earth that encompasses exact atom-for-atom and molecule-for-molecule replicas of us. Our replicas have exactly the same life histories as we do, utter the same word forms, encounter the same perceptual experiences, consume the same food, and so on. For example, the Earthian Oscar has a Doppelgänger on Twin Earth, who is referred to as Oscar$_2$. Oscar speaks English; Oscar$_2$ speaks Twin English, a language indistinguishable from our English. If Oscar senses a pain in his leg, Oscar$_2$ does, too. When Oscar utters, 'My leg hurts', Oscar$_2$ does, too. Oscar and Oscar$_2$ are "exact duplicates in appearance, feelings, thoughts, interior monologue etc." (Putnam 1973: 702, 1975: 141)[34]. The physical environment of the Twin Earth is also indistinguishably similar to that of Earth in every respect, with replicas of the Sahara desert, Mount Everest, the Pacific Ocean, the Nile River, and so on. The sole difference between the two planets is that on Twin Earth the stuff called 'water' has a complicated molecular structure abbreviated as XYZ, instead of H_2O, even though it is superficially indistinguishable from Earthian water[35]. The Pacific Ocean and the Nile are filled with H_2O, whereas the Twin Pacific Ocean and the Twin Nile contain XYZ. On our planet, H_2O falls as rain, whereas on Twin Earth XYZ falls from the sky. The difference is not consciously accessible to the inhabitants of the two planets. Both Oscar and Oscar$_2$ associate the word form 'water' with descriptions such as a 'liquid which is colorless, transparent, tasteless, thirst-quenching, found in lakes, etc.' (Putnam 1975: 191).

Nevertheless, Putnam argues, the extension of the English word 'water' is H_2O, whereas the extension of the Twin English word 'water' (translated as 'twater' in our English; see Burge 1982: 100/2007: 85) is XYZ. Both words are spelled as 'water' and pronounced as ['wɔːtə(r)] but the Earthian word 'water' is not true of XYZ and the Twin-Earthian word 'water' is not true of H_2O (Segal 2000: 23). Kripke (1980) expressed a similar view:

---

34) This assumption will be called into question later.

35) Some may doubt that Oscar$_2$ is an exact replica of Oscar, because Oscar's body contains a significant amount of H_2O (cf. Burge 2013: 269). As Stich (1978: 589, n. 16), Brown (2004: 11) and Farkas (2006: 326) remark, those who think that this fact is detrimental to the thought experiment are urged to construct a case in which the difference between the two planets concerns kinds of substances that are not found in the human body. In any case, as Burge (1986b: 22/2007: 236) clarifies, "[t]he empirical implausibility of the thought experiments is irrelevant to their philosophical point".

We identified water originally by its characteristic feel, appearance and perhaps taste, (though the taste may usually be due to the impurities). If there were a substance, even actually, which had a completely different atomic structure from that of water, but resembled water in these respects, would we say that some water wasn't H_2O? I think not. We would say instead that just as there is a fool's gold there could be a fool's water ; a substance which, though having the properties by which we originally identified water, would not in fact be water. And this, I think, applies not only to the actual world but even when we talk about counterfactual situations. If there had been a substance, which was a fool's water, it would then be fool's water and not water (Kripke 1980: 128)

The natural conclusion is that "[t]he extension of our terms depends upon the actual nature of the particular things that serve as [local] paradigms, and this actual nature is not, in general, fully known to the speaker" (Putnam 1973: 711, 1975: 164). To acquire the word 'water', one must learn that water is whatever has the same nature as the normal examples of *this* liquid called 'water' (Putnam 1975: 152, 162), i.e. what Donnellan (1993: 156) called local paradigms. In Putnam's (1973: 710, 1975: 152) words, "'water' is stuff that bears a certain similarity relation to the water *around here*". Gasparri and Marconi (2021: Section 3.3) stipulate that the use of indexicals such as 'this' and 'here' (Bar-Hillel 1954) is essential because mere descriptions cannot help us determine the extension of 'water'. Local paradigms of 'water' are associated with stereotypes such as 'liquid which is colorless, transparent, tasteless, thirst-quenching, found in lakes, etc.' (Putnam 1975: 191). Although such stereotypes serve to identify local paradigms of water (Segal 2000: 27), they cannot fully determine the extension of 'water' because the extension of 'twater' (XYZ) equally matches the stereotypes. Put simply, natural kind terms do not have Fregean senses (Schwartz 1977: 13, Bromberger 1997: 153). Putnam concluded that "the extension of the term 'water' […] is not a function of the psychological state of the speaker by itself" (Putnam 1973: 702, Putnam 1975: 141). Since, as stated in Section 1.1, the intension of a word determines its extension, a difference in extension entails a difference in intension and it is impossible for two words to share the same intension when they differ in extension. It then follows that the word form 'water' has not only different extensions but also different intensions for Oscar and Oscar$_2$, even though the two speakers understand the word form in exactly the same manner (Sainsbury and Tye 2011: 108)[36]. As

26

remarked by Rey (1983: 246), natural kind concepts provide "cases in which we would expect the epistemological and metaphysical roles of concepts to diverge". The meaning of 'water' is not determined by what we know about the word but by the metaphysical nature of what the word denotes. As Goosens (1977: 150) puts it, "a knowledge of the meaning of [natural kind] terms provide very little linguistic competence". This is in sharp contrast with words like 'bachelor', whose meaning is determined by their corresponding descriptions and objects that happen to satisfy the descriptions are contingent. As Abbott (1989: 285) states, "[s]urely we can be said to know the meaning of *bachelor* even though its extension is not in anybody's head". Conversely, the extension is essential to the meaning of a natural kind term like 'water' (Putnam 2013: 272-273)[37].

Putnam's view of natural kind terms embodies what Wikforss (2008) calls foundational externalism (FE), a form of semantic externalism:

> **Foundational Externalism (FE):** The set of all facts that determine the meaning of a term include external facts; that is, features of the external environment are included in the determination basis. (Wikforss 2008: 161)

If FE is true, then two speakers who are atom-for-atom and molecule-for-molecule identical could nevertheless mean different things by employing exactly the same word forms. FE exhibits two principal varieties, depending on the types of

---

36) If intension is defined to be something that individual speakers have in their mind, the conclusion to be drawn is that, contrary to the traditionary conception of meaning, intension can fail to determine extension and that two terms can differ in extension even if they have the same intension (Putnam 1973: 700, 1975: 164). Instead of giving up the assumption that intension determines extension, Putnam chose to divorce the intension of a term from the psychological state (in the narrow sense) corresponding to the term. (Putnam 1975: 164). This move has been criticized by several philosophers (Burge 1982/2007, 1993/2007, McDowell 1992), as will be discussed shortly.

37) Sainsbury and Tye (2011, 2012) propose to individuate concepts in terms of their origins. Like Rey's (1983), their view entails externalism about concepts (Sainsbury and Tye 2011: 108) and, hence, a distinction between the metaphysics and epistemology of concepts (ibid.: 105). Note, however, that Sainsbury and Tye's position is more thoroughly externalist than Rey's. Thus, if people on Twin Earth used the word 'bachelor' to mean 'unmarried man', that word would express a concept different from our word 'bachelor', due to their different origins. The originalist view makes it difficult to understand how concepts can be shared not only within specific linguistic communities but also across different communities (Onofri 2016: 14).

'external facts' or 'external environment' at issue. Putnam's argument demonstrates that the meaning of the term 'water' depends on the physical environment in which the speaker is positioned. This type of FE is called physical externalism. The other major form of externalism is social externalism, which will be discussed in the next section. As Katz (1997: 2) noted, Putnam's and Kripke's arguments "spearheaded an empiricist and externalist takeover in the philosophy of language".

There is good reason to be skeptical about Putnam's assumption that Oscar and Oscar$_2$ think exactly the same thought. Putnam's Twin Earth thought experiment concerns linguistic content much more than mental content (Burge 1978: 138, n. 18, Burge 1982: 101/2007: 86, 1993: 319/2007: 300 Noonan 1984: 216-217, McDowell 1992, Stalnaker 1993: 299-300, Woodfield 2000: 434, Liu 2002: 386, Farkas 2006: 190, Sainsbury and Tye 2012: 4, n. 5, Brown 2022: 2.1). Putnam evinced that meaning was non-individualistically individuated but his opinions on thought and concept remained individualistic (McDowell 1992, Burge 1993/2007, Liu 2002). For Putnam (1975: 152), meanings are not concepts because concepts are supervenient on an individual's physical histories (Burge 1986b: 4/2007: 222). However, Burge (1986a: 718/2007: 272) highlights that meaning and thought "are interwoven in complex ways which render it impossible fully to analyze one in terms of the other". Consequently, a difference in meaning yields a difference in thought. As Sainsbury and Tye (2011: 104) remark, "[l]inguistic immersion is also conceptual immersion". Given that thoughts (or more generally, propositional attitudes) are intentional or representational (Burge 1986b: 3/2007: 221) in the sense that they are about objects in the world, it is difficult to comprehend the claim that an individual's thoughts remain the same even when environments vary (Burge 1986b: 24, 34, 43-45/2007: 237, 245, 252-253). McGinn (1977: 531) states that "a correct specification of the mental states of the two groups of speakers in respect of H_2O and XYZ would mention those very substances", making it impossible to claim that the mental states of Oscar and Oscar$_2$ are identical. Suppose that Oscar and Oscar$_2$ uttered (9):

(9)   There is some water within twenty miles, I hope. (Burge 1982: 101/2007: 86)

According to FE, Oscar's utterance of (9) is true if and only if there is water (H_2O) within twenty miles; Oscar$_2$'s utterance of (9) is true if and only if there is twater

Chapter 1 The (Lack of) Impact of Externalism on Cognitive Linguistics

(XYZ) within twenty miles. If water but not twater were found in the proximity of the two speakers, only Oscar's utterance of (9) would be true. As Segal (2000: 24) remarks, "the content of the belief they express is just the content of the sentence they utter" (see also Stich 1978: 581, Crane 1991: 4 and Owens 1992: 89-90, Sainsbury and Tye 2011: 121-122). It is not cogent to say that Oscar's utterance of (9) and Oscar$_2$'s utterance of (9) differ in meaning (and hence in the truth condition) while Oscar's thought expressed by (9) and Oscar$_2$'s thought expressed by (9) share the same truth value. Rather, Oscar's thought corresponding to (9) is true if and only if there is water (H_2O) within twenty miles and Oscar$_2$'s thought corresponding to (9) is true if and only if there is twater (XYZ) within twenty miles. If there were water but no twater within twenty miles of the two thinkers, only Oscar's thought corresponding to (9) would be true. In principle, the same thought cannot be both true and false (Stich 1978: 578-579, Elugardo 1993: 372). Therefore, Oscar's thought differs from Oscar$_2$'s despite their internal identity[38]. Burge (1982: 102/2007: 87) claims that "the two are in no sense exact duplicates in their thoughts", contrary to Putnam's assumption. The assertion that they are internally identical is not equivalent to the assertion that their thoughts or psychological state are the same (Farkas 2003: 190). Ultimately, Oscar and Oscar$_2$ are not psychologically identical from the outset[39]. As Nuccetelli (2003: 5) remarks, "[i]ndiscernibility with respect to internal properties does not entail indiscernibility with respect to mental properties with content".

Such considerations imply that the psychological state of speakers cannot be

---

38) We can also ask whether Oscar's and Oscar$_2$'s actions are the same, given that Oscar drinks H_2O while Oscar$_2$ drinks XYZ. The answer depends on how we individuate actions (Grabarczyk 2016: 166).

39) Perhaps it is a matter of terminology to some extent even though several authors (McDowell 1992, Burge 1993/2007, Liu 2002) opine that the issue is substantial. Putnam (1975: 137-139) explicitly discussed the psychological state 'in the narrow sense'. He never claimed that Oscar and Oscar$_2$ are in the same psychological state in the broad sense (Crane 1991: 4). By 'being in a psychological state' Putnam means 'being in a state internally or individualistically described', while Burge construes the phrase to mean 'having concepts not describable independently of one's relations to the environment'. Another terminology is adopted by Aydene (1997: 425), who says that "twins are in different mental states despite their psychological identity". Hunter (2003: 724) describes the situation in a slightly different way: "a person's mental states are not fixed by his intrinsic bodily states". There are still other formulations (Nuccetelli 2003: 2-9). Be that as it may, both Putnam and Burge reject the internalist assumption that knowing the meaning of an expression is a matter of being in a certain psychological state as internally or individualistically described.

described independently of their relations with the environment external to their mind (Burge 1993/2007: 300-301). This view is called psychological externalism (PE):

> **Psychological Externalism (PE):** For all psychological states of type S, the individual is in a state of this type only if she stands in an appropriate relation to external fact E. (Wikforss 2008: 175)

FE commonly accompanies PE[40]. As Wikforss (2008: 162) makes clear, the fundamental premise of PE is that "the external determination of truth-conditions will carry over to the level of mental content". According to PE, the states of mind of Oscar and $Oscar_2$ differ solely because they stand in relation to different external facts. The meaning of the terms spelled as 'water' and the concept corresponding to the term are both distinct for the two individuals (Haukioja 2017: 868-869, Sainsbury and Tye 2012: Chs. 3 and 5). To facilitate intelligibility, I will henceforth use the terms 'semantic externalism' or 'externalism' to indicate both FE and PE.

1.3.2 Social Externalism[41]

Putnam's Twin Earth thought experiment on the word 'water' evinced that meaning and mental content depend on the physical environment of speakers. This form of semantic externalism is called physical externalism. Burge (1979a/2007) employs the word 'arthritis' to establish social externalism, which is another form of semantic externalism. According to social externalism, meaning and mental content depend on the social environment of speakers as well as their internal states[42].

Burge's (1979a/2007) best-known thought experiment comprises three steps. First, we are asked to suppose that Adam, a rational person who is generally competent in English, expresses his fear to his doctor by uttering (10):

(10) I have arthritis in my thigh.

---

40) Although PE "is very widely endorsed", Wikforss (2008: 176) argues that FE does not generally support PE.
41) Section 1.3.2 is based on Sakai (2022b: Section 1.1).
42) De Brabanter and Leclercq (2023: Section 1.2) call this type of externalism 'conventional externalism'.

Adam harbors several beliefs about the disease called 'arthritis'. Thus, he thinks correctly "that he has had arthritis for years; that his arthritis in his wrists and fingers is more painful than his arthritis in his ankles, that it is better to have arthritis than cancer of the liver, that stiffening joints is a symptom of arthritis, that certain sorts of aches are characteristic of arthritis, that there are various kinds of arthritis, and so forth" (Burge 1979a: 77/2007: 104). Among such beliefs about arthritis is the one expressed by the sentence in (10). The doctor tells Adam that this cannot be the case, because arthritis is specifically an inflammation of the joints. The patient relinquishes his view and now believes that some disease other than arthritis is lodged in his thigh.

In the second step, we must conceive of a hypothetical community in which Adam$_2$, an exact replica of Adam, expresses his fear to his doctor by uttering (10). Up to this point Adam and Adam$_2$ have had identical experiences. A major difference emerges when the doctor replies to Adam$_2$. In the hypothetical community, the word 'arthritis' applies to varied rheumatoid ailments, including arthritis and other ailments that can afflict a person's thigh. It follows that, unlike Adam's fear expressed by (10), Adam$_2$'s fear expressed by (10) is well grounded and could even be true.

Finally, the counterfactual situation is interpreted. According to Burge, we can reasonably suppose that the community in which Adam$_2$ resides has no concept of *arthritis*. Adam's 'arthritis' and Adam$_2$'s 'arthritis' are merely two homonymous words that happen to share a phonological form. The hypothetical community utilizes a word that is spelled as 'arthritis' and pronounced as /ɑːɹθˈɹaɪtɪs/. Nevertheless, it lacks the concept of *arthritis*. Adam$_2$'s 'arthritis' denotes a disease distinct from arthritis, say *tharthritis*[43]. In the standard conception of meaning, intension or concept uniquely determines extension (but not vice versa) and a difference in extension entails a difference in intension or concept (Schroeter and Schroeter 2016: 196, 199). Therefore, as Burge (1979a: 79/2007: 106) states, "[t]he word 'arthritis' in the counterfactual community does not mean *arthritis*", because it is "not even extensionally equivalent" to the actual word 'arthritis' (see also Noonan 1984: 2019). Given that a thought consists of concepts, it follows that Adam and Adam$_2$ have different thoughts about what they call 'arthritis'. Even though Adam and Adam$_2$ are molecularly identical, their thoughts differ, due to the sole fact that different meanings are associated with the same phonological

---

43) A term coined by Burge (1979a: 94/2007: 123).

form:

> The upshot of these reflections is that the patient's mental contents differ while his entire physical and non-intentional mental histories, considered in isolation from their social context, remain the same[44]. (We could have supposed that he dropped dead at the time he first expressed his fear to the doctor.) The differences seem to stem from differences "outside" the patient considered as an isolated physical organism, causal mechanism, or seat of consciousness. The difference in his mental contents is attributable to differences in his social environment. (Burge 1979a: 79/2007: 106)

Meaning and mental content are not in the mind; they are dependent for their individuation on an individual's social environment. As Schroeter and Schroeter (2016: 200) put it, "sameness of concept depends on sameness of social context".

Semantic externalism as originally proposed by Putnam (1973, 1975) is generally considered to concern natural kind terms such as 'beech', 'cat', 'elm', 'beech', 'gold', 'molybdenum', 'tiger', 'water', etc. Putnam (1975: 160-163) extended his theory to encompass names of artefacts such as 'pencil' as well. Burge (1979a: 79) explicitly rejects the view that externalism, or anti-individualism as he calls it, is only applicable to natural kind terms:

> The argument has an extremely wide application. It does not depend, for example, on the kind of word 'arthritis' is. We could have used an artifact term, an ordinary natural kind word, a color adjective, a social role term, a term for a historical style, an abstract noun, an action verb, a physical movement verb, or any of various other sorts of words. I prefer to leave open precisely how far one can generalize the argument. But I think it has a very wide scope. (Burge 1979a: 79/2007: 106-107)

Burge (1986b: 6/2007: 222, 1989: 181/2007: 283) similarly treats words like 'baby', 'bread', 'chair', 'knife', 'shadow', 'walk' or 'water'. If Burge is right, as Haukioja (2017: 869) says, a similar argument could establish semantic externalism in relation to

---

44) A mental state is said to be intentional when it is about objects or events in a world (McGeer 1994: 451, Rowlands et al. 2020: Section 3). For this reason, intentionality is often called 'aboutness'. Mental states such as beliefs, desires, fears and hopes have intentionality or aboutness and are called propositional attitudes.

virtually all linguistic expressions[45]. The same generalization applies to psychological externalism. According to Fodor (1987: 29), Burge's thought experiment "shows that if the Putnam story raises *any* problems for the notion of content, then the problems that it raises are completely general and affect all content-bearing mental states". This consequence stems naturally from the fact that "the content of many kinds of concepts, not merely those of natural kinds, depends in part on the social environment, on the way other people use words" (Segal 2000: 61).

It is not that social externalism subsumes physical externalism. The impossibility of reducing all forms of physical externalism to social externalism can be demonstrated by Putnam's (1973: 701-703, 1975: 141-146) discussion of what the word 'water' meant before 1750. Henri Cavendish discovered only in the late eighteenth century that water was not an element but a compound (Barber 2003: 25). At that time, no one knew that water was constituted of hydrogen and oxygen; rather, water was considered merely a colorless, transparent, tasteless, and thirst-quenching liquid found in lakes. Nevertheless, in Putnam's (1973: 702, 1975: 141) view, "the term 'water' had the same extension in 1750 and in 1950 (on both Earths)". The same point is made by Noonan (1984: 218-219). As previously mentioned, Putnam assumed that "'water' means 'whatever is like water, bears some equivalence relation, say the same liquid relation to *our* water'" (Putnam 1974: 451). According to Putnam (1973: 702-703, 1975: 142), we must conduct substantial scientific investigation to determine whether or not the sameness relation holds. What changed between 1750 and 1950 is not the meaning of 'water' but our understanding of what the sameness relation consists in. This perspective is orthogonal to social externalism, because, even if the meaning of words one employs is dependent "on the way other people use words" (Segal 2000: 61), it does not follow that the meaning of 'water' remained constant between 1750 and 1950. After all, the way in which people, or at least experts, use the term 'water' has changed over the course of time, altering the social environment on which the meaning of 'water' is constitutively dependent. Social externalism hinges upon the fact that other people know better about the extension of the relevant word, but physical externalism does not. According to physical externalism, meaning and mental content may depend on physical factors of which no community member

---

45) Haukioja (2017: 865) is more cautious when he states, "The central and distinctive externalist claim is, roughly, that the meanings of *at least some* linguistic expressions are not wholly determined by, or supervenient on, the intrinsic features of the speaker" (emphasis mine). See also Cohnitz and Haukioja (2013: 476).

is aware.

These delineated differences disclose that social externalism and physical externalism pose different sets of problems in addition to a problem common to both. The problem shared by social externalism and physical externalism is how they can account for the fact that Adam and Adam$_2$ think different thoughts about what they call 'arthritis' despite their internal identity and that Oscar and Oscar$_2$ think different thoughts about what they call 'water'. The problem specific to social externalism is how Adam and his doctor can talk and think about the same disease. It is not a simple matter of the doctor knowing more about arthritis than Adam does. In Burge's depiction of the situation, Adam believes erroneously that arthritis can afflict his thigh. To employ Burge's terminology, Adam understands the concept of *arthritis* incompletely[46]. Given Adam's and his doctor's mutually incompatible conceptions of what they call 'arthritis', it should be expected that Oscar's utterance of 'arthritis' is homonymous with the doctor's utterance of 'arthritis', in the same way that 'bank' in the sense of 'river edge' is true of objects which 'bank' in the sense of 'financial institution' is not. The two subjects may be said to talk and think about distinct things when they employ the same phonological form. Contrary to this expectation, however, it is not difficult for us to think of Adam and his doctor as talking about the same disease when Adam expresses the fear that arthritis could afflict his thigh. Without assuming the identity of the subject matter under discussion, we could not make sense of the fact that Adam is willing to correct his view when his doctor tells him that arthritis affects only joints. Adam would never correct any of his ideas about banks in the sense of river edges even if a financial planner told him something about banks in the sense of financial institutions about which he was ignorant. The conceptions of 'arthritis' of Adam and his doctor are so different that they almost contradict each other. Nevertheless, Adam and his doctor must be considered to share the concept of *arthritis*. Onofri (2016) indicates this necessity in reference to the principle of publicity:

Publicity (PUB): Whenever a group of subjects communicates successfully, genuinely agrees, or is covered by the same intentional generalization, then

---

46) Burge (1979a/2007) gives the term 'incomplete understanding' a more specific meaning than commonly understood. This issue will be addressed in Chapter 2. It suffices here to understand the term in the ordinary or intuitive sense.

those subjects must share the corresponding concepts. (Onofri 2016: 5)

Loar (1988/2017) explained that this is another lesson to be drawn from Burge's (1979a) thought experiment. On the one hand, both Adam and Adam$_2$ think, 'I have arthritis in the thigh', but the contents of their thoughts differ, as is proven by the fact that only Adam$_2$'s thought is true. It follows that "sameness of conceptual role is not *sufficient* for sameness of content" (Loar 1988/2017: 154, emphasis in the original). On the other hand, Adam and his doctor mean the same thing by employing the word form 'arthritis', despite their contradicting beliefs. We can therefore assert that "sameness of conceptual role is not *necessary* for sameness of psychological content" (ibid.). As Pollock (2015: 3231) remarks, if social externalism is right, "content and understanding can come apart". This potential sets a challenge for internalism, as will be discussed below. The 'water' case can be similarly understood if experts know more about water than Oscar does, that is, if, for Oscar, water is merely a colorless, transparent, tasteless, thirst-quenching liquid that is found in lakes for Oscar but experts also know that the molecular structure of water is H$_2$O.

What distinguishes social externalism from physical externalism is not the nature of the terms considered, but the presence or absence of experts in the community. Burge (1982/2007) suggests that social externalism can also be established through a 'water'-type thought experiment if some members of the community know more about the subject matter than others. The problem specific to physical externalism occurs when no experts exist in society vis-à-vis the subject under discussion, as was the case with water before 1750. Physical externalism holds that the extension of a term is determined by the nature of the physical environment, even in such situations:

When it comes to natural-kind terms, Putnam thinks that neither the individual's concepts, nor the socially defined intensions (the Fregean *sense*), could determine their meaning. The meaning of such a term is partially determined by the nature of the physical environment that surrounds us. In the original dubbing (supposedly there was one) a natural-kind term was coined to pick out a particular set of things that have in common a certain *stuff*. This term thereupon designates this particular set of things. (Liu 2002: 385)

As regards social externalism, it can be assumed that the community as a whole possesses the Fregean sense associated with the relevant term, not its individual members. Physical externalism cannot rely on this assumption because no community member knew before 1750 the correct descriptions which could determine the extension of 'water'.

Although linguists tend to regard externalism as a non-starter, Cohnitz and Haukioja (2013: 477) and Haukioja (2017: 866) indicate that most philosophers, subscribe to some form or other of externalism. Wikforss (2008: 158) goes even further, stating that in philosophy "externalism has been so successful that the primary focus of today's debate is not so much on whether externalism is right or wrong, but rather on what its implications are". As Hunter (2003: 724) and Farkas (2006: 187) put it, externalism constitutes an "orthodoxy in the philosophy of mind". The same remark applies to the philosophy of language (Häggqvist and Wikforss 2018: 912).

1.3.3 What Externalism Is Not (Necessarily)[47]

Burge (2013: 263) points out that the popularity of the term 'externalism' is "inversely proportional to its clarity". It is vital not to confuse externalism as construed here with other seemingly similar positions. First of all, externalism (as opposed to internalism) is not equivalent to mechanism (as opposed to mentalism) presented in Section 1.1. Externalism as applied to the linguistic realm represents the belief that the knowledge of meaning cannot be fully determined through individualistic notions, whether psychological states or physical actions. Thus, no matter how much we adhere to structuralist recommendations to minutely scrutinize the individual's "speech-utterances and other observable actions" (Bloomfield 1933: 143), we can never identify his "mental processes or internal bodily processes" (ibid.) that allow us to distinguish his thought from his twin's, insofar as the objects of our observations are described in individualistic terms.

Second, externalism is not the view that the acquisition of concepts necessarily involves interactions with the environment. The mere emphasis on interaction with the environment cannot serve as the hallmark of externalism, because few internalists would say that all our concepts are innate and we do not need to acquire them through any interaction with our environment. Hunter (2003: 727) remarks that "such interaction is surely needed (in the ordinary run of things)

---

47) Section 1.3.3 is mostly a reproduction of Sakai (2023a), which is based on Sakai (2022a: Section 3) and Sakai (2022b: Section 5).

Chapter 1   The (Lack of) Impact of Externalism on Cognitive Linguistics

simply for us to develop the neural complexity needed for us to have a mind". Langacker (2008: 31 inter alia) congruently emphasizes from an internalist perspective that the diffusion of neural activation is implicated in many linguistic phenomena. It is obvious that people cannot acquire concepts with total autonomy from the environment in which they are tokened. The internalist/externalist debate rather pertains to whether concept individuation depends on the environment.

Third, externalism does not maintain that no mental entity is involved in understanding a word (Wikforss 2008: 178, n. 2). As previously noted, Putnam (1973, 1975) and Kripke (1980) opined that the meaning of the word 'water' is not solely defined in terms of the description of the superficial properties of water and that we must take into account the possibly unknown underlying nature of the local paradigms of the substance. This makes Oscar's and Oscar$_2$'s uses of the same word form 'water' occurrences of two distinct words, even though the two speakers are molecule-for-molecule identical. This view does not entail, however, that extension or reference exhausts what we intuitively label as 'word meaning'. Even though Kripke emphasized that the meaning of a natural kind term cannot be equated with any description, Soames (2002: 241) states that "he did not provide a positive doctrine that identifies what the semantic contents" of such terms are[48]. Häggqvist and Wikforss (2020: 225) interpret Kripke (1980) as claiming that the semantic content of a natural kind term "is exhausted by the term's extension (across possible worlds), just like reference is held to exhaust the semantic content of proper names". This construal could convey the impression that externalism is none other than what Lakoff (1987: 157ff) calls "objectivist" semantics, which generally equates meaning with extension or reference. However, this interpretation misrepresents externalism. In fact, Lakoff (1987: 169) notes that Putnam's (1973, 1975) view is presented "in a somewhat different form" from Kripke's (1980) and Hacking (2007a: 3) indicates that "unlike Kripke, Putnam did offer an explicit meaning of 'meaning'". Lakoff (1987: 169) acknowledges that "Putnam's [...] account of meaning is objectivist in most, but not quite all, ways". Besides its reference, the meaning of a word includes what Putnam calls its stereotype (Poncinie

---

48) Soames is discussing the semantics of proper names, but the same point applies to natural kind terms because Kripke (1980) intended to extend his views on proper names to a wider class of terms including natural kind terms (Soames 2002: 242, Wikforss 2010: 69-70, 2013: 243).

37

1985: 416-417)[49] and Hacking (2007a: 3) describes as "some sort of common (if possibly mistaken) knowledge associated with the [word]"[50]. Thus, Putnam stated that "speakers are required to know something about (stereotypical) tigers in order to count as having acquired the word 'tiger'; something about elm trees (or, at least, about the stereotype thereof) to count as having acquired the word 'elm'; etc." (Putnam 1975: 168). On Putnam's view, "'meaning' never means 'extension'" (Putnam 1975: 140), even though "[t]he extension is included in the meaning" (Hacking 2007a: 3, cf. McCulloch 1995: 170)[51]. As Abbott (1997: 313) remarks, "Putnam's theory is less radical than Kripke's view". If we assume that the extension is included in the meaning, we must distinguish between acquiring a word and learning its meaning (Putnam 1975: 167). One can acquire a word, that is, store a word in one's mental lexicon, without learning its meaning. The minimum level of knowledge necessary for a speaker to be considered to have acquired a word differs from word to word and from culture to culture. Speakers of English must be able to differentiate tigers from leopards but are not required to distinguish between elm and beech trees (Putnam 1975: 168). As Goosens (1977:

---

49) Goosens (1977: 153) resists the idea that stereotypes represent an aspect of meaning on the grounds that the stereotypes associated with a term are open to modifications while the meaning of the term remains unaltered. Putnam partially acknowledged this point:

Sometimes change in a stereotype might not be considered a change in meaning; yet it does seem to me that if we no longer associate tigers with *stripes* at all, that should count as a change in the 'meaning' of the term. (Putnam 2013: 273)

50) Putnam defined a stereotype as "a description of what a typical speaker thinks a paradigmatic 'elm', or whatever, is (or is conventionally assumed to be) like" (Putnam 1992: 386). According to Putnam (1975: 170), one of the examples of radically mistaken stereotypes is the stereotype associated with the word 'witch', namely "witches enter into pacts with Satan" or "they cause sickness and death". Even though such mistaken stereotypes exist, "[m]ost stereotypes do in fact capture features possessed by paradigmatic members of the class in question" (Putnam 1975: 170, cf. Dupré 1993: 23).

51) Not every externalist shares this view. Bilgrami (1992: 2), for instance, states that one can "be an externalist and yet deny that reference in *any* standard sense has anything to do with content". This version of externalism will not be the primary object of the present discussion, because, as Putnam (1992: 386-397) clarified, it has little to do with linguistic semantics:

But Bilgrami's interests are quite different. In his recent *Belief and Meaning* [= Bilgrami (1992)] he makes it clear that his purpose is not to explicate the concept of meaning at all; indeed, he argues that for the purpose of psychological explanation, what we want is *not*, in general, a knowledge of the meaning of the thinker's words. *Meaning* is not all that important a notion, he thinks. But be that as it may, it is the notion I was trying to explicate in MoM [= Putnam (1975)]! (Putnam 1992: 386-387)

151-153) and Recanati (1993: 148) observe, the learning of word meaning is a matter of degree. At one end of the spectrum there are words such as 'phoneme' which are unknown to average users of the language. There are also words such as 'molybdenum' that average speakers may know to exist without knowing much about their meaning. At best, speakers of English are expected to know that molybdenum is a metal (Goosens 1977: 151). In other cases, the stereotypes associated with words are very poor, as with words such as 'elm' and 'beech' (Poncinie 1985: 418-419), both of which are associated with the stereotype "common sort of deciduous tree" (Putnam 1992: 386; see also Putnam 1975: 143, 147)[52]. At the other end of the spectrum there exist words such as 'water' with which average speakers associate fairly rich stereotypes. Speakers unfamiliar with the stereotype of a word required by the community are not deemed competent in the use of the word. For instance, as Putnam (1975: 168) states, there is no point in talking about tigers with a person who points to a snowball and asks, 'Is that a tiger?' (Putnam 1975: 168). The right thing to say in such a case is that the person fails to refer with the utterance of 'tiger'. The Twin-Earth thought experiment rests on the assumption that both Oscar and Oscar$_2$ are familiar with the stereotype associated with the word form 'water'; otherwise there would be reference failure when they employed 'water', and no thesis about the public meaning of 'water' would follow. The gist of Putnam's (1975) argument is that, although stereotypes are, or ought to be, in the mind, they are often insufficient, or even inappropriate, in determining the extension of the word in question and the content of the thought the subject entertains in using that word. In particular, the stereotype associated with a natural kind term constitutes neither its intension nor its sense (Linsky 1977: 819, Keil 1989: 27). Fodor (1975: 61) summarizes that, if Putnam is right, "either the semantic properties of a word aren't what you learn when you learn the word, or the semantic properties of a word don't determine its extension". This summary is correct if the first occurrence of 'semantic properties' is intended to mean 'extension' and the second 'stereotype'[53].

Needham (2011: 2-4) maintains that the use of 'etc.' in Putnam's (1975: 191) description of the stereotypical conception of 'water' as a 'liquid which is colorless,

---

52) Pincinie (1985: 419) distinguishes between the ordinary stereotype and the expert stereotype. The second notion, but not the first, enables botanists or foresters to tell elm trees from beech trees.

53) To be more faithful to Putnam's (1975: 167) terminology, we should say that the semantic properties of a word aren't what you learn when you *acquire* the word.

transparent, tasteless, thirst-quenching, found in lakes, etc.', is problematic because it leaves open the possibility that the description could be completed into the necessary and sufficient condition for something to be water. This would, Needham argues, undermine Putnam's and Kripke's claim that the meaning of 'water' can be defined only in terms of the microstructure of water, because the completion of the stereotypical description could be accomplished solely by appealing to the macroscopic properties of the substance. This argument may be adequate if it is directed at microessentialism, according to which a chemical substance can only be defined by its microstructure. However, the use of 'etc.' in the stereotypical descriptions of 'water' does not undermine the notion of a stereotype or the externalist thesis that what is in the head is insufficient for the determination of the meaning of a word. Ultimately, the use of 'etc.' indicates that we are not required to expound on the 'etc.' to competently use the word 'water'. We must know the stereotype associated with 'water' but this stereotype need not be specific enough to determine the meaning of the term.

The fourth point, which is the reverse of the third just rehearsed, is that the externalist position does not consist in reducing the meaning of every word to an indexical meaning exhibited by pure indexicals such as 'I', a meaning which is generally assumed to reside in the head. Pure indexicals are words whose content varies with context (Bar-Hillel 1954: 365-366). The pronoun 'I', for instance, refers to different people depending on the context of use; 'I' refers to Mary when uttered by Mary, and refers to John when uttered by John. Nevertheless, despite the variations in its content, 'I' always means 'the utterer', independent of the context of use (Benveniste 1956/1966: 252, Recanati 1993: 4.3). Kaplan (1989a: 505ff, 1989b: 574) labels this constant linguistic meaning of indexicals as their 'character'. Competent speakers of English know the character of 'I', which enables them to pick out a particular individual in each context. We can say with regard to indexicals that what is in the mind (i.e. the character) fails to determine the extension and the extension is determined only with respect to particular contexts[54] (Burge 1979a: 86/2007: 114-115). This does not mean that what is in the mind fails to determine the meaning, because the character is in the mind. The linguistic meaning of a pure indexical word like 'I' is its character, and not the object picked out in a given context. This reasoning is not applicable to natural kind terms, because, as

---

54) Kaplan (1989a, 1989b) calls the reference of an indexical expression 'content', rather than 'extension'.

Burge (1982: 103/2007: 88) emphasizes, "it is clear that 'water', *interpreted as it is in English*, or as we English speakers standardly interpret it, does not shift extension from context to context in this way" (see also Wikforss 2008: 169). Unlike pure indexicals, natural kind terms are context-insensitive (Salmon 1981: 105). If Oscar says, 'there is some water within twenty miles', the reference of 'water' is water (H_2O), and his utterance is true only and only if there is water within twenty miles. Even if Oscar uttered the same sentence on Twin Earth, the reference of 'water' would remain water (H_2O) rather than twater (XYZ) (Farkas 2006: 333)[55], and his utterance would be false because no water exists on Twin Earth. The extension of 'water' remains constant across contexts, unlike the contents of pure indexicals like 'I' or 'here' (Putnam 165, Bach 1987: 263, Burge 1989: 181/2007: 283).

What is puzzling, as Bach (1987: 263) puts it, is that Putnam states in several instances that 'water' is indexical (Putnam 1973: 710-711, 1974: 451-452, 1975: 152, 162, 187, 188, 193). De Brabanter and Leclercq (2019: 4ff, 2023: 1.2ff) employ the term 'indexical externalism' (externalisme indexical) in congruence with Putnam to allude to physical externalism. However, it could be argued in opposition to externalism that, if 'water' is as indexical as 'I' is, the meaning (character) of 'water' is in the mind just as the meaning (character) of 'I' is, and that 'water' has the same meaning on Earth and on Twin Earth (Putnam 1975: 164-165). Indeed, some internalists have contended that 'water' is indexical in the relevant sense. Thus, Jackson (1998a: 213) claims that "the description theory is committed

---

55) If Oscar is transported to Twin Earth without his knowledge and stays there long enough to think constantly about the watery stuff around him, the reference of his use of the term 'water' could shift to twater (XYZ) (Boghossian 1992: 18, 1994: 37-38, Millikan 1993: 313, Braddon-Mitchell 2004: 147-148, Brown 2004: 39-40, 48-49, Farkas 2006: 337, Schroeter 2008: 118, Sainsbury and Tye 2012: 92-93). Burge calls this shift 'slow switching':

> [...] if one were stealthily shifted back and forth between actual situations that modeled the counterfactual situations, one would not notice some feature in the world or in one's consciousness which would tell one whether one was in the "home" or the "foreign" situation. [...] The thoughts would switch only if one remained long enough in the other situation to establish environmental relations necessary for new thoughts. So quick switching would not be a case in which thoughts switched but the introspection remained the same. But slow switching could be such a case. (Burge 1988: 652)

As Grabarczyk (2016: 157) states, "the longer the user uses the term in contact with XYZ the more the context shifts towards Twin Earth". Conversely, pure indexicals do not need any interval to change their references. For instance, Oscar's use of 'this liquid' on Twin Earth would immediately pick out twater.

to 'water' in our mouths referring to whatever has the property we associate with 'water', and the test for being the property we associate with 'water' is that it is the, possibly disjunctive, feature common to the possible cases we describe as water" (see also Jackson 1998b: 39, 49, Chalmers 1996: 57-58). Likewise, Egan (1995: 201, n. 21) remarks that "a computational theory of belief would type-identify my *water* beliefs and my Twin Earth doppelgänger's *twater* beliefs, although intentional interpretations appropriate to our respective worlds might assign different broad contents to our type-identical beliefs".

Nonetheless, Putnam's (1975) claim that natural kind terms are indexicals does not imply that 'water' is endowed with a context-independent character in the manner of 'I' (Putnam 1975: 165). As Liu (2002: 400, n. 3) points out, "Putnam is using 'indexical' in a way different from the standard usage of the term". Arguably, Putnam intended to state that the reference of 'water' cannot be determined unless we take into account local paradigms of 'water', which are identified only through ostensive definitions such as "'water' means 'whatever is like water, bears some equivalence relation, say the same liquid relation to *our* water'" (Putnam 1974: 451) or "this liquid is called water" (Putnam 1973: 702, 1975: 141). According to Wikforss (2008: 160), "indexical elements play a role when these terms are introduced into the language". Putnam's notion of indexicality alludes to the fact that the local paradigms of a term can be fixed only via direct references (Liu 2002: 399). The indexical elements 'our' and 'this' occurring in the definition of the word 'water' refer to the environment in which 'water' is tokened (Linsky 1977: 823). This enables Oscar's and Oscar₂'s uses of 'water' to mean different kinds of substances, despite their internal identity. While the meaning of 'water' per se is non-indexical, the determination of the meaning of 'water' necessarily involves an indexical component by which a particular kind of substance is picked out on each planet and without which Oscar's and Oscar₂'s uses of 'water' would remain indistinguishable (Donnellan 1993: 159). Otherwise, 'water' bears scant resemblance to indexicals such as 'that', 'now' or 'today' (Wiggins 1995: 61-62). Indeed, Putnam distinguished between natural kind terms and 'obviously indexical' words or 'absolutely indexical' words such as 'I' and 'here' (Putnam 1973: 710, 1974: 148, 1975: 152, 165, Wikforss 2008: 160). Burge (1982: 103/2007: 88) is thus right to say that "[t]here is nothing at all indexical about 'water' in the customary sense of 'indexical'", as long as 'customary' indexicals are identified with what Putnam called 'absolutely' indexicals (cf. Schroeter 2008: 112). As Donnellan (1993: 157) points out following Salmon (1981: 106), "the importance of indexicality in the

Chapter 1　The (Lack of) Impact of Externalism on Cognitive Linguistics

Table 1-1: Indexicality of 'I' and 'water'

	Absolute indexicals e.g. 'I'	Natural kind terms e.g. 'water'
The initial determination of the extension depends on the context of the utterance.	✔	✔
The meaning of the term, and therefore its extensions in all situations, depend on the initially determined extension.	*	✔
The subsequent determination of the extensions depends on the context of the utterance.	✔	*

Putnam thought experiments really shows up at a deeper level, at the level of 'explaining the meaning of natural kind term'". Linsky (1977: 822) remarks that natural kind terms and indexicals have in common that the extension "is not determined by any properties it expresses but rather by the situation of its utterance". Once determined, the extension of a natural kind term plays a prominent role in defining its meaning. Haukioja (2015: 2144) characterizes the term 'water' as being actuality-dependent in the sense that "some feature of the object [...] in its *actual* extension enters into determining its extension in *non-actual* contexts of interpretation"[56]. Arguably, this is what Putnam (1973: 710, 1975: 152) meant by saying that "words like 'water' have an unnoticed indexical component". Table 1 compares how the indexicality becomes operational in the interpretation of absolute indexicals and natural kind terms:

The fifth point to be made is that externalism does not necessarily force us to embrace natural kind essentialism, according to which natural kinds such as water, cat or gold have essential properties, namely properties that are instantiated in all possible worlds. Natural kind essentialism holds, for example, that "in any possible world anything that is not an animal is not a cat and that in any possible world anything that is not composed of molecules of H_2O is not water" (Robertson Ishii and Atkins 2020: Section 4). On this view, being H_2O is the essential property of water, while being transparent, thirst-quenching, etc. is merely accidental. Essentialism incorporates such modal notions as 'possible world', 'rigid designation'

---

56) Actuality-dependent expressions generally display an externalist semantics, because the relevant feature of the object in its extension may not be accessible to speakers (Haukioja 2015: 2146).

43

and '(metaphysical) necessity'. Some externalists are committed to essentialism in this sense and convey the impression that 'externalism' and 'essentialism' are two names of the same doctrine. Thus, Kripke (1980) deliberated on necessary truths about natural kinds such as cow, tiger, water and gold, defined in terms of the underlying essential properties that they have in all possible worlds, in some of which the actual physical laws even do not hold. For Kripke, the statements in (11) express necessary or metaphysical truths, that is, truths that would remain valid in all possible worlds (cf. Salmon 1981: 84-86, Soames 2002: 244)[57]:

(11) a. Water is H_2O.
      b. Flashes of lightening are flashes of electricity.
      c. Cats are animals.
      d. Whales are mammals.
      e. Heat is the motion of molecules.

Necessary statements must be distinguished from analytic statements, which are true solely by virtue of their meaning (Schwartz 1977: 25). The analytic statement 'bachelors are unmarried', for instance, is *a priori* because its validity can be confirmed without any empirical investigation. Conversely, necessary statements may be *a posteriori* because they are solely empirically confirmed (Deutsch 1993: 392, Hanna 1998: 498-500). According to Kripke (1980: 128), "science can discover empirically that certain properties are *necessary* of cows, or of tigers" and the statements in (11) are necessarily true if they are true in the actual world, because, like proper names, natural kind terms are rigid designators, i.e. terms that designate the same object or kind in all possible worlds (Schwartz 1977: 30)[58]. If water = H_2O in the actual world and both 'water' and 'H_2O' are rigid designators, then there can be no world in which the two terms designate different things. Therefore, the statement 'water = H_2O' would remain true in all possible worlds. Kripke's view resembles Putnam's in dictating that superficial properties of a substance may fail to define the substance[59]:

Let us suppose the scientists have investigated the nature of gold and have found that it is part of the very nature of this substance, so to speak, that it

---

57) Jackson (1998b: 69) claims that 'Water is H_2O' is necessary in the same sense that 'Water is water' and 'H_2O is H_2O' are necessary.

have the atomic number 79. Suppose we now find some other yellow metal, or some other yellow thing, with all the properties by which we originally identified gold, and many of the additional ones that we have discovered later. An example of one with many of the initial properties is iron pyrites, 'fool's gold.' As I have said, we wouldn't say that this substance is gold. (Kripke 1980: 124)

The distinction drawn between gold and iron pyrites (fool's gold) is analogous to the distinction between water and twater: the sole difference is that twater is an imaginary substance but iron pyrites is not[60]. Mellor (1977: 301) characterizes Putnam's and Kripke's views as anti-Fregean because "Putnam's theory of the extension of kind terms, and Kripke's theory of their reference, are alike in denying traditional accounts that make the reference (or extension) of terms a function *inter alia* of something like their Fregean sense". Donnellan (1983/2012: 179) even implied that there is a logical relationship between Putnam's and Kripke's views: "[t]he theory of natural kinds terms developed by Saul Kripke and Hilary Putnam is seen by both authors, I believe, as being intimately connected to Kripke's views about reference, perhaps even a consequence of them". Based on the putative

---

58) Kripke (1980: 122, 127, 134) stressed the similarity between proper names and natural kind terms:

> We use terms such as 'gold' and 'tiger' rigidly, as applying to 'that kind of thing'; consequently, the meaning of a natural kind term cannot be given a descriptivist construal any more than the meaning of a proper name. (Kripke, 1980, p. 122)
>
> According to the view I advocate, then, terms for natural kinds are much closer to proper names than is ordinarily supposed. The old term 'common name' is thus quite appropriate for predicates marking out species or natural kinds, such as 'cow' or 'tiger'. My considerations apply also, however, to certain mass terms for natural kinds, such as 'gold', 'water', and the like. (Kripke 1980: 127)

Kripke's doctrine of proper names, however, cannot be so straightforwardly extended to other terms (Donnellan 1973, Schwartz 1977: 37-38, Abbott 1989: 276, Soames 2002 and Wikforss 2010, 2013, cf. Haukioja 2015: 2144).

59) As Hanna (1998) and Sainsbury and Tye (2012: 30-31) make clear, Kripke's view was meant to represent an antithesis to Kant's, according to which the judgment 'Gold is a yellow metal' is analytically true, necessary, and *a priori*.

60) Putnam also offered examples of actual kinds. Thus, normal speakers of English associate with both 'elm' and 'beech' the stereotype 'common deciduous trees' (Putnam 1975: 143, 147), which does not even allow us to determine the local paradigms. In fact, gold and iron pyrites are not good examples of twin-substances, because, as Ben-Yami (2001: 161) points out, "iron pyrites has only a *faint* resemblance to gold".

similarity, the two authors' views are often labeled as the 'Kripke-Putnam' view or the 'Putnam-Kripke' view (Hacking 2007a: 1-2, Wikforss 2013: 242). For example, Donnellan (1983/2012: 180) discusses "the Kripke-Putnam treatment of natural kind terms" and Lakoff (1987: 173) regards "the Putnam-Kripke view" as "objectivist". Kripke's (1980) emphasis on necessary truths seems to suggest that endorsing externalism is none other than endorsing essentialism:

> So if this consideration is right, it tends to show that such statements representing scientific discoveries about what this stuff *is* are not contingent truths but necessary truths in the strictest possible sense. It's not just that it's a scientific law, but of course we can imagine a world in which it would fail. Any world in which we imagine a substance which does not have these properties is a world in which we imagine a substance which is not gold, provided these properties form the basis of what the substance is. In particular, then, present scientific theory is such that it is part of the nature of gold as we have it to be an element with atomic number 79. It will therefore be necessary and not contingent that gold be an element with atomic number 79. (Kripke 1980: 125)

This may appear to provide a sufficient reason for considering Putnam an essentialist, as Mellor (1977: 299) does: "Kripke and Putnam claim that natural kinds have essential properties; that is, properties which nothing can lack and still be of the kind" (see also Hanna 1998: 499-500). Kripke (1980) and Putnam (1973, 1975) certainly shared the idea that the extension of a term is included as part of its meaning, the descriptions attached to the term being often insufficient to determine its extension, contrary to Frege's idea that the sense of a term grasped by a speaker determines its reference. As Hacking (2007a: 11) points out, however, "Putnam seldom dabbled in essences". Hacking (2007a: 11-12, 2007b: 228) observes that Putnam almost always placed 'essence' and 'essential nature' in scare-quotes, presumably "indicating amusement or irony" (ibid.: 12). This subtle difference between Kripke and Putnam stemmed from their attitudes toward the notion of rigid designation, which was, according to Hacking (2007a: 5), "integral to Kripke's approach" but "at most incidental to Putnam's". Putnam (1992) was very clear about the difference between 'water' and 'H_2O'[61]:

> [...] competence in the use of "H_2O" presupposes competence in the use of 'H' (hydrogen) and 'O' (oxygen), as well as in the use of the notions 'molecule' and

'atom'. The very different form of entry for 'water' makes it clear that the ability to characterize the extension of 'water' in some other way than simply by using the word 'water' (e.g., by a scientific definition) is not presupposed by competence in the use of the word (notwithstanding the fact that the extension of 'water', in one sense of that word, is 'H_2O give or take certain impurities' [...] (Putnam 1992: 388)

Even though 'water' and 'H_2O' have the same extension, the two terms in no way express the same concept or intension. To say simply that both are rigid designators does not allow us to account for the fact that one can be competent in the use of 'water' without yet being competent in the use of 'H_2O'. Fodor (1994: 57, 105-106) made a similar point, claiming that "despite their synonymy, the conditions for *having* the concepts [of *water* and *H_2O*] are different" (Fodor 1994: 57). This perspective is orthogonal to the simple idea that the meaning of a word can be defined in purely scientific terms, as illustrated by Bloomfield's (1933: 239) remark that "[w]e can define the names of minerals, for example, in terms of chemistry and mineralogy, as when we say that the ordinary meaning of the English word *salt* is 'sodium chloride (NaCl)'".

Putnam extended this contention by saying that 'water' and 'H_2O' differ not only in their intension but also in their extension, because the extension of H_2O "is the set of all substances that consist entirely of molecules consisting of two hydrogen atoms and one oxygen atom", to which most water does not belong (Putnam 1992: 406, n. 62). The two terms are synonymous for Fodor, but not for Putnam. As noted by Gasparri and Marconi (2021: Section 3), it is in principle possible to imagine, following Mates's (1951) remark, that our chemistry is seriously mistaken in assuming that water is H_2O:

It must be admitted that if we have a knowledge of physics there may be certain general physical laws such that it would be very difficult for anyone to present facts which we would accept as evidence against them; nevertheless, we will have no great difficulty in *imagining* conditions under which they would be false. However strongly established the law may be, we feel no disposition to rule out all future evidence; we do not have the feeling that "things could

---

61) Putnam (1992: 388) also says that, unlike 'water', 'H_2O' is a one-criterion term. This notion will play some part in subsequent chapters.

not have been otherwise." (Mates 1951: 531)

Importantly, even if water turned out not be H_2O, Putnam's claim that the meaning of 'water' depends on the physical environment in which the word is tokened would not be undermined, insofar as there are some important properties which, unbeknownst to competent speakers, distinguish water from twater. For Putnam, water is "whatever is of the same character, whatever has the same important physical properties, as *our* water" (Putnam 1974: 452). As Häggqvist and Wikforss (2018: 914) point out, 'H_2O' is "a mere placeholder" in Putnam's argument (cf. Haukioja 2015: 2147-2148, 2150, n. 9), albeit "a bit less explicitly so than XYZ"[62]. Burge (2003: 457) claims in a similar vein that the force of Putnam's Twin Earth thought experiment "does not depend on the assumption that water is H_2O". It is not essential whether the important physical properties of water involve hydrogen and oxygen:

> Importance is an interest-relative notion. Normally the "important" properties of a liquid or solid, etc., are the ones that are structurally important: the ones that specify what the liquid or solid, etc., is ultimately made out of – elementary particles, or hydrogen and oxygen, or earth, air, fire, water, or whatever – and how they are arranged or combined to produce the superficial characteristics. (Putnam 1975: 157)

Putnam's position is characterized by interest in interest. As Hacking (2007a: 9) nicely puts it, two words separate Kripke's and Putnam's views: "essence for Kripke, and interest for Putnam". Putnam's non-essentialist position is clearly articulated in the following passage:

> [...] we discover 'tigers' on Mars. That is, they look just like tigers, but they have a silicon-based chemistry instead of a carbon, based chemistry. (A remarkable example of parallel evolution!) Are Martian 'tigers' tigers? It depends on the context. (Putnam 1975: 157-158)

---

62) Häggqvist and Wikforss (2018) do not endorse Putnam's externalism even when 'H_2O' is interpreted as a mere placeholder. Rather, they rebel against Putnam's and Kripke's view on natural kind terms, concluding that "[t]ime is ripe to cut the cord with the legacy of Kripke and Putnam, and start afresh" (ibid.: 929). I shall return to this issue in Chapter 5.

Chapter 1   The (Lack of) Impact of Externalism on Cognitive Linguistics

Putnam's answer to the question "Are Martian 'tigers' tigers?" strikingly contrasts with Kripke's (1980: 121), according to which "anything not of this species, even though it looks like a tiger, is not in fact a tiger". If Martian tigers can be tigers, one can naturally assume that twater can be deemed a kind of water in contexts in which the superficial characteristics of substances are more important than their chemical structures (McCulloch 1995: 172-173). Indeed, Putnam espouses this position:

> And structure may sometimes be unimportant; thus one may sometimes refer to XYZ as water if one is using it as water. (Putnam 1975: 157)

The Twin Earth thought experiment requires only the assumption that there could be contexts in which twater is not water and that the differences between water and twater could be inaccessible to competent speakers. We do not have to appeal to modal notions such as 'possible world', 'rigid designation' or '(metaphysical) necessity'.

What complicates the matter is that, as Hacking (2007a: 5) and Wikforss (2013: 250) point out, Putnam (1975: 146-152) seems to fully endorse Kripke's natural kind essentialism in a section entitled 'Indexicality and Rigidity':

> Kripke calls a designator 'rigid' (in a given sentence) if (in that sentence) it refers to the same individual in every possible world in which the designator designates. If we extend the notion of rigidity to substance names, then we may express Kripke's theory and mine by saying that the term 'water' is *rigid*. (Putnam 1975: 148):

> Suppose, now, that I discover the microstructure of water – that water is H_2O. At this point I will be able to say that the stuff on Twin Earth that I earlier *mistook* for water isn't really water. In the same way, if you describe not another planet in the actual universe, but another possible universe in which there is stuff with the chemical formula XYZ which passes the 'operational test' for water, we shall have to say that that stuff isn't water but merely XYZ. You will not have described a possible world in which 'water is XYZ,' but merely a possible world in which there are lakes of XYZ, people drink XYZ (and not water), or whatever. In fact, once we have discovered the nature of water, nothing counts as a possible world in which water doesn't have that nature. Once

49

we have discovered that water (in the actual world) is H_2O, *nothing counts as a possible world in which water isn't H_2O*. In particular, if a 'logically possible' statement is one that holds in some 'logically possible world,' it isn't logically possible that water isn't H_2O. (Putnam 1975: 150)

Why was Putnam (1975: 146-152) so sympathetic toward Kripke's modal claim at the risk of misrepresenting his own view? According to Wikforss (2013: 252), this affinity has to do with Putnam's distrust of the traditional positivist account of meaning and necessity, which was famously challenged by Quine (1951)[63]. For logical positivism, necessary statements are nothing but analytic statements that are true by virtue of their meaning. If the statements in (11) are analytic, the word 'water' certainly underwent a semantic change when it was discovered that water is H_2O. Before this discovery, 'water' was defined by the superficial characteristics of water, but the term is now defined by the chemical structure of the substance. This line of reasoning would easily be coupled with incommensurability, a notion promoted by Kuhn and Feyerabend, among others (Ambrus 1999: 2). Thus, the theory of relativity and Newtonian physics both utilize the term 'mass' but do not discuss the same subject matter through the use of this word. Similarly, the Copernican revolution changed the meaning of the term 'planet' so drastically that it is illusory to think that astronomers have always referred to the same thing by the term (ibid.: 2-3). Putnam thought of incommensurability as a serious threat to scientific realism and attempted to explain "why there is no change of reference following a change of theories" (ibid.: 3). In Putnam's (1975: 142, 153, 1990: 60) account, the meaning of 'water' remains constant even after the discovery that water is H_2O (cf. Valente 2019: 321). Reference discharges a pivotal role in Putnam's theory of meaning and "the man who initially introduced a term designating water made reference to the source of identity of this substance, even though he did not know that this was H_2O" (Ambrus 1999: 4). This statement indicates that, unlike 'bachelors are unmarried', 'water is H_2O' is not analytic, and is hence not *a priori*. Putnam thought that the separation of necessity from analyticity and *a priori* aligned with Kripke's theory, according to which the statement 'water is H_2O' is necessary and metaphysical but is neither analytic nor *a priori*. As previously indicated, however, Kripke's view entails essentialism, with which Putnam's emphasis on interest is obviously incompatible (cf. Hanna 1998: 498-499, n. 5).

---

63)]s argument will be presented in Chapter 2.

Whatever the reason for Putnam's sympathy toward Kripke's modal claim, Hacking (2007a: 16) maintains that "[a]lthough in the pages just cited, Putnam heartily endorsed possible worlds, rigid designation and necessity, those pages can be deleted without affecting any position to which Putnam was himself later committed". Hacking's interpretation accords with Putnam's (1990) remark:

I do not think that a criterion of substance-identity that handles Twin Earth cases will extend handily to 'possible worlds'. In particular, what if a hypothetical 'world' *obeys different laws* ? […] Is it clear that we would call a (hypothetical) substance with quite different behavior *water* in these circumstances? I now think that the question, 'What is the necessary and sufficient condition for being water *in all possible worlds?*'makes no sense at all. And this means that I now reject 'metaphysical necessity'. I won't insist (any more) that 'it is conceivable that water may turn out not to be H_2O but it isn't logically possible that water isn't H_2O'. (Putnam 1990: 69-70)

Externalism as such makes no commitment to reducing linguistic semantics to essentialism, which maintains that chemical substances exhibit some invariable microscopic properties, namely their essences, in all possible worlds. Although Putnam principally distanced himself from modal claims, it is nonetheless true that Putnam was committed to the view that water is distinct from twater even if the distinction is not accessible to anyone. This view poses its share of problems, and I will return to this issue in Chapter 5[64].

Finally, and perhaps most notably, externalism is not a view about the locus of meaning and thought, despite its name; at stake is not whether meaning and thought are inside or outside the mind (Burge 2003: 454-455), but whether a person's intrinsic properties are sufficiently rich to individuate what the person means by his words vis-à-vis what his twin means by his words. It would then be possible,

---

64) Chapter 5 will address problems with the Twin Earth experiment, including the one pointed out by Needham (2011):

What could Putnam's twin earth fantasy show beyond the triviality that sufficiently ignorant people might not be able to distinguish similar substances? If it assumes that two substances are distinct at the microlevel and yet share all their macroproperties, so that they can't be distinguished in terms of macroproperties, then the scenario is wildly implausible. Assuming that it is in some sense possible doesn't show it to be possible. (Needham 2011: 11)

for example, to be a Platonist regarding meaning and thought without being an externalist in the relevant sense. As previously stated in Section 1.2, Frege famously (or infamously) considered senses and thoughts to belong neither to the inner world nor to the outer world of material, perceptible things, but to what he called the third realm (cf. Dummett 1991: Ch. 12). In Frege's opinion, meanings are not mental entities but abstract entities that exist outside a thinker's mind (Putnam 1973: 699, 1975: 134). Such a belief does not make Frege an externalist in the relevant sense, however, because he definitely equated grasping or apprehending the sense of an expression with being in a certain state of mind. Frege never mentioned the thinker's external environment as a factor that contributed to the determination of the person's thoughts[65]. Although I have used the term 'externalism' throughout this chapter in the interest of intelligibility, it is not the term Burge prefers. Rather he utilizes the term 'anti-individualism' in his arguments (Burge 2003: 453). 'Internalism vs. externalism' and 'individualism vs. anti-individualism' are "approximately interchangeable" and their "[u]sage here is obviously a matter of taste" (Burge 2007: 154). Still, Burge prefers the terms 'individualism' and 'anti-individualism' chiefly because the terms 'internalism' and 'externalism' would erroneously indicate that "the main issue is essentially concerned with spatial location" (ibid.). The actual issue concerns "the role of the individual and the individual's relations to a wider order" and not spatial location. The social environment is "a prominent subclass" of such relations (Burge 2007: 155). Externalism is not the standpoint that meaning and mental content are located outside the mind; it offers the perspective that the individuation of meaning and mental content depends on "relations that are not reducible to matters that concern the individual alone" (ibid.: 154; see also Schroeter 2008: 108, n. 6). Rowlands et al. (2020) elucidates this point:

---

65) As will be seen in Section 4.2 below, Frege did refer to the context of utterance as a factor contributing to the expression of a thought (Frege 1918-1919a: 64/1956: 296). Thus, John's utterance of 'I am hungry' and Mary's utterance of the same sounds express different thoughts. But this merely suggests that Frege was aware of the existence of what Kaplan (1989a, 1989b) and Putnam (1973, 1975) called (absolutely) indexical words as opposed to natural kind terms like 'water'. At stake in the internalist/externalist debate is whether the meaning of a non-indexical term can be determined in total independence of the nature of the environment within which it is tokened. Both parties accept the obvious fact that the reference of an absolutely indexical term can only be determined with respect to the context of an utterance.

Despite some initially over-exuberant formulations of Putnam (1975) – of the "Cut the pie any way you like, meaning just ain't in the head", variety – the correct conclusion of this thought experiment does not concern the *location* of (some) mental states but, rather, a claim about their *individuation*. External individuation does not entail external location. Sunburn, as Davidson (1987) pointed out, is externally individuated: individuation dependent on factors that lie outside the skin. Nevertheless, it is still located on the skin. That some mental states are individuation dependent on circumstances that exist outside the skin of an individual does not entail that those mental states are located outside the individual's skin. (Rowlands et al. 2020: Section 3.1, emphases in the original)

We must rhetorically interpret Putnam's (1973: 700, 1975: 139) question, "Are meanings in the head?" (Nuccetelli 2003: 3). In Burge's opinion, this is why 'individualism / anti-individualism' are more appropriate terms in characterizing the issue than 'internalism / externalism'. I shall continue to use the terms 'internalism / externalism' but it should be borne in mind that the internalist-externalist debate concerns whether or not the individuation of meaning and thought can be accomplished without taking into account the nature of an environment about which the utterer or thinker may be unaware.

Properly understood, externalism is probably better placed than internalism from inception: externalism stakes merely an existential claim while internalism commits us to a stronger universal claim (Hunter 2003: 733). What Putnam's and Burge's thought experiments are designed to establish is that there *can* be twins who are molecularly identical but have differing concepts and thoughts or, equivalently, that a person's intrinsic properties *can* fail to individuate that person's concepts and thoughts vis-à-vis her twin's. As Burge (1993: 318/2007: 300) states, "[a]nti-individualism is the view that *not all* of an individual's mental states and events can be type-individuated independently of the nature of entities in the individual's environment to which the individual bears not purely conceptual relations" (emphasis mine). Similarly, as Schroeter (2008: 107) states, anti-individualism maintains that "whether a mental state involves a particular concept is determined *in part* by contingent facts about the subject's actual environment (about which she may be ignorant or mistaken)" (emphasis mine). Externalism is merely committed to the claim that "*[n]ot all* of Adam's [...] obliquely ascribable attitudes supervene on his bodily properties" (Elugardo 1993: 373, emphasis mine). To refute this view, it must be shown that no two people who are internally identical but have different concepts and thoughts can exist, or, in Segal's (2000: 28) words, that "[a]ny twin of mine in any environment would have a concept with the same extension condition". This contrast is emphasized by Haukioja (2017) and Rowlands et al. (2000)[66]:

> [...] internalism holds that propositional content is *always* supervenient on intrinsic properties – externalism, as the negation of internalism, holds that the corresponding expressions (i.e. expressions which are phonetically or orthographically identical) used by duplicates may *at least in some* cases differ in *some* of their semantic properties" (Haukioja 2017: 866, emphases in the original).

> [...] externalism is the view that an individual's bodily (including neural) events, states, processes, etc. do not always, on their own, determine the mental, states, processes had or undergone by that individual. The qualifier *not always* permits there to be cases – perhaps many – in which mental occurrences are fixed by bodily occurrences. Externalism, generically at least, is merely committed to the claim that this does not *always* happen. The qualifier *on its own* is intended to convey that even if an individual's bodily occurrences do not *completely* determine which mental occurrences are had or undergone by that individual, the former will at least *partially* determine the latter and, indeed, can play an important role in such determination. (Rowlands et al. 2020: Section 1, emphases in the original)

It follows that, as Hunter (2003: 733) states, "the opponent of Internalism has the prima facie easier case". Suppose that on Twin Earth there is iron pyrites but no gold and that iron pyrites is called 'gold' in Twin English. Suppose also that Oscar cannot distinguish gold and iron pyrites, both of which are found on his planet, Earth. Assuming that Oscar and Oscar$_2$ are atom-for-atom and molecule-for-molecule identical, this implies that their psychological states as individualistically described

---

66) Likewise, Brown (2004: ix) characterizes anti-individualism as the view that "a subject's thought contents are *partly* individuated by her environment" (emphasis mine; see also Brown (2004: 4, 11, 18)). The antithesis of this view, i.e., individualism, holds that "a subject's thoughts are *wholly* individuated by her 'internal' states, such as her brain states." (ibid., emphasis mine).

are indistinguishable when they talk or think about what they call 'gold'. It would still be reasonable to suppose that Oscar's utterance of 'gold', but not Oscar$_2$'s utterance of 'gold', can refer to gold (cf. Newman 2005: 154-155)[67]. Since Oscar$_2$ has never come into any contact with gold nor with those who have had contact with gold, he has no means through which to think about gold, and his utterance of 'gold' refers exclusively to iron pyrites. The sameness of the internal states of the twin speakers does not *ipso facto* make their meanings of 'gold' identical. If Oscar$_2$ visited Earth and attempted to sell his 'gold' as gold, he would be charged with fraud. This single example suffices to refute the claim that no two people can exist who are internally identical but have different concepts and thoughts. According to Segal (2000: 27), the internalist view quoted above that "[a]ny twin of mine in any environment would have a concept with the same extension condition" is "[t]he less extreme version" of internalism. Confronted with the challenge set by Putnam's and Burge's thought experiments, the internalist could even find it difficult to defende a moderate version of his own claim. Perhaps, it would surprise some philosophers to know that most linguists commit to what Segal (2000: 27) calls 'radical internalism'.

1.3.4 (Ir)relevance of Externalism to Linguistics[68]

Barber (2003: 26) expounds that "[l]inguistics is no longer a branch of individualist psychology if it must consider an individual's physical and social environment before it can identify the content of the theory supposedly known by speakers". Nevertheless, linguistics has generally opted to align with individualist psychology, as evidenced by Deutsch's (1993: 410) remark that "[r]elatively little has been written by linguists on the Kripke-Putnam view". One of the reasons why linguistics has historically expressed scant interest in externalism is that externalism is primarily couched in terms of the notion of 'truth', a notion related not only to 'truth condition' (Burge 1982: 110, 115/2007: 93, 97, Boghossian 1992: 34, Haukioja 2017: 869, Wikforss 2008: 162, 169, 179) and 'truth value' (Burge 1979a: 99/2007: 128), but also to 'extension' (Quine 1951: 21, Putnam 1975: 134,

---

67) Newman (2005) argues that the position called 'weak internalism', which holds both that beliefs are in the head and that microphysical duplicates can differ mentally (ibid.: 155), is untenable because it renders impossible the communication of *de se* beliefs between the duplicates (ibid.: 167). If Newman's argument is correct, "we must choose between internalism and externalism full-stop" (ibid.: 156).

68) Section 1.3.4 is based on Sakai (2022a: Section 2) and Sakai (2023a).

154). Truth and extension are inseparable from each other insofar as "[t]he extension of a term is just what the term is *true of*" (Putnam 1975: 154, emphasis in the original). As noted in Section 1.1.1, the externalist argument hinges on the fact that the stereotype associated with a word fails to fully determine the extension of the word. What Oscar knows about 'water' is insufficient in determining the extension of 'water' to the exclusion of twater. What Adam understands about 'arthritis' is inadequate in determining the extension of 'arthritis' to the exclusion of tharthritis. This indicates that, ultimately, externalism can only be justified by appealing to the notion of truth. Another term closely related to 'extension' is 'reference'. Although, in general, 'extension' is used for general terms while 'reference' is used for proper names, this distinction is often blurred because, as Kripke (1980: 134) argued, "certain general terms, those for natural kinds, have a greater kinship with proper names than is generally realized". It would then be natural to talk about the reference of 'tiger', the reference of 'gold', the reference of 'water', and so on (Kripke 1980: 135-136, Hacking 2007a: 3). Further, as Frege (1918-1919a: 68/1956: 301) emphasized, truth does not belong to individual speakers. It would make scarcely any sense to say, for example, that my Pythagorean theorem is true while yours is false. It could then be legitimately claimed that truth-related notions are external to the language faculty of competent language users, which contemporary linguistics seeks to elucidate. This partially explains why Chomsky (1955) discredits reference, which, for him, is opposed to meaning:

> The distinction between the theory of reference and the theory of meaning is an important one [...] The citation of Quine and Tarski in support of the theory of meaning must itself be a confusion of meaning and reference, since both Tarski and Quine have done important work in the theory of reference. This is the branch where real progress has been made; but it is also the branch that has little interest for linguists. (Chomsky 1955: 40-41)

Chomsky adheres to the position Segal (2000: 27) refers to as 'radical internalism', which "dispenses with the notions of extension and extension conditions altogether"[69]. The radical internalist dismisses not only the terms 'reference' and 'extension' but also the notions of reference and extension. If Chomsky is a radical internalist, Abbott's (1999) following remark is off the point:

> Chomsky also complains that normal speakers do not have intuitions about

theoretical semantic relations like reference and extension (1995, p. 42), but to get Putnam's results one does not need to use terms like "reference" or "extension" which, indeed, ordinary speakers may not be familiar with in their technical uses. All one needs to ask is whether, for example, under such-and-such conditions such-and-such a substance would be water or such-and-such an animal would be a tiger. In this respect gathering semantic data is no different from gathering syntactic data, where native speakers who do not (consciously) know anything about Principle B Binding Theory will nevertheless agree with Chomsky's intuition that somebody who says "John expects to like him" is saying that John expects to like some male person other than himself (cf. Chomsky, 1995, p. 36). (Abbott 1999: 312-313)

In fact, Chomsky complains that the gathered semantic data build on the notions of reference and extension. Such data, according to Chomsky (1995: 24-25), are irrelevant to linguistics to the extent that competent speakers generally have no clear intuition about reference and extension:

A good part of contemporary philosophy of language is concerned with analysing alleged relations between expressions and things, often exploring intuitions about the technical notions "denote", "refer", "true of", etc., said to hold between expressions and something else. But there can be no intuitions about these notions, just as there can be none about "angular velocity" or "protein". These are technical terms of philosophical discourse with a stipulated sense that has no counterpart in ordinary language-which is why Frege had to provide a new technical meaning for "Bedeutung", for example. If we re-run the thought experiments with ordinary terms, judgments seem to collapse, or rather, to become so interest-relative as to yield no meaningful results. (Chomsky 1995: 24-25; see also Chomsky 2000: 172, 188/2003: 266, 280)[70]

---

69) Segal (2000: 157, n. 2) notes that radical internalism is upheld by Chomsky and "some other prominent linguists". Even though Segal makes no reference to cognitive linguistics, such prominent linguists include Langacker, among others, as we will be discussed below. Of course, radical internalism is not accepted by every linguist. Thus, Higginbotham (1998a: 160) says that "semantics is a matter of knowledge of conditions on reference".

70) Chomsky also makes a more specific point about Putnam's Twin Earth thought experiment (Chomsky 1995: 22-23/2000: 127-128). This point will be addressed in Chapter 5.

True, as Abbott (1997: 312) points out, Chomsky (1995, 2000) does not challenge the major result of Putnam's thought experiment. On Chomsky's view, however, the putative main result has no significance for the scientific study of language because the intuitions elicited by the thought experiment rest on notions such as reference and extension. Chomsky denies for the same reason that social factors surrounding an individual have any bearing on the characterization of the individual's I-language:

> Communities, cultures, patterns of deference, and so on, are established in human life in all sorts of ways, with no particular relation to anything we call "languages" in informal discourse. There is no meaningful answer to the question whether Bert should refer to the pain in his thigh as arthritis; or whether he should use the word "disinterested" to mean "unbiased", as the dictionary says, or "uninterested", as virtually every speaker believes; or whether he should pronounce words as in Boston or London. (Chomsky 1995: 49/2000: 155)

Neither Putnam's nor Burge's thought experiments have any direct implications for the study of I-language. As Barber (2003: 26) summarizes, Chomsky regards intuitions mined from externalist thought experiments merely as "folk intuitions with no more than sociological interest, belonging to 'ethnoscience'" as opposed to natural science. In a similar vein, Segal (2000: 122), one of the few philosophers aligned with the 'heterodox' faction (Hunter 2003: 724), claims that "[t]he Externalist intuitions generated by the focal Twin Earth experiments are simply misleading" and that they reveal "only an accidental and adventitious strand of our psychological thinking" that we should not take "too seriously".

Several researchers have questioned Putnam's and Burge's judgment of the Twin Earth situation (Fodor 1987: 28-29). Thus, Bach (1987: 276) comments that "[n]ot everyone shares Putnam's and Burge's intuitions that there is no water on Twin Earth" and that "[i]nstead of denying that there is water on Twin Earth, some people are inclined to say that there are two kinds of water, one kind here and one kind there" (cf. Wikforss 2005: 72). For such individuals, "what is essential to water is not its chemical make-up but its functional role" (Bach 1987: 276, n. 9). It would be plausible to regard twater as a kind of water to the extent that twater performs the same functional role in Oscar$_2$'s life as water does in Oscar's life. This intuition is shared by Mellor (1977: 303), who claims that, if an Earthian scientist investigated a sample of the liquid Twin Earthians called 'water', she would discover that "not all water has the same microstructure". If we assume that both Oscar and Oscar$_2$ talk and think about water, albeit of different kinds, there remains no compelling reason, as against Putnam and Burge, to attribute different meanings and thoughts to the two subjects. At best, as Lewis (1994: 424) puts it, "we are in a state of semantic indecision about whether it deserves the name 'water'". On this account, twater is water in one sense, but not in another, as LaPorte suggests:

> I do not think that the essence of water is H_2O. On the contrary, I think that we might conclude, if confronted by XYZ, "XYZ is water." We might also conclude, if confronted with H_2O that has unusual characteristics, "Some H_2O is not water." I do not argue that if we were confronted by XYZ then we would *have* to conclude, "XYZ is water," on pain of error. It is not that we would be right to affirm 'XYZ is water' and wrong to reject that statement, as a well-known *minority* response to Putnam would have it: According to this minority response (e.g. Mellor [1977]), XYZ would simply be water. I argue instead that XYZ is neither clearly in nor clearly out of the extension of the vague word 'water'. (LaPorte 2004: 93, emphases in the original)

The varying intuitions should not be dismissed as irrelevant to semantics if, as Braddon-Mitchell (2004: 149) claims, "we are masters of our meanings in the final instance, in that what it takes to *determine* the reference of our words at least is up to us".

Katz (1997) impugns Putnam's (1973, 1975) assumption inherited from Frege, that sense (intension) determines reference (extension). The upshot of Putnam's Twin Earth argument is that whatever is in the speaker's mind is weaker than the Fregean sense because it cannot determine reference (cf. McCulloch 1995: 170). Without the Fregean assumption that sense determines reference, Katz (1997: 7) ironizes, "the famous Twin Earth argument would be an infamous Twin Earth fallacy". Insofar as the Twin Earth argument rests on that Fregean assumption, the putative internalist-externalist debate is merely "a Fregean family squabble" (ibid.). Katz (1978: 63) expresses his aversion to the construal of his internalist theory of semantic representation as "a linguisticized version of Frege's theory of sense". For Katz (1972: Ch. 1, 1978: 66, 68, 94, 1997: 8), the genuine internalist definition of sense should run as follows:

The sense of an expression is that aspect of its grammatical structure which is responsible for its sense properties and relations, i.e., having a sense (meaningfulness), sameness of sense (synonymy), multiplicity of sense (ambiguity), repetition of sense (redundancy), opposition of sense (antonymy), and so on. (Katz 1997: 8)

The relevant properties and relations are all "*internal* to language" (Katz 1978: 66, emphasis in the original) and Katz's definition of sense "makes no reference to reference" (Katz 1997: 8). Katz (1997: 14) argues that the proper construal of sense turns the "great strength of Putnam's arguments into a fatal weakness". If we jettison the Fregean assumption that sense determines reference, it will no longer follow that the speaker's psychological state cannot individuate sense.

Most cognitive linguists share the dismissive attitude of generativists toward truth-related notions, despite the otherwise drastic oppositions between the two camps. George Lakoff, a founder of cognitive linguistics, argues extensively against disciplines which build on truth and reference (Lakoff 1987: Book I; Part II). According to Lakoff, such disciplines have developed an 'objectivist paradigm' (ibid.: 157ff) that contrasts diametrically with the cognitive approach. Likewise, Fauconnier (1985/1994: 152) comments toward the end of the book in which he advances Mental Space theory, a widely acknowledged cognitive linguistic frameworks:

As mentioned before, there are differences between the objectives and adequacy criteria of the research carried out here and those usually adopted in philosophical investigations of the same phenomena. In particular, two crucial questions from a standard philosophical point of view, truth and reference, have not played a central role in the study of mental spaces. It has not been my primary concern here to discover under what conditions an utterance would count as true in a certain state of a real or fictional world. Linguistic expressions help to set up and identify space elements, but do not *refer* to them. Reference would be another connection, presumably relating space elements and real (or perhaps fictional or possible) entities. (Fauconnier 1985/1994: 152, emphasis in the original)

Langacker (2008: 28) similarly highlighted that the notion of truth condition pertains to "what the world is like objectively" and falls short of capturing the fact that "meaning derives from embodied human experience". Virtually all cognitive linguists categorically reject Lewis's (1970: 18) (in)famous statement that "[s]emantics with no treatment of truth conditions is not semantics".

Nevertheless, a nonnegligible difference exists between Chomsky's and Langacker's distrust of truth-related notions utilized in the study of semantics. This disparity emanates from their divergent definitions of language, or more specifically, meaning. For Chomsky, the I-language comprises a lexicon and a syntax (Chomsky 1995: 15). The lexicon contains lexical items (i.e. words and idioms) each of which incorporates phonological features such as 'bilabial stop' along with semantic features such as 'artifact'. Syntax is a computational system that combines lexical items to form a complex expression that encompasses an array of phonological and semantic features. It is important to realize that such an array of phonological and semantic features belongs to the syntax, contrary to the indications we may receive from the names:

> [...] the computational procedure maps an array of lexical choices into a pair of symbolic objects, phonetic form and LF, and does so in a way that is optimal, from a certain point of view. The elements of these symbolic objects can be called "phonetic" and "semantic" features, respectively, but we should bear in mind that all of this is pure syntax, completely internalist, the study of mental representations and computations, much like the inquiry into how the image of a cube rotating in space is determined from retinal stimulations, or imagined. (Chomsky 1995: 19/2000: 125)[71]

Chomsky (1995: 43/2000: 159) cautions that his use of the term "'representation' is not to be understood relationally, as 'representation of'"[72]. Semantics or representation in the ordinary sense of the term, namely the study of language/mind-

---

71) Chomsky has repeatedly expressed the opinion that semantics in the purely internal sense should rather be called 'syntax'. Thus, Chomsky (2003a) remarks:

> Peter Ludlow opens by observing that I am not 'hostile towards semantics.' That's correct. Most of my work on language, from the outset, has an effort to explore the form and meaning of expressions and principles that determine them, core problems of semantics. It's true that I prefer to call this work 'syntax,' and think the same term might well be used for other investigations that keep to symbolic systems that are internal to the mind-brain, the faculty of language FL or others. (Chomsky 2003a: 287)

world relations, is fundamentally orthogonal to the study of the I-language:

> As for semantics, insofar as we understand language use, the argument for a reference-based semantics (apart from an internalist syntactic version) seems to me weak. It is possible that natural language has only syntax and pragmatics; it has a "semantics" only in the sense of "the study of how this instrument, whose formal structure and potentialities of expression are the subject of syntactic investigation, is actually put to use in a speech community" [...] (Chomsky 1995: 26/2000: 132)

> An expression such as "I painted my house brown" is accessed by performance systems that interpret it, on the receptive side, and articulate it while typically using it for one or another speech act, on the productive side. How is that done? The articulatory-perceptual aspects have been intensively studied, but these matters are still poorly understood. At the conceptual-intentional interface the problems are even more obscure, and may well fall beyond human naturalistic inquiry in crucial respects. (Chomsky 1995: 20/2000: 125)

It was noted in Section 1.1 that even Burge acknowledges that purely internalist approaches would not adversely affect the study of syntax in Chomsky's sense[73]. Such approaches to the syntax are made possible by the fact that, as Fodor (1980: 65) maintains, purely computational mental processes "have no access to the *semantic* properties of [mental] representations, including the property of being true, of having referents, or, indeed, the property of being representations *of the environment*" (emphases in the original). Consequently, the externalist thesis on the semantic properties of mental states does not undermine the basis of generative linguistics. As remarked in Section 1.1, cognitive linguistics holds that

---

72) See Rey (2003) for a critical review of Chomsky's use of 'represent(ation)'. To precisely understand Chomsky's intentions in using the term is, to say the least, "extremely difficult" (Rey 2003: 144).

73) Stich (1992: 258) raises a suspicion about the naturalistic approach to phonology in Fodor's (1987) sense on the grounds that there is no available definition of phonemes couched in terms that are generally accepted in physics or biology. This is not a knock-down argument to naturalism, however, because, as Crane (1991: 6) states, naturalism is not physicalism, to the extent that it holds that "theories can define their own laws and concepts in their own terms" as distinct from physicalist terms.

"[m]eaning is what language is all about" and that "[g]rammar is simply the structuring and symbolization of semantic content" (Langacker 1987: 12). For the cognitive linguist, the syntax as construed in generative linguistics has no role to play in semantics nor even in grammar. One of the basic tenets of cognitive linguistics is that "grammar is meaningful" (Langacker 2008: 3) and that studying grammar inevitably helps unravel the nature of "both meaning and cognition" (ibid.: 5). Of particular relevance here is that, for Langacker, grammar is "an integral part of cognition" and "reflects our basic experience of moving, perceiving, and acting on the world" (ibid.: 4). Cognition, which integrates both grammar and meaning, is what mediates a person's engagement in the world:

> Some have questioned whether a "cognitive" approach to language can accommodate either its social function (as a means of interaction) or its referential function (as a means of describing the world). These concerns are unfounded. They stem from the erroneous idea that what goes on inside the skull is isolated from everything outside it, including other minds. But this is simply not so. In the sense that cognition resides in activity of the brain, it does indeed take place inside the skull. The brain, however, is the nexus of a nervous system that runs all through the body, connecting with the sensory and motor organs through which we perceive and act on the world. Neither is the brain's activity isolated from other minds. An essential aspect of cognition is our awareness of other people and our recognition that they, too, are cognitive agents. We are quite adept at reading their intentions, as well as imagining the nature of their mental experience. Thus cognition, far from being insulated from the world and the other people in it, is our primary means of engaging them. (Langacker 2008: 500)

According to the cognitive linguistic conception of language, drastically different from the generative linguistic perspective, the study of the relationship between the semantic content of an expression and the environment in which it is tokened should constitute part and parcel of genuine linguistic inquiry. Despite the reticence of most researchers working within the framework, the internalist/externalist debate should directly influence the overall organization of linguistic theory.

Some preliminary remarks are mandated before we approach the core of this subject. First, an emphasis on reference or other truth-related notions (as opposed to meaning) does not entail externalism. As I have remarked in Section 1.2, truth-related notions play a pivotal role in Frege's theory. Frege (1969: 135/1979: 128) further asserted that "there is no one property by which their [= sciences such as physics and chemistry] nature is so completely characterized as logic by the word 'true'"[74]. Frege's conception of thought is intuitively sensed as bearing greater affinity to meaning than to reference. Nevertheless, it is grounded essentially on the notion of truth:

In thinking we do not produce thoughts but we apprehend them. For what I have called thought stands in the closest relation to truth. What I recognize as true I judge to be true quite independently of my recognition of its truth and of my thinking about it. That someone thinks it has nothing to do with the truth of a thought. 'Facts, facts, facts' cries the scientist if he wants to emphasise the necessity of a firm foundation for science. What is a fact? A fact is a thought that is true. But the scientist will surely not recognise something which depends on men's varying states of mind to be the firm foundation of science. The work of science does not consist of creation but of the discovery of true thoughts. (Frege 1918-1919a: 74/1956: 307-308)[75]

We must recognize that Frege's insistence on reference and truth did not deter him from endorsing what is now called semantic internalism. When applied to Frege's theory, semantic internalism amounts to the idea that grasping or apprehending the sense of an expression is being in a certain state of mind and that this state determines the reference of the expression[76]. Conversely, the repudiation of truth-related notions does not guarantee internalist conceptions of semantics. In

---

74) „[…] durch keine einzige [Eigenschaft] so vollkommen in ihrem Wesen gekennzeichnet sind, wie die Logik durch das Wort ‚wahr'." (Frege 1969: 135)

75) „Beim Denken erzeugen wir nicht die Gedanken, sondern wir fassen sie. Denn das, was ich Gedanken genannt habe, steht ja im engsten Zusammenhange mit der Wahrheit. Was ich als wahr anerkenne, von dem urteile ich, dass es wahr sei ganz unabhängig von meiner Anerkennung seiner Wahrheit, auch unabhängig davon, ob ich daran denke. Zum Wahrsein eines Gedankens gehört nicht, dass er gedacht werde. ‚Tatsachen! Tatsachen! Tatsachen!' ruft der Naturforscher aus, wenn er die Notwendigkeit einer sicheren Grundlegung der Wissenschaft einschärfen will. Was ist eine Tatsache? Eine Tatsache ist ein Gedanke, der wahr ist. Als sichere Grundlage der Wissenschaft aber wird der Naturforscher sicher nicht etwas anerkennen, was von den wechselnden Bewusstseinszuständen von Menschen abhängt. Die Arbeit der Wissenschaft besteht nicht in einem Schaffen, sondern in einem Entdecken von wahren Gedanken." (Frege 1918-1919a: 74)

Chapter 1   The (Lack of) Impact of Externalism on Cognitive Linguistics

fact, Bilgrami (1992: 32), an advocate of a version of externalism, contends that the notion of reference has nothing to do with meaning and content. A detailed discussion is required to determine whether Langacker's dismissive attitude toward truth-related notions vindicates his version of internalism.

Langacker identifies meaning with conceptualization, a notion designed to enfold all aspects of mental experience:

> [...] meaning is not identified with concepts but with conceptualization, the term being chosen precisely to highlight its dynamic nature. Conceptualization is broadly defined to encompass any facet of mental experience. It is understood as subsuming (1) both novel and established conceptions; (1) not just "intellectual" notions, but sensory, motor, and emotive experience as well; (3) apprehension of the physical, linguistic, social, and cultural context; and (4) conceptions that develop and unfold through processing time (rather than being simultaneously manifested). (Langacker 2008: 30, emphasis in the original)

In a nutshell, externalism is the view that meaning transcends conceptualization. The internalism/externalism debate in linguistics should then center around the question whether meaning and conceptualization can be individuated independently from a person's environment. Although Langacker does not directly address this question, he seems to side with internalism in thinking that the collective knowledge of a community depends on the knowledge of individual members but not vice versa:

> We can validly distinguish, however, between what a single speaker knows and the collective knowledge of a whole society. The former is arguably more basic, since collective knowledge consists in (or at least derives from) the knowledge of individuals. For purposes of studying language as part of cognition, an expression's meaning is first and foremost its meaning for a single (representa-

---

76) This does not mean, of course, that all versions of internalist semantic theory hinges on the notion of reference. As stated earlier, in defending his internalist semantic theory, Katz (1997) disputed both Putnam's externalism and Frege's internalism. While, in Frege's theory, sense determines reference, Katz advanced a notion of sense which "makes no reference to reference" (ibid.: 8). On Katz's view, "sense *mediates* rather than determines reference" (ibid.: 9).

tive) speaker. (Langacker 2008: 30, emphasis in the original)

This perspective contemplates external factors only after individual knowledge is in place. This seems to entail that differences described by Putnam (1973, 1975) and Burge (1982/2007) between the mental states of the twin subjects transgress cognitive linguistic studies because no one has cognized them. We could posit by the same token that the difference Burge (1979a/2007) posits in the truth value of Adam's and Adam$_2$'s beliefs is not the primary object of linguistic inquiry because the falsity of Adam's belief only emerges when his belief is compared against the collective knowledge of his community. Langacker proposes that the term 'meaning' should be reserved for an individual speaker's understanding of a linguistic expression:

> Countless aspects of our surroundings do carry meaning potential [...]. Thus, if a doctor extends a tongue depressor toward my mouth and says *Open wide*, my understanding of what the doctor intends and what I am supposed to do is far more comprehensive than anything derivable from the linguistic expression alone. (I know, for example, that I will not satisfy the request by approaching a cabinet and pulling a drawer out all the way.) It would not be unreasonable to describe the relevant circumstances as being "imbued with meaning" or as "part of the meaning" an expression has in context. Yet I think we gain in clarity and analytical precision by reserving the term "meaning" for how a speaker understands an expression (in either a speaking or a listening capacity). It thus incorporates a speaker's apprehension of the circumstances, and exploits the meaning potential they carry, but cannot be identified with those circumstances. So defined, an expression's meaning resides in the conceptualizing activity of individual speakers. (Langacker 2008: 29)

According to this recommended standpoint, a speaker's conceptualization is determined by the speaker's personal properties which are considered in isolation from her environment. This stance opposes externalism because all unknown differences between the Earth and the Twin Earth are excluded from the semantic descriptions of the words the speaker employs. Langacker would sympathize with Unger (1983), who argues against the opinion that philosophical thought experiments as envisaged by Putnam impact the semantics of natural language. Unger asserts that "it is doubtful whether any semantic theory is actually doing much to explain our responses to any of these cases" (ibid.: 83)[77]. On this view, Oscar and Oscar$_2$ would be considered to share the same meaning of 'water' because they understand the word and apprehend their circumstances in exactly the same way. This would also be true of Adam and Adam$_2$, who, if Langacker's view is validated, would be viewed as thinking the same thought, even though one of them thinks truthfully and the other falsely.

In fact, these considerations have motivated some philosophers to postulate varied conceptions of narrow content that can be individuated in total isolation of external factors (Burge 1986b: 6, 10/2007: 223, 226, Rey 1992: 319, Prinz 2002: 264, Grabarczyk 2016: 156-157)[78] as opposed to wide content or intentional content (Prinz 2002: 264). As Grabarczyk (2016: 169) puts it, it is plausible to characterize such propositions of narrow content as "a form of damage control after the Fregean project of linguistic meaning proved to be unsuccessful". In brief, the externalist is broad-minded, whereas the internalist is narrow-minded (Crane 1991: 1-2). Thus, Fodor (1987) proposed that the narrow content represents a partial function from contexts to broad or wide contents[79]. Even though Oscar and Oscar$_2$ have the same function from contexts to broad contents, their positioning in different contexts yields different broad contents[80]:

[…] by this criterion, my Twin's 'water'-thoughts are intentionally identical to my water-thoughts; they have the same contents even though, since their contexts are de facto different, they differ, de facto, in their truth conditions. In effect, what we have here is an extensional criterion for 'narrow' content. The 'broad content' of a thought, by contrast, is what you can semantically evaluate;

---

77) However, Langacker would disagree with Unger's proposal to the effect that semantics should be immune to psychological factors. Unger (1983: 33) remarks that questions posed by philosophical thought experiments "are psychological, not semantic, and the responses are to be explained psychologically".

78) Narrow content corresponds to what Chomsky (2000/2003) calls "I-meaning", as indicated by his paraphrasing (Chomsky 2000: 170ff/2003: 264ff). Rey (2003: 167, n. 24) points out that Chomsky's stance toward narrow content is ambiguous.

79) For a critical view, see Aydene (1997).

80) Roughly speaking, you are an externalist if you acknowledge that broad content serves to characterize mental state. Whether you acknowledge that, in addition to broad content, narrow content also characterizes mental state is another problem. Some but not all externalists agree with this bifurcation of content. Thus, defending a version of externalism, Bilgrami (1992) argues for the unity of content.

it's what you get when you specify a narrow content *and fix a context*. (Fodor 1987: 48, emphasis in the original)

If Oscar were born on Twin Earth, he would have acquired the concept of *twater* just as $Oscar_2$ did; if $Oscar_2$ were born on Earth, he would have acquired the concept of *water* just as Oscar did (Segal 2000: 18). The basic idea behind this proposal is that Oscar behaves exactly like $Oscar_2$, despite their environmental differences. Evidently, behavior is explained not by what holds in the environment but by what one believes holds in the environment. Oscar and $Oscar_2$ inhabit different environments but their understanding of the environments is the same, which renders their behaviors indistinguishable. As Fodor (1994: 17) states, "narrow content is ipso facto *not* externalist"[81]. Fodor (1987: 47) neutralizes the externalist claim by saying that "Twin Earth examples didn't break the connection between content and extension; they just relativize it to context" (cf. Aydene 1997: 427).

Segal (2000: 33-41) argues that the notion of narrow content can be substantiated by the existence of empty natural kind terms[82]. The concept *ghost* influences behavior in some people not because ghosts exist but because such people believe in the existence of ghosts. The same applies to more scientific concepts such as *phlogiston* or *ether*. Importantly, the explanation of behavior is not affected by whether or not the terms in question are empty. Grabarczyk (2016: 167) stresses that "[d]ismissing beliefs about non-existing objects as less important or second-rate beliefs (contrary to ones which are cognitively successful) would have been a huge mistake". Although the concept *water* is nonempty unlike *phlogiston* or *ether*, Oscar's behavior is determined not by what water is like but by what he believes water is like, and $Oscar_2$'s behavior is determined not by what twater is like but by what he believes twater (which he calls 'water') is like. Their understanding of what they each call 'water' is the same; thus, the concept of 'water' is narrow in the relevant sense of the term: "[i]f S has concept C, then S's having C

---

81) Fodor (1994) calls into question the need for the narrow content he defended in Fodor (1987), saying, "There aren't any narrow contents, and, a fortiori, there aren't any narrow content laws" (Fodor 1994: 25), or at least, "narrow content is *superfluous*" (ibid.: 28). As Horst (1996: 243) points out, Fodor (1994) does not quite endorse broad content; his new view merely implies that broad content does not threaten his individualist psychology. Aydene (1997) argues that Fodor's (1994) attempt to eliminate narrow content is unsuccessful because Fodor's alleged broad content is in fact equivalent to narrow content.

82) For a brief summary, see Brown (2022: Section 2.3).

Chapter 1   The (Lack of) Impact of Externalism on Cognitive Linguistics

is *narrow* just in case every physically possible twin of S also has C" (Hunter 2003: 726)[83]. This formulation disputes the idea that the mental states of Oscar and Oscar$_2$ differ and accords plausibility to Langacker's proposal of excluding what is not in the mind from the definition of meaning[84]. As Rey (1983: 249) suggests, positing two levels of content and concept, "one metaphysical and the other epistemological", may represent "the temptation behind the view of meaning as 'conceptual role'".

However, this option is not available to Langacker. As mentioned earlier, for Langacker, "cognition, far from being insulated from the world and the other people in it, is our primary means of engaging them" (Langacker 2008: 500). Given that meaning is identified with conceptualization in Langacker's framework, "conceptualization should be seen as a primary means of engaging the world" (Langacker 2008: 29). If we accept this conception of cognition and meaning, it seems pointless to separate narrow content from broad content. At best, such a

---

83) Hunter applies the term 'narrow' to one's having a concept rather than a concept *per se*:

> More accurately, the issue is whether a person's *having* some concept is fixed or determined by his bodily states. For the question concerns what makes it the case that someone, say, S, has the concepts she does. The debate is not over what concepts themselves are. (Hunter 2003: 725, emphasis in the original)

This conception is congruent with cognitive linguistics, which identifies meaning with conceptualization. Conceptualization differs from concept and more resembles having a concept.

84) Hunter (2003: 731-732) doubts that the existence of empty natural kind terms operates in favor of internalism:

> Everyone, Internalists and Externalists alike, has to admit that there are empty concepts, and so has the problem of saying what their semantics are. And the notorious problems here are the same for everybody. So I do not see why the Internalist is better off in this respect.

As Rey (2003: 142) reminds us, it is one of the oldest problems about intentionality (aboutness) or content how we should understand the fact that "one can bear the representation 'relation' to 'things', like Zeus, that do not exist". The problem of nonexistence usually does not arise for terms expressing features or properties rather than things, "for the unsurprising reason that the ontological commitments of people who talk about features and properties are often wholly obscure" (Rey 2003: 149). Thus, people tend to assume that the property of being a mountain higher than Everest exists, but is uninstantiated, even though it is a more controversial question whether there exist uninstantiable properties such as being round and square. Be that as it may, I grant for the sake of argument that cognitive semantics provides a satisfactory semantics for empty terms, somewhat along the lines indicated by Sainsbury and Tye (2011: 111, 119, 2012: 49, 139-144).

move would merely salvage the thesis that meaning is conceptualization. If conceptualization is a primary means of engaging the world, we should assume that the putative narrow content is merely an artificial abstraction of the wide content, which is more fundamental (McDowell 1992: 41-42).

As Jackendoff (1989: 68) stresses, the correctness of a notion is not generally an all-or-nothing affair but is relative to one's purpose. As Keil (1989: 25) says, "it is difficult to design and motivate empirical studies on concept acquisition without first committing oneself to a set of assumptions about what concepts are and how they are represented". This perspective has led researchers to endorse different notions of concept (Margolis 1994: 74, Grabarczyk 2016: 159-160), Peacocke (1992) summarizes:

In the literature of the cognitive sciences, the term "concept" is often assigned a different sense from that chosen here. Sometimes it is used to mean mental representation. Thus, for instance, Jackendoff 1989, 73. Sometimes it is used to capture what I would call central but inessential beliefs involving the concept. This use is found in both artificial intelligence (Hayes 1979) and psychology (Keil 1989). Yet again, it was once frequently used to mean *prototype*. All these notions are of great interest and importance, but they each are to be distinguished from concepts in my sense. (Peacocke 1992: 3)

Jackendoff's goal is "the characterization of the mental resources that make possible human knowledge and experience of the world" (Jackendoff 1989: 69). To this end, we should prefer Chomsky's notion of I-language to his notion of E-language. The notion of I-language requires the notion of I-concept[85]:

If, for my purposes and Chomsky's, the notion of I-language rather than E-language is the suitable focus of inquiry, then on the face of it one should also choose I-concepts rather than E-concepts as the focus for a compatible theory of knowledge. (Jackendoff 1989: 70):

Jackendoff exploits the distinction between I-concepts and E-concepts to dismiss Putnam's (1973, 1975) Twin Earth thought experiment as irrelevant to his purpose:

---

85) Jackendoff (1989: 74ff) similarly distinguishes I-semantics from E-semantics.

I have identified the notion of *I-concept* with the formal notion of *conceptual constituent* as developed in Conceptual Semantics[86]. Furthermore, I have sketched a number of the major elements of the internal structure of concepts, showing how the approach accounts for various basic phenomena in the semantics of natural language [...] In evaluating this approach, I think two things must be borne in mind. First, it does not address what are taken to be some of the standard hurdles for a theory of concepts, for example Putnam's Twin Earth problem. What must be asked with respect to such problems, though, is whether they are relevant at all to a theory of I-concepts, or whether they are germane only to the theory of E-concepts, as I believe is the case with the Twin Earth problem. If they are problems only for E-conceptual theory, they play no role in evaluating the present approach. [...] (Jackendoff 1989: 100)

The question of whether Putnam's thought experiment is external to the purpose of cognitive linguistics remains unanswered. As Bilgrami (1992: 194; see also 1992: 5) expounds, it is generally agreed that the challenge set by externalism is how we can reconcile the assumption that "the content of intentional states explains behavior (in the commonsense psychological explanation)" and the assumption that "this content, specified in that-clause, is externally constituted". Applied to the Twin Earth case, the first assumption says that the mental content of Oscar and Oscar$_2$ is identical because their behavior is indistinguishable. However, the second assumption would lead us to the conclusion that the mental states of Oscar and Oscar$_2$ differ because of the disparate intentional objects of their mental states, namely water and twater, respectively. The proposal that there be two types of content, narrow and broad, purports to settle this conundrum by allocating divergent roles to narrow content and broad content. It might be tempting to think that internalism as embraced by cognitive linguistics can be salvaged if we restrict the object of linguistic inquiry to the narrow content entertained by individual speakers. Narrow content, however, is too narrow to explain behavior. If Oscar's behavior is explained solely by the narrow content of his belief,

---

86) In Jackendoff's Conceptual Semantics, "a level of mental representation called conceptual structure is seen as the form in which speakers encode their construal of the world" (Jackendoff 1989: 74). In Higginbotham's (1998a: 160) interpretation, "it seems safe to say that conceptual structure in this sense is a level of representation, a syntax".

it is predicted that his behavior is never effected by what is inaccessible to his mind. This prediction is not borne out. Suppose that Oscar looks for water and finds a bottle of twater and that a scientist tells him that it is twater, not water. In such a context, Oscar is more likely to say (12a) than (12b) (Sainsbury and Tye 2012: 6).

(12) a. Oh I see.
      b. For me, it's water.

As noted in Section 1.3.1, 'water' is nothing but a 'liquid which is colorless, transparent, tasteless, thirst-quenching, found in lakes, etc.' for Oscar. The response in (12b) would be more aligned with this understanding because the substance present in front of Oscar fits this description. Nevertheless, the response in (12b), although not impossible, sounds less natural than the response in (12a)[87]. This seems to indicate that Oscar's behavior can be affected by something he does not understand. Oscar utters (12a) precisely because he knows that there is something he does not know about water. Similarly, if what Adam understands about arthritis is all that explains his behavior about arthritis, there is no reason for him to abandon his opinion when the doctor tells him that arthritis is specifically an inflammation of the joints. Schroeter (2008: 138) notes in a different but related context that "[o]ur commitment to anti-individualism is integral to our own epistemic agency". The internalist conception of meaning under consideration appears incapable of handling the fact that speakers are disposed to revise their original application of a term (Sainsbury and Tye 2012: 6, Greenberg 2014: 162, Haukioja 2017: 875). A similar point is made by Marconi (1997: 84). Let us imagine a hypothetical scene in which a modern chemist indicates to Archimedes that some of the samples he believes to be gold, or χρῡσός (khrūsós), are not really gold based on the results of varied chemical tests now known to be valid. Archimedes would accept the correction instead of saying (13), if he recognized that the chemist commanded a superior knowledge of gold:

(13) Ah, but that's according to *your* notion of gold; according to *my* criteria, they are indeed gold! (Marconi 1997: 84)

---

87) The fact that (12b) is not completely excluded needs some explanation. This problem will be addressed in Chapter 5.

As Boyd (213: 226) puts it, "individual rationality is essentially social". This type of social interaction is among the phenomena that cognitive linguistics seeks to investigate:

> It is pointless to ask whether language is cognitive or sociocultural in nature, for it is obviously both. A linguistic system comprises a vast array of skills employed in talking. Ultimately, those skills reside in recurrent patterns of neural and neurally guided processing activity. They do not develop in isolation, but as the product of social interaction in a cultural context (Tomasello 2003). In learning to talk, an individual's linguistic system converges on those of other individuals the learner interacts with. Acquisition is never really completed, for the system a person acquires continues to be refined, adjusted, and extended throughout linguistic life. These adaptations as well are effected through socio-cultural interaction, and are thus coordinated to some extent among individuals who interact with one another. (Langacker 2008: 218)

Putnam's Twin Earth and Burge's 'arthritis' thought experiments are therefore by no means irrelevant to cognitive linguistics, even though, as Chomsky (1995, 2000) and Jackendoff (1989) clarify, it can mostly be ignored in the study of I-language and I-concepts.

One might object on behalf of Langacker that the disposition of speakers to amend their use of words does not threaten internalism, on the grounds that their knowledge of meaning can change through their interactions with others. Oscar's utterance in (12a), so goes the objection, merely indicates the obvious fact that "the use of words can be taught" (Putnam 1970: 136). Oscar's conceptualization of water changes when the scientist tells him that the substance in question is not water because its molecular structure is not H_2O. Adam's conceptualization of arthritis is altered when the doctor apprises him that arthritis afflicts only the joints. Such an interactive character of language use is precisely what cognitive linguistics focuses on, and it is hardly conceivable that Langacker fails to take it into account. Moreover, this objection seems to be in line with Donnellan's (1983/2012: 180) remark that "[w]hile the theory calls for a certain relationship between the semantics of these terms and science, the terms obviously are not borrowed from the vocabulary of science and were part of English long before the advent of modern science". Meanings encompasses individualistic and scientific aspects. Thus far, the objection appears appropriate.

However, the behavior of speakers cannot be adequately elucidated by meaning change. The English word 'beads', for instance, underwent a semantic change from 'prayers' to 'small balls on a rosary' (Stern 1931: 352-354, Taylor 2012: 251-252). The alleged semantic change of the word 'water' from a 'liquid which is colorless, transparent, tasteless, thirst-quenching, found in lakes, etc.' to a 'liquid whose molecular structure is H_2O' is different in character from the case of 'beads'. Speakers of English would evaluate (14a) to be more acceptable than (14b):

(14)　a.　Before 1750, people did not know that water was H_2O.
　　　　b.　Before the 13th century, people did not know that beads were small balls on a rosary.

The obvious truth that "the use of words can be taught" (Putnam 1970: 136) cannot be assimilated to typical instances of semantic change. Rather, the statements in (12a) and (14a) favor Putnam's (1975: 155-156) idea that, even if Oscar cannot tell what the underlying physical nature of water is, the extension of the word 'water' is as much H_2O for Oscar as for the scientist. Oscar understands more about water through his interactions with others, and this process does not alter the meaning of 'water', which is fixed independently of Oscar's conceptualization of water. Putnam (1973: 702-703, 1975: 142) was very clear about this point from the outset:

[…] the necessary and sufficient condition for being water is bearing the relation $same_L$ to the stuff in the glass […] The key point is that the relation $same_L$ is a *theoretical* relation: whether something is or is not the same liquid as this may take an indeterminate amount of scientific investigation to determine. Moreover, even if a "definite" answer has been obtained either through scientific investigation or through the application of some "common sense" test, the answer is *defeasible*: future investigation might reverse even the most "certain" example. Thus, the fact that an English speaker in 1750 might have called XYZ "water," while he or his successors would not have called XYZ water in 1800 or 1850 does not mean that the "meaning" of "water" changed for the average speaker in the interval. In 1750 or in 1850 or in 1950 one might have pointed to, say, the liquid in Lake Michigan as an example of "water." What changed was that in 1750 we would have mistakenly thought that XYZ bore the relation same$_L$ to the liquid in Lake Michigan, while in 1800 or 1850 we would have known that it did not [...] (Putnam 1975: 142)

Putnam (1990: 60) reemphasized in a later work that it is illegitimate to presume that scientists "*changed the meaning of the word 'water'* upon discovering that water is H$_2$O" (emphasis in the original).

Conceivably, in asserting that meaning is in the head, Langacker is mistaken in taking literally the question, "Are meanings in the head?", posed by Putnam (1973: 700, 1975: 139), which, as Nuccetelli (2003: 3) points out, is only a metaphor. Literally speaking, it is evident that all mental states are housed in the head. Even Burge (1993: 453) agrees with this claim, stating that externalism, or in his terms anti-individualism, "is about the nature of 'internal' psychological state". To say that meaning is in the head in the literal sense of the term cannot sufficiently show that meaning is in the head in the metaphorical sense of the term. The former claim amounts to a truism endorsed by both internalists and externalists, while the latter claim is incompatible with internalism[88]. If we literally interpret the term 'in', it is patently obvious that Oscar's mental state is located in his mind and that Oscar$_2$'s mental state is located in his mind. It would be ludicrous to claim that their mental states are housed outside their mind, say, in a lake or in a conference hall. Far from repeating such truisms, externalists claim that what distinguishes the mental states of Oscar and Oscar$_2$ should not to be sought in their minds and that "the existence and nature of certain psychological kinds depends necessarily on the existence and nature of certain relations to specific kinds or situations in the environment" (Burge 2003: 454). It is difficult to distinguish the

---

88) Alternatively, we could follow Burge (2013: 264) and assert that for both internalists and externalists meaning is not in the head, because "meaning is an abstraction, hence not located anywhere". The same applies to mental content (Burge 2013: 265). As remarked in Section 1.2, Frege held that sense and thought are located in the third realm which is distinct from the physical and mental realms, while grasping the sense or thought is an individual mental act. If we accept this idea, along with the view that the Fregean sense is an aspect of the meaning of an expression, it will be more accurate to say that it is a truism that the mental process of understanding the meaning of an expression occurs in the individual's mind. Burge (2003) accepts this truism:

> Meaning is abstract and hence not anywhere. But the psychological state of understanding a meaning is naturally seen "in" the mind or brain. Nothing anti-individualism requires rejecting this natural view. I accept it (Burge 1982). (Burge 2003: 455)

externalist thesis thus formulated from Langacker's (2008: 28-29) remark made from the internalist perspective: "[t]he conceptualizations we entertain are undeniably internal, in the sense of taking place in the brain, yet reach beyond it in the sense of being conceptualizations **of** some facet of the world" (emphasis in the original). In this context, we could ask whether it is possible to count Langacker among externalists, by construing his apparently internalist claim that meanings are in the speaker's mind in such a manner that it could be reduced to a truism. If such an interpretation is feasible, then the internalism-externalism debate will ultimately be relegated to a matter of terminology, as far as linguistics is concerned.

This conclusion may appear plausible, in light of the fact that, as pointed out by Bilgrami (1992: 2), Owens (1992: 89), Rey (1992: 315), Burge (1986b: 4/2007: 222) and Rowlands et al. (2020: Section 2), among others, externalism emerged as an antithesis to the Cartesian thesis that "the mental processes had by an individual are always, and completely, determined by what is going on inside that individual's body" (Rowland et al. 2020: Section 2). This Cartesian principle can be pushed so far as to entail what Putnam (1975: 136) called 'methodological solipsism', namely the doctrine that "no psychological state presupposes the existence of the subject's *body* even: if P is a psychological state, properly so called, then it must be logically possible for a 'disembodied mind' to be in P". The Cartesian assumption conflicts with cognitive linguistics, which views the physical properties of language users as essential to the comprehension of the nature of language insofar as cognition is "grounded in perception and bodily experience" (Langacker 2008: 28). Langacker shares with the externalist the anti-Cartesian idea that "[a]n individual's notion of what an expression means develops through communicative interaction" (Langacker 2008: 30). Langacker is certainly not committed to the Cartesian thesis that "our states of mind are the way they are regardless of what the external world is like" (Crane 1991: 5).

Nevertheless, an obstacle remains to the reduction of the cognitive linguistic view to a version of externalism: it would be incoherent to follow Langacker (2008: 30) and simultaneously espouse (15a), (15b) and (15c):

(15) a. Meaning is identified with conceptualization. (Langacker 2008: 30)
b. Conceptualization is broadly defined to encompass any facet of mental experience. (Langacker 2008: 30)
c. Conceptualizations are internal in the sense of taking place in the

brain, and yet reach beyond it in the sense of being conceptualizations of some facet of the world. (Langacker 2008: 28-29)

Given (15c), Oscar's conceptualizations correspond to certain states of his brain, but transcend them insofar as his conceptualizations involve objects located in his environment. Given (15b), Oscar's conceptualization of water can change through his interactions with others and evoke novel mental experiences. However, this statement is at odds with (15a). Oscar's statement in (12a) cannot be accounted for unless he thinks that the meaning of 'water' is fixed independently from his conceptualization of water. If meaning is identified with conceptualization, the progression of Oscar's conceptualization of water can only be described as a semantic change of 'water' for him. On the one hand, this would make it difficult to differentiate between (14a) and (14b). That speakers of English evaluate (14a), but not (14b), to be perfectly acceptable considerably strains the identification of conceptualization with meaning. On the other hand, this identification requires that meaning encompass all facets of mental experience, which in turn would mandate that no meaning can be defined in isolation from a person's mental experience. Thus, the meaning of 'water' for Oscar cannot transcend his experiences of water. This would counter the possibility of Oscar uttering (12a), which presupposes the existence of something he does not understand about the meaning of 'water'. Either meaning should not be identified with conceptualization, or the definition of conceptualization should be even broader than Langacker assumes and encompass a portion of the environment outside a speaker's mental experience. Either way Oscar's understanding of the word 'water' would transcend his mental state as individualistically or narrowly individuated. Evidently, Langacker's commitment to internalism must be compromised in some way or other.

Chapter 2

Social Externalism and Prototype Semantics

This chapter attempts to demonstrate that, contrary to the official view of the school, cognitive linguistics, coupled with prototype semantics, can provide stronger support for part of social externalism than Burge's (1979a/2007) thought experiments.

2.1 Partial Compatibility of Social Externalism and Cognitive Linguistics

Chapter 1 has shown that the cognitive linguistic framework defended by Langacker (2008) has difficulty handling the 'water' case (Putnam 1973, 1975) and the 'arthritis' case (Burge 1979a/2007). Langacker's proposal to reserve the term 'meaning', identified with 'conceptualization', for what is in the speaker's mind is at odds with Putnam's and Burge's externalist claims that meaning and mental content cannot be determined without considering factors to which individualist psychology may be blind. If externalism is correct, two internally identical subjects may nevertheless express different meanings and thoughts by using the same terms (Schroeter 2008: 108), a situation difficult for cognitive linguistics to accommodate. The purpose of this chapter is to demonstrate that, contrary to the official view of the school, cognitive linguistics can provide stronger support for part of social externalism than Burge's (1979a/2007) thought experiments[1].

I say 'part of' because as it stands cognitive linguistics can meet only one of the two challenges posed by social externalism. Burge's thought experiment is designed to establish, on the one hand, that Adam and Adam$_2$ may have different concepts of what they call 'arthritis' even though they are molecule-for-molecule identical, and, on the other, that Adam and his doctor have the same concept of

---

1) Parts of the material presented in this chapter are borrowed from Sakai (2022b). However, I shall make some qualifications to the conclusions reached in that paper.

arthritis even though Adam's conceptualization of the disease is remarkably deviant from the community standard. What will be shown in this chapter is that cognitive linguistics can accommodate the former case, namely, the case in which two internally identical subjects nevertheless have different concepts. The latter case, in which two contradictory beliefs nevertheless concern the same object, will be addressed in Chapter 4.

I say 'stronger support' because, if properly understood, cognitive linguistics, unlike Burge's thought experiments, is immune to Wikforss's (2001, 2004, 2006, 2014) attack on the notion of incomplete understanding which played a prominent role in establishing social externalism (Greenberg 2014). Wikforss argues that incomplete understanding, as assumed by Burge, does not do the job it is supposed to do, and a far stronger version of incomplete understanding is needed to defend the externalist thesis. Incomplete understanding in the stronger sense, however, entails an undesirable dichotomy between 'analytic' and 'synthetic', famously criticized by Quine (1951). What makes cognitive linguistics seemingly immune to the analytic-synthetic problem is that the notion of conceptualization it assumes incorporates the notion of prototype.

2.2 Social Externalism and Incomplete Understanding

Let us rehearse Burge's (1979a/2007) thought experiment in defense of social externalism, as sketched in Section 1.3.2. We are asked to suppose that Adam is a rational person generally competent in English and has a number of correct beliefs about arthritis. He thinks correctly "that he has had arthritis for years; that his arthritis in his wrists and fingers is more painful than his arthritis in his ankles, that it is better to have arthritis than cancer of the liver, that stiffening joints is a symptom of arthritis, that certain sorts of aches are characteristic of arthritis, that there are various kinds of arthritis, and so forth" (Burge 1979a: 77/2007: 104). One day, Adam feels pain in his thigh. Fearing that arthritis has spread to his thigh, he goes to see his doctor and utters (1):

(1) I have arthritis in my thigh.

The doctor tells Adam that this cannot be the case, because arthritis is an inflammation of the joints only. Then, Adam relinquishes his view and now believes that some disease distinct from arthritis is lodged in his thigh. As a second step, we are

Chapter 2   Social Externalism and Prototype Semantics

to conceive of a hypothetical community in which Adam$_2$, an exact replica of Adam, expresses his fear to his doctor by uttering (1). In the hypothetical community, the word 'arthritis' is defined to apply to various rheumatoid ailments, including not only arthritis but also ailments afflicting a person's thigh. It follows that, unlike Adam's fear expressed by (1), Adam$_2$'s fear expressed by (1) can be true. Finally, the counterfactual situation is interpreted. Burge maintains that the community in which Adam$_2$ lives has no concept of *arthritis*, Adam's 'arthritis' and Adam$_2$'s 'arthritis' being two homonymous words which happen to share the same form. According to the traditional conception of meaning, intension or concept uniquely determines extension (but not vice versa) and a difference in extension entails a difference in intension or concept. Therefore, as Burge (1979a: 79/2007: 106) puts it, "[t]he word 'arthritis' in the counterfactual community does not mean *arthritis*", since it is not even extensionally equivalent to the actual word 'arthritis'. Given that a thought consists of concepts, it also follows that Adam and Adam$_2$ have different thoughts about what they refer to as 'arthritis'. Even though Adam and Adam$_2$ are molecule-for-molecule identical, the contents of their thoughts are different due to the fact that different meanings are attached to the same word form. Burge concludes that meaning and mental content are not in the head but dependent for their individuation on one's social environment.

2.3 Incomplete Understanding of Concepts

Based on the traditional conception, an individual's understanding of meaning is either (2) and (3).

(2)   The individual associates the correct or standard meaning/concept C with the word W.

(3)   The individual associates an incorrect or non-standard meaning/concept C' with the word W.

An example of (3) is illustrated in (4), as discussed by Burge (1979a: 90-91/2007: 119-120).

(4)   I have been drinking orangutans for breakfast for the last few weeks.

We would not reasonably ascribe to a man who utters (4) the belief that he has

81

been drinking orangutans for the last few weeks (cf. Bilgrami 1992: 258, n. 12). A more reasonable move would be to take his 'orangutans' to express the concept of *orange juice*[2]. In this move, the word 'orangutan' is reinterpreted as 'what he calls 'orangutans', in conformity with the principle of charity[3]. As a result of the reinterpretation, the man is taken to express, with the utterance of (4), the true belief that he has been drinking what he calls 'orangutans', namely orange juice, for breakfast for the last few weeks, rather than the irrational belief that he has been drinking orangutans. Therefore, in uttering (4), the man is not talking about orangutans but about orange juice (cf. Valente 2019: 320). The same would apply to cases in which someone believes 'arthritis' to be the name of a tree or fish.

The gist of Burge's (1979a/2007) thought experiment is that there is a third possibility distinct from both (2) and (3), namely (5) (Greenberg 2014: 147-148; see also Sainsbury and Tye 2011: 119, 2012: Section 3.8, and Wikforss 2014):

(5) The individual associates the correct or standard meaning/concept C with the word W and understands C only incompletely.

As noted earlier, Adam in the actual community believes that arthritis may afflict his thigh. This belief is not empirically but conceptually false, because arthritis is by definition an inflammation found only in the joints. It is a conceptual truth that no disease that lodges in one's thigh can be arthritis. Nevertheless, the option in (5) allows Adam to use a concept which he understands only incompletely. When uttering (1) above, Adam expresses the belief in (6), and not the belief in (7).

(6) Adam has arthritis in his thigh.
(7) Adam has what he calls 'arthritis', namely tharthritis, in his thigh.

---

2) Burge (1979a/2007) qualifies this conclusion:
>   Contrary to philosophical lore, I am not convinced that such a man cannot correctly and literally be attributed a belief that an orangutan is a kind of fruit drink. (Burge 1979a: 91/2007: 120)
>
> But I shall not pursue the possibility suggested by his remark.
3) The *Routledge Encyclopedia of Philosophy* defines the principle of charity as follows:
>   The principle of charity governs the interpretation of the beliefs and utterances of others. It urges charitable interpretation, meaning interpretation that maximizes the truth or rationality of what others think and say.
>   (DOI: 10.4324/9780415249126-P006-1)

Both Adam and his doctor talk about arthritis, even though they conceptualize the concept differently (Valente 2019: 319). As Greenberg (2014: 147) puts it, Burge's argument indicates "how little is required to have a concept".

Langacker (2008) seems to be aware that there are cases in which meaning should be separated from conceptualization:

> We can validly distinguish [...] between what a single speaker knows and the collective knowledge of a whole society. The former is arguably more basic, since collective knowledge consists in (or at least derives from) the knowledge of individuals. For purposes of studying language as part of cognition, an expression's meaning is first and foremost its meaning for a single (representative) speaker. This is not to deny or diminish the social aspect of linguistic meaning. An individual's notion of what an expression means develops through communicative interaction and includes an assessment of its degree of conventionality in the speech community. By their nature, moreover, certain questions have to be studied at the population level (e.g. how norms are established and maintained, the extent to which consensus is achieved, and the range of variation actually encountered). (Langacker 2008: 30)

This passage can plausibly be taken to indicate that social externalism focuses on meanings which "have to be studied at the population level", whereas cognitive linguistics addresses "more basic" issues. A problem with the putative division of labor between social externalism and cognitive linguistics is that cases which Langacker regards as less basic, that is, cases in which we "use the words without knowing very much about the referent" (Saeed 2016: 34), are the rule rather than the exception. Burge (1979a: 79/2007: 107) says that "[o]ne need only thumb through a dictionary for an hour or so to develop a sense of the extent to which one's beliefs are infected by incomplete understanding" and that "[t]he phenomenon is rampant in our pluralistic age". In the postscript to Burge (1979a/2007), Burge (2007: 175) goes so far as to say that incomplete understanding is part of the human condition:

> Reading 'Individualism and the Mental' again, I was struck by my insistent emphasis on the idea that one can have thoughts that one incompletely understands. This emphasis had an autobiographical root. A primary impetus for my discovering the thought experiments was recognizing how many words or

concepts I went around using which I found, on pressing myself, that I did not fully understand. I came to realize that this was not just a personal weakness. It was part of the human condition, at least in complex societies. (Burge 2007: 115)

Now, a question arises as to whether the thought experiment *essentially* makes use of the notion of incomplete understanding. The following remark suggests that Burge considers the possibility of incomplete understanding to be sufficient for the establishment of social externalism:

> For purposes of defending the thought experiment and the arguments I draw from it, I can afford to be flexible about exactly how to generalize about these various phenomena. The thought experiment depends only on there being some cases in which a person's incomplete understanding does not force rein-terpretation of his expressions in describing his mental contents. Such cases appear to be legion. (Burge 1979a: 92/2007: 121)

Wikforss (2001, 2004) maintains that incomplete understanding is not only suffi-cient but also necessary for the externalist thesis to follow. On Wikforss's (2008: 164) construal, "what is distinctive about social externalism is not so much that it represents a break with traditional accounts of the determination of meaning (and content), as that it represents a break with traditional accounts of linguistic (and conceptual) competence". This is to say that the validity of the thought experiment goes with that of the notion of incomplete understanding illustrated in (5). If Adam's error were merely empirical rather than conceptual as in (8), the externalist thesis that Adam and Adam$_2$ think differently would not follow:

(8) a. My grandfather had arthritis. (Segal 2000: 79)
   b. Arthritis afflicts more than one percent of the population per year.

Suppose that Adam's grandfather did not have arthritis but Adam$_2$'s grandfather did, and that both Adam and Adam$_2$ hold the belief expressed by (8a). Although, in this situation, only Adam$_2$'s belief is true, it does not follow that the two subjects have different concepts corresponding to the word form 'arthritis'. In having a belief characterized by (1) above, Adam makes a conceptual error, whereas he merely makes an empirical error in (8a). What makes (1) false is the conventional meaning of 'arthritis' adopted in Adam's community, whereas what makes (8a) false is what happens to hold in the world, and hence it requires an empirical investigation to know that (8a) is false. The difference in truth value between Adam's and Adam$_2$'s thoughts corresponding to (8a) derives not from a conceptual difference but from a factual difference between their communities (Valente 2019: 320). The factual difference in question is perfectly compatible with Adam's full grasp of the concept of *arthritis*. If so, the case at hand is an example of (2) above. In (8b), we have a more global factual difference between the two communities. Suppose that arthritis is estimated to afflict less than one percent of the population per year in Adam's community, while tharthritis (i.e. what Adam$_2$ calls 'arthritis') is estimated to afflict more than one percent of the population per year in Adam$_2$'s community. In this scenario, Adam's thought corresponding to (8b) is false, while Adam$_2$'s thought corresponding to (8b) is true. Does this discrepancy show that Adam and Adam$_2$ express distinct thoughts by uttering (8b)? The answer is negative, because the scenario is perfectly compatible with the possibility that arthritis and tharthritis may be one and the same disease. In this construal, Adam's community and Adam$_2$'s community adopt different theories about the same disease. What makes the truth values of Adam's and Adam$_2$'s utterance of (8b) different is not the difference in meaning between Adam's 'arthritis' and Adam$_2$'s 'arthritis', but the fact that their communities assess the same statement in (8b) with respect to different theories. There is no incomplete understanding here; both Adam and Adam$_2$ understand the concept of *arthritis* perfectly. Adam's thought corresponding to (8b) is false simply because he makes an empirical error rather than a conceptual one; he merely adopts a non-standard theory about arthritis. If (8b) is an empirical claim, Adam's mistake is empirical, failing to establish that Adam's and Adam$_2$'s mental contents differ. Wikforss concludes that what is needed in the thought experiment supporting social externalism is the possibility of incomplete understanding illustrated in (5):

> An ordinary empirical error appears not to be sufficient. It should be clear why this is so. If Burge's arthritis-patient in uttering 'I have arthritis in my thigh' does not make a conceptual error, and if 'Arthritis afflicts the joints only' is an empirical claim, then the fact that the counterfactual community rejects this claim would imply not that their word 'arthritis' must have a different meaning, but that the disagreement between the two communities is one of theory. That is, the conclusion to be drawn would be that the counterfactual community has

developed a slightly different theory about the same disease, not that the counterfactual community has a different 'arthritis'-concept and speaks of a different disease. There would then be no reason to say that the speaker in the counterfactual world, when uttering 'I have arthritis in my thigh', expresses a belief different from that of the speaker in the actual world. (Wikforss 2001: 220)

The types of errors discussed so far can be summarized in Figure 2-1:

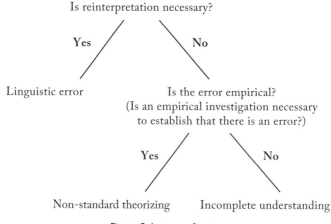

Figure 2-1: types of errors

Genuine cases of incomplete understanding are detected only when the possibility of linguistic error and non-standard theory is carefully set aside. A person makes a linguistic error if, in uttering 'X', he refers to and thinks about non-X, as in (4) above. A person adopts a non-standard theory about X if, in uttering 'X', he refers to and thinks about X, but disagrees with his community as to whether the proposition that X is Q, where 'Q' is a predicate conceptually independent from 'X', is empirically valid, as in (8a-b). In this case, it is in principle possible that the proposition that X is Q will prove true, contrary to the community standard. For instance, further investigations conducted in the actual community may someday establish the validity of the propositions in (8a-b), which, unlike other members of the community, Adam believes to true. Finally, a person has an incomplete understanding of the concept X if, in uttering 'X', he refers to and thinks about X, but accepts the proposition that X is P, where 'P' is a predicate conceptually incompatible with 'X' in light of the standard dictionary definition of 'X', as in (1). In this case, no empirical investigation will be needed to show that the proposition that X is P is false.

In what follows, I will argue that social externalism rests on the possibility of incomplete understanding, but not in the way Wikforss thinks. Wikforss worries that the notion of incomplete understanding entails that of analytical truth, a notion which has been dismissed by many philosophers since Quine's (1951) influential work. This worry is allayed if we take into account the notion of prototype, which allows for the possibility that one can partially misunderstand a concept without misunderstanding the corresponding linguistic meaning in the narrow sense of the term, as required for the notion of analytic truth.

2.4 Sawyer's (2003) Objection to Wikforss (2001): 'sofa'

Sawyer (2003) objects to Wikforss (2001) that thought experiments in support of social externalism do not essentially rest on the notion of incomplete misunderstanding, on the ground that Burge presents elsewhere a thought experiment which makes no use of that notion (Burge 1986a/2007). According to Sawyer (2003), Wikforss should have looked more in detail into Burge's (1986a/2007) thought experiment concerning 'sofa', instead of Burge's (1979) thought experiment concerning 'arthritis'. Burge (1986a: 707ff/2007: 263ff) invites us to imagine that Adam, a rational person competent in English, begins to doubt the truism that sofas are pieces of furniture and hypothesizes that sofas are religious works of art. Adam's hypothesis is rationally based on the observation that, like other religious artifacts, sofas "are generally given a prominent location in private and public places, [that] they are expensive, and [that] most people who care usually take good care of them" (Elugardo 1993: 369). While admitting that some sofas have been sat upon, Adam suspects that most sofas will collapse under any considerable weight. He then tests his hypothesis using reasonable methods and concludes that his theory is mistaken. The second step of the thought experiment consists in imagining that $Adam_2$, a duplicate of Adam living in some other community, comes up with the same hypothesis, which he tests using reasonable methods. But in $Adam_2$'s community, that sofas are pieces of furniture is not a truism. In his community, what are called 'sofas' are indeed religious artifacts, and his hypothesis is borne out. According to Burge (1986a: 708/2007: 263), it is reasonable to say that there are no sofas in $Adam_2$'s community and that the word form 'sofa' denotes objects different from sofas, translated into our English as 'safos'[4]. Adam's utterance of (9) then expresses the truism that sofas are pieces of furniture, whereas Adam$_2$'s utterance of (9) expresses the false proposition that safos are pieces of furniture.

(9)   Sofas are pieces of furniture.

Although Adam and Adam$_2$ are internally identical, the contents of their thoughts are different. This thought experiment may at first glance appear similar to the thought experiment concerning 'arthritis'. But, as Burge (1986a/2007) and Sawyer (2003) point out, there is one crucial difference: when Adam and Adam$_2$ utter (9), neither of them makes any conceptual error:

> The arguments of "Individualism and the Mental" [= Burge (1979a/2007)] and "Other Bodies" [= Burge (1982/2007)] ascribe incomplete linguistic understanding and ignorance of expert knowledge (respectively) to the relevant protagonists. By contrast, A [= Adam] may be a sophisticate. He need not lack linguistic understanding or be unapprised of expert or common opinion. The present argument features not incomplete understanding or ignorance of specialized knowledge, but nonstandard theory. (Burge 1986a: 709/2007: 264)

> An ability to discriminate some but not all Fs from non-Fs typically betrays a partial grasp of the concept F. If a subject were to apply the term 'sofa' to overstuffed armchairs as well as to sofas, for example, it would be most plausible to diagnose an incomplete grasp of the concept *sofa*. This kind of error is surely best thought of as conceptual. In contrast, ability to discriminate Fs from non-Fs combined with inability correctly to characterize the nature of Fs typically signals incorrect empirical theory. Thus in the second thought experiment above, A is able reliably to distinguish sofas from non-sofas, but characterizes the nature of sofas incorrectly. In this case it is most plausible to attribute to A a full grasp of the concept *sofa*, but an incorrect empirical theory of sofas. (Sawyer 2003: 271)

When Adam doubts the alleged necessary truth that sofas are pieces of furniture,

---

4) A term coined by Burge (1986a: 708/2007: 263).

Chapter 2   Social Externalism and Prototype Semantics

"there need not be any failure or incompleteness of understanding on [Adam]'s part" (Burge 1986a: 711/2007: 266). Sawyer (2003: 273) concludes that social externalism is not essentially dependent upon incomplete misunderstanding[5].

This argument is fallacious, however. Adam certainly has the ability to discriminate sofas from non-sofas. This allows us to say that he correctly understands the extension of the term 'sofa'. But it does not follow that he has a full grasp of the concept *sofa*, because the sameness of extension does not entail that of intension or concept. Thus, a person who associates with the word 'cat' the intension characterized by descriptions such as 'x is a cat or a round square' would have the ability to discriminate cats from non-cats, but he would not be considered fully competent with the concept *cat*. In the case at hand, it may be difficult to attribute a full grasp of the concept *sofa* to a person who associates with the word 'sofa' the intension characterized by descriptions such as 'x is not a piece of furniture to be sat upon, but a work of art'. That sofas are pieces of furniture would plausibly be considered part of what Putnam (1970) called core facts about sofas. Core facts about the term 'X', Putnam says (1970: 197), are facts "such that one can convey the use of ['X'] by simply conveying those facts" and that "one cannot convey the approximate use *unless* one gets [those] facts across" (emphasis in the original). But we may grant, for purposes of the argument, that it is not a core fact about the term 'sofa' that sofas are pieces of furniture to be sat upon. After all, Adam perfectly knows that in his community sofas are conventionally defined as pieces of furniture to be sat upon.

Still, the externalist thesis does not follow without begging the question. Wikforss (2004) remarks that the real problem arises from what Sawyer (2003) takes to be "the unifying principle of externalism" (Sawyer 2003: 272). Sawyer (2003: 272) contends that "[t]he notion of conceptual error is secondary and derivative" and that the unifying principle underlying various externalist thought experiments is the claim that "[c]oncepts are individuated partly by their referents rather than entirely by what the subject thinks is true of the referents"[6], incomplete understanding being just "[o]ne way to bring out our commitment to the

---

5) Sawyer (2003: 267, n. 7) leaves open the question whether Burge held this view at the time of his 1979a paper. Burge's following remark in that paper seems to suggest a negative answer:
  It would be a mistake, however, to think that incomplete understanding, in the sense that the argument requires, is in general an unusual or even deviant phenomenon. [...] The sort of "incomplete understanding" *required* by the thought experiment includes quite ordinary, nondeviant phenomena. (Burge's 1979a: 83-84/2007: 112, emphases mine)

89

claim". Sawyer's unifying principle can be formulated as "a difference in reference (extension) implies a difference in concepts" (Wikforss 2004: 75). As Wikforss (2004: 291, n. 6) and Schroeter (2008: 111) point out, this principle is explicitly defended by Burge:

> On any systematic theory, differences in the extension – the actual denotation, referent, or application – of counterpart expressions in that-clauses will be semantically represented, and will, in our terms, make for differences in content. (Burge 1979a: 75/2007: 102)

> Although the reference of these words is not all there is to their semantics, their reference places a constraint on their meaning, or on what concept they express. In particular, any such word w has a different meaning (or expresses a different concept) from a given word w' if their constant referents, or ranges of application, are different. That is part of what it is to be a non-indexical word of this type. (Burge 1989: 181/2007: 283)

Schroeter (2008: 111, 133) refers to this principle as the 'Semantic Difference Principle'. Since, according to Burge (1986/2007), the term 'sofa' has different extensions in the actual and hypothetical communities, it follows from the Semantic Difference Principle that Adam and Adam$_2$ associate different concepts with the term. This argument begs a question, however. What makes the extensions of 'X' in the two communities different in the first place? A moment's reflection will reveal that a difference in extension does not suffice for a conceptual difference. Following Wikforss (2004: 191), let us imagine a world in which all sofas are made of leather. Given that, as a matter of fact, there are not only sofas made of leather but also sofas made of cloth, the term 'sofa' has different extensions in

---

6) Sawyer (2003: 272) acknowledges that "[t]he so-called 'empty case', in which a concept lacks a referent, poses special problems" which she sets aside. Thus, her alleged unifying principle does not enable one to distinguish between the concept of *centaur* and that of *unicorn*. But the problems raised by empty cases are not specific to Sawyer's position; they threaten virtually any theory of meaning. Goodman (1949: 5) reminds us that "[a] centaur-picture differs from a unicorn-picture not by virtue of its resemblance to a centaur and lack of resemblance to a unicorn; for there are neither centaurs nor unicorns". Any theory of meaning must take into account the fact that "although two words have the same extension, certain predicates composed by making identical additions to these two words may have different extensions" (Goodman 1949: 5). See Sainsbury and Tye (2011: 111) for some suggestions.

Chapter 2   Social Externalism and Prototype Semantics

the actual and imagined worlds. Wikforss (2004: 191) points out that this "does not yield the externalist conclusion that the word has a different meaning and expresses a different concept" in the imagined world. Such a reasoning would lead to conceptual and referential fragmentation, as Wikforss (2001: 218) calls it, resulting in a thesis that is completely orthogonal to externalism to the effect that no two communities or individuals would share the same concept. In order to avert such a ludicrous consequence, we might interpret 'a difference in reference (extension)' in Sawyer's principle in such a narrow way that our word 'sofa' never applies to any object found in the hypothetical world. Arguably this is the correct interpretation of the thought experiment, in view of Burge's (1986a: 708/2007: 263) remark that "[t]here are no sofas in [Adam₂'s] situation" and that "the word form 'sofa' does not mean *sofa*". This may also be what Sawyer has in mind when she states that the two communities "do not have different theories about the same things, but have, rather, different theories about *different* things" (Sawyer 2003: 272, emphasis in the original). But, again, the question arises as to what makes the extensions of 'sofas' in the two communities different in this narrow sense. Wikforss (2004: 292-293) contends that this question cannot be answered without appealing to the notion of incomplete understanding:

It is no doubt true that many people share the view that 'sofa' does not apply to the objects in [Adam₂]'s world. The most straightforward explanation of this is that the belief that sofas are to be sat upon is so central to the meaning of our word 'sofa' that the objects in [Adam₂]'s world could not possibly fall within its extension, since they are so brittle that they cannot be sat upon. After all, terms for artefacts are typically given functional definitions, and it is not implausible that 'sofa' should be given such a definition. However, it is obvious that this reply is not available to Sawyer. If this is the reason why our term 'sofa' does not apply to the objects in [Adam₂]'s world, then it follows that [Adam], who doubts that sofas are furnishings to be sat upon, *does* display an incomplete understanding of the concept of sofa. That is, the thought-experiment would rely on the assumption of incomplete understanding after all. The challenge Sawyer faces (along with Burge) is therefore to show that the objects in [Adam₂]'s world are not sofas, without appealing to the conventional meaning of 'sofa'. I think this is a formidable challenge, and that it is one reason why Burge's later externalism [= Burge (1986a/2007)] has achieved much less attention than his earlier social externalism [= Burge (1979a/2007)]. (Wikforss

2004: 292-293; see also Elugardo 1993: 377-381)

What Wikforss calls "formidable challenge" is specific to social externalism, because this challenge can be met by physical externalism, insofar as it deals with natural kinds. As discussed in Section 1.3.1, physical externalism rests on the assumption that "[t]he extension of our terms depends upon the actual nature of the particular things that serve as paradigms" and that "this actual nature is not, in general, fully known to the speaker" (Putnam 1975: 164). What determines the meaning of the term 'water' is not the linguistic convention adopted by the community but the important physical properties, usually the underlying microstructure, of the local paradigms of 'water' (Liu 2002: 388-390). Thus, according to Putnam (1973: 702, 1975: 141), "the extension of the term "water" was just as much H_2O on Earth in 1750 as in 1950". Conversely, no stuff which has a molecular structure distinct from H_2O is water, no matter how similar it is to water. Kripke defends a similar view concerning the term 'tiger':

> We might find animals in some part of the world which, though they look just like a tiger, on examination were discovered not even to be mammals. Let's say they were in fact very peculiar looking reptiles. Do we then conclude on the basis of this description that some tigers are reptiles? We don't. We would rather conclude that these animals, though they have the external marks by which we originally identified tigers, are not in fact tigers, because they are not of the same species as the species which we called 'the species of tigers'. Now this, I think, is not because, as some people would say, the old concept of tiger has been replaced by a new scientific definition. I think this is true of the concept of tiger *before* the internal structure of tigers has been investigated. (Kripke 1980: 120, emphasis in the original)

Wikforss's argument can be interpreted as demonstrating that the meaning of 'sofa' does not depend on the physical (as opposed to the social) environment. Physical externalism holds that something which all community members consider samples of water can turn out to be samples of a different substance. The meaning of 'water' is not fully determined by what community members have in their mind and depends on the physical environment in which they happen to be located. The conventional meaning of 'water' may not exhaust the metaphysical nature, or 'essence', of water, which can only be uncovered by scientific investigation. It is

Chapter 2   Social Externalism and Prototype Semantics

therefore possible for someone to fully understand the conventional meaning of 'water' while doubting that the liquid that all community members call 'water' really is water. This is not the case with 'sofa'. As remarked by Bloom (2000: 162), "humans are naive essentialists about entities such as birds and water, but not about chairs and clocks". If the community members agree that something is a sofa, then it is a sofa. It makes little sense to suppose that something which all community members consider a sofa may fail to satisfy a putative metaphysical definition of 'sofa' possibly unknown to the community members. The contrast between words like 'water' and words like 'sofa' is stressed by Schwartz (1978)[7]:

> The fact that several examined chairs are upholstered, say, does not support the claim that all chairs are upholstered. The fact that the examined chairs are wooden does not support the contention that all chairs are wooden and so on. In fact if a scientist were interested in chairs as a subject of scientific study and got himself a good specimen and started to examine it closely in order to discover the nature of chairs, we would think that he was crazy. Compare this with the zoologist interested in snakes, and so obtains a fine specimen and begins to dissect it. (Schwartz 1978: 573)

The meaning of 'sofa' is in the mind of community members and competent speakers are required to know it. When Adam doubts that the objects which his fellows call 'sofas' are really sofas, he doubts nothing but the conventional meaning of 'sofa', displaying an incomplete grasp of the concept *sofa*. Schwartz (1978: 571-572) provides a similar argument about the word 'pencil', originally discussed by Putnam (1975: 160-162). Putnam (1975: 162) suggests that, just like 'water', 'pencil' denotes "whatever has the same *nature* as the normal examples of the local pencils in the actual world". Schwartz (1978: 571) rejects Putnam's suggestion on the grounds that, unlike water, pencils have no underlying nature. What makes

---

7)   Note that the contrast does not turn on the fact that, unlike water and snakes, sofas and chairs are artifacts. Even if it were discovered, as Putnam (1975: 161) imagined about pencils following Rogers Albritton, that sofas and chairs were organisms, the discovery would not alter the fact that sofas and chairs are pieces of furniture to be sat upon. In this situation, it would simply be the case that some sofas and chairs were organisms. As Schwartz (1978: 572) argues, "it is not analytic that chairs, pencils, and lamps are artifacts". The contrast between 'water' and 'sofa' should not be attributed to the artifactual character of sofas, which happen to be constantly observed in the actual world.

something a pencil is not its alleged underlying nature but "superficial characteristics such as a certain form and function" (ibid.). To the extent that these characteristics "are analytically associated with the term 'pencil,' not disclosed by scientific investigation (ibid.)", doubting that pencils have the characteristics in question would be displaying an incomplete understanding of the concept of *pencil*. Even if it is true that, as Burge (1986a: 707/2007: 262-263) claims, "[s]ome mental states [...] depend for their identity on the nature of the physical environment, in complete independence of social practices" and that social practices "are often not the final arbiter", applying this view to sofas and pencils is likely to yield undesirable results. Wiggins (1995: 62) comments that Putnam's attempt to extend his doctrine of natural kind terms to words like 'pencil' "was a pity". Wikforss's argument is so convincing as to leave little doubt that thought experiments in support of social externalism are *essentially* dependent upon some notion or other of incomplete understanding, even though different notions of incomplete understanding may be at play in the 'arthritis' and 'sofa' cases.

One may now wonder why the presence or absence of incomplete understanding matters so much to the externalist, or at what cost incomplete understanding comes. The answer has to do with the fact that, construed in a straightforward manner, that notion seems to presuppose an unwelcome distinction between the analytic and the synthetic.

2.5 Conceptual or Analytic Truth

2.5.1 Incomplete Understanding and Conceptual Truth

In Burge's (1979a/2007, 1986a/2007) view, in uttering (1) above, Adam displays an incomplete understanding of the concept of *arthritis*. While Burge (1979a/2007) uses the term 'incomplete understanding' dozens of times to characterize his thought experiments, the same does not hold for the term 'conceptual error'. Although Wikforss (2001: 219) insists that "[a] central component of Burge's reasoning is the notion of a non-empirical or conceptual error", Burge (1979a/2007) seems rather skeptical about the philosophical significance of the distinction between empirical and conceptual errors:

In fact, I do not believe that understanding, in our examples, can be explicated as independent of empirical knowledge, or that the conceptual errors of our subjects are best seen as "purely" mistakes about concepts and as involving no

Chapter 2   Social Externalism and Prototype Semantics

"admixture" of error about "the world." With Quine, I find such talk about purity and mixture devoid of illumination or explanatory power. But my views on this matter neither entail nor are entailed by the premises of the arguments I give [...] Those arguments seem to me to remain plausible under any of the relevant philosophical interpretations of the conceptual-ordinary-empirical distinction. (Burge 1979a: 88/2007: 117)

This passage suggests that, when Burge (1979a: 100/2007: 129) says that "[t]here is nothing irrational or stupid about the linguistic or conceptual errors we attribute to our subjects", the term 'linguistic or conceptual error' should be understood in the ordinary non-technical sense. Nevertheless, Wikforss (2001, 2004) construes Burge's thought experiments as relying on the notion of conceptual error in the strict sense of the term, on the grounds that without that notion "the externalist conclusions are blocked" (Wikforss 2001: 226). For Wikforss (2001, 2004), the notion of incomplete understanding entails that of conceptual error in the strict sense of the term, and "Burge must rely on the assumption that the speaker in the actual world [= Adam] makes a conceptual error" (Wikforss 2001: 226). If, in uttering (1) above, Adam makes a conceptual error in the technical sense of the term, the sentence in (10) must be interpreted as expressing a conceptual truth:

(10)   Arthritis does not afflict one's thigh.

Wikforss equates conceptual truths in the strict sense of the term with analytic truths, stating that "Burge's talk of *conceptual* errors and *conceptual* truths seems to suggest that he rejects Quine's criticisms of the analytic/synthetic distinction" (Wikforss 2001: 221, emphases in the original). As Jackson (1998b: 52) remarks, Quine's rejection of full-blown analyticity is close to orthodoxy, at least in America. If Wikforss is right, Burge's view rests essentially on the notorious notion of analyticity, without which the notion of conceptual error as construed by Wikforss would have no essential role to play (Sainsbury and Tye 2012: 82, n. 24).

Intuitively, analytic statements are defined as statements whose negation reduces to contradiction (Quine 1951: 20, Putnam 1983: 87, 95)[8]. This definition is at odds with Burge's official view on analyticity, which entails no specific philosophical position, as suggested by his remark:

Both the 'analytically' true and the 'analytically' false attitudes are linguistic in

95

the sense that they are tested by consulting a dictionary or native linguistic intuitions, rather than by ordinary empirical investigation. (Burge 1979a: 100/2007: 129)

In elaborating her argument Wikforss is fully aware that Burge's view is different from hers:

Burge's suggestion, therefore, is that we can endorse what might be called a 'weak' notion of analytic or conceptual truths, one which is quite compatible with Quine's rejection of the analytic/synthetic distinction. 'Arthritis afflicts the joints only' is a conceptual truth in the sense that this is what the dictionary tells us. To say that the speaker uttering 'I have arthritis in my thigh' makes a conceptual error is just to say that he goes against the dictionary definition. It does not require a commitment to a strong notion of conceptual truths. (Wikforss 2001: 222)

The dictionary definition is not strongly analytic to the extent that it may be mistaken. What is needed for the thought experiments, in Burge's assumption, is this weaker notion of analyticity. Wikforss (2001: 222) dismisses Burge's view as "clearly unsatisfactory", because the mere fact that (10) is what the dictionaries tell us in the actual community does not allow us to conclude that there is a difference in meaning between Adam's and $Adam_2$'s 'arthritis'. The dictionary description in (10)

---

8) The notion of analyticity is notoriously difficult to define. The definition presented here is the one which served as the starting point for Quine's (1951) long argument. Quine (1951: 20) is suspicious about the explanatory value of this definition, which can be traced back to Kant, because analyticity and self-contradictoriness are "the two sides of a single dubious coin", both standing in "exactly the same need of clarification". Mates (1951: 525-527) points out that White's (1950) and Quine's (1951) arguments are potentially targeted at all of the definitions of analyticity given in (i)-(viii):
(i) S is analytic if and only if S is true in all possible worlds.
(ii) S is analytic if and only if S could not possibly be false.
(iii) S is analytic if and only if "not S" is self-contradictory.
(iv) S is analytic if and only if S is true by virtue of meanings and independently of fact.
(v) S is analytic if and only if either S is logically true or S can be turned into a logical truth by putting synonyms for synonyms.
(vi) S is analytic if and only if S comes out true under every state-description.
(vii) S is analytic if and only if S can be reduced to a logical truth by definition.
(viii) S is analytic in L if and only if S is true according to the semantical rules of L.

might turn out to be false as a result of scientific investigation, just as the dictionary description in (11) did turn out to be false (Putnam 1962a: 396, Burge 1993: 316/2007: 297-298).

(11) Atoms are indivisible.

The fact that Dalton's definition of an atom given in (11) turned out to be false after some scientific investigation suggests that the actual community once adopted a theory which is now considered a non-standard theory. Accordingly, a person who believes (11) today can plausibly be viewed as developing a non-standard theory illustrated in Figure 2-1 above. The present community which rejects (11) and the past community which accepts (11) talk about one and the same concept of *atom*. No one would say that the present word 'atom' and the past word 'atom' are homonyms which happen to share the same word form. Likewise, it is perfectly conceivable that the actual community which accepts (10) and the hypothetical community which rejects (10) talk about one and the same concept of *arthritis*. Both Adam and Adam$_2$ may well be developing a theory about arthritis which is deemed non-standard in the actual community but conforms to the conventions followed by the hypothetical community. It does not follow that they have different concepts corresponding to the word form 'arthritis'; they are rather developing the same theory about the same disease, which only the hypothetical community evaluates as true. The fact that (10) is evaluated to have different truth values in the actual and hypothetical communities is not sufficient for the externalist thesis to follow; what yields a difference in truth value must be a difference in meaning rather than a difference in theory. For there to be a difference in meaning, it must be the case that (10) expresses a conceptual truth in the strict sense of the term, namely an analytic truth, in the actual community but not in the hypothetical community. If (10) expresses an analytic truth (in the actual community), no empirical investigation can ever invalidate (10), and anyone who denies or doubts (10) (in the actual community) betrays an incomplete understanding of the concept of *arthritis*. Burge (1986a: 714/2007: 268) rightly points out that"[t]he consensus of the most competent speakers can be challenged" and that "truths of meaning are dubitable". But this undermines his very point. What is needed is neither the consensus of the most competent speakers nor the dictionary compiled on the basis of their consensus, but analytic truths such that denying or doubting them entails making a conceptual error as opposed to developing a non-standard theory. Or equivalently, in Burge's (1993/2007) terminology, what is needed is not "epistemic definitions" (Burge 1993: 316/2007: 297)[9] but "metaphysical or essence-determining definitions" (Burge 1993: 311/2007: 293)[10]. This is what Wikforss means by saying that "Burge's talk of *conceptual* errors and *conceptual* truths seems to suggest that he rejects Quine's criticisms of the analytic/synthetic distinction" (Wikforss 2001: 226).

2.5.2 Overview of Quine's Criticism of the Analytic-Synthetic Distinction

Quine's (1951) argument is widely known to have attacked the analytic-synthetic distinction (Putnam 1983: 87) and is generally considered a "very satisfactory demolition" of that distinction (Haiman 1980: 349). Quine's argument extends White's (1950) in a more radical manner (Mates 1951: 527, Kaufman 1953: 421). White (1950) claimed that no behavioral criteria can properly characterize the notion of analyticity on the grounds that such criteria, if any, are "as much in need of explanation as the notion of *analytic* itself" (ibid.: 328). Quine (1951) reinforced White's claim by demonstrating that no other criteria, behavioral or not, do the job. His argument is divided into two parts. The first half of the argument consists in showing that "all attempts to define the distinction are *circular*" (Putnam 1983: 87, emphasis in the original), or more specifically that "[a]nalyticity within a language can be defined only in terms of synonymy [...], which in turn, however, can be defined within a language only in terms of analyticity" (Haiman 1980: 349). The argument starts from the statement in (12).

(12) No unmarried man is married.

This statement is equivalent to the logical truth given in (13a), and, more generally, that given in (13b), each of which "is true and remains true under all reinterpreta-

---

9) "Where they are possible, epistemic definitions do articulate the meanings of a speaker's words in one important sense. They articulate what the word means for the speaker, and what conception he associates with his concept. They constitute a summary or explanation of speaker usage that provides the speaker's most considered explication of his term." (Burge 1993: 316/2007: 297)

10) "A metaphysically correct definition – one that states actual necessary and sufficient conditions, indeed essential or fundamental individuating conditions for instantiating a kind – need not be known, or knowable on mere reflection, by someone who has the concept." (Burge 1993: 314-315/2007: 296)

tions of its components other than the logical particles" (Quine 1951: 23).

(13) a. ¬∃x (¬ married (x) ∧ man (x) ∧ married (x))
     b. ¬∃x (¬ P (x) ∧ Q (x) ∧ P (x))

Quine has little to say about this type of analytic statement which is equated with logical truth (Mates 1951: 528). The problem for him lies in the second class of analytic statements exemplified by (14):

(14) No bachelor is married.

The statement in (14) is not a logical truth, since (15a) and (15b) do not remain true under all reinterpretations of their components other than the logical particles:

(15) a. ¬∃x (bachelor (x) ∧ married (x))
     b. ¬∃x (Q (x) ∧ P (x))

Intuitively, however, (14) is analytically true, because its negation seems to reduce to contradiction. This intuition is buttressed by the fact that (14) "can be turned into logical truth by putting synonyms for synonyms" (Quine 1951: 23; see also White 1950: 321)[11]. The intuitive equivalence between (12) and (14) is thus assured by the synonymy between the expressions 'unmarried man' and 'bachelor'.

---

11) Katz (1997) counters this characterization of analyticity for a different reason from that provided by Quine. While, as will be discussed shortly, Quine mainly calls into question the notion of synonymy (Mates 1951: 528), it is the notion of logical truth that Katz rejects. Katz (1997: 2) states that Quine's characterization of (14) "is a virtual paraphrase of Frege's definition". Since, as remarked in Section 1.3.4, Katz (1972, 1997) excludes truth-related notions from semantic theory, he insists that the definition of analyticity should make no reference to logical truth. He proposes the definition in (i):

(i) A sense of a simple sentence is analytic if that sense is fully contained in the sense of (any) one of its terms. (Katz 1997: 12)

Cohen (2000) argues that Katz's impoverished notion of sense, neatly divorced from reference, prevents (i) from doing the job it is supposed to do. According to Cohen (2000: 132-133), we are faced with a dilemma: either we accept both a purely internal sense, which fails to determine reference, and false analytic sentences, or we accept an external sense, which determines reference, and give up on Katz's internalist conception of analyticity.

This means that analyticity may possibly be defined in terms of synonymy. Quine cautions that "we are not concerned here with synonymy in the sense of complete identity in psychological associations or poetic quality; indeed no two expressions are synonymous in such a sense" and that "[w]e are concerned only with what may be called *cognitive* synonymy" (Quine 1951: 28, emphasis in the original). This remark anticipates Taylor's (2003: 59) declaration, made from a cognitive linguistic perspective, that "perfect synonyms – lexical items with the same meaning and which are therefore interchangeable in all contexts – are exceedingly rare"[12]. Now, the question is how to define cognitive synonymy. In the first half of the twentieth century, Rey (2022: 1.2) states, the notions of synonymy, definition and meaning were thought "to be sufficiently obvious notions whose clarification didn't seem particularly urgent until W.V.O. Quine [(1951)] raised serious questions about them much later".

Arguably the most promising idea is that "the [cognitive] synonymy of two linguistic forms consists simply in their interchangeability in all contexts without change of truth value" (Quine 1951: 27, cf. Mates 1951, Naess 1957, Burge 1978)[13]. One may think that to say that 'bachelor' and 'unmarried man' are interchangeable in all contexts *salva veritate* is to say that (16) is true.

(16) All and only bachelors are unmarried men.

But the truth of (16) is no more sufficient for the cognitive synonymy between 'bachelor' and 'unmarried man' than the truth of (17) is for the cognitive synonymy between 'creature with a heart' and 'creature with a kidney'.

---

12) The first edition of Taylor (2003) was published in 1989.

13) Quine (1951: 27-28) carefully sets aside the cases in which the expression in question occurs within a complex word or within quotation marks. Thus, 'bachelor of arts' (cf. Quine 1960: §11, n. 1) and 'bachelor's button' cannot be turned into 'unmarried man of arts' and 'unmarried man's button', and (i) cannot be turned into (ii) *salva veritate*.

(i) 'Bachelor' has less than ten letters.

(ii) 'Unmarried man' has less than ten letters.

Quine (1951: 27-28) proposes to treat a complex word and the whole of 'noun + quotation marks' as a single indivisible word, applying the interchangeability *salva veritate* to single indivisible words but not to subparts thereof. He admits that this approach has the drawback of presupposing a prior definition of words. What counts as a word is far from evident (Quine 1960: 13). See also Kaplan (1990, 2011), Hawthorne and Lepore (2011) and Stojnić (2022).

Chapter 2   Social Externalism and Prototype Semantics

(17)   All and only creatures with a heart are creatures with a kidney.

The notion of interchangeability *salva veritate* needed for the definition of cognitive synonymy is that of interchangeability *salva veritate* in a language whose vocabulary contains intensional expressions such as 'necessarily'. In the case at hand, what is required is the truth of (18):

(18)   Necessarily, all and only bachelors are unmarried men.

The fact that (18) is intuitively true while the addition of 'necessarily' to (17), as in (19), makes the sentence intuitively false enables us to say that 'bachelor' and 'unmarried man' are synonyms while 'creature with a heart' and 'creature with a kidney' are not:

(19)   Necessarily, all and only creatures with a heart are creatures with a kidney.

The crucial point is that a language whose vocabulary contains intensional expressions "is intelligible only if the notion of analyticity is already clearly understood in advance" (Quine 1951: 30), because to say that (18) is true is to say that (16) is analytically true[14]. In this attempt to define analyticity, analyticity is reduced to synonymy, which is reduced to interchangeability, which is reduced to analyticity. Quine (1951: 29) states that "[o]ur argument is not flatly circular, but something like that".

Even though Quine's argument helps recognize that the notion of synonymy is far from obvious (Rey 2022: 1.2), it remains unclear whether it leads to the demise of the analytic-synthetic distinction. As Putnam (1983: 87) puts it, "Quine's

---

14)   Quine defines necessity in terms of analyticity in several places. Thus, according to Quine (1943: 121), (i) is equivalent to (ii):
(i)   9 is necessarily greater than 7.
(ii)   '9 > 7' is analytic.
Quine (1960: 196) states that "'necessarily' amounts to 'is analytic' plus an antecedent pair of quotation marks". As discussed in Section 1.3.3, the identification of necessity with analyticity was disputed by Kripke (1980). Necessary statements such as 'Water is H$_2$O' are *a posteriori* in that its confirmation requires scientific investigation, whereas analytic statements are *a priori* in that the validity of 'Bachelors are unmarried' can be confirmed without any empirical evidence.

101

argument is little more than that Quine cannot think how to define 'synonymy'". As Grice and Strawson (1956: 142) point out, "[t]here are doubtless plenty of distinctions, drawn in philosophy and outside it, which still await adequate philosophical elucidation, but which few would want on this account to declare illusory". The notion of grammaticality in Chomsky's (1957, 1965, 1975) sense is a case in point. Although grammaticality has never been defined in a satisfactory manner, Putnam (1983: 89) says, "no one proposes to do linguistics without the notion". Furthermore, as Mates (1951: 528) remarks, "circular definitions are often very effective in creating understanding; i.e., it often happens that after being subjected to such definitions people are able to make the various decisions which we regard as indicative of the psychological phenomenon called 'understanding'". Likewise, Kaufman (1953: 423) states that "the difficulty in establishing criteria, behavioral or otherwise, is not sufficient reason for abandoning the analytic-synthetic distinction". Putnam (1983: 89) concludes that the first part of Quine's argument is a bad argument because it cannot convince anyone to do philosophy and linguistics without analyticity and synonymy.

The first part of Quine's argument is, on Putnam's (1983: 87) construal, directed against "the linguistic notion of analyticity", which is defined such that "a sentence is analytic if it can be obtained from a truth of logic by putting synonyms for synonyms" (Putnam 1983: 87). The second half of Quine's argument, on the contrary, is directed against "the notion of an analytic truth as one that is *confirmed no matter what*" (Putnam 1983: 87, cf. Quine 1951: 35, 1960: 66). According to Putnam, this part of Quine's argument, which is even less familiar to linguists, is "of historical importance" (Putnam 1983: 87), but here Quine should have talked about the "distinction between *a priori* and *a posteriori* truths" (Putnam 1983: 89) instead of analytic and synthetic truths. In Putnam's (1983: 92) view, Quine's equation of analyticity and apriority stems from the positivist assumption that *a priori* statements are true by meaning alone. For positivism, "a priori truths must be necessary" and "if there is necessity, it has to be linguistic/conceptual" (Fodor 1998a: 86). Quine accepts this positivist assumption (cf. Quine 1960: 66)[15]. In order to argue against the second notion of analyticity, Quine calls into question reductionism endorsed by empiricism, namely "the belief that each meaningful

---

15) Putnam (1983: 96) raises a question whether it is possible to endorse the first notion of analyticity (= analytic truths *qua* linguistic notion) without endorsing the second one (= *a priori* truths), to which he provides an affirmative answer.

Chapter 2   Social Externalism and Prototype Semantics

statement is equivalent to some logical construct upon terms which refer to immediate experience" (Quine 1951: 20). This belief goes with "the supposition that each statement, taken in isolation from its fellows, can admit of confirmation or infirmation at all" (Quine 1951: 38). Reductionism in this sense lends support to the (second notion of) analyticity in such a way that "as long as it is taken to be significant in general to speak of the confirmation and infirmation of a statement, it seems significant to speak also of a limiting kind of statement which is vacuously confirmed, *ipso facto*, come what may" (Quine 1951: 38). To be sure, this definition of analyticity "comes to naught unless we independently circumscribe the 'what may'" (Quine 1960: 66). Someone might say that (14) would be falsified if we encountered a married bachelor. One way to convince her that there can be no married bachelor without appealing to the assumption that (14) is analytic is "to take 'come what may' as 'come what stimulation […] may'" (ibid.). On this view, statements like (14) are analytic because they are vacuously confirmed come what stimulation may. Quine (1951) claims that this view is misguided, because "our statements about the external world face the tribunal of sense experience not individually but only as a corporate body" (ibid.). As Putnam (1983: 91) puts it, "[o]pen-mindedness even to the extent of being prepared to revise logical laws is necessary in the scientific enterprise":

[…] no statement is immune to revision. Revision even of the logical law of the excluded middle has been proposed as a means of simplifying quantum mechanics; and what difference is there in principle between such a shift and the shift whereby Kepler superseded Ptolemy, or Einstein Newton, or Darwin Aristotle? (Quine 1951: 40)

The following passage at the end of the first part of Quine's (1951) argument anticipates the conclusion of the whole argument:

It is obvious that truth in general depends on both language and extralinguistic fact. The statement 'Brutus killed Caesar' would be false if the world had been different in certain ways, but it would also be false if the word 'killed' happened rather to have the sense of 'begat'. Hence the temptation to suppose in general that the truth of a statement is somehow analyzable into a linguistic component and a factual component. Given this supposition, it next seems reasonable that in some statements the factual component should be null; and these are the analytic statements. But, for all its a priori reasonableness, a boundary between analytic and synthetic statements simply has not been drawn. That there is such a distinction to be drawn at all is an unempirical dogma of empiricists, a metaphysical article of faith. (Quine 1951: 33)

A similar remark can be found in the second half of the paper as well:

My present suggestion is that it is nonsense, and the root of much nonsense, to speak of a linguistic component and a factual component in the truth of any individual statement. Taken collectively, science has its double dependence upon language and experience; but this duality is not significantly traceable into the statements of science taken one by one. (Quine 1951: 39)

This picture, now called 'confirmation holism', "expresses a tremendously influential view of Quine's that led several generations of philosophers to despair not only of the analytic-synthetic distinction, but of the category of *a priori* knowledge entirely" (Rey 2022: 3.4). On this view, which accords with White's (1950: 330) earlier conjecture that "a suitable criterion is likely to make the distinction between analytic and synthetic a matter of degree", analytic statements are merely statements which are "at the center of an interconnected set of beliefs" (Keil 1989: 268). If one wishes to be open-minded, one should treat the statement in (10) as a revisable theoretical statement rather than an analytic truth which is not subject to disproof by counterexample. Wikforss's (2001, 2004) argument demonstrates that Burge's (1979a/2007) thought experiments leave no room for such open-mindedness, contrary to his own remark to the effect that his thought experiments do not presuppose analyticity.

2.5.3 One-Criterion Words, Nominal Kind Words and Cluster Words

As pointed out by Hale (1997: 487), Quine (1951) "is not claiming that any statement accepted at any time is one which we *will* at some time *in fact* reject; what he is denying is the existence of statements which we *could not* be led to reject" (emphases in the original). In this connection, Putnam (1962a, 1962b, 1970, 1975, 1983) provides more linguistic considerations for the issue than Quine (1951). Putnam (1962a: 360) takes as his point of departure Grice and Strawson's (1956: 143) observation that those who know the terms 'analytic' and 'synthetic' "apply the term 'analytic' to more or less the same cases, withhold it from more or

Chapter 2   Social Externalism and Prototype Semantics

less the same cases, and hesitate over more or less the same cases" and that "[t]his agreement extends not only to cases which they have been *taught* so to characterize, but to new cases"[16]. The claim that there is an analytic-synthetic distinction should be kept apart from the fact that one cannot offer a satisfactory account of the nature of that distinction. It is beyond any doubt that there is an intuitive distinction between (20a) and (20b).

(20)   a. All bachelors are unmarried. (for the analytic side of the dichotomy)
       b. There is a book on this table. (for the synthetic side)
                            ((20a-b): Putnam 1962a: 360)

Anyone who undertakes an empirical investigation to test the validity of (16) or (20a) would not be deemed competent in English. As Fodor (1998a: 86) notes, "intuitions deserve respect"[17]. Quine is certainly wrong in not respecting intuitions (Putnam 1962a: 361). Quine is right, however, "in a deeper sense", i.e. in the sense that "it is less of a philosophic error, although it is an error, to maintain that there is no distinction at all than it is to employ the distinction in the way that it has been employed by some of the leading analytic philosophers of our generation" (ibid.). Putnam's point is that there are only a few hundred words in English that have an analytic definition (Putnam 1962b: 659, 1970: 189, 1983: 89, cf. Keil 1989: 28, Valente 2019: 314). What is the case with these words has wrongly been taken to hold for tens of thousands of words (Putnam 1970: 189). Putnam (1962a: 396) introduced the term 'one-criterion word' to distinguish such a small class of words from other words called 'cluster words'[18]. Among the one-criterion words in English are 'bachelor' and 'vixen', whose characteristics Putnam (1983: 89) articulates in some detail:

---

16)   Mates (1951) makes a similar remark and concludes that "we have at least *some* understanding of 'analytic'" (ibid.: 531, emphasis in the original) and that "there are 'intuitive' notions of analyticity and synonymy" (ibid.: 532). Naess (1957) points out that this does not entail that one and the same intuitive notion of synonymy is shared by everyone. In particular, the requirement of universal interchangeability *salva veritate* proposed by a number of philosophers "is more in agreement with certain preconceived conceptions of synonymity than with usage itself" (Naess 1957: 91).

17)   Fodor goes on to say that intuition-based arguments are not decisive, because "*that As* and *Bs* are different is one thing; what they differ *in* is quite another" (Fodor 1998a: 86, emphases in the original).

105

The idea, in a nutshell, is that there is an exceptionless 'law' associated with the noun 'bachelor', namely, that someone is a bachelor *if and only if* he has never been married; an exceptionless law associated with the noun 'vixen', namely, that something is a vixen *if and only if* it is a female fox; etc. Moreover, this exceptionless law has, in each case, two important characteristics: [(i)] that no other exceptionless 'if and only if' statement is associated with the noun by speakers; and [(ii)] that the exceptionless 'if and only if' statement in question is a *criterion*, i.e., speakers can and do tell whether or not something is a bachelor by seeing whether or not it is an unmarried man; whether or not something is a vixen by seeing whether or not it is a female fox; etc. (Putnam 1983: 89)

If someone disagrees with (21), we should say that she does not understand the sentence, probably because she is not competent with the word 'vixen':

(21) Every vixen is a female fox.

As far as one-criterion words are concerned, Williamson (2007: 73) suggests, "failure to assent is not merely *good evidence* of failure to understand; it is *constitutive* of such failure" (emphases in the original). In Putnam's view, one-criterion words have what Williamson (2007: 74ff) calls 'understanding-assent link'; failure to assent to a sentence such as (21) constitutes failure to understand the meaning of the sentence[19]. In one-criterion words, "the core fact is just the analytical necessary and sufficient condition" (Putnam 1970: 201)[20]. This implies that, insofar as conceptual errors are errors about core facts, alleged conceptual errors about one-criterion words are always reduced to linguistic errors illustrated in Figure 2-1. Thus, a person who utters (22a) or (22b) makes a linguistic error:

(22) a. I saw a married bachelor.

---

18) Among the cluster concepts are what Putnam (1962a) calls 'law-cluster concepts'. Law-cluster concepts are concepts of science such as *energy* which "are constituted not by a bundle of properties as are the typical general names like 'man' and 'crow,' but by a cluster of laws which, as it were, determine the identity of the concept" (Putnam 1962a: 379).

19) Wikforss (2013: 244, n. 5) points out that Williamson's view departs from Putnam's in generalizing Quine's holism to one-criterion words as well. Williamson denies that even one-criterion words have understanding-assent links.

b. I have a fear of male vixens.

If the utterer is rational, the word forms 'bachelor' / 'vixen' in (22) do not express the concepts of *bachelor* / *vixen* and some reinterpretation is called for. Williamson (2007: 118) imagines speakers who assert the propositions in (23):

(23) a. A man who has lived with a partner for several years without getting married is not a bachelor.

b. Someone who underwent a sex-change operation after giving birth is a mother without being a female parent.

According to Williamson (2007: 118), such speakers "fall well within the range of permissible variation for linguistically competent speakers" and "are only giving more weight than others to an inclination that most speakers feel in some degree to classify the cases that way". In (23a), the word 'bachelor' is used in a derived sense as observed in the sentence in (24), which "might be said of a married man who acts like a bachelor – dates a lot, feels unbound by marital responsibilities, etc." (G. Lakoff 1973: 474, 1987: 138; see also R. Lakoff 1973: 66-67):

(24) John is a regular bachelor.

As Putnam (1962a: 380) puts it, "'All bachelors are unmarried' cannot be rejected unless we change the meaning of the word 'bachelor' and not even then unless we change it so radically as to change the extension of the term 'bachelor'".

The word 'mother' is commonly held to express a one-criterion concept, namely 'a person who gives birth to a child'. If this is true, a person who denies (25) does not understand the meaning of the sentence:

(25) A mother is a person who gives birth to a child.

---

20) Wikforss (2001: 222) states that one-criterion words "are not caught up with theory but could plausibly be given simple definitions". This characterization is erroneous, however, because one-criterion words as well as cluster words can be (and usually are) associated with theories. Indeed, Putnam (1962a: 395) observes that "there are various things that we might call indications of bachelorhood: being young, high spirited, living alone". The theory about 'bachelor' characterized by these indications plays an essential role when the word is modified by the adjective 'regular', as discussed in the text.

Contrary to this common assumption, G. Lakoff (1987: 74-76) maintains that the concept of *mother* involves a cluster model consisting of the cognitive models outlined in (26):

(26) a. The birth model: A mother is a person who gives birth to a child.
b. The genetic model: A mother is a female who contributes the genetic material.
c. The nurturance model: A mother is a female adult who nurtures and raises a child.
d. The marital model: A mother is the wife of the father.
e. The genealogical model: A mother is the closest female ancestor.
(adapted from Lakoff 1987: 74)

In Lakoff's view, the statement in (25) corresponds to the characterization of *mother* based on the birth model in (26a), one of the cognitive models which jointly define the concept in question. Since no single model provides the defining properties of mothers, it is possible to accept some without accepting the others, depending on the context. The sentence in (23b) presupposes that someone who fulfills (26a) may fail to fulfill (26c). In other words, the utterer of (23b) regards *mother* as a cluster concept. (23b) is therefore not a counterexample to the idea that failure to assent to a sentence characterizing a one-criterion concept constitutes failure to understand the meaning of the sentence. Insofar as one-criterion words are used as one-criterion words, those who fail to deny the statements in (22) and (25) would be charged with linguistic errors. As a consequence, there can be no incomplete understanding of one-criterion concepts.

The cases of incomplete understanding in the sense discussed here, if any, must be sought for in statements in which cluster words (as opposed to one-criterion words) are employed. If, as discussed in 2.5.1, incomplete understanding presupposes analyticity, however, there can hardly be incomplete understanding of cluster words, because, on Putnam's view, the notion of analyticity is in tension with the notion of the cluster word. Putnam (1970: 189) claims that "[t]here are no *analytic* truths of the form *every lemon has P*", except for the trivial truth that every lemon is a lemon. Or suppose that cats turn out to be robots remotely controlled from Mars. Putnam (1975: 162) observes that, to report this scenario, (27a) is more natural than (27b) and (27c).

Chapter 2   Social Externalism and Prototype Semantics

(27)   a. Cats have turned out not to be animals, but robots.
     b. The things I am referring to as 'cats' have turned out not to be animals, but robots.
     c. It has turned out that there are no cats in the world.

That (27a) is a natural statement suggests that (28a) does not express an analytic truth (Schwartz 1977: 27, Goosens 1977: 149, Ambrus 1999: 5):

(28)   a. Cats are animals.
     b. Whales are mammals.

As remarked by Schwartz (1978: 569), we would not say that (28a) was false when only one or two of the things that had been thought to be cats turned out to be robots. In this situation, we would simply say that this robot is not a cat. But if we discovered that all of the things that had been thought to be cats were robots, Schwartz suggests, we would reject the statement in (28a) (see also Abbott 1989: 273-274). More subtle cases are discussed by Putnam (1962b: 660-661). These thought experiments reveal that even competent speakers of English have no firm intuition about the use of the word 'cat'[21]. A similar point was made by Donnellan (1962) concerning (28b):

> There is no reason, a priori, why our present usage should legislate for all hypothetical cases. Given present circumstances, the correct thing to say is that all whales are mammals. But whether this is, as we intend it, a necessary truth or contingent is indeterminate. It is indeterminate because the decision as to which it is would depend upon our being able to say now what we should say about certain hypothetical cases. And evidently we are not prepared to do that. (Donnellan 1962: 658)

Donnellan nevertheless did not doubt the necessity of (28a):

---

21) Unger (1983: 119) attributes our tendency to judge (27a) as more natural than (27b-c) to the fact that "our *existence* belief, that there are or have been cats, is stronger than our *property* belief, that cats are animals" (cf. Abbott 1989: 273-274).

109

One may know what whales are and what mammals are without being aware of the connection. But if one knows what cats are and what animals are, I believe he must see that cats are animals. (Donnellan 1962: 652-653)

Donnellan (1962: 653) says that a person who seriously asks whether (28a) is true fails to grasp either the concept of *cat* or the concept of *animacy*. Putnam's (1962b, 1975) argument calls into question the necessity and analyticity of (28a) as well as (28b). After all, as Katz (1997: 5) states, it seems inconsistent to endorse the necessity of (28a) without endorsing the necessity of (28b)[22]. To be sure, we can decide which hypothetical use of a word keeps its original meaning, but this decision has no bearing upon the notion of meaning relevant to the everyday use of language, because, as suggested by Putnam (1962b), any decision would make 'meaning' a technical term:

Today it doesn't seem to make much difference what we say; while in the context of a developed linguistic theory it may make a difference whether we say that talking in one of these ways is changing the meaning and talking in another of these ways is keeping the meaning unchanged. But that is hardly relevant here and now; when linguistic theory becomes that developed, then 'meaning' will itself have become a technical term, and presumably our question now is not which decision is changing the meaning in some future technical sense of 'meaning', but what we can say in our present language. (Putnam 1962b: 661)

From a cognitive linguistic perspective, Taylor (2003: 86) states that (29) does not express an analytic truth, because it is possible that, "as a consequence of scientific discoveries, our understanding of life forms [may] undergo radical change, resulting in a major re-classification of biological kinds":

(29) Dogs are animals.

Textbooks on semantics sometimes say that 'Fido is a dog' (semantically) entails

---

22) Although I will not go into the matter, Katz (1997: 14) qualifies this diagnosis in the course of defending his own view of analyticity. On the assumption that sense does not determine reference but merely mediates it, Katz claims, "the possibility of 'cat' referring to non-animals is entirely consistent with the analyticity of [(28a)]" (ibid.).

Chapter 2   Social Externalism and Prototype Semantics

'Fido is an animal'. A closer examination reveals, however, that even a sentence like (29) is not analytic, "in that its truth is ultimately dependent on real-world contingencies and of [sic.] our understanding of them" (ibid.). In short, "the dictionary is encyclopaedic" (ibid).

Some nouns which commonly denote artifacts exhibit an apparent similarity to animate nouns just discussed. At first sight, the sentences in (30) may appear analytic:

(30)   a. Pencils are artifacts.
       b. Sofas are artifacts.

Schwartz (1978) argues, however, that this intuition is not correct, because we can imagine, as in the thought experiment Putnam (1975: 161) owed to Rogers Albritton, that pencils turn out to be organisms or even that, in some community, people grow and harvest pencils in the same way we grow and harvest apples (Schwartz 1978: 570). Even if pencils turned out to be organisms, contrary to the common wisdom, we would not say that it was discovered that there were no pencils in the world. Likewise, we would not say that the people in the imagined community grew pencil-like plants, insofar as they used the objects to write letters or to draw pictures. We would rather say that pencils in the community have very different properties from our pencils. The same holds for 'sofa'. If this intuition is correct, the cases under consideration will provide counter-examples to the statements in (30). Schwartz (1978: 571-572) concludes that it is neither necessary nor analytic that pencils, sofas, chairs and lamps are artifacts.

So far, words like 'pencil' and 'sofa' resemble words like 'dog' and 'lemon'. Complicating the matter is that Schwartz insists that there are analytic truths about words like 'pencil' and 'sofa'. After all, even in a hypothetical community in which people grow and harvest pencils, the statement in (31a) holds:

(31)   a. Pencils are instruments for writing or drawing.
       b. Sofas are pieces of furniture to be sat upon.

If it turned out that the pencil-like plants in the community were never used for writing or drawing but were merely fed to dogs, we would judge the plants not to be pencils, as Abbott (1989: 281) suggests in relation to a similar hypothetical setting. The same point can be made for (31b), whose truthfulness makes Adam in

111

Burge's 'sofa' thought experiment a deviant speaker.

Due to their dual nature, nouns such as 'pencil' and 'sofa' cannot neatly be classified into one-criterion words or cluster words (Schwartz 1978: 573). According to Schwartz (1978: 572), objects like chairs, pencils and lamps belong to 'nominal kinds' as opposed to natural kind (Keil 1989: Ch. 3). Nominal kinds, Schwartz (1977: 39) suggests, "have what Locke would call a nominal essence but lack a biological, chemical, or atomic essence". Locke (1690: Book III, Ch. III, 15) states that "things are ranked under names into sorts or species, only as they agree to certain abstract ideas, to which we have annexed those names". Such abstract ideas constitute the nominal essence of the things under consideration. As Dupré (1981: 67) makes clear, the nominal essence roughly corresponds to "the means whereby we distinguish things as belonging to that kind". Nominal kind concepts such as *pencil* and one-criterion concepts such as *bachelor* have in common that they possess no 'essence' which may be unknown to the public (ibid.: 572) and that they are associated with "an analytic specification in terms of form and function" (ibid.: 572). Nominal kind terms include "the names of kinds of furniture, household articles, implements, tools, ornaments, and so on" (ibid.: 573). Schwartz illustrates the contrast between natural kinds and nominal kinds with the help of nominals which intuitively denote animals:

> "Dog" and "cat" are natural kind terms, but "pet" is a nominal kind term. Something is a pet if it satisfies certain descriptions. We do not presume that pets share a common underlying nature, other than being animals, perhaps. Something is a pet not because of its nature but because of its relationship to other things, its function or role, and so on. (Schwartz 1978: 573)

Since pets are not artifacts, it is a mistake to equate nominal kind terms with nouns which commonly denote artifacts[23].

On the other hand, nominal kind terms have in common with cluster words that even their alleged core features may fail to characterize them. The statements in (30) may turn out to be false, just as the statements in (28)-(29) fail to characterize the terms in question. As regards 'sofa', Burge (1986a: 715/2007: 270) proposes the definition "sofas are all and only pieces of furniture of a certain

---

23) The qualification 'commonly' is added because, as discussed in the text, 'pencil', 'chair' and 'lamp' can also denote organisms.

Chapter 2   Social Externalism and Prototype Semantics

construction meant or made for sitting" and Sawyer (2003: 269) proposes the definition "Sofas are upholstered pieces of furniture for two or more people ... used for
sitting on". These descriptions cannot be considered a criterion for 'sofa' unless the
content of "certain" and "..." are specified. It is disputable whether ordinary speakers can and do tell what further specifications are needed.

To summarize, one-criterion terms are defined in terms of necessary and sufficient conditions which competent speakers are supposed to know. Nominal kind
terms are associated with partial analytic specifications which serve as necessary
conditions for something to belong to the categories. Cluster terms are distinguished from both one-criterion terms and nominal kind terms in that there can
be no analytic specifications for them. Putative cases of an incomplete understanding of a cluster concept thus are reduced to non-standard theorizing. Now, it is
fairly obvious that 'arthritis' is a cluster term, given Putnam's (1962c/1975: 310-
311) suggestion that 'multiple sclerosis' is a cluster term. If Putnam's view is correct, it follows that, except for trivial analytic statements such as 'arthritis is arthritis' (Schwartz 1978: 566), there can hardly be any analytic truth about arthritis.
This is the reason why the statement in (1) above, which Burge takes to be a case
of incomplete understanding, can turn out to be a case of non-standard theorizing,
as discussed in Section 2.3.

2.6 Prototypes and Incomplete Understanding

2.6.1 A Forever Absolutely True Synthetic Statement

As discussed in Section 2.3, thought experiments in support of social externalism are *essentially* dependent upon the notion of incomplete understanding. As
discussed in Section 2.5.1, the notion of incomplete understanding entails the
notion of conceptual error in the technical sense of the term, that is, the notion of
conceptual error which presupposes the existence of analytic truths – truths characterized either as statements which are "true by virtue of meanings and independently of fact" (Quine 1951: 21) or as *a priori* statements which are "confirmed
no matter what" (ibid.: 35). As discussed in Section 2.5.3, conceptual errors in this
sense can hardly be found, because, in the case of one-criterion words and nominal
kind words, alleged conceptual errors are almost always reduced to linguistic errors,
while, in the case of cluster words, alleged conceptual errors are in most cases
reduced to non-standard theorizing, as illustrated in Figure 2-1. Thus, even the
negation of 'Cats are animals' can be interpreted as a statement based on a

113

non-standard theory which can prove to be true. As is the case with 'lemon' discussed by Putnam (1970), there may be no analytic truth about cats. What has been discussed so far then suggests (i) that conceptual errors, if any, can most probably be found in statements containing cluster words, (ii) that conceptual errors, if any, must be distinguished from non-standard theorizing in that it is impossible (in the ordinary as opposed to the philosophical sense of the term) that what is considered a conceptual error will turn out not to be one, and (iii) that conceptual errors about cluster words, if any, presuppose no analytic truth. Given (i)-(iii), the notion of incomplete understanding on which thought experiments supporting social externalism are essentially dependent must be independent from analyticity. So the question to be asked is whether there can be incomplete understanding without analyticity.

It may at first blush appear that the desiderata stated in (ii) and (iii) are mutually incompatible to the extent that the combination of the two clauses requires that there be forever absolutely true synthetic statements. A moment's non-philosophical and non-scientific reflection, however, will reveal that there are such facts everywhere: Emmanuel Macron is the President of the French Republic in 2023, Japan has a constitution in 2023, I am writing this sentence in 2023, and so on. Someday, some people may doubt the truthfulness (and even be convinced of the falsity) of these sentences, but such doubt (or confidence) will never alter their truthfulness. The real challenge lies rather in the desideratum stated in (i). Together with (ii) and (iii), (i) requires that there be forever absolutely true synthetic statements which conceptually characterize the entities denoted by the cluster word under consideration. The statement that Emmanuel Macron is the President of the French Republic in 2023, for instance, fails to conceptually characterize Emmanuel Macron, because Emmanuel Macron will be Emmanuel Macron even after his retirement. Forever absolutely true synthetic statements which conceptually characterize the entities in question, if any, concern what Putnam (1970) called core facts about cluster terms. Among the few statements satisfying the desiderata, it seems to me, is (32), a statement to which the following discussion in this chapter is devoted exclusively.

(32) Birds fly.

(32) is obviously not an analytic statement, because there are many birds that do not fly. Indeed, there can hardly be any analytic truths about birds. Hampton (2015:

131) says that "BIRD has a clear-cut definition – 'feathered bipedal creature' – and no borderline cases". But this alleged clear-cut definition does not seem to fulfill clause (ii) of the definition of an exceptionless law, reproduced here as (33):

(33) (ii) that the exceptionless 'if and only if' statement in question is a *criterion*, i.e., speakers can and do tell whether or not something is bachelor by seeing whether or not it is an unmarried man; whether or not something is a vixen by seeing whether or not it is a female fox; etc. (Putnam 1983: 89)

It is doubtful that ordinary speakers can and do tell whether or not something is a bird by seeing whether or not it is a feathered bipedal creature. The feature in question is not sufficient to define 'bird', because we would hesitate to say that a feathered bipedal creature we encountered was a bird if it were more than ten meters in body length, for example. The feature is certainly necessary for the definition of 'bird', but, as Hampton (2006: 11) points out, when describing birds, people will commonly start with 'have wings' and 'fly', instead of 'have feathers', "in spite of the fact that there are well-known examples of flightless birds, and many species of insect that fly, whereas all birds (at least before they are prepared for the oven) and only birds have feathers". This indicates that the word 'bird' does not satisfy (33ii), one of the conditions imposed on one-criterion words. In this respect, as Hampton (2006: 11) remarks, birds may be "a rather special" case. There is another fact that may support this conclusion. As we have seen in Section 2.5.3, the core facts about a one-criterion word can be equated with the analytical necessary and sufficient condition for something to fall within the extension of the word. It is hardly the case, however, that one can convey the use of 'bird' by simply conveying the fact that birds are feathered bipedal creatures, or that one cannot convey the approximate use unless one gets this fact across. The word 'bird' does not seem to be a nominal kind term, either, because, unlike the case of 'sofa' discussed earlier, one can rationally ask whether there is a hidden nature that makes something a bird. 'Bird' is neither one-criterion word nor a nominal kind word but a cluster word.

The remaining question is whether (32) is a forever absolutely true statement which conceptually characterizes birds. This question is divided into two parts: (i) Is (32) a forever absolutely true statement?, and (ii) Does (32) conceptually characterize birds? As regards (i), it must be noticed, first, that the sentence in (32) is largely idiomatic in Taylor's (2012) sense. In addition to the traditional notion of idiomaticity which characterizes idioms as "expressions whose properties (phonological, syntactic, or semantic) cannot be derived from more general principles and which therefore have to be learned" (Taylors 2012: 282), Taylor puts forward another notion of idiomaticity, according to which "understanding the idiomatic concerns the appropriate thing to say in a given context" (ibid.: 283). To ask a person's age in English, for instance, the appropriate expression to employ is 'How old are you', rather than 'What is your age?' (ibid.). To give another example, when reporting what they did, 'They swam across the river' is more appropriate than 'They crossed the river by swimming' (ibid.; see also Talmy 2000). Likewise, one may note that (32) is a more appropriate thing to say than (34a-d)[24].

(34)　a. Birds usually fly.
　　　b. Normally birds fly.
　　　c. Most birds fly.
　　　d. Typical birds fly.

A person who seriously says in response to (32), 'That's false. There are birds that do not fly', would not be deemed competent in English; the ability to assent to (32) is part of competence in English. This competence does not concern syntax or semantics, but the way to talk about birds. Competent speakers are required to recognize "the fact that many sentences may be neither universally true, nor simply false, but may instead be true under some notion of 'generally true' or 'typically true'" (Hampton 2006: 11). The second point to be made about (i) is that (32) concerns what Putnam (1975) refers to as the stereotype of a bird, namely a conventional idea of what a bird looks like or acts like or is (cf. Putnam 1975: 169)[25].

---

24)　Idioms (in both senses) may differ from language to language. For instance, the Japanese counterpart of (32) is either (i) or (ii), with the latter sounding somewhat more idiomatic in Taylor's (2012) sense:
(i)　Tori　wa　tobu.
　　　bird TOP　fly
　　　Lit.: A bird flies. / Bird fly.
(ii)　Tori　wa　sora　o　tobu.
　　　bird TOP　sky ACC　fly
　　　Lit.: A bird flies the sky. / Bird fly the sky.
25)　Putnam (1975: 369) stresses that stereotypes may be "malicious" or "widely inaccurate". This is not to say that every stereotype is malicious or inaccurate.

According to Putnam (1975: 171), "[w]hat it means to say that being striped is part of the (linguistic) stereotype of "tiger" is that it is obligatory to acquire the information that stereotypical tigers are striped if one acquires the word "tiger"". The same holds for (32); it seems to be obligatory to acquire the information conveyed by (32) in order to be competent in the use of the word 'bird' and the concept of *bird*. By putting together the two points that have been just made, it can be concluded that a competent speaker of English is expected to assent to the statement in (32) by interpreting it as expressing the truth literally conveyed by (34). The statement in (32) interpreted in this manner is indisputably a forever absolutely true statement. It will never turn out that birds do not fly, in contrast to the case of arthritis, where it is possible to imagine that, contrary to common wisdom, the disease turns out to afflict one's thigh under certain circumstances.

The second question, namely, (ii) Does (32) conceptually characterize birds?, is closely tied to the consideration provided for the first question. Since 'bird' is one of the most basic words of English, anyone who wishes to be competent in the language is required to acquire the concept of *bird* expressed by that word. If (32) does not conceptually characterize birds, the understanding of (32) is not needed for competence in English. As has just been shown, however, (32) is a core fact about the word 'bird', to the extent that one cannot convey the approximate use of the word unless one gets across the fact represented by (32). True, (32) is not part of the meaning of 'bird' in the sense of intension and extension, as evidenced by the fact that penguins, emus and ostriches are included in the extension of the word, too (Rey 1992: 322, Stich 1992: 249, Fodor 1998a: 92). In this respect, (32) is arguably different from (31a-b), which may plausibly be taken to constitute the intension of the words 'pencil' and 'sofa', so that denying (31a-b) would evince an incomplete understanding of the concepts of *pencil* and *sofa*. Understanding the meaning of a word, however, is sometimes insufficient for acquiring the concept expressed by the word. As Haiman (1980: 348) puts it, "analytic is to synthetic as dictionary is to encyclopedia". Sticking to the pure notion of meaning to the exclusion of encyclopedic knowledge is tantamount to reviving the analytic-synthetic distinction even for cluster words. It is one of the main tenets of cognitive linguistics that there is "no strict dichotomy between linguistic and extralinguistic knowledge" (Langacker 2008: 464). The sharp dichotomy between dictionary and encyclopedia is unwarranted, because, as Taylor (2003: 87) points out, "[t]he acceptability – and interpretability – of linguistic expressions depends, very often, on the activation of knowledge about the world". There is good reason to suppose that this "very often" includes the cases concerning (32). First of all, a person ignorant of the truth expressed by (32) would not be able to understand the meaning of such simple sentences as (35a) and (35b).

(35) a. If I were a bird, I would fly to you.
     b. I wish I could fly like a bird.

This confirms the point that encyclopedic knowledge affects the interpretability of basic linguistic expressions that any competent speaker is expected to understand. Secondly, a person who dissents from (32) would not share with other speakers the judgment about sentences containing a 'hedge', an expression which signals the "degree of category membership" (Taylor 2003: 79)[26]. G. Lakoff (1973) famously provided the following data:

(36) a. A robin is a bird par excellence. (true)
     b. A chicken is a bird par excellence. (false)
     c. A penguin is a bird par excellence. (false)
                               ((36a–c): G. Lakoff 1973: 473)
(37) a. A robin is sort of a bird. (False – it is a bird, no question, about it)
     b. A chicken is sort of a bird. (True, or very close to true)
     c. A penguin is sort of a bird. (True, or close to true)
                               ((37a–c): G. Lakoff 1973: 471)

Psychological experiments show that robins and sparrows are good examples (Rosch 1975: 232), or prototypes (Rosch 1977: 2), of birds, while penguins, ostriches and chickens are not (cf. Rey 1992: 328). One of the relevant factors is, obviously, whether or not the bird in question flies. Such judgments about the typicality of examples are not purely psychological, but are mirrored in linguistic judgments as illustrated in (36) and (37). In Taylor's (2003: 87) words, "encyclopaedic knowledge is crucially involved in the way in which words are used".

2.6.2 Prototype Semantics and Cognitive Linguistics

Influenced by Rosch's work, virtually every linguist working within the

---

26) Hedges are originally defined by G. Lakoff (1973: 471) as "words whose meaning implicitly involves fuzziness – words whose job is to make things fuzzier or less fuzzy".

Chapter 2   Social Externalism and Prototype Semantics

cognitive linguistic framework has accepted prototype semantics as a basic principle, rejecting classical Montague semantics which rests on what Langacker (1987)
calls "the criterial-attribute model", according to which categories are defined in
terms of necessary and sufficient conditions and "class membership is thus an all-
or-nothing affair" (ibid.: 16). Langacker (1987) asserts that "the prototype model
has considerable linguistic and cognitive plausibility" (ibid.: 17) on the grounds
that "[m]uch in language is a matter of degree" (ibid.: 14). In disputing the criterial-attribute model, Langacker appeals, for one thing, to the fact that the putative
criteria are often neither necessary nor sufficient. Being able to fly is not necessary
for something to count as a bird because there are flightless birds (ibid.: 16).
Laying eggs is not sufficient because there are egg-laying mammals (ibid.). For
another, Langacker points out that the alleged necessary and sufficient conditions
can fail to fully characterize the category. Thus, even though the specifications
[FEATHERLESS] [BIPED] allow us to define the extension of humans, "we
would nevertheless hesitate to accept these two features as a comprehensive or
revealing description of our species" (ibid.). This is reminiscent of the point made
earlier, namely the point that the specifications [FEATHERED] [BIPEDAL]
[CREATURE] do not seem to correspond to our understanding of birds even if
they are necessary and sufficient for something to be a bird. Langacker draws on
Rosch's work to defend the prototype model:

Experimental work in cognitive psychology (pioneered by Rosch, e.g. 1973,
1975, 1977, 1978) has demonstrated that categories are often organized
around prototypical instances. These are instances people accept as common,
run-of-the-mill, garden-variety members of the category. They generally occur
the most frequently in our experience, tend to be learned the earliest, and can
be identified experimentally in a variety of ways (e.g. responders accept them
as class members with the shortest response latencies). Nonprototypical
instances are assimilated to a class or category to the extent that they can be
construed as matching or approximating the prototype. Membership is therefore a matter of degree: prototype instances are full, central members of the
category, whereas other instances form a gradation from central to peripheral
depending on how far and in what ways they deviate from the prototype.
(Langacker 1987: 16-17)

Although in cognitive linguistics it is generally assumed that the prototype

119

model is in no need of justification, it is not widely accepted in philosophy. Thus, Peacocke (1992: 3) worries that the prototype model is not suitable for the elucidation of concepts of proper philosophical interest, even though it may serve for other purposes. Unlike ordinary concepts, prototypes are characterized by their variability. In some culture, grandmothers may typically be small, old or fragile, etc. But we would not want to say that the concept of *grandmother* has been replaced by another when the 'grandmothers' are no longer small, old, fragile, etc., thanks to the development of anti-aging technology. A concept may persist even when its prototype undergoes a drastic change. Peacocke (1992: 3) states:

> And it is well known that it need not even be true, let alone uninformative, that all and only grandmothers fall under the prototype (small, old, fragile, etc.) associated in some cultures with the concept *grandmother*. [...] Recognition of the level of concepts in the present sense is [...] needed for a proper description of cases in which there is a change of prototype or relatively central beliefs associated with a concept. Indeed, as elsewhere, describing a case as one of change, rather than as one of replacement, is correct only if there is something that persists through the change, and it is the concept in my sense that so persists. (Peacocke 1992: 3)

The change of the prototype does not affect the concept of which it is the prototype. To employ Segal's (2000: 77) metaphor, the concept remains the same 'organic unity'. The process in question should rather be described as a theory change which the organic unity has survived. If such is the case, it may be objected that what the data in (36) and (37) mirror is the standard theory about birds, rather than the concept of *bird* per se.

The objection is certainly valid for 'bachelor' or 'grandmother'. The prototype of 'bachelor' or 'grandmother' does not meet the condition of 'conceptual stability' or 'content publicity' proposed by Löhr (2020: 2183-2184). "Being young, high spirited, living alone" (Putnam 1962a: 395) may constitute the prototype of 'bachelor' at a given time and place. Nevertheless, these properties are not among the core facts about 'bachelor' which contribute to the definition of the concept of *bachelor*. We do not have to think that those who believe that bachelors are usually high-spirited have a different concept expressed by the word form 'bachelor' from those who believe that bachelors are usually low-spirited; it is just that they have different theories about the same concept. Such a difference in theory would best be accounted for by what Löhr (2020: 2183) calls a 'theory of categorization' as opposed to 'theory of conceptualization'. To say that understanding what typical birds look like is central to the concept of *bird* is not to say that all concepts are characterized by prototypes. The view defended here does not commit one to what Weiskopf (2009: 149) refers to as the 'Uniformity Assumption', namely the assumption that "all concepts belong to the same psychological kind". As Weiskopf (2009: 155, 158) stresses, "the conceptual system is structured to employ a variety of different representational tools" (ibid.: 155), of which the prototype model is only one example.

Fodor (1998a, 1998b) offers an argument against the view that some concepts are characterized by prototypes, claiming that "[c]oncepts can't be prototypes, *pace* all the evidence that everybody who has a concept is highly likely to have its prototype as well" (Fodor 1998a: 93). Fodor's argument rests on the assumption that concepts are compositional (Fodor 1998a: 25-27, 94, 99-100, 105, 1998b: 3, Löhr 2020: 2184-2186). For Fodor, compositionality is what explains the systematicity and productivity of concepts (cf. Weiskopf 2009: 148). Denying that concepts are compositional, Fodor (1998b: 3) argues, "leaves it open that one could have the concept RED APPLE and not have the concept RED". Prototypes do not fulfil this condition imposed on concepts. For instance, a goldfish (or a guppy) is a prototypical example of 'pet fish' but is neither a good example of 'pet' nor of 'fish' (Osherson and Smith 1981: 45, Fodor 1998a: 102, 1998b: 4-6). Since the typicality of 'pet fish' contains something which the typicality of 'pet' and the typicality of 'fish' lack, "prototypes don't compose" (Fodor 1998a: 94, 101). This is to say that the ability to discern good instances of a category does not compose (Fodor 1998b: 5-6). It follows that "concepts can't be prototypes" (Fodor 1998a: 93, 94, 100).

One of the problems with Fodor's view is that, even if it is conceded that concepts are generally compositional, it does not follow that concepts must actually compose. As Prinz (2002: 294) states, "the strong interpretation we can defend is that they are *potentially* compositional" (emphasis in the original). Another problem is that the idea that concepts cannot be prototypes cannot account for the fact that competent speakers of English are required to have the prototype of 'bird'. What is characteristic of 'bird' is that it is not only that everybody who has the concept of *bird* is highly likely to have its prototype as well but also that everyone who fails to have its prototype is likely to fail to fully understand the concept as well. Recanati (2006: 254-256) raises an objection to Fodor (1998a, 1998b) by saying that the non-compositionality of epistemic properties does not entail that these are not essential to concepts. The claim that the reference of a concept is compositionally determined is compatible with the claim that epistemic properties do not compose. According to Recanati, Fodor's argument conflates composition and inheritance. Even if it is right to say that the ability to recognize red things does not compose, it does not follow that one can have the ability to discern red apples without having the ability to discern red things. Epistemic properties are inherited, though not composed. This weak notion of inheritance (simple inheritance as opposed to compositional inheritance) is sufficient to guarantee that one cannot have the concept *red apple* without having the concept *red*. Although Recanati does not discuss prototypes, a similar argument can be made to demonstrate that both compositionality and prototypicality can be essential to concepts. It is not incoherent to say both that the reference of 'pet fish' is compositionally determined and that understanding the typicality of 'pet fish' presupposes understanding the typicality of 'pet' as well as that of 'fish'. Thus, a person who does not know that dogs are typical pets cannot be considered competent with the concept of *pet fish*. Consequently, the claim that the prototype of 'bird' essentially constitutes part of the concept of *bird* does not conflict with the thesis that concepts are compositional.

In fact, the objection that what the data in (36) and (37) mirror is the standard theory about birds, rather than the concept of *bird* per se, fails to recognize that the sentences in (36) and (37) concern what counts as birds, and not what birds look like or act like. To this one may still object that (36) and (37) are not statements about birds, on the ground that, at least from a semantic point of view, 'bird par excellence' in (36) and 'sort of bird' in (37) can be analyzed as complex predicates denoting the concepts of, say, *typical bird* and *marginal bird*, respectively. This view may be adequate, but it does not help solve the problem at hand. While hedges like 'par excellence' and 'sort of' serve to tighten the category, so that *typical bird* and *marginal bird* are narrower concepts than *bird*, there are also hedges operating in the opposite direction. Thus, 'loosely speaking' serves to "[extend] the category by accommodating things that would not ordinarily be considered members" (Taylor 2003: 80).

(38) a. Loosely speaking, a whale is a fish. (G. Lakoff 1973: 475, Kay 1983: 131)
      b. Loosely speaking, a bat is a bird. (true, or at least not patently false) (Taylor 2003: 80)

As Kay (1983: 132) states, 'loosely speaking' has "nothing to do with the modification of a category", since no intersection of the category of fish with any other category includes whales as members and no intersection of the category of birds with any other category includes bats as members. A similar remark can be made for 'in a manner of speaking':

(39) In a manner of speaking, a bat is a bird. (true, or close to true)

(G. Lakoff 1973: 473)

One might think that hedges like 'loosely speaking' and 'in a manner of speaking', when applied to 'bird' for instance, generate the category of, say, *bird in an extended sense*, just as the adjectival construction 'fake N' serves to extend the category of N, as seen in 'fake dollar' or 'fake gun' (Recanati 2010: 72). I have nothing to say about this analysis insofar as it is intended as a semantic description of the phenomena under consideration. What is important to realize is that this analysis as such cannot answer the question about why the concept of *bird* is extended so as to include *bat* but not *cow*, as shown by the data in (40):

(40) a. Loosely speaking, a cow is a bird. (false)
  b. In a manner of speaking, a cow is a bird. (false)

((40a-b): G. Lakoff 1973: 473)

The answer to the question is fairly obvious. As Taylor (2003: 80) maintains, hedges such as 'loosely speaking' and 'in a manner of speaking' are used to accommodate "things that would not ordinarily be considered members, but which might nevertheless be associated with the category on the basis of one or two non-essential attributes which they share with it". The fact that bats but not cows share with birds the attribute of flying determines the truthfulness or falsity of the statements in (40). Indeed, Taylor (2003: 80) observes that (38b) above, not acceptable for some speakers, can be improved by making explicit the reason for the extension of the category as in (41):

(41) Loosely speaking, a bat is a bird, in that it has wings and can fly.

(Taylor 2003: 80)

This suggests that the statement in (32) plays an essential role in determining what falls under the concept expressed by the word 'bird', whether the concept be *bird*, *typical bird*, *marginal bird* or *bird in an extended sense*.

There is yet another point to be made about the idea that what the data in (36) and (37) mirror is the standard theory about birds, rather than the concept of *bird* per se. The point cannot be fully developed in this book and it is more a story than an argument pertaining to how, on the prototype-semantic view, categories come into existence and are organized. Langacker (1987: 371) depicts a scenario in which "[a] prototype is a typical instance of a category[27] and other elements are assimilated to the category on the basis of their perceived resemblance to the prototype". A similar view is defended by Peacocke (1992: 12) and Hampton (2006: 9-11). If this picture captures the reality, albeit partially, then what triggers the formation of a category is the prototype. This implies that the category, and hence the concept, of birds cannot come into being unless the state of affairs expressed by the statement in (32) holds. If such is the case, it is reasonable to conclude that (32) is a forever absolutely true statement which conceptually characterizes birds.

If the argument so far is on the right track, the statement in (32) is what may yield an incomplete understanding without analyticity, a notion needed for thought experiments in support of social externalism. Suppose, as a first step, that Adam, a rational person competent in English, believes (42):

(42) Birds are feathered bipedal creatures that live on the ground.

Although birds fly, Adam has never seen birds fly. When he encountered birds, they happened to be on the ground, walking or running. For him, flying things include insects, bats and airplanes, but not birds. People have never told Adam that birds fly, because it is so obvious that it has never occurred to them that he is ignorant of the fact. The second step of the thought experiment consists in imagining that Adam$_2$, a near duplicate of Adam living in some other community, believes (42) just as much as Adam in the actual community does. The only

---

27) As pointed out by Taylor (2003: 63-64), the term 'instance' here should be interpreted in a more or less abstract manner (see also Prinz 2002: Ch. 3). In most (but not all) cases, the prototype of a category cannot be equated with any specific instance. Thus, no specific person can be the prototype of tallness, no matter how tall she may be. The typical instance of a category is often a specific *kind* of entity, or, more abstractly, an unspecific entity that is mentally represented as having certain attributes.

Chapter 2 Social Externalism and Prototype Semantics

difference between the two communities resides in the habits of birds. In Adam$_2$'s community, ordinary people believe that birds do not fly. Still, what are called 'birds' in that community are birds. The nature of birds is exactly the same in the actual and hypothetical communities as far as biology is concerned, and the word 'bird' has exactly the same meaning, namely the same intension and extension. The situation is thus different from those imagined in Burge's thought experiments concerning 'arthritis' and 'sofa', in which the same word form has different meanings for the two communities. The situation is also different from that imagined in Putnam's thought experiment concerning 'cat', in which cats turn out to be automata remotely controlled from Mars. The peculiar habits of birds supposed in the present thought experiment are ultimately attributed to the policy adopted by the government of Adam$_2$'s community, rather than the genetic properties of birds. The hypothetical government gives an order, unknown to the general public, to its special forces to administer a drug to every bird as soon as it is born in order to prevent it from flying. Every year there are a few birds that successfully escape from the injection, but their number is not large enough to undermine the widely accepted idea that birds do not fly. It is a truism in the community of Adam$_2$ that birds do not fly. Finally, the imagined situation is interpreted. Intuitively, Adam's thought that birds do not fly is false, while Adam$_2$'s thought that birds do not fly is true. Although Adam and Adam$_2$ are internally identical and the meanings of the words they employ are the same, the contents of their thoughts are different due to the difference of the conceptual truths accepted by their communities. Adam, but not Adam$_2$, betrays an incomplete understanding of the concept of *bird* insofar as he dissents from the forever absolutely true statement which conceptually characterizes birds. In conclusion, social externalism essentially relies on incomplete understanding without analyticity. Wikforss (2001, 2004) is right in claiming that social externalism essentially relies on incomplete understanding, but is mistaken in claiming that incomplete understanding presupposes analyticity.

2.6.3 Conclusion and Qualification

The argument developed in this chapter suggests the classification of errors illustrated in Figure 2-2.

125

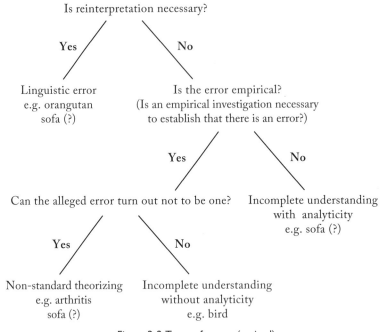

Figure 2-2: Types of errors (revised)

It is not clear under which category the 'sofa' case falls. If, as Burge (1986a/2007) suggests, it is possible to reasonably doubt that sofas are pieces of furniture, then the 'sofa' case will fall under non-standard theorizing. If, as Wikforss (2004) suggests, Adam necessarily evinces an incomplete grasp of 'sofa' when doubting that sofas are pieces of furniture, then it will fall under either incomplete understanding with analyticity or a linguistic error. If one can grant Adam the concept of *sofa* even though he misunderstands the definition of 'sofa', then we have a case of incomplete understanding with analyticity. If Adam is not considered to possess the concept of *sofa*, he will be considered to be making a linguistic error in saying that sofas are religious works of art. This indecision suggests that the types of error are not neatly separate categories but placed on a continuum. Speakers are more or less competent with the use of a term and the concept it expresses. We will return to this problem in Chapter 3.

Social externalism essentially relies on the notion of incomplete understanding. This notion seems to presuppose the notion of analyticity. A person who thinks that arthritis can be found in one's thigh, Burge (1979a/2007) says, betrays an

Chapter 2   Social Externalism and Prototype Semantics

incomplete understanding of the concept of *arthritis*. According to Wikforss (2001, 2004), Burge's view requires that it be a conceptual truth in the strong sense of the term, namely an analytic truth, that arthritis strikes the joints only. Insofar as 'arthritis' is a cluster word, however, it is both theoretically and empirically difficult to postulate any analytic truths about arthritis. It is theoretically difficult because "a boundary between analytic and synthetic statements simply has not been drawn" and "[t]hat there is such a distinction to be drawn at all is an unempirical dogma of empiricists" (Quine 1951: 33). It is empirically difficult because further scientific investigations may reveal that arthritis can afflict the thigh in exceptional cases and dictionary descriptions may be revised accordingly. A person who thinks that arthritis afflicts one's thigh may be more plausibly be characterized as developing a non-standard theory about arthritis.

A person who thinks that sofas are religious works of art, Burge (1986a/2007) says, has a full grasp of the concept of *sofa* and she should merely be credited with a non-standard theory about sofas. This idea rests on the assumption that "ability to discriminate Fs from non-Fs combined with inability correctly to characterize the nature of Fs typically signals incorrect empirical theory" (Sawyer 2003: 271). That person's theory is incorrect because sofas are not religious artifacts but pieces of furniture to be sat upon. According to Burge (1986a/2007: *passim*), a statement such as 'Sofas are pieces of furniture to be sat upon' is a "meaning-giving normative characterization" for the term 'sofa'. Meaning giving normative characterizations, Burge claims, are not analytic truths in that they are dubitable (Burge 1986: 701/2007: 258). As Burge (1986a: 714/2007: 269) puts it, "truths of meaning are dubitable". However, as Wikforss (2001, 2004) points out, rightly I think, an analytic truth is smuggled into the thought experiment concerning 'sofa' when Burge (1986a: 708/2007: 263) says that "[t]here are no sofas" in his hypothetical community in which what are called 'sofas' are "objects that look like sofas but are, and are widely known to be, works of art or religious artifacts sold in showrooms and displayed in people's houses". As suggested by Schwartz (1978), it is a necessary and analytic truth that sofas are pieces of furniture to be sat upon. This implies that a person in the actual community who thinks that sofas are works of art believes non-sofas to be sofas. There seems to be no fundamental difference between this case and the case of 'arthritis'; both cases appeal to analyticity.

Incomplete understanding without analyticity, if any, stems from misunderstanding of certain (but not all) prototypes. A person who does not think that birds fly displays an incomplete grasp of the cluster concept of *bird* while perfectly

127

understanding the meaning of the word 'bird', as long as 'meaning' is equated with 'intension and extension'. That birds fly is a conceptual truth about birds, but it is nonetheless not an analytic truth. Social externalism can thus be vindicated by appealing to incomplete understanding without analyticity.

Prototype semantics is generally considered part of cognitive linguistics, as illustrated by the fact that virtually every textbook on this discipline has a chapter devoted to that semantics. Prototype semantics favors social externalism, contrary to the official view of cognitive linguistics, commonly known an internalist theory or a group of internalist theories. For Langacker, "language is part of cognition" (Langacker 2008: 7) and "meanings are in the minds of the speakers who produce and understand the expressions" (ibid.: 27). The idea that the misunderstanding of typicality is what is necessary and sufficient for the social externalist thesis to follow is prima facie at odds with the official view of this school. How are we to reconcile social externalism with the thesis that meanings, equated with various processes of conceptualization (Langacker 2008: 30), are in the head (ibid.: 27)? One simple answer suggests itself: this is the wrong question, because there is no threat at all. As noted in Section 1.3.3, externalism is not the view that meaning and thought are outside the subject's mind, but the view that the subject's intrinsic properties are not sufficient to individuate the meaning and thought she entertains. For this reason, Burge prefers the term 'anti-individualism' to 'externalism'. Burge (2003) expounds the correct construal of externalism and internalism:

Anti-individualism or externalism, in my sense, need not affect the way psychology studies the structures and mechanisms of internal psychological states. I am happy to agree that all psychological states, properly so-called, are "in" the individual's mind. Anti-individualism is about the nature of "internal" psychological states. Anti-individualism is the view that an individual's being in a significant range of particular intentional psychological states (beliefs, understandings, and so on) necessitates that the individual bear certain causal, functional, or historical relations to an environment beyond the individual. Further, the natures and identities of those states are constitutively dependent on certain relations between individual and environment. [...] Internalism, in *my* sense, concerns not the locus of the psychological states, or the best ways to study them, but whether being in them presupposes individual-environmental relations. It concerns whether the existence and nature of certain psychological kinds depends necessarily on the existence and nature of certain relations to

Chapter 2   Social Externalism and Prototype Semantics

specific kinds or situations in the environment. (Burge 2003: 454-455)

Conceived in this manner, externalism seems highly compatible with cognitive linguistics. When Langacker (2008: 27) says that "meanings are in the minds of the speakers who produce and understand the expressions", he may well be talking about spatial location. At the same time, Langacker (2008: 28) says that "[s]ince mental development is stimulated and guided by social interaction, the skills and knowledge acquired are very much attuned to the sociocultural surroundings". Here Langacker apparently "presupposes individual-environmental relations" in Burge's (2003: 455) sense, in accordance with what Boyd (2013) suggests:

> [...] it is not possible for a person to learn all the subtleties of even one com-
> munity's norms and to apply them effectively in the absence of social interac-
> tions within her own community. In so far as her community's norms change
> in response to interactions with the relevant subject matters, her ability to fol-
> low those norms will depend on her continuing involvement with that com-
> munity. (Boyd 2013: 223)

If this interpretation is correct, there is no reason to suppose that Langacker embraces internalism as construed by Burge. Now, when Adam and $Adam_2$ utter or think, "Birds do not fly" and dismiss nearly as categorically the thought(s) expressed by 'In a manner of speaking, a bat is a bird' as the thought(s) expressed by 'In a manner of speaking, a cow is a bird', there is a sense in which their skills and knowledge are not equally attuned to their sociocultural surroundings. This makes Adam's utterance and thought, but not $Adam_2$'s utterance and thought, false. Adam's skills and knowledge are not attuned to the generally accepted theory that birds fly. Langacker's view can thus accommodate the externalist thesis that two internally identical people may nevertheless have different mental states, due to the fact that their skills and knowledge may be attuned to their environments in different degrees.

What then becomes of Langacker's claim that meaning is conceptualization? It is important to realize that conceptualization is not defined in total isolation from the physical and social environment in which the conceptualizer is situated. After all, Langacker (2008: 539) states that "[c]onceptualization is seen (without inconsistency) as being both physically grounded and pervasively imaginative, both individual and fundamentally social". Adam's and $Adam_2$'s conceptualizations of

129

'bird' are grounded in the practices of their respective communities. Although they are intrinsically identical, their conceptualizations of 'bird' are different, insofar as they are supposed to comply with different social practices. Langacker's notion of conceptualization is compatible with the externalist thesis that "sameness of conceptual role is not *sufficient* for sameness of content" (Loar 1988/2017: 154, emphasis in the original).

What really is problematic for Langacker's assumption that meaning is conceptualization is the fact that Adam and his doctor mean the same thing by employing the word form 'arthritis', despite their contradicting beliefs. This fact is commonly assumed to support another externalist thesis, namely the thesis that "sameness of conceptual role is not *necessary* for sameness of psychological content" (ibid.). But this thesis seems incompatible with the idea that meaning is conceptualization. In the situation under consideration, Adam believes about arthritis what the doctor disbelieves; Adam's conceptualization of arthritis includes the belief that the disease can afflict one's thigh, whereas the doctor's conceptualization includes a contradictory belief. Given these mutually incompatible conceptualizations, it should be expected that Adam's word 'arthritis' is homonymous with the doctor's word 'arthritis', in the same way that 'bank' in the sense of 'river edge' is true of objects which 'bank' in the sense of 'financial institution' is not true of. In short, the two subjects may be said to be talking about distinct things by employing the same phonological form. Contrary to this expectation, it is not difficult for us to think of Adam and his doctor as talking about the same disease when the patient expresses his fear that arthritis may afflict his thigh. We would not be able to make sense of Adam's willingness to stand corrected without assuming the identity of the subject matter being talked about (Burge 1978: 130-131, cf. Schroeter and Schroeter 2016: 194). Adam would never correct any of his ideas about banks in the sense of 'river edges' even if a financial planner told him something of which he was ignorant about banks in the sense of 'financial institutions'. While Adam's conceptualization of 'arthritis' and the doctor's conceptualization of 'arthritis' are so different as to contradict one another, the meaning of the word remains identical for them. Apparently, meaning and conceptualization diverge. This problem will be addressed in Chapter 4.

A more fundamental problem for both social externalism and cognitive linguistics is that the discussion in this chapter assumes that concepts, but not necessarily meanings, are individuated by prototypes. It is not an analytic truth that birds fly because the extension of the word 'bird' includes flightless members. It is nevertheless a core fact about 'bird', or equivalently, a conceptual truth about birds that birds fly, because a person ignorant of the fact is not deemed competent with the use of the word 'bird' and the concept of *bird*. This makes room for incomplete understanding without analyticity, a notion needed for the establishment of social externalism. There are a number of researchers who resist this conclusion by saying that concepts are not individuated by prototypes. Thus, Peacocke (1992: 3), as we have seen in Section 2.6.2, insists that the notion of concept should be defined without any reference to the notion of prototype while acknowledging that the latter notion is "of great interest and importance". Much more critical of proto-types, Rey (1983: 283) contends that the prototype conception of concept "hope-lessly confuses metaphysical issues of conceptual *identity* with (roughly speaking) epistemological issues of conceptual *access*" (emphases in the original) (cf. Sainsbury and Tye 2011: 105). In other words, the prototype conception blurs the distinction between how the world is and how we know, believe and infer how the world is (ibid.: 243). The prototype of a concept merely serves as a convenient means to access the concept, since, as Langacker (2008: 66) states, "[w]ithin a cat-egory, the prototype has greater prominence than its various extensions". Rey (1985: 299) claims that "a theory of concepts is a theory of competence not performance". The fact that prototypes are more readily accessible than other members merely concerns performance (ibid.: 300). This point is confirmed by Armstrong et al.'s (1983) observation that people tend to judge some odd numbers to be odder than others even though they consider *odd number* to be a well-defined concept. Graded responses should not be taken as a symptom of graded membership (Keil 1989: 29-30). A similar remark can be made about *bird*. As stated earlier, birds are feath-ered bipedal creatures and there are no borderline cases (Hampton 2015: 131).

It may be objected that the prototype of bird may not be the prototype of the prototype category in that the category of bird has a clear-cut boundary. Although, as Sainsbury (1990/1996/2002: 82) rightly points out, prototypicality is orthogo-nal to vagueness, as evidenced by penguins, non-prototypical but genuine examples of birds (Rey 1992: 322), prototypicality is typically instantiated in vague catego-ries. Indeed, prototype semantics can also handle categories with borderline cases in a straightforward fashion:

[...] the members are not necessarily a uniquely defined set, since there is no specific degree of departure from the prototype beyond which a person is absolutely incapable of perceiving a similarity. The best we can say, as a general matter, is that substantial dissimilarity to the prototype greatly diminishes the probability that a person will make that categorization. (Langacker 1987: 17)[28]

A well-known case is the distinction between cups, mugs, bowls and vases, as reported by Labov (1973), but the point generalizes if, as Sainsbury (1990/1996/2002: 72) maintains, "almost all concepts lack boundaries, so that the classical picture is of very little use to us"[29]. Even though, as remarked earlier, Peacocke (1992) prefers to exclude prototypes from concepts, he concedes that, when a concept lacks clear boundaries, mastery of the concept "may involve knowledge of a prototype, a similarity relation, and a means of classifying objects in respect of such similarity to the prototype" (ibid.: 12). The existence of the vague categories Labov discusses may thus lend support to prototype semantics. Nevertheless, it makes no room for the notion of incomplete understanding without analyticity, because there can be no conceptual truths about such vague categories. Suppose that typical cups have property F. It is not an analytic truth about 'cup' that cups are F, since the extension of 'cup' includes non-F members. Neither is it a conceptual truth about cups, because competent speakers of English are not expected to know that cups are F in the same way that they are expected to know that birds fly. It may certainly be true that typical cups are F but it is nonetheless not true that cups are F. A person ignorant of the fact that cups are F does not display an incomplete grasp of the concept of *cup*. Of course, it is a conceptual truth about cups that cups, typical or not, are more or less F. But this is also an analytic truth about 'cup', because a person who judges an object which completely lacks F to be a cup would rather be making a linguistic error.

The lesson to be drawn is that, for there to be incomplete understanding without analyticity, there must be a conceptual, but not analytical, truth, and that such

---

28) Likewise, Taylor (2003: 87) says that "a prototype semanticist should have no problems in dealing with categories with fuzzy boundaries".

29) Sainsbury (1990/1996/2002: 78) observes that "boundaryless concepts come in groups of contraries". There is good reason for this:

> Not just any clear case of the non-applicability of a concept will serve to help a learner see what the concept excludes. Television sets, mountains and French horns are all absolutely definite cases of non-children; but only the contrast with *adult* will help the learner grasp what *child* excludes. (Sainsbury 1990/196/2003: 78)

This explains that, in Labov's (1973) report, the meaning of 'cup' is examined in relation to the meaning of words such as 'mug', 'bowl' and 'vase'. These words can naturally be taken to be contraries to each other.

a truth cannot be found in vague categories like 'cup', unlike in clear-cut categories like 'bird' and 'odd number'. When we have a clear-cut category boundary, however, the prototype may be taken, as Rey (1983, 1985, 1992) claims, to serve merely as a convenient means to access the concept. We have now returned to the starting point: how are we to justify the notion of incomplete understanding without appealing to analyticity?

Chapter 3

Incomplete Understanding and Construal

This chapter argues that not only grammar (as claimed by cognitive linguistics) but also incomplete understanding (on which social externalism essentially rests) provide the bases for our ability to construe the same situation in different fashions, an ability intrinsically tied to the individuation of a concept.

3.1 Twin Cases and Frege Cases

The discussion in Chapter 1 has demonstrated that the thesis in (1), defended in cognitive linguistics, is apparently in tension with the consequences of social externalism outlined in (2a-b) (cf. Grabarczyk 2016: 162-163):

(1)   Meaning is conceptualization.

(2)   a. Although Adam and $Adam_2$ conceptualize what is called 'arthritis' (or 'bird' as discussed in Chapter 2) in exactly the same fashion, the meaning of 'arthritis' ('bird') and the thought content containing 'arthritis' ('bird') are different for them.

b. Although Adam and his doctor conceptualize what is called 'arthritis' in a mutually incompatible way, the meaning of 'arthritis' and the thought content containing 'arthritis' are the same for them.

(2a) represents what Fodor (1994: 23) calls Twin cases, while (2b) is intuitively similar to what Fodor calls Frege cases (cf. Prinz 2002: 6, 8, 15, 263-264, Heck 2012: 135ff, Onofri 2016: 6ff), in which 'the morning star' and 'the evening star' for instance, refer to the same planet despite the difference in sense:

Twin cases show that more than one intentional state (F1, F2) can correspond to the same implementing mechanism (M1), hence that identity of implementation can't be sufficient for identity of intentional content. Frege cases show that more than one implementing mechanism (M1, M2) can correspond to the same intentional state (F1), hence that identity of intentional state can't be sufficient for identity of implementation. (Fodor 1994: 23)

Both Twin cases and Frege cases are among the seven puzzles of thought explored by Sainsbury and Tye (2012). These cases apparently pose problems for cognitive linguistics as well, because conceptualization as individualistically described seems unable to capture the possible divergences between an individual's internal state and the intentional content of her thought. The challenge for cognitive linguistics is, then, how to preserve, in the face of such divergences, the identity between conceptualization and meaning.

In Chapter 2, it has been shown that Twin cases are compatible with cognitive linguistics, to the extent that an individual's conceptualization is more or less grounded in, or attuned to, her environment. This allows for the possibility that two individuals who have exactly the same intrinsic properties nevertheless have different conceptualizations, due to their differing degrees of adaptation to their respective environments. When an individual's knowledge and skill are attuned to the environment only partially, the individual is said to have an incomplete understanding of the word and concept in question. Thus, Burge (1979a/2007) claims that Adam, who thinks that he has arthritis in his thigh, has an incomplete grasp of the concept of *arthritis*, since arthritis is by definition an inflammation of the joints. By contrast, Adam$_2$, who is molecule-for-molecule identical to Adam, has a full grasp of the concept corresponding to the word form 'arthritis', because, in his community, the disease is believed to afflict one's thigh as well as one's joints. The disease called 'arthritis' in Adam$_2$'s community is not arthritis but something else, say, tharthritis, because it does not fulfill the definition of arthritis. It follows that Adam and Adam$_2$ attach different concepts to the word form 'arthritis' despite their internal identity. They have different concepts not because their intrinsic states are different but because the social practices they are supposed to abide by are different.

The possibility of incomplete understanding of a concept is of great importance for social externalism, because neither linguistic errors nor empirical errors are sufficient for the conclusion that the two subjects in question have different concepts. If Adam believes that what he calls 'arthritis' is a kind of insect, for instance, then his use of the word form 'arthritis' has little to do with the public word 'arthritis'. This is a case of linguistic error. Adam's thought corresponding to the sentence 'I have arthritis in my thigh' is true if and only if he has a certain insect in his thigh. Even if the same holds for $Adam_2$, it does not follow that their thoughts differ. Their thoughts are identical and both true independently of their social environments.

Next, if Adam wrongly believes that his father had arthritis, his thought corresponding to the sentence 'My father had arthritis' is false. If, on the contrary, $Adam_2$'s father did have arthritis, his thought corresponding to that sentence is true. Adam, but not $Adam_2$, makes an empirical error in thinking that his father had arthritis. But this does not imply that they have different concepts corresponding to the word form 'arthritis', because whether or not their father had arthritis is irrelevant to the definition of 'arthritis'; the word form 'arthritis' may refer to the same ailments in both communities. Social externalism can therefore be vindicated only if the notion of incomplete understanding as opposed to linguistic error and empirical error is in place.

Wikforss (2001, 2004) makes a case against Burge's argument, claiming that it is possible for Adam to fully understand 'arthritis' contrary to Burge's assumption. Medical scientists in Adam's community may find someday that arthritis also afflicts one's thigh, i.e. arthritis is nothing but tharthritis. In this situation, the correct conclusion to draw is that Adam and $Adam_2$, who are intrinsically identical, have the same concept of *tharthritis*. Social externalism does not follow. In Chapter 2, I have appealed to the notion of prototype to respond to Wikforss's objection. The statement that birds fly conceptually characterizes birds because Adam, who does not know that birds fly and fails to employ hedges like 'sort of' and 'in a manner of speaking' appropriately, can be considered to have an incomplete grasp of the concept of *bird*. Still, Adam cannot be charged with any linguistic error, because the definition of 'bird' does not include the notion of flight, as illustrated by birds such as penguins and ostriches. Moreover, unlike in the case of 'arthritis', no one will ever find out that birds are flightless. Thus, a genuine Twin case in support of social externalism seems to come from the notion of prototype.

3.2 Prototype and Concept or Epistemology and Metaphysics

The argument based on the notion of prototype is not decisive, because, if Rey (1983) is right, prototypes serve merely as cognitive reference points and as such do not define the concept in question. On this view, appealing to prototype only obscures the distinction between metaphysics (concepts) and epistemology (access to concepts) (cf. Sainsbury and Tye 2011: 105)[1]. As remarked in Section 1.3.3, some philosophers, most notably Kripke (1980), have emphasized the distinction between the metaphysics and epistemology of concepts. For Kripke, it is necessary but not *a priori* that water is H_2O. Or equivalently, as Putnam (1975: 150) stated, it is conceivable, but not logically possible, that water is not H_2O[2]. It might be said that metaphysics has nothing to do with linguistics, i.e. empirical studies of language. As argued in Section 1.3.4, however, the dismissal of truth-related notions may have a fatal effect on semantics, since, as Rey (1983: 247) notes, the distinction between epistemology and metaphysics is psychologically real, as seen in the fact that people distinguish 'looking like a bird' and 'actually being a bird'. In a sense, Rey (1983: 245-247) suggests, prototype semantics revives logical positivism which identified metaphysics with epistemology by postulating 'Verification Principle', according to which "the meaning of a sentence consists in the methods by which people employ in verifying it" (ibid. 245). The observation that something is a creature and flies provides a good reason for supposing that it is a bird. But this method, no matter how effective it may be, does not define 'bird'. Rey (1983) states:

> If the features by which I identify birds have to do with their songs, while those you go by have to do with their feathers, then, since you and I have different sets of properties 'in mind', you and I have different concepts associated with 'bird'. That is – to recall precisely the work concepts are to do in their Stability and Linguistic roles – you and I could not have beliefs and preferences with the same content [bird]; our uses of the word 'bird' would be mere homonyms; our agreements and disputes about *birds* illusory. (Rey 1983: 249)

Access to the concept and the concept per se must be kept apart. When Langacker (2008: 66) says that "[w]ithin a category, the prototype has greater prominence than its various extensions", he may well be talking about high accessibility to a category exhibited by the prototype, despite his intention. Rey's claim that

---

1) Conversely, Margolis (1994) holds that prototype theory is a purely metaphysical thesis about categories with no psychological implications. For Margolis (1994: 76), concepts are psychological constructs, while categories are what concepts are about. In this view, prototype theory obscures the distinction between concepts and categories, wrongly taking a view about categories to be a view about concepts.

2) As remarked in Section 1.3.3, Putnam (1990: 70) retracted this view.

Chapter 3   Incomplete Understanding and Construal

metaphysics and epistemology must be distinguished seems compelling, at least as far as categories with sharp boundaries such as *bird* (Hampton 2015) or *odd number* (Armstrong et al. 1983) are concerned. Although Rey acknowledges the existence of boundaryless categories in Sainsbury's (1990/1996/2003) sense, he stresses that unclear categories should not be confused with unclear judgments:

> [...] a corresponding distinction needs to be drawn between two sorts of 'unclear cases': those, like that of *euglena* (p. 31), which may well be on the borderline between animal and plant; and those, like that of *tomatoes* (p. 59), which may *be* (metaphysically) clear cases of fruit (check the dictionary!), even though people may be (epistemologically) confused about them. The fact that subjects might be unclear about whether something falls under a particular concept will not show anything one way or another about whether there are metaphysically defining conditions for that concept unless it can be shown that the unclarity is metaphysical and not merely epistemological. (Rey 1983: 248)

In Sections 2.6.1 and 2.6.2, I have argued that linguistic data concerning the use of hedges mirror not the standard theory about the concept in question but the nature of the concept per se. Now, if Rey is right, we should rather say that what is mirrored in the use of hedges is the standard means to access the concept. As Quine (1960: 5) put it, "we are little more aware of a distinction between [...] cues and conceptualizations than we are of a distinction between the proteins and the carbohydrates of our material intake". An incomplete understanding of the standard cues to access the concept must be distinguished from an incomplete understanding of the concept itself. With this distinction in place, it is possible to say that Adam, who believes that birds do not fly, has a complete grasp of the concept of *bird*, merely ignorant of the most prominent cue to identify birds. In short, Adam and Adam$_2$, who are internally identical, may have the same concept of *bird* in the metaphysical sense. Again, social externalism does not follow. The situation is worse for social externalism than in the case of arthritis, because, if the notion of prototype is extraneous to the identity of a concept (at least when the concept has a sharp boundary), then Adam's and Adam$_2$'s community should be taken to share the same concept of *bird*, at this very moment. No reference to any future discovery is called for.

The question to be asked is, again, where to find incomplete understanding without analyticity. The question is relevant not only to social externalism but also

139

to cognitive linguistics, because, as will become clearer in due course, it is closely tied to how we should understand semantic and conceptual competence, a problem which will have implications for the cognitive linguistic conception of meaning .

3.3 Conceptual Content vs. Construal

The general idea behind Rey's (1983) argument may be that Adam, who believes that birds do not fly, and his community members, who believe that birds fly, think about the same objects in the world despite their divergent beliefs. This view makes it possible to define concepts in total independence from the subjects' beliefs about them. Following this line of reasoning, Rey (1983: 255, 1985: 298) proposes the hypothesis of external definitions of concepts outlined in (3):

(3)   *Hypothesis of External Definitions*: the correct definition of a concept is provided by the optimal account of it, which need not be known by the concept's competent users. (Rey 1983: 255)

By 'optimal account' Rey means an account of a concept obtained by taking into account "all relevant issues and possible evidence" (ibid.). Roughly speaking, (3) says that competent users of a concept need not know the correct or metaphysical definition of the concept[3]. In this view, both Adam and Adam$_2$ can be held to have the concept of *bird* (in the metaphysical sense), and what they believe about birds, or in Rey's (1983: 260, 1985: 297-298, 302), Burge's (1993: 316/2007: 298) and Higginbotham's (1998a) terminology, their conception of birds, is ultimately irrelevant to the identity of the concept. The same point applies to other community members. The fact that Adam's fellows believe that birds fly while Adam$_2$'s fellows believe that birds do not fly does not prevent them from sharing one and the same concept of *bird*. It seems that Wikforss's (2001, 2004) argument against Burge's (1979a/2007) 'arthritis' thought experiment turns on the possibility, implied by (3), that even experts may be ignorant of the nature of the phenomena they investigate. Adam believes that he has arthritis in his thigh, while experts in his community believe that arthritis cannot afflict one's thigh. Burge assumes that,

---

3) Rey is in fact more cautious about what the optimal account amounts to:
   For realists, that might be the true account; for those more idealistically inclined, it may simply be the account human beings will eventually agree upon. (Rey 1983: 255)

Chapter 3   Incomplete Understanding and Construal

in this situation, Adam betrays an incomplete understanding of the concept of *arthritis*. It is possible, however, that it is the experts who are mistaken, since, according to (3), competent speakers including experts need not know the optimal account of the ailments. We can imagine that arthritis in fact can afflict one's thigh and that Adam fully understands the concept of *arthritis*. In this scenario, the experts in Adam's community have wrongly assessed his understanding as deviant. As remarked by Kimbrough (1998: 479), "[j]ust as an anti-individualist should be open to discovering that members of the 'counterfactual' community are mistaken in their usage of the term 'arthritis', so should he be open to discovering that our actual usage may be corrected in relation to theirs". Burge's (1979a/2007) 'arthritis' thought experiment seems to preclude this possibility from the outset[4]. The assumption that experts always have a full grasp of a concept should now be challenged. Higginbotham (1998a) expresses a view similar to Rey's (1983) hypothesis of external definitions presented in (3):

Hilary Putnam especially has promoted the view that reference can remain constant through changes in theory. To the extent that we take scientific advancement issuing in more adequate conceptions of a concept, we have the sequence that the concept itself remains constant through changes in theory. Do we conclude that not only the reference of 'gold', but even the concept GOLD itself, is something of which we had no adequate conception until at least the nineteenth century? An affirmative answer to this question is not as radical as it might appear, however, if concept possession does not have an epistemic basis. The nature of some of our concepts may then be beyond the reach even of most sophisticated conceptions. (Higginbotham 1998a: 161)

If the nature of arthritis is beyond the reach of Adam's community members, Adam's putative incomplete understanding of the concept, or anyone's for that matter, is unable to substantiate the claim that Adam's community possesses a different concept corresponding to the word form 'arthritis' than Adam$_2$'s community. The same concept is understood more or less incompletely by everyone. Burge (1990/2007) points out that Frege shared this view. Frege held, according to Burge

---

4) This possibility is taken into account in Burge's (1986a/2007) 'sofa' thought experiment, where a fully competent speaker doubts the definition of 'sofa' generally agreed upon in his (and our) community. But this thought experiment fails for another reason, as given in 2.4.

141

(1990: 32/2007: 246), that "all of the expressions in conventional mathematics and natural science, and some of the same terms in ordinary discourse, are not sharply understood – are not backed by a sharp grasp of a definite sense – even by their most competent users" (cf. Frege 1969: 240/1979: 222, Burge 2012: 60).

To respond to this metaphysical challenge, we have to deny the idea that both Adam and Adam$_2$ have a complete understanding of the concept of *bird* in believing that birds do not fly. Intuitively, Adam, but not Adam$_2$, fails to discern what is central to the concept of *bird*. If access to *bird* is allowed into the definition of the concept, we can legitimately say that the two subjects possess different concepts corresponding to the word form 'bird'. Adam, but not Adam$_2$, has an incomplete grasp of *bird* to the extent that he fails to grasp the most effective cues to access the concept. It is irrelevant to the notion of incomplete understanding thus construed whether Adam has a full grasp of the concept *per se*, because, if access to the concept is part of the concept, incomplete understanding of the access entails incomplete understanding of the concept. We do not have to go into metaphysics to ascribe incomplete understanding to the thinking subject. In this connection, Higginbotham (1998a) proposes a threefold distinction between the concept, the conception of the concept, and the conscious view of the concept. What concerns us here is the distinction between the concept and the conception of the concept. Higginbotham describes concept acquisition as a sophistication of how the learner conceptualizes the concept:

[…] if there is a distinction between the concept that a person possesses and her conception of it, it will be appropriate to ascribe to that person thoughts involving the concept that she only partly apprehends, or even misconceives; and the distinction allows us to view a person's increased sophistication with a concept as a consequence, not of progressive replacement in thought of one concept by another, but of acquiring a more adequate conception (Higginbotham 1998a: 153)

What we are after is the possibility that the conception of a concept may be incorporated into the definition of the concept, that is, concepts may be partly individuated by the way in which they are conceptualized.

Papineau (1996: 426-428) takes issue with Peacocke's (1992) use of the expression '*the* concept ϕ'. The singular definite article is unsuitable here because "different individuals would seem to employ different notions, constituted by

142

Chapter 3   Incomplete Understanding and Construal

different possession conditions, when they form beliefs to the effect that certain things are ϕ " (Papineau 1996: 426). If the way in which a subject conceptualizes ϕ is part of her concept ϕ, there is no such thing as *the* concept of ϕ shared by all subjects. Indeed, this is the view held by Langacker and other cognitive linguists. When Langacker says that meaning is conceptualization, his 'conceptualization' can be equated neither with Higginbotham's 'concept' nor with his 'conceptualization'. Langacker's 'conceptualization' essentially consists of 'conceptual content' and 'construal', both constituting an integral whole. Every linguistic expression, be it a word or a clause, is associated with a construal, a particular way of viewing the content it evokes:

> Most broadly, a meaning consists of both conceptual content and a particular way of construing that content. The term construal refers to our manifest ability to conceive and portray the same situation in alternate ways. (Langacker 2008: 43, emphases in the original; see also Langacker 1976: 345, 347-348, 355)

For instance, the general terms in (4a-c) describe the same figure, and the sentences in (5a-b) depict the same situation.

(4)   a. triangle
      b. three-angled polygon
      c. three-sided polygon   ((4a-c): Langacker 2008: 62)
(5)   a. The glass is half-full.
      b. The glass is half-empty.   ((5a-b): Langacker 2008: 43)

To employ the traditional terminology, (4a), (4b) and (4c) have the same truth-conditional meaning and (5a) and (5b) have the same truth-conditional content. Nevertheless, intuitively, (4a), (4b) and (4c) differ in meaning and so do (5a) and (5b). Such differences in meaning, Langacker claims, are attributed to differences in construal as opposed to conceptual content. Thus, the concepts of *three* and *angle* are profiled in both (4a) and (4b), but their salience is lower in (4a) than in (4b) because few speakers of English analyze 'triangle' into 'three' and 'angle'. Such a contrast can be seen more clearly in (6a-b):

(6)   a. pork

143

b. pig meat ((6a-b): Langacker 2008: 61)

Although (6a) and (6b) have the same extension, they are semantically distinct because they arrive at the extension "via different compositional paths" (Langacker 2008: 61-62). Up to this point, the contrast between (6a) and (6b) is the same as that between (4a) and (4b). The former contrast can be viewed as more radical, however, because, unlike (4a), (6a) has "no individually symbolized components" (Langacker 2008: 62). Turning to the difference between (4b) and (4c), the concept of *figure* is highlighted in both (4b) and (4c), but this concept is combined with the concept of *angle* in (4b) while it is combined with the concept of *side* in (4c). A related example is (7):

(7) a. roe
b. caviar ((7a-b): Langacker 1987: 64-65)

According to Langacker (1987: 164-165), (7a) and (7b) are distinguished with respect to the relative prominence of certain domains evoked by these expressions, even though both designate the same mass of eggs. Central to (7a) is the reproductive cycle of fish, while in (7b), the construal of the same mass of eggs as an item of consumption is far more salient. The same holds for (8a) and (8b), which designate the same creature:

(8) a. snail
b. escargot ((8a-b): Langacker 2008: 49)

With 'escargot,', Langacker (2008: 49) suggests, the domain of fancy cuisine is ranked very high, while with 'snail', the domain of garden pests is more prominent but the domain of fancy cuisine is still fairly accessible. This accounts for the difference in acceptability between (9a) and (9b):

(9) a. The snails were delicious.
b. *My garden is crawling with escargots ((9a-b): Langacker 2008: 49)

For Langacker (2008: 62), such contrasts indicate that the expressions under consideration "are semantically distinct, despite their referential identity".

Conceptual content (as opposed to construal) is not necessarily equivalent to truth-conditional content. (4a), (4b) and (4c) are interchangeable *salva veritate*, and (6a) is true if and only if (6b) is true. This may give the impression that construal is external to truth-conditional content. It is often the case, however, that "[t]he distinction between content and construal is not at all a sharp one" (Langacker 2008: 43). Thus, although both (10a) and (10b) can be employed to describe one and the same object, they are in no way truth-conditionally equivalent:

(10) a. the glass with water in it
      b. the container with liquid in it ((10a-b): Langacker 2008: 43)

This is easily confirmed by the fact that (11b) can be true without (11a) being true:

(11) a. Mary saw the glass with water in it.
      b. Mary saw the container with liquid in it.

If Mary saw a cup with coffee in it, for instance, (11b) is true while (11a) is false. In cognitive linguistics, it is commonly (and often implicitly) assumed that there is no conceptual content independent of any construal: a conceptual content is necessarily construed in some way or other. This means that conceptual content cannot be determined in total isolation from the subject who conceptualizes it. Conceptual content is a thing or state of affairs to which the speaker intends to refer in some way or other.

Langacker's two-dimensional model of conceptualization may, in a sense, be viewed as a rehabilitation of Leibniz's view on meaning and concept. Ishiguro (1990) points out that, for Leibniz, concept (or term, in Leibniz's terminology) is clearly distinct from meaning:

> We can now understand Leibniz's claim that the terms [= concepts] "triangle" and "trilateral" are identical, because they can be substituted *salva veritate* [= without affecting truth]. Many people would claim that the notion of "triangle" and the notion of "trilateral" are different, since if "triangle" means "the shape which has three angles" and "trilateral" means "the shape which has three sides," the meaning of the words and hence the concepts expressed by them may be thought to be different. For Leibniz, however, the problem of the identity of concepts is not one of the synonymy of the corresponding words. The concept of a triangle or a trilateral is not the meaning of these words which

145

express the concepts. Both concepts are complex, one being a function of the concepts of three and of angle, and the other a function of the concepts of three and of side. A concept may be specified by different expressions with different senses. Even if the meanings of the expressions "triangle" and "trilateral" are different, so long as the meanings are related in such a way that anything that is a triangle is necessarily a trilateral, then the concept of a triangle is the concept of a trilateral. (Ishiguro 1990: 27)

Leibniz's concept (or term) corresponds approximately to Langacker's conceptual content[5]. Leibniz says that sameness in conceptual content does not entail sameness in meaning, or equivalently, that difference in meaning does not entail difference in conceptual content. Leibniz's idea is congenial to Langacker's view that 'triangle' and 'three-angled polygon' differ in meaning even though the two expressions share the same conceptual content (Langacker 2008: 62). The reason that cognitive linguists generally show little interest in Leibniz's philosophy despite their striking affinity is, I think, that Leibniz highlights the identity of the conceptual content expressed by the words 'triangle' and 'trilateral', whereas one of the aims of cognitive linguistics is to unearth the various ways in which the same conceptual content can be construed. The sentences in (5) serve to highlight the difference in construal rather than the identity in conceptual content. Langacker (2008: 43) states that (5a) designates the relationship wherein the volume occupied by the liquid is just half of its potential volume, while (5b) designates the relationship wherein the volume occupied by the void is just half of its potential volume. The contrast between (5a) and (5b) illustrates "our manifest ability to conceive and portray the same situation in alternate ways" (Langacker 2008: 43). As remarked in Section 1.3.4, Jackendoff (1989: 68) maintains that the choice of a technical notion is only justified relative to one's purpose. Given that Langacker's main purpose lies in underlining our ability to construe the same object or situation in various ways, admittedly, the best notion of concept for Langacker is that which incorporates both conceptual content and its construal.

Langacker's emphasis on various construals is closely related to his downplay of veracity of construals. Researchers working in the cognitive linguistic framework never say that construal determines conceptual content. This is to say that

---

5) For Leibniz, a term is neither a linguistic expression nor a thing but a concept (Ishiguro 1990: 21-22).

Chapter 3   Incomplete Understanding and Construal

construal cannot be assimilated to intension in the traditional sense of the term or to mathematical function in any sense. Rather, construal is a way of portraying a thing or a situation from the speaker's point of view. Since its early days, cognitive linguistics has directed attention to a number of linguistic expressions which reflect speakers' subjective construals of the situations depicted. Among such phenomena is fictive motion. Thus, according to Talmy (1983: 235), the use of the motion verbs 'run', 'extend' and 'go' in (12) suggests that the road, a stationary linear figure, "is conceptualized as having a leading edge that is in virtual motion, or as being scanned along its length by one's focus of attention":

(12)   a. This road runs past the factory.
       b. This road extends through the tunnel.
       c. This road goes from Burney to Redding.   ((12a-c): Talmy 1983: 236)

If veracity were the primary concern for speakers, (13a) would be a more appropriate way of depicting the state of affairs in question than (13b-c), since the mountain range is clearly not set in motion:

(13)   a. That mountain range lies (longitudinally) between Canada and Mexico.
       b. That mountain range goes from Canada and Mexico.
       c. This mountain range goes from Mexico to Canada.
                                           ((13a-c): Talmy 1996/2000: 104)

In fact, (13b) and (13c) are no less natural descriptions of the state of affairs than (13a). As Talmy (1996/2000: 104) states, "languages systematically and extensively refer to stationary circumstances with forms and constructions whose basic reference is to motion". The construals observed in sentences in (13) are usually even less veridical than those in (14):

(14)   a. The Linguistic Hall of Fame is across the plaza, through the alley, and over the bridge.
       b. There was a fire last night across the river, through the canyon, and over the mountain.   ((14a-b): Langacker 1987: 170)

Langacker (1987: 170-171) remarks that, depending on the context, the sentences in (14) can express either objective motions or subjective motions. When the

147

motions are construed objectively, each sentence in (14) represents a state of affairs in which the addressee or a hypothetical traveler moves along the path described. When the motions are construed subjectively, on the contrary, the speaker "mentally traces along this path for purposes of computing the location of the subject" (Langacker 1987: 171). Subjective construal is the only option available in such sentences as (13b-c), since, as Langacker (2008: 529) states, the situation these sentences describe "is static and has no inherent directionality". It is also worth noting that subjective construal cannot be reduced to metaphor to the extent that, in (13), what moves fictively is not the mountain but the imaginary trajectory (Fauconnier 1997: 177). What is at play in (13), and sometimes in (14), is the process Langacker (2008: 528, 537) calls 'subjectification', a process in which "mental operations inherent in a certain kind of experience are applied to situations with respect to which their occurrence is extrinsic" (ibid.: 528). This process enables motion verbs to represent static situations:

Through subjectification, the dynamicity inherent in the apprehension of events is transferred to the conception of static scenes. A verb like *run*, which profiles objectively construed motion by its trajector, comes instead to designate a configuration apprehended through subjectively construed motion (i.e. sequential mental access) by the conceptualizer. (Langacker 2008: 530)

The ability to construe a thing or situation subjectively is indisputably part of a speaker's linguistic and conceptual competence. After all, as Langacker (1976: 343) remarks, "[v]irtually all language is figurative to some degree" (see also Langacker 1976: 355). Whether the construal is veridical or fictional has nothing to do with the adequacy of the relevant conceptualization. Construals need not be veridical, in the same way that Putnam's (1975) stereotype may distort reality. The word 'witch', Putnam says, is associated with a radically mistaken stereotype such as 'witches enter into pacts with Satan" or "they cause sickness and death' (Putnam 1975: 170). Nevertheless, competent speakers are required to know something about the stereotype associated with the word in question (Putnam 1975: 168, Putnam 1992: 386, cf. Burge 2013: 268). It should now be clear that stereotypes, veridical or not, are among the construals associated with linguistic expressions. Taylor (2003: 90) states that "Putnam's stereotypes also appear to coincide with our notion of a prototype seen in the context of the relevant domain matrix".

The notion of concept defended in cognitive linguistics enables one to rebut

Chapter 3   Incomplete Understanding and Construal

the metaphysical objection raised by Wikforss (2001, 2004) to the effect that Adam and Adam$_2$ may share one and the same concept expressed by 'arthritis'. As discussed in Section 2.3, Burge's (1979a/2007) claim that Adam displays an incomplete grasp of the concept *arthritis* falls back on the assumption that Adam's thought, but not Adam$_2$'s thought, corresponding to (15) is false:

(15)   I have arthritis in my thigh.

It is because, Burge argues, Adam and Adam$_2$ are supposed to comply with different social practices that their thoughts have different truth values. In Adam's community, arthritis is by definition an inflammation of the joints only, whereas what is referred to as 'arthritis' in Adam$_2$'s community does not fulfill this definition. From this, Burge concludes that Adam and Adam$_2$, despite their intrinsic identity, possess different concepts both of which are associated with the word form 'arthritis'. As noted in Section 2.5.1, Wikforss (2001, 2004) contends that Burge's argument is not successful in establishing that Adam and Adam$_2$'s thoughts differ in truth value, because it may turn out that (16a) is no more a conceptual truth about arthritis than (16b) is a conceptual truth about atoms:

(16)   a. Arthritis does not afflict one's thigh.
       b. Atoms are indivisible.

Just as rejection of (16b) is more appropriately described as a change in theory than as a replacement of a concept by another (Putnam 1962a: 396, Burge 1993: 316/2007: 297-298), Adam's dissent from (16a) can be taken to merely indicate that he is developing a theory about arthritis which his contemporary community members happen to assess as false. For Burge's thought experiment to successfully establish that Adam understands *arthritis* incompletely, (16a) must express an analytic truth about 'arthritis', which by definition cannot be false. In other words, it must be guaranteed that Adam has a metaphysically different concept from Adam$_2$. As Kimbrough (1998) makes clear, when Adam's and Adam$_2$'s thoughts are said to have different truth values, what is at issue is not the truth evaluation of their thoughts but the truth in the metaphysical sense:

To sustain the conclusion of the thought experiment, the anti-individualist is committed to maintaining that contents differ when they involve concepts that

149

are truly applied in different circumstances. At the same time, however, differences of opinion regarding the correct application of a concept are insufficient on their own to establish a difference of content. [...] the notion of content cannot be tied to the acceptance of certain opinions (e.g., the opinion of the 'experts'), but must instead be connected to truth-conditions. (Kimbrough 1998: 474)

[...] the notion of content is tied to the notion of truth-conditions: contents differ when they involve concepts that are truly applied in different circumstances, though differing *opinions* about the conditions for applying a given term do not similarly imply a difference in the concepts and contents expressed. (Kimbrough 1998: 477, emphasis in the original)

Kimbrough's remark casts doubt on the conclusion reached in Chapter 2 that Adam and $Adam_2$ have different concepts expressed by the word form 'bird', due to the fact that in Adam's community, but not in $Adam_2$'s community, it is commonly assumed that birds fly. The difference between the communities stems solely from the peculiar policy adopted by $Adam_2$'s community, consisting in administering a drug to every bird as soon as it is born in order to prevent it from flying. Birds in the two communities have no biological difference. There can therefore be no difference in truth value, in the metaphysical sense of the term, between the putative conceptual truths about birds assumed in the two communities. This objection fails, however, now that the concept of *bird* involves its construal, as suggested by Langacker (1987, 2008). The notion of truth as raised by Kimbrough (1998) merely concerns conceptual content, having no effect on the construal. Adam's and $Adam_2$'s communities construe the alleged same creature in different fashions. This is sufficient to substantiate the claim that Adam and $Adam_2$ have different concepts, regardless of whether the creatures in question are biologically the same.

Furthermore, Adam betrays an incomplete grasp of *bird* to the extent that he is ignorant of his community's construal of birds, namely, what the prototype of bird consists of. Burge (1990: 51/2007: 266) remarks that "there are some expressions in ordinary discourse for whose understanding we would simply refuse to recognize any further authority than communal practice". 'Bird' is among such expressions. As discussed in Section 2.6.2, what is characteristic of 'bird' is that everyone who fails to have its prototype is likely to be judged to understand the concept only incompletely. A similar argument applies to the 'arthritis' case. We can say that Adam understands the concept of *arthritis* incompletely to the extent that he is ignorant of a conceptual truth about arthritis agreed upon by the experts, namely, the construal of arthritis as an inflammation of the joints only. Burge's (1979a/2007) conclusion is therefore right, contrary to what I have suggested in Chapter 2. What Burge is wrong about is that, as Kimbrough (1998) points out, he ties the notion of incomplete understanding to the notion of truth, which is more congenial to conceptual content than the construal. This move makes Burge's (1979a/2007) thought experiment succumb to the metaphysical argument defended by Kimbrough (1998) and Wikforss (2001, 2004). We have only to appeal to the notion of construal, to which the metaphysical truth is orthogonal, in order to vindicate the notion of incomplete understanding needed for social externalism.

There are two remaining issues regarding the 'arthritis'/'bird' cases. Firstly, it might be objected that the inclusion of the construal into the definition of a concept would yield what Wikforss (2001) refers to as conceptual and referential fragmentation. Adam's construal of 'arthritis' and the doctor's construal of 'arthritis' are so different as to contradict each other. The same holds for 'bird', for which Adam and his fellows have mutually incompatible construals. How, then, can they think about the same concept and reference? This issue will be taken up in Chapter 4.

Secondly, it might be said, on behalf of Kimbrough and Wikforss among others, that the conception of concepts defended in this section is at best question-begging. The construal is considered to contribute to the individuation of a concept, so goes the objection, only to fend off the metaphysical argument which purports to demonstrate that Adam and Adam$_2$ share the same concepts of *arthritis* and *bird*. The idea that a concept consists of conceptual content and its construal enables us to say that a person who, in light of the community standards, misconstrues the relevant conceptual content *ipso facto* displays an incomplete grasp of the concept, automatically establishing social externalism (cf. Boyd 2013: 205). The question whether it is the experts who are mistaken simply does not arise. This line of reasoning would leave the nature of the statement in (16) unaccounted for. According to Burge (1986a/2007, 1993/2007), the revisability of (16) suggests that we should distinguish the conventional meaning of 'atom' and its real definition, or, in Burge's words, cognitive value:

Dalton and his predecessors *defined* 'atom' (and its translations) in terms of indivisibility. Major theoretical changes intervened. The definition was discarded. Despite the change, we want to say, Dalton wrongly thought that *atoms* were indivisible: despite his erroneous definition, he had the "concept" of atom (not merely the referent of 'atom'). I think that this sort of attribution is defensible in a wide variety of central examples of scientific developments, even in the light of Kuhnian insights into scientific revolutions. Although I cannot develop the point here, the distinction between theoretical meaning and cognitive value is in many ways analogous to that between conventional meaning and cognitive value. (Burge 1986a: 716/2007: 270)

The statement in (16b) gives the conventional meaning of 'atom' accepted by Dalton and his predecessors. When (16b) was revised, Burge suggests, the meaning of 'atom' underwent a change without affecting the concept of *atom*[6]. As Wikforss (2014: 2.2) states, "even if the expert has a complete grasp of conventional meaning she may not have a complete grasp of the concept expressed". The metaphysical notion of concept seems to have a role to play in the individuation of a concept, whether or not the construal may be relevant to the individuation. My answer to this objection is that the metaphysical notion of concept has only to do with physical externalism, which will be discussed in Chapter 5. In fact, Wikforss (2014: 2.2) remarks that "[t]he appeal to environmental factors, and the suggestion that even the experts may be wrong about the essential nature of a kind picked out by a general term, is reminiscent of what Kripke (1980) and Putnam (1975) says [sic.] about natural kind terms". As far as social externalism is concerned, conceptual competence can be equated with linguistic competence, since conceptual competence in the communal sense as opposed to the metaphysical sense is assessed in relation to the community standards. Indeed, in cognitive linguistics, the construal is commonly assumed to be conventionally associated with a linguistic expression, as illustrated by Langacker's (2008: 55) remark that "[a]s part of its conventional semantic value, every symbolic structure construes its content in a certain fashion". Accordingly, incomplete understanding in the metaphysical sense, which concerns physical externalism, must be distinguished from incomplete understanding in the communal sense, which substantiates social externalism. After all, as Burge (2012: 65) puts it in a different context, "[t]here are many kinds

---

6) Wikforss (2014: Section 2.2) remarks that Burge's (1986a/2007) 'sofa' thought experiment falls back on the idea that even experts can display an incomplete grasp of a concept.

Chapter 3　Incomplete Understanding and Construal

of incomplete understanding, just as there are many kinds of understanding". The notion of incomplete understanding relevant to social externalism, stemming from failure to properly construe the relevant conceptual content, is independently motivated by Frege's notion of sense presented in Chapter 1.

3.4 Construal and Frege's Sense[7]

One may have noticed that Langacker's 'construal' bears a striking similarity to Frege's 'sense' presented in Section 1.2.2. Frege (1892a) introduced the notion of sense (*Sinn*) to account for the difference in cognitive value (*Erkenntniswert*) or information content (Dummett 1973: 94) between (17a-18a) and (17b-18b):

(17)　(Let a, b, c be the lines connecting the vertices of a triangle with the midpoints of the opposite sides.)

　　a. the point of intersection of a and b = the point of intersection of a and b

　　b. the point of intersection of a and b = the point of intersection of b and c

(18)　a. the morning star (Phosphorus) = the morning star (Phosphorus)

　　b. the morning star (Phosphorus) = the evening star (Hesperus)

The references of 'the point of intersection of a and b' and 'the point of the intersection of b and c' are the same. If the meaning of these expressions were exhausted by their reference, say, A, both (17a) and (17b) would mean that A = A, a trivial truth. Intuitively, this is not the case. While (17a) holds *a priori* as does 'A = A', (17b) contributes to an extension of our knowledge[8]. It is in this sense that (17a) and (17b) are considered to differ in cognitive value[9]. The difference in

---

7) Section 3.4 is based on Sakai (2017).

8) Burge (2012: 55) notes that Frege never wrote that (17a) lacked cognitive value. What is in fact needed here is a weaker claim which Burge says that Frege actually made, namely, the claim that (17a) and (17b) differ in cognitive value.

9) Salmon (1986: Ch. 6) challenges this assumption and claims that 'a = b' is semantically equivalent to 'a = b'. In his view, the observation that unlike 'a = a' 'a = b' is (or sounds) informative results from failure to distinguish between semantics and pragmatics. The nontrivial information carried by 'a = b' but not by 'a = a' is "pragmatically imparted information" (Salmon 1986: 79). I shall not pursue this line of thought, however, because the sheer dichotomy between semantics and pragmatics is incompatible with the cognitive linguistic framework developed by Langacker (1987, 2008).

cognitive value between (17a) and (17b), Frege claims, derives from the difference in sense between 'the point of the intersection of a and b' and 'the point of the intersection of b and c'[10]. By the principle of compositionality, according to which the meaning of a complex expression is determined solely by the meanings of its constituents and the way they are put together, the differing senses of these expressions yields those of the sentences in (17a) and (17b). A similar remark can be made about (18). Perhaps some might object that the reference of 'the morning star' is not identical with that of 'the evening star', on the grounds that, unlike (19a), (19b) sounds false.

(19) a. I saw the morning star this morning.
b. I saw the evening star this morning.

The two expressions in question are not interchangeable *salva veritate*, suggesting that their references are not the same. Two remarks are in order. First, this objection overlooks the fact that Frege (1892a: 27/1997: 153) cautions that the term 'reference' (Bedeutung) should be taken in the widest range ("dies Wort [= Gegenstand] im weitesten Umfange genommen"). This makes the dispute mostly a matter of terminology. Frege urges us to construe the term 'reference' so that the reference of 'the morning star' may be identical with that of 'the evening star'. Second, if one nevertheless claims that the references of the two expressions are substantially (rather than terminologically) different as in (20a), a difficulty arises in accounting for the intuitive difference between (20b-c) and (20d):

(20) a. the morning star ≠ the evening star
b. the morning star ≠ Venus
c. the evening star ≠ Venus
d. the morning star ≠ Mars

If, as assumed here, you accept (20a), you must also accept (20b-c), since the negation of (20b-c), namely (21a-b), would entail (21c):

---

10) Sainsbury and Tye (2012: Section 3.7) contend that Frege's argument is not convincing and that the informativeness of 'A is B' must be attributed to the distinct origins of the concepts *A* and *B*. Sainsbury and Tye's approach allows us to account for the informativeness of 'A is B' without postulating any additional semantic layer over and above reference.

Chapter 3   Incomplete Understanding and Construal

(21)   a. the morning star = Venus
       b. the evening star = Venus
       c. the morning star = the evening star

But (21c) is exactly what we are assuming here that you reject. This indicates that
the acceptance of (20a) entails the acceptance of (20b-c). Now, there is an intuitive
difference between (20b-c) and (20d). Whereas (20d) is obviously true, (20b-c) are
felt not to be as obviously true. If the occurrences of '≠' in (20b-d) are all assigned
the same meaning, the origin of the difference between (20b-c) and (20d) must be
sought for elsewhere. But where? It is not an easy task to answer this question.
This naturally leads us to assume that the reference of 'the morning star' is identical with that of 'the evening star'.

Returning to the main issue, as Dummett (1973: 293) points out, "'sense' is
first introduced as a correlative of 'understand': the sense of an expression is what
we know when we understand it". In a nutshell, "[t]he notion of sense has to do
with the speakers' understanding of their language, that is, their grasp of meaning"
(Dummett 1991: 321). Bromberger (1997: 153) characterizes the sense of a term
as "that which speakers know about the word by virtue of which they can discern
members of its extension". This interpretation comports with Frege's (1892a) well-
known remark that "[t]he sense of a proper name is grasped by everybody who is
sufficiently familiar with the language or totality of designations to which it
belongs"[11]. Less known but more eloquent is Frege's (1918-1919b/1997) following
remark:

> The being of a thought may also be taken to lie in the possibility of different
> thinkers' grasping the thought as one and the same thought. In that case the
> fact that a thought had no being would consist in several thinkers' each associ-
> ating with the sentence a sense of his own; this sense would in that case be a
> content of his particular consciousness, so that there would be no common
> sense that could be grasped by several people. (Frege 1918-1919b: 146/1997:
> 349)[12]

To the extent that we can understand each other by using an expression, it must be

---

11) „Der Sinn eines Eigennamens wird von jenem erfasst, der die Sprache oder das Ganze von
     Bezeichnungen hinreichend kennt, der er angehört." (Frege 1892a: 27)

155

the case that we share the sense of that expression and the thoughts expressed by the sentences in which the expression occurs. As Noonan (1984: 205) states, "thoughts are psychologically real: they are the objects of the propositional attitudes and it is by reference to an agent's propositional attitude that his rational actions are to be explained" (see also Heck 2002: 2).

The notion of sense has yet another aspect. As remarked in Section 1.2.2, Frege characterized the sense as containing a mode of presentation of the reference:

> It is natural, now, to think of there being connected with a sign (name, combination of words, letter), besides that to which the sign refers, which may be called the reference of the sign, also what I should like to call the sense of the sign, wherein the mode of presentation is contained. (Frege 1892a: 26/1997: 152)[13]

In this view, 'the morning star' and 'the evening star', for example, correspond to different modes of presentation of the same planet. Now, how is the characterization of the sense as a correlative of 'understand' related to the characterization of the sense as a container of the mode of presentation of the reference? The answer lies in the fact that understanding a singular term involves thinking of its reference in a particular way, as Evans (1982) put it:

> Frege's idea was that it may be a property of a singular term as an element of a public language that, in order to understand utterances containing it, one must not only think of that object, its Meaning [= reference], but one must think of that object *in a particular way* [...]. (Evans 1982: 16, emphasis in the original)

---

12) „Man kann unter dem Sein eines Gedankens auch verstehen, dass der Gedanke als derselbe von verschiedenen Denkenden gefasst werden könne. Dann würde das Nichtsein eines Gedankens darin bestehen, dass von mehreren Denkenden jeder seinen eigenen Sinn mit dem Satze verbände, der dann Inhalt seines besonderen Bewusstseins wäre, so dass es einen gemeinsamen Sinn des Satzes, der von mehreren gefasst werden könnte, nicht gäbe." (Frege 1918-1919b: 146)

13) „Es liegt nun nahe, mit einem Zeichen (Namen, Wortverbindung, Schriftzeichen) außer dem Bezeichneten, was die Bedeutung des Zeichens heißen möge, noch das verbunden zu denken, was ich den Sinn des Zeichens nennen möchte, worin die Art des Gegebenseins enthalten ist." (Frege 1892a: 26)

Chapter 3 Incomplete Understanding and Construal

In saying that (17a)-(18a) and (17b)-(18b) differ in sense and hence in mode of presentation, Frege assumed the constraint outlined in (22a), or more simply, (22b)[14]:

(22) a. Necessarily, if *m* is a mode of presentation under which a minimally rational person *x* believes a thing *y* to be *F*, then it is not the case that *x* also believes *y* not to be *F* under *m*. In other words, if *x* believes *y* to be *F* and also believes *y* not to be *F*, then there are distinct modes of presentation *m* and *m'* such that *x* believes *y* to be *F* under *m* and disbelieves *y* to be *F* under *m'*. (Schiffer 1978: 180)

b. If it is possible to rationally believe that *p* and not believe that *q*, then the contents of *p* and *q* are distinct. (Brown 2004: 165, 197, 205)

Schiffer (1978) calls the constraint in (22) 'Frege's Constraint'[15]. Frege's Constraint is what connects the notion of cognitive value with that of the mode of presentation. If a minimally rational person believes (23a) while rejecting (23b), she thinks of the morning star and the evening star under different modes of presentation; otherwise she would be deemed irrational[16]:

(23) a. The morning star is a body illuminated by the sun.
          (Der Morgenstern ist ein von der Sonne beleuchteter Körper.)
      b. The evening star is a body illuminated by the sun.

---

14) The definition in (22) corresponds to what Recanati (2016, p. xv) calls the modal formulation of Frege's Constraint, as opposed to the non-modal one, according to which the contents of *p* and *q* are distinct if the subject actually entertains doubt as to whether *p* and *q* involve the same object.

15) Frege's Constraint is also called 'the Intuitive Criterion of Difference for thoughts' (Evans 1982: 18), 'the differential dubitability test (DDT)' (Kimbrough 1998: 470), 'Frege's test (for differential dubitability)' (Burge 1979b: 10/1990: 223, 1986a: 717/2007: 271, 1993: 317/2007: 298), 'the Frege test' (Goldberg 2008: 165), 'the (Fregean) Cognitive Difference Principle (CDP)' (Schroeter 2008: 110-111), 'Frege's principle' (Wikforss 2006) or the Fregean Constraint (FC) (Onofri 2016: 6). The intuition that (23a) and (23b) express different thoughts derives from the fact that there can be someone who rationally believes (23a) and disbelieves or doubts (23b). Note that it is controversial whether 'if' in (22) cannot be strengthened into 'if and only if'. As Burge (2012: 56) remarks, even if no rational subject takes different attitudes toward (i) and (ii), these nevertheless constitute different thoughts:

(i) $2^2 = 4$
(ii) $2 + 2 = 4$

157

(Der Abendstern ist ein von der Sonne beleuchteter Körper.)

((23a-b): Frege 1892a: 32/1997: 156)

The qualification 'minimally rational' in Frege's Constraint is needed for this reason. An irrational person would assert, for instance, both that the morning star is a body illuminated by the sun and that the morning star is not a body illuminated by the sun. One would not want to conclude from this alone that 'the morning star' is associated with two different modes of presentation. This assertion does not reveal anything about the meaning of the expression, which merely suggests that the utterer is in a troubled state of mind. This is not to say that the notion of (minimal) rationality poses no problem in Frege's theory. I will have more to say about this in 3.5.

Parallel to the contrast between (23a) and (23b), Frege (1918-1919a: 297-298) claimed that (24a) and (24b) express distinct thoughts, even when (24c) holds:

(24) a. Dr. Lauben has been wounded.

   b. Gustave Lauben has been wounded.

   c. Dr. Lauben = Gustave Lauben

Despite the truth-conditional equivalence between (24a) and (24b), Frege took (24a) and (24b) to correspond to different modes of presentation:

Accordingly, with a proper name, it depends on how whatever it refers to is presented. This can happen in different ways and every such way corresponds

---

16) Komorjai (2006: Section 4.2) argues against attributing Frege's Constraint to Frege. For Komorjai (2006), Frege's notion of sense, thought and even cognitive value (ibid.: 147) have little to do with epistemology and must be understood in an objective or non-cognitive way (ibid.: 137, 165). His dissatisfaction with Frege's Constraint derives from the fact that the constraint bases differences between thoughts to different epistemic attitudes that a subject takes toward them. Thoughts are individuated, Komorjai claims, not in terms of attitudes but in terms of objective contents (ibid.: 148, 153). It seems to me that Komorjai's argument is confused. No one claims that, as Komorjai (2006: 151) suggests, thoughts differ "*because* the same person might have different attitudes toward them" (emphasis in the original). Frege's Constraint says that the speaker's epistemic attitudes toward a pair of thoughts constitute a reliable test for determining whether the two thoughts have the same objective content. This is obviously compatible with the assumption that a thought has objective content independently from how the speaker construes it.

with a particular sense of a sentence containing a proper name. The different thoughts which thus result from the same sentence correspond in their truth-value, of course; that is to say, if one is true then all are true, and if one is false then all are false. Nevertheless their distinctness must be recognized. So it must really be demanded that a single way in which whatever is referred to is presented be associated with every proper name. (Frege 1918-1919a: 65-66 /1956: 298)[17]

Given this account, the thought expressed by a sentence comprises, but is not exhausted by, its truth-condition in the ordinary sense of the term as explained in standard textbooks on semantics[18]. As Recanati (2008: 69) remarks, the Fregean thought expressed by a sentence is not the truth-condition of the sentence; it

---

17) „Demnach kommt es bei einem Eigennamen darauf an, wie der, die oder das durch ihn Bezeichnete gegeben ist. Das kann in verschiedener Weise geschehen, und jeder solchen Weise entspricht ein besonderer Sinn eines Satzes, der den Eigennamen enthält. Die verschiedenen Gedanken, die sich so aus demselben Satze ergeben, stimmen freilich in ihrem Wahrheitswerte überein, d. h. wenn einer von ihnen wahr ist, sind sie alle wahr, und wenn einer von ihnen falsch ist, sind sie alle falsch. Dennoch ist ihre Verschiedenheit anzuerkennen. Es muss also eigentlich gefordert werden, dass mit jedem Eigennamen eine einzige Weise verknüpft sei, wie der, die oder das durch ihn Bezeichnete gegeben sei." (Frege 1918-1919a: 65-66)

18) This is arguably the reason that Bell (1984: 371, my emphasis) states that "the sense of a sentence *comprises* the condition = the True, i.e. its truth-condition", rather than that the sense of a sentence *is* its truth-condition. A more fine-grained notion of the truth condition is proposed by Donnellan (1974). The sentences in (i) and (ii) are commonly taken to have the same truth condition as long as Henry is identical with George.

(i)   Henry is bald.
(ii) George is bald.

If Henry is George, (i) cannot be true without (ii) also being true, making (i) and (ii) truth-conditionally equivalent. Contrary to this prevalent view, Donnellan (1974) claims that (i) and (ii) differ in the truth condition, even though they express the same proposition:

> [...] we express the same proposition if the person you referred to by using the name "Henry" and I by using the name "George" are the same person. But what you say is true if and only if the person you referred to – that is, the person historically connected – when you used the name "Henry" has the property of being bald; whereas what I say is true if and only if what I referred to by using the name "George" has the property of being bald. The truth conditions are different because they must be stated in terms of what is referred to by different expressions, in the one case my use of the name "George" and in the other your use of the name "Henry." Yet we may express the same proposition. (Donnellan 1974: 28-29)

corresponds to the truth-condition under a certain mode of presentation[19]. This is illustrated by such pairs as in (23) and (24). The thought expressed by (23a) and that expressed by (23b) are truth-conditionally equivalent, since (23a) cannot be true without (23b) also being true. Nevertheless, the two sentences express different thoughts, insofar as they present one and the same planet from different perspectives. The same holds for (24a) and (24b).

Here emerges a non-negligible parallel between Frege's notion of grasping a sense or thought and Langacker's notion of construing a conceptual content. Every singular term, Frege says, is associated with a particular way of thinking of its reference, and a competent speaker of the language must understand it. This particular way of thinking of the reference may naturally be taken to correspond to what Langacker (2008: 43) calls the construal, namely "our manifest ability to conceive and portray the same situation in alternate ways". In fact, no substantial difference can be found between Frege's and Langacker's accounts of the morning star / evening star problem.

Classic examples illustrating the Fregean sense / reference distinction are treated similarly: *the morning star* designates an entity construed in relation to the stellar configuration of the morning sky, and *the evening star*, to that of the evening sky. For a person who knows that the morning star and the evening star are the same, both expressions include these abstract domains in their encyclopedic characterizations; they differ in their choice of primary domain, through which access to the overall knowledge system is achieved. *Venus* is yet another expression with the same designatum but a different primary domain. (Langacker 1987: 165, n. 13)

Just as grasping the sense of 'the morning star' and grasping the sense of 'the evening star' correspond to different ways of thinking of the planet, so construing the two expressions evokes distinct cognitive domains. The parallel goes further. In the same way that, as we have seen in Section 1.2.2, Frege stressed the public nature of the sense as opposed to the idea (*Vorstellung*), Langacker (2008: 55) repeatedly talks about the conventionality of construal, as we have seen in Section

---

19) "La « pensée » frégéenne n'est donc pas identique à ce que j'ai appelé la condition de vérité : la pensée frégéenne correspond à la condition de vérité *sous un certain mode de présentation*." (Recanati 2008: 69, emphasis in the original)

3.3. As far as singular terms are concerned, the cognitive linguistic approach is no different from the Fregean approach. In fact, as Aydene (1997) points out, it was Frege cases that originally motivated the bifurcation of content sketched in Section 1.3.4:

> It is usually believed that Frege cases are an important test for any scheme of psychological explanation proposed to be carried out in terms of the intentional properties of mental states, since such cases involve states with the same broad content but quite different internal behaviour. Hence the usual lesson drawn is that appealing to only denotational content can't be sufficient to explain the quite different psychological behaviour of the mental states involved in Frege cases. And the usual solution has been to appeal to some notion of narrow content of such states in the explanation of their behaviour. (Aydene 1997: 427-428)

Both Frege's and Langacker's theories can be characterized as varieties of two-dimensional semantics, namely, semantic models which, understood in the broadest sense, "[ascribe] two systematic aspects of meaning" (Sainsbury and Tye 2012: 30)[20]. For Frege, meaning consists of sense and reference, and for Langacker, meaning consists of construal and conceptual content.

An apparent obstacle to assimilating Frege's sense to Langacker's construal is that, as we have seen in Section 1.2.2, one of the functions of the sense attached to a term is held to determine the term's reference, while, as said in Section 3.3, construal is often fictive. It is obvious that false descriptions attached to a term fail to determine the term's reference, insofar as 'determine' is construed in the mathematical sense. If Frege's sense is to be assimilated to Langacker's construal, the conception of sense as the determiner of the reference in the metaphysical sense of the term must be compromised. Although I shall not delve into Frege's exegesis here, two remarks are in order. First, when Frege says that 'the morning star' and 'the

---

20) Various two-dimensional systems proposed in the literature have in common that the first-dimensional notion, i.e. Frege's (1892a) sense, Kaplan's (1989a) character, Langacker's (2008) construal, etc., is designed to better account for the cognitive significance carried by a linguistic expression than the second-dimensional notion (Chalmers 2006: 63). More narrowly construed, the term 'two-dimensional semantics' often refers to semantic theories that try to reconcile externalism with descriptivism, as exemplified by Chalmers (1996, 2006) and Braddon-Mitchell (2004).

evening star' present the same planet (or star) from different perspectives, as in (25) (cf. Sainsbury and Tye 2012: 3), he thereby acknowledges that the sense attached to an expression can be wrong:

(25) a. The morning star (or Phosphorus) is the planet seen only at position y in the morning sky.
b. The evening star (or Hesperus) is the planet seen only at position x in the evening sky.

The descriptions in (25) are erroneous, since the morning star is also visible in the evening and the evening star is also visible in the morning. This relates to the second remark to be made about the assimilation of sense to construal: as pointed out by Burge (1990: 31/2007: 242-243), Frege is far from eloquent about how the sense of a term determines its reference, in contrast to the other two functions fulfilled by the sense, namely that of accounting for cognitive value and that of serving as the denotation of expressions in oblique contexts:

Frege explicates the notion of fixing a *Bedeutung* in a purely logical way: for each sense there is at most one *Bedeutung*. It is also clear, partly from the first function [= the function of accounting for cognitive value], that a sense is a way of thinking of *Bedeutung*. Beyond the foregoing, Frege says little. (Burge 1990: 31/2007: 243)

That there is at most one reference allows for the possibility that there is no reference determined by the sense. Indeed, Frege concedes that a name and a sentence can have a sense without having any reference:

Is it possible that a sentence as a whole has only a sense, but no *Bedeutung*? At any rate, one might expect that such sentences occur, just as there are parts of sentences having sense but no *Bedeutung*. And sentences which contain proper names without *Bedeutung* will be of this kind. The sentence 'Odysseus was set ashore at Ithaca while sound asleep' obviously has a sense. But since it is doubtful whether the name 'Odysseus', occurring therein, has a *Bedeutung*, it is also doubtful whether the whole sentence does. (Frege 1892a: 32/1997: 156-157)[21]

162

Chapter 3 Incomplete Understanding and Construal

As far as natural language is concerned, it seems that Frege did not conceive the sense of an expression as a reliable determiner of its reference. In the glossary at the end of his 2012 book, Chalmers defines 'Fregean sense' as "[a] meaning or content associated with an expression that captures its cognitive significance" (Chalmers 2012: 470). In this definition, there is no explicit reference to reference. Likewise, for Chalmers (2006: 55), sense "is constitutively tied to cognitive significance".

Now that the affinity between Frege's and Langacker's theories is in place, we can appeal to Frege's Constraint to substantiate the claim that the definition of a concept involves its construal. From Frege's Constraint in (22) Peacock (1992) draws the criterion for individuation of concepts outlined in (26):

(26) Distinctness of Concepts: Concepts C and D are distinct if and only if there are two complete propositional contents that differ at most in that one contains C substituted in one or more places for D, and one of which is potentially informative while the other is not. (Peacock 1992: 2, cf. Papineau 1996: 425, Sainsbury and Tye 2012: 55-56)

This criterion is a consequence of Frege's Constraint. As mentioned above, Frege's Constraint enables one to say whether two (or more) truth-conditionally equivalent statements express distinct thoughts by relating the possibility to rationally embrace only one of the statements to the presence of distinct modes of presentation. Thus, as long as one can reasonably embrace (23a) while rejecting (23b), (23a) and (23b) can be said to express different thoughts. Since the only difference between (23a) and (23b) resides in the subject nominal, we can safely attribute the differing thoughts to the differing senses or construals attached to 'the morning star' and 'the evening star'. Insofar as a concept includes its sense or construal, we can conclude that 'the morning star' and 'the evening star' express different concepts. Now, from an uninformative statement like (18a), we can obtain an

---

21) „Hat vielleicht ein Satz als Ganzes nur einen Sinn, aber keine Bedeutung? Man wird jedenfalls erwarten können, dass solche Sätze vorkommen, ebensogut, wie es Satzteile gibt, die wohl einen Sinn, aber keine Bedeutung haben. Und Sätze, welche Eigennamen ohne Bedeutung enthalten, werden von der Art sein. Der Satz "Odysseus wurde tief schlafend in Ithaka ans Land gesetzt" hat offenbar einen Sinn. Da es aber zweifelhaft ist, ob der darin vorkommende Name ‚Odysseus' eine Bedeutung habe, so ist es damit auch zweifelhaft, ob der ganze Satz eine habe." (Frege 1892a: 32)

163

informative statement like (18b) by replacing a term with another coreferential term. In this case, it is fairly obvious that (18a), but not (18b), is embraced by everyone. Peacock's proposal in (26) is tantamount to saying that 'the morning star' and 'the evening star' express different concepts precisely because it is possible to construct a pair consisting of an uninformative statement and an informative statement. For any concepts C and D, we can construct such a pair insofar as C and D are distinct concepts.

By applying Frege's Constraint in (22) and Distinctness of Concepts in (26) to statements in which the word 'arthritis' occurs, we can confirm that Adam$_2$ and his fellows have a different concept corresponding to the word form 'arthritis' than the experts in Adam's community. After all, Adam$_2$ and his fellows accept (27a) while rejecting (27b), an obviously false statement:

(27) a. Arthritis may occur in the thigh.
      b. A rheumatoid disease of the joints only may occur in the thigh.

This suggests that (27a) and (27b) express different thoughts, the difference between (27a) and (27b) deriving from the differing senses attached to the one-place predicates 'arthritis' and 'a rheumatoid disease of the joints only'. Not only singular terms and sentences but also predicates or general terms have a sense in addition to a reference. That the predicates or general terms 'arthritis' and 'a rheumatoid disease of the joints only' express different concepts is confirmed by the possibility of constructing a pair consisting of an uninformative statement and an informative statement, as in (28):

(28) a. Arthritis is arthritis.
      b. Arthritis is a rheumatoid disease of the joints only.
          ((28a-b): Wikforss 2006: 171, cf. Burge 1993: 317/2007: 298)[22]

This is in line with Burge's (1979: 79/ 2007: 106) assumption that "[t]he word 'arthritis' in the counterfactual community does not mean *arthritis*". The two communities construe the conceptual content denoted by the word form 'arthritis' in different fashions. As pointed out by Sainsbury and Tye (2012: 73), "[Frege's]

---

22) Wikforss (2006) disagrees with the view defended in this section, as will be discussed in the next section.

Chapter 3 Incomplete Understanding and Construal

argument for sense, as a semantic property additional to reference, was non-de-monstrative" and Frege was presumably aware of this, judging from Frege's (1892a: 26/1997: 152) remark quoted above that it is "natural" (*naheliegen*) to posit sense in addition to reference. Combined with Langacker's conception of concepts, however, Frege's two-dimensional semantics provides a compelling argument for the idea that Adam's community and Adam$_2$' community possess different concepts.

3.5 Frege's Constraint and Incomplete Understanding[23]

The issue is far from settled. True, if we accept Frege's Constraint, it follows that 'the morning star (Phosphorus)' and 'the evening star (Hesperus)' express different concepts despite their identity in reference, and that Adam's community and Adam$_2$'s community possess different concepts expressed by the word form 'arthritis', regardless of whether or not the two concepts ultimately determine the same reference. So far so good. But the same reasoning seems to warrant, wrongly for the social externalist, that Adam possesses a different concept expressed by 'arthritis' from his fellows, since he attaches to the word a different construal or sense. This would make his 'arthritis' and his fellows' 'arthritis' homonymous and the communication between them illusory. As discussed in Section 3.2, Rey (1983: 249) proposes to exclude from the definition of a concept any methods whatsoever to access the concept precisely because such methods are unstable, varying from person to person. Far from constraining concepts, Frege's Constraint seemingly makes room for conceptual fragmentation. Indeed, Brown (2003, 2004) and Wikforss (2006) claim that Frege's Constraint misfires if it is combined with incomplete understanding. A similar point is made by Falvey and Owens (1994) without explicitly invoking Frege's Constraint. Falvey and Owens depict a scenario in which a speaker of English, Rudolf, believes cilantro and coriander to be distinct kinds of herbs:

Suppose that Rudolf is acquainted with cilantro. He knows it to be an herb that figures prominently in Mexican cuisine, and he is familiar with its distinctive aroma. He says to himself, "cilantro should be used sparingly," thereby expressing the thought that cilantro should be used sparingly. In addition,

---

23) Part of Section 3.5 is a reproduction of Sakai (2017).

165

Rudolf frequently employs dried coriander in his cooking; indeed he is as familiar with coriander as he is with cilantro. Coriander, too, he thinks should be used sparingly, and he says so to himself, "coriander should be used sparingly." Is Rudolf's thought that cilantro should be used sparingly the same as or different from his thought that coriander should be used sparingly? According to externalism, this question may not be answerable in terms of the mental images or descriptions Rudolf associates with cilantro and coriander, or anything else that is "in his head." (Falvey and Owens 1994: 110)

Two contradicting results can follow from the scenario under consideration. On the one hand, since, as a matter of fact, cilantro is coriander, (29a) is truth-conditionally equivalent to (29b), suggesting that Rudolf is entertaining one and the same thought without recognizing that he is:

(29) a. Cilantro should be used sparingly.
      b. Coriander should be used sparingly.
                              ((29a-b): Falvey and Owens 1994: 110)

On the other hand, Frege's Constraint tells us that (29a) and (29b) express different thought contents, because it is possible for Rudolf to throw away one of the thoughts while retaining the other (cf. Sainsbury and Tye 2012: 95-96). Combined with the notion of incomplete understanding, externalism invites us to choose the first option; Rudolf fails to see that (29a) and (29b) express one and the same content. This option coheres with the externalist thesis that the identity of a thought is partly determined by the relevant features of the environment in which the thought is tokened. Cilantro actually is coriander in the environment in which Rudolf entertains the thought(s) expressed by (29), but this fact is not represented in his mind. The lack of relevant information prevents him from recognizing that he thinks the same thought twice when he entertains (29a) and (29b). Falvey and Owens (1994: 110) state that this argument suggests that the principle in (30) is false:

(30) Introspective knowledge of comparative content:
     With respect to any two of his thoughts or beliefs, an individual can know authoritatively and directly (that is, without relying on inferences from his observed environment) whether or not they have the same con-

Chapter 3   Incomplete Understanding and Construal

tent. (Falvey and Owens 1994: 109-110)[24]

Brown (2004: 160, 195) calls the principle in (30) 'transparency of sameness of content' [25]. According to Brown (2003: 442-443, 2004: 161-162) and Wikforss (2006: 175), Falvey and Owens's argument demonstrates that the externalist is committed to the antithesis of the principle of the transparency of sameness of content, namely, the principle of the opaqueness of sameness of content (OSC):

(31)   Opaqueness of sameness of content (OSC):
A subject may have two thoughts, or thought-constituents, with the same content at a single time, although she supposes that they have different contents, and is unable to realize that they have the same content without using empirical information. (Brown 2003: 442)

Rudolf does not know, Wikforss (2006: 171-172) argues, that he is so irrational as to believe that only one of the statements in (29) can cease to be true. It is therefore not possible to apply here Frege's Constraint, which involves an assumption of rationality. If, nevertheless, one applies Frege's Constraint to Rudolf's case, the proper conclusion to draw is that Rudolf rationally attaches to the terms 'cilantro' and 'coriander' distinct concepts, say *schmilantro* and *schmoliander*, respectively (Wikforss 2006: 172). Insofar as the distinctness of these concepts is transparent to Rudolf, there is no role left for incomplete understanding to play. We are faced

---

24) A similar principle can be proposed for linguistic meaning. Thus, Dummett (1978) famously wrote that an individual can know introspectively, or in Goldberg's (2015: 3, 5) words, from the armchair, whether any two of the meanings she attaches to linguistic expressions are the same (Boghossian 1994: 33, Wikforss 2015: 146, 151-152):
It is an undeniable feature of the notion of meaning – obscure as that notion is – that meaning is transparent in the sense that, if someone attaches a meaning to each of two words, he must know whether these meanings are the same. (Dummett 1978: 131)
25) Boghossian (1994: 36) proposes to break up the transparency of mental content into two subparts:
(i)   *Transparency of Sameness*: If two of a thinker's token thoughts possess the same content, then the thinker must be able to know *a priori* that they do.
(ii)   *Transparency of Difference*: If two of a thinker's token thoughts possess distinct contents, then the thinker must be able to know *a priori* that they do.
Frege cases and Twin cases provide prima facie challenges to (i) and (ii), respectively (Boghossian 1994: 39, Wikforss 2015: 148).

with a dilemma: either the sameness of content is transparent and the thinker is rational or the sameness of content is opaque and the thinker is irrational. Since the notion of incomplete understanding entails that the sameness of content is opaque, Wikforss (2006: 171) maintains that "Burge's commitment to the idea that someone can believe a content despite misunderstanding this content, is incompatible with Frege's [Constraint]". Assuming, as the social externalist does, that Adam has an incomplete grasp of *arthritis* rather than a complete grasp of *tharthritis*, his different attitudes toward (27a)-(28a) and (27b)-(28b) show at best that he is irrational, unable to see that both express the same thought. Frege's Constraint has no work to do here. Neither construal nor mode of presentation is relevant to the identity of a concept. Social externalism may be established even on this assumption, because Adam is held to possess the concept of *arthritis* without recognizing that he does. However, this version of social externalism is incompatible with the internalist conception of concepts held by Frege and Langacker, according to which concepts are partly individuated by a rational individual's construals. Incomplete understanding threatens rationality. Brown (2004: 230) concludes that "[t]he standard arguments for Fregean sense rely on assumptions about transparency and rationality that are hard to motivate if one also accepts anti-individualism".

Wikforss's (2006) and Brown's (2003, 2004) arguments, in my view, rest on the failure to sufficiently discriminate between understanding a concept incompletely and being irrational. True, Rudolf's incomplete grasp of *cilantro* and *coriander* makes room for the possibility that he is too irrational to be credited with these concepts. But, crucially, it does not compel us to conclude that he really is. As Millikan (1997: 511) reminds us, "[a]n ability is not, in general, something one either has or has not and "[m]ost abilities come in degrees". Incomplete understanding does not entail irrationality. In effect, Frege's Constraint, I submit, embodies the possibility for a person to be rational or competent in the use of some linguistic expression E while being ignorant of some aspects of the meaning, or more specifically, construal, expressed by E. Although Burge (2012: 60-61) contends that this reading of Frege's Constraint is non-Fregean because, according to Burge, "Frege takes *fully* understanding expressions to be a condition on individuating their senses" (ibid.: 60, emphasis in the original), it is the only way, as far as I can see, to reconcile Frege's Constraint and social externalism. Then, it is certainly a mistake to apply Frege's Constraint to anyone, rational or not, but it is also a mistake to reserve it for those who fully understand the meaning of the relevant

Chapter 3   Incomplete Understanding and Construal

expression. One can understand a concept incompletely without being irrational in the relevant sense.

Evans (1982) formulates Frege's Constraint, or in his terminology, the Intuitive Criterion of Difference for thoughts, as in (32):

(32) The Intuitive Criterion of Difference for thoughts: The thought associated with one sentence S as its sense must be different from the thought associated with another sentence S' as its sense, if it is possible for someone to understand both sentences at a given time while coherently taking different attitudes toward them, i.e. accepting (rejecting) one while rejecting (accepting), or being agnostic about, the other. (Evans 1982: 18-19)[26]

Evans (1982: 19, n. 19) notes that the word 'somebody' is crucial in this definition, because "it is not true that *anyone* who understands" the sentences in (23a-b), for instance, "take different attitudes to them" (emphasis in the original). Those who know that the morning star is identical with the evening star would accept both statements as true. Evans's interpretation is supported by textual evidence. Frege (1892a: 32/1997: 156) stated that anybody who did not know that the evening star is the morning star might hold the one thought to be true and the other false[27]. The restriction "who did not know that the evening star is the morning star" indicates that the difference between the thought expressed by (23a) and that expressed by (23b) is solely guaranteed by the attitudes taken by those who fail to find out the identity between the evening star and the morning star. Too much emphasis on 'someone' in (32), however, may make us easily distracted from 'understand both sentences'. When we apply Frege's Constraint to someone, it must be the case that this someone understands the pair of sentences in question. If (32) is compared with (22), one may notice that Evans equates understanding a linguistic expression with being rational about the use of that expression. Crucially, understanding comes in degrees (Quine 1960: 13, Dupré 1981: 70, Burge 1986a/2007: 713, 718, Dummett 1991: 321, Wiggins 1995: 71-72, Millikan 1997:

---

26) More simply, S and S' have differing cognitive value if and only if "it is possible for someone who understands S and S' to accept one as true, while not accepting the other" (Recanati 1993: 63).

27) „Jemand, der nicht wüsste, dass der Abendstern der Morgenstern ist, könnte den einen Gedanken für wahr, den anderen für falsch halten." (Frege 1892a: 32)

169

514, Recanati 1997: 88, 94, Stanley 1999: 17-18, Woodfield 2000: 447-448, De Brabanter et al. 2005: 27, 2007: 15-16, Boyd 2013: 206, 209-211, 214-215, Wikforss 2014: Section 2.1). How much understanding is required for rationality in the relevant sense? As Papineau (1996: 427) makes clear, Peacocke (1992: 32) suggests, as does Burge (2012), that Frege's Constraint should only be applied for "one who fully understands the word". This proposal is question-begging unless we make clear what counts as full understanding. Thus, it would be reasonable to say that, on some construal of full understanding, those who fully understand 'the morning star' and 'the evening star' surely know that the morning star is the evening star. This would make Frege's Constraint inapplicable, or, even if it is applied to such people, the result is that 'the morning star' and 'the evening star' share both sense and reference, leaving behind the difference in cognitive significance between (23a) and (23b).

The question of how much understanding is required for rationality is inseparably tied to the question of what kind of rationality is at issue. The type of rationality at stake here, in my view, is, or at least involves, what Millikan (1993) calls semantic rationality, which includes the epistemic givenness of meaning identity and difference defined as in (33):

(33) The epistemic givenness of meaning identity and difference:
A rational person has the capacity to discern a priori whether or not any two of her thoughts comprehend the same term or proposition, the same meaning. (Millikan 1993: 287)[28]

Semantic rationality can be considered to constitute part of linguistic competence. It might be said that semantic competence cannot be equated with, or included in, Frege's rationality, given that, as Burge (1979b/2005, 1990: 31, 56, n. 5/2005: 244,

---

28) Millikan (1993: 287) mentions two other conditions imposed upon meaning rationalism:
The epistemic givenness of univocity:
A rational person has the capacity to discern a priori when she is entertaining a thought with double or ambiguous meaning (if ambiguous thoughts are possible at all).
The epistemic givenness of meaningfulness:
A rational person has the ability to discern a priori whether she is meaning a term or proposition or whether her thought is empty of meaning.
Of the three conditions for meaning rationalism, Millikan claims, the epistemic givenness of meaning identity is the most central. What is relevant to the present discussion is this central type of givenness.

245, n. 5, 2012: Section I) points out, Frege's notion of sense is distinct from conventional linguistic meaning and deeply rooted in epistemology. What lends support to the view that Frege's Constraint constrains the range of semantic competence is Frege's distinction between sense (*Sinn*) and tone (*Beleuchtung, Färbung*), discussed in Section 1.2.2. In Section 3.4, I have shown that Frege's and Langacker's frameworks have a remarkable affinity. Both authors maintain that the sense or construal of a singular term corresponds to a particular way of thinking or viewing its reference and that the sense or construal is public or conventional. For both authors, the conceptual content expressed by a linguistic expression cannot be equated with the truth-conditional meaning, because it is always presented under a certain mode of presentation. Sentences containing singular terms apart, however, Frege seems to have equated thoughts with truth conditions. Frege (1918-1919a: 60/1956: 295) characterized (but did not define) a thought as something for which the question of truth arises. Based on this characterization of thought, Frege embarked on excluding from thought everything orthogonal to the question of truth. Quite naturally, Frege (1918-1919a: 63-64/1956: 295) threw away the idea and the tone, which, as discussed in Section 1.2.2, he took to be external to the question of truth.

Complicating the matter is that Frege (1918-1919a: 63/1956: 295) regarded the difference between 'horse' (Pferd) and 'steed' (Ross) and the difference between 'cart-horse' (Gaul) and 'mare' (Mähre) as external to the thought, just like the difference between 'and' (und) and 'but' (aber). Frege thereby drew a distinction between singular terms and predicates; whereas the difference between 'Dr. Lauben' and 'Gustave Lauben' belongs to the sense, that between 'horse' and 'steed' belongs to the tone, thus making no difference to the thought containing these predicates (Burge 2012: 63).

This line of demarcation has no counterpart in cognitive linguistics. Langacker (1987: 164-165) advances the view that 'roe' and 'caviar' are distinguished with respect to the relative prominence of certain domains evoked by these expressions, even though they designate the same mass of eggs. The meaning of a predicate is not exhausted by its extension, comprising a construal of its extension. The divergence between Frege's sense and Langacker's construal is most clearly seen in their treatment of grammatical constructions. The hallmark of the cognitive linguistic approach is the way it handles the meaning of various grammatical constructions which are truth-conditionally equivalent. Langacker (2008: 70) maintains that "[e] xpressions can have the same content, and profile the same relationship, but differ in meaning because they make different choices of trajector and landmark", where the trajector corresponds to the primary focus of the profiled relationship and the landmark to the secondary focus. For instance, the passive combines with a verb to derive a higher-level verb representing a different type, Langacker (2008: 361) argues, by adjusting the focal prominence of processual participants, conferring trajectory status on what would otherwise be the landmark. Thus, in the active in (34a), the stimulus X and the experiencer Y appear as the subject and the object, respectively:

(34) a. X frightened Y.
      b. Y was frightened by X.

The passive in (34b), by contrast, focuses on the experiencer Y instead of the stimulus X (Langacker 2008: 126). A similar contrast can be observed in (35) (Langacker 2008: 75-76):

(35) a. The rock is in front of the tree.
      b. The tree is behind the rock.

Even though (35a) and (35b) serve to describe the same situation, they differ in the choice of the trajector and the landmark. In (35a), the trajector is the rock and the landmark is the tree. The alignment is reversed in (35b), resulting in a different construal.

Frege was fully aware of the alternations observed in such pairs as (34) and (35) (Burge 2012: 59). Frege (1982b/1997) states that "[l]anguage has means of presenting now one, now another, part of the thought as the subject; one of the most familiar is the distinction of active and passive forms" (Frege 1892b: 200/1997: 188)[29]. Frege (1918-1919/1956) makes a similar point: "[a] sentence can be transformed by changing the verb from active to passive and making the object the subject at the same time" (Frege 1918-1919a: 64/1956: 296). The active and the resulting passive "have the same logical structure and sense" (Burge 2012: 59). Another means to transform a sentence is to replace the verb with another. Thus,

---

29) „Die Sprache hat Mittel, bald diesen, bald jenen Teil des Gedankens als Subjekt erscheinen zu lassen. Eins der bekanntesten ist die Unterscheidung der Formen des Aktivs und des Passivs." (Frege 1892b: 200)

Chapter 3   Incomplete Understanding and Construal

"[i]n the same way the dative may be changed into the nominative while 'give' is replaced by 'receive'" (ibid.)[30]. Clearly incompatible with the cognitive linguistic framework, however, is Frege's view that these alternations have no bearing upon the thoughts expressed by the sentences (cf. Katz 1972: 121, Dummett 1991: 291):

[W]e must not fail to recognize that the same sense, the same thought, may be variously expressed; thus the difference does not here concern the sense, but only the apprehension, shading, or colouring of the thought, and is irrelevant to logic." (Frege 1892b: 196, n. 7/1997: 184, n. G)[31]

We know that even in speech the same thought can be expressed in different ways, by making now this proper name, now that one, the grammatical subject. No doubt we shall say that these different phrasings are not equivalent. This is true. But we must not forget that language does not simply express thoughts; it also imparts a certain tone [Beleuchtung] or colouring [Färbung] to them. And this can be different even where the thought is the same." (Frege 1969[1906]: 209/1979: 192-193)[32]

A sentence can be transformed by changing the verb from active to passive and making the object the subject at the same time. In the same way the dative may be changed into the nominative while "give" is replaced by "receive". Naturally such transformations are not indifferent in every respect; but they do

---

30) „Man kann einen Satz umformen, indem man das Verb aus dem Aktiv ins Passiv umsetzt und zugleich das Akkusativ-Objekt zum Subjekte macht. Ebenso kann man den Dativ in den Nominativ umwandeln und zugleich „geben" durch ‚empfangen' ersetzen." (Frege 1918-1919a: 64)

31) „[E]s darf nicht verkannt werden, dass man denselben Sinn, denselben Gedanken verschieden ausdrücken kann, wobei denn also die Verschiedenheit nicht eine solche des Sinnes, sondern nur eine der Auffassung, Beleuchtung, Färbung des Sinnes ist und für die Logik nicht in Betracht kommt." (Frege 1892b: 196, n. 7)

32) „Auch die Sprache kann ja denselben Gedanken in verschiedener Weise ausdrücken, indem sie bald diesen, bald jenen Eigennamen zum grammatischen Subjekt macht. Man sagt wohl, dass diese verschiedenen Ausdrucksweisen nicht wertig seien. Das ist richtig. Es ist aber zu beachten, dass die Sprache den Gedanken nicht nur ausdrückt, sondern ihm eine besondere Beleuchtung oder Färbung gibt. Und diese kann verschieden sein, auch der Gedanke derselbe ist." (Frege 1969[1906]: 209)

not touch the thought, they do not touch what is true or false[33]. If the inadmissibility of such transformations were generally admitted then all deeper logical investigation would be hindered. It is just as important to neglect distinctions that do not touch the heart of the matter as to make distinctions which concern what is essential. (Frege 1918-1919a: 64/1956: 296)[34]

Nowhere does Frege include distinctions in meaning as observed in (34)-(35) in the thoughts expressed by the sentences. For Frege, the distinctions bear only on the tone. The parallel between sense and construal finally collapses.

Now, one may ask what motivated Frege to refuse to include the contrast between 'horse' and 'steed', 'X is in front of Y' and 'Y is behind X', and the active and the passive in the thought expressed by a sentence in which these expressions occur. Indeed, this is the place where Frege's Constraint comes into play. Any speakers of English competent with the use of the words 'horse' and 'steed' judge (36a) and (36b) to have the same truth value:

(36) a. This is a horse ridden by the Queen.
b. This is a steed ridden by the Queen.

---

33) This observation is not quite correct, because a passive sentence sometimes has a different truth condition from the corresponding active sentence, as Chomsky (1957) famously observes:

> […] we can describe circumstances in which a 'quantificational' sentence such as "everyone in the room knows at least two languages" may be true, while the corresponding passive "at least two languages are known by everyone in the room" is false, under the normal interpretation of these sentences – e.g., if one person in the room knows only French and German, and another only Spanish and Italian. This indicates that not even the weakest semantic relation (factual equivalence) holds in general between active and passive. (Chomsky 1957: 100-101)

34) „Man kann einen Satz umformen, indem man das Verb aus dem Aktiv ins Passiv umsetzt und zugleich das Akkusativ-Objekt zum Subjekte macht. Ebenso kann man den Dativ in den Nominativ umwandeln und zugleich ‚geben' durch ‚empfangen' ersetzen. Gewiss sind solche Umformungen nicht in jeder Hinsicht gleichgültig; aber sie berühren den Gedanken nicht, sie berühren das nicht, was wahr oder falsch ist. Wenn allgemein die Unzulässigkeit solcher Umformungen anerkannt würde, so wäre damit jede tiefere logische Untersuchung verhindert. Es ist ebenso wichtig, Unterscheidungen zu unterlassen, welche den Kern der Sache nicht berühren, wie Unterscheidungen zu machen, welche das Wesentliche betreffen." (Frege 1918-1919a: 64)

Chapter 3   Incomplete Understanding and Construal

Evans (1982: 18) proposed to interpret Frege's Constraint as "the single constraint Frege imposed upon his notion of thought". If there is no other criterion of difference for thoughts, Evans (1982: 20) argued, the fact that there is no difference in cognitive value between (36a) and (36b) implies that the thought expressed by (36a) is the same as that expressed by (36b), in conformity with Frege's (1918-1919a: 63/1956: 295) view. It is because Frege's Constraint gives the result that 'horse' (*Pferd*) and 'steed' (*Ross*) or 'cart-horse' (*Gaul*) and 'mare' (*Mähre*) do not differ in sense that Frege (1918-1919a: 63/1956: 295) considered the difference between these pairs of words external to the thought[35].

The most plausible interpretation of Frege's distinction between the 'morning star / the evening star' cases and the 'horse / steed' cases is that it is semantic competence that sustains Frege's Constraint. It is part of semantic competence in German to be able to recognize the cognitive synonymy between 'Pferd' and 'Ross' or 'Gaul' and 'Mähre', whereas competent speakers of German are not required to assent to the cognitive synonymy between 'Morgenstern' and 'Abendstern'. The contrast between 'X is in front of Y' and 'Y is behind X' in English belongs to the 'horse / steed' cases. Even if someone judges (35a) to be true while rejecting (35b), it is not justified to conclude that 'X is in front of Y' and 'Y is behind X' have different senses in English. Rather, this would suggest that the person has no ability to recognize that the two sentences have the same sense. Any person competent in English is required to know that 'in front of' is an antonym of 'behind'. If Frege's 'rationality' did not refer to semantic competence, Frege's treatment of the 'horse / steed' cases would remain a mystery. Suppose that Frege's 'rationality' refers to rationality in the non-linguistic sense of the term. Anyone is rational in the non-linguistic sense if "[her] head is intact, in good mechanical order, not diseased, not broken" (Millikan 1993: 289) or if she has the "ability and disposition to conform to the principles of logic on an *a priori* basis" (Boghossian 1994: 42). In this construal, if someone rational happened not to know that 'steed' was synonymous with 'horse', thus taking different attitudes toward (36a) and (36b), we would be compelled to say that the two sentences express different thoughts. But this is not what Frege says. Frege's Constraint thus serves to deprive those who are not

---

35) This interpretation raises a problem for mathematical statements such as (i)-(ii).
  (i) $2^2 = 4$
  (ii) $2 + 2 = 4$
Burge (2012: 56) points out that (i) and (ii) express different thoughts even if no rational subject takes different attitudes toward them. I will leave this issue open.

175

semantically competent with the relevant terms of the right to determine the identity of concepts. It does not matter whether there is anyone who accepts (35a)-(36a) while rejecting (35b)-(36b). Such a person, if any, will simply be deemed semantically irrational.

The interpretation that the applicability of Frege's Constraint depends on semantic competence has a textual basis, albeit an indirect one. It is in the course of the discussion concerning poetic devices exploited by various languages that Frege mentions the words under consideration, namely 'horse' (*Pferd*), 'steed' (*Ross*), 'cart-horse' (*Gaul*) and 'mare' (*Mähre*):

> An indicative sentence often contains, as well as a thought and the assertion, a third component over which the assertion does not extend[36]. This is often said to act on the feelings, the mood of the hearer or to arouse his imagination. Words like "alas" and "thank God" belong here. Such constituents of sentences are more noticeably prominent in poetry, but are seldom wholly absent from prose. […] On the other hand, the constituents of language, to which I want to call attention here, make the translation of poetry very difficult, even make a complete translation almost always impossible, for it is in precisely that in which poetic value largely consists that languages differ most. It makes no difference to the thought whether I use the word "horse" or "steed" or "cart-horse" or "mare". The assertive force does not extend over that in which these words differ. What is called mood, fragrance, illumination in a poem, what is portrayed by cadence and rhythm, does not belong to the thought. (Frege 1918-1919a: 63/1956: 295)[37]

Here Frege evidently talks about poetic effects produced by the use of natural languages rather than mental processes. Mental processes have neither cadence nor

---

36) For Frege (1918-1919a: 62/1956: 294, 1918-1919b: 152/1997: 356), an indicative sentence contains a thought and an assertion, although language usually has no special marker for assertion. The corresponding interrogative sentence contains the same thought and, in addition, a request. It follows that grasping a thought, in Frege's view, means entertaining a thought without necessarily judging or asserting it as true or false (Heck 2002: 5). Frege's view is a forerunner of Austin's (1962/1975) distinction between meaning and force. Contrary to Frege's remark, however, language apparently has an expression which expresses assertion. As Austin (1962: 90) states, 'I state that P' is unambiguously an assertion. Frege's remark must be held to mean that language has no special morpheme that is a constituent of P and indicates, within the same clause, that P has the force of an assertion (Sakai 2019: 266, n. 6).

Chapter 3   Incomplete Understanding and Construal

rhythm; expressions of natural language do (when used). Mental processes are not translated; expressions of natural languages are. What distinguishes 'horse' from 'cat' can readily be translated into another language, whereas what distinguishes 'horse' from 'steed' can hardly be preserved in any pair of expressions of the target language(s). It does not make sense to talk about poetic value where there is no language. It is the word 'steed', not any mental processes supervenient on uses of the word, that has a different poetic value from the word 'horse'. If so, whatever distinguishes (36a) and (36b) is something linguistic intrinsically tied to the English words 'horse' and 'steed'. Following Evans (1982: 20), let us call this something 'poetic coloring'. Evans says that the difference in poetic coloring between (36a) and (36b) can never be the basis for holding only one of the statements to be true (see also Burge 2012: 59-60, 63, 66). Frege's Constraint therefore allows us to conclude that (36a) and (36b) express the same thought.

What is of particular interest here is that this conclusion cannot be obtained if someone can rationally take different attitude toward the two statements. Anyone who takes different attitudes towards (36a) and (36b) must be considered irrational. But in what sense? The deviant person in question believes the difference in poetic coloring to affect the truth values taken by the statements in (36). As Frege (1892a/1997) suggests, it is irrelevant to rationality considerations whether the subject discerns a difference in poetic coloring in given pairs of sentences:

We can now recognize three levels of difference between words, expressions, or whole sentences. The difference may concern at most the ideas, or the sense but not the *Bedeutung*, or, finally, the *Bedeutung* as well. With respect to the

---

37) „Ein Behauptungssatz enthält außer einem Gedanken und der Behauptung oft noch ein Drittes, auf das sich die Behauptung nicht erstreckt. Das soll nicht selten auf das Gefühl, die Stimmung des Hörers wirken oder seine Einbildungskraft anregen. Wörter wie ‚leider‘, ‚gottlob‘ gehören hierher. Solche Bestandteile des Satzes treten in der Dichtung stärker hervor, fehlen aber auch in der Prosa selten ganz. […] Dagegen erschweren die Bestandteile der Sprache, auf die ich hier aufmerksam machen möchte, die Übersetzung von Dichtungen sehr, ja machen eine vollkommene Übersetzung fast immer unmöglich; denn gerade in ihnen, auf denen der dichterische Wert zu einem großen Teile beruht, unterscheiden sich die Sprachen am meisten. Ob ich das Wort ‚Pferd‘ oder ‚Roß‘ oder ‚Gaul‘ oder ‚Mähre‘ gebrauche, macht keinen Unterschied im Gedanken. Die behauptende Kraft erstreckt sich nicht auf das, wodurch sich diese Wörter unterscheiden. Was man Stimmung, Luft, Beleuchtung in einer Dichtung nennen kann, was durch Tonfall und Rhythmus gemalt wird, gehört nicht zum Gedanken.“ (Frege 1918-1919a: 63)

first level, it is to be noted that, on account of the uncertain connection of ideas with words, a difference may hold for one person, which another does not find. The difference between a translation and the original text should properly not overstep the first level. To the possible differences here belong also the colouring and shading which poetic eloquence seeks to give to the sense. (Frege 1892a: 30-31/1997: 155)[38]

We cannot tell a lie by replacing 'horse' with 'steed', in the same way that substituting 'but' for 'and' leaves the truth of the statement intact (Frege 1892a: 45/1997: 167, Grice 1989: 361, Blakemore 2002: 12ff, Carston 2002: 108, Burge 2012: 59-60, 63, 66). Since poetic coloring is what linguistic expressions more or less have, the deviance in question should be considered linguistic in character. At stake in Frege's Constraint is minimal semantic competence. The subject who dissents from only one of the statements in (36) may be rational otherwise, but she is linguistically irrational.

I am not claiming that Frege's notion of sense or mode of presentation should be identified with conventional linguistic meaning. The point made here is perfectly compatible with the view that not all senses are conventionally associated with a particular linguistic expression or that senses are what linguistic expressions have when employed in context. The claim that minimal semantic competence is sufficient to see the truth-conditional equivalence between (36a) and (36b), for instance, merely implies that 'horse' and 'steed' share the same sense in this particular pair of statements, not implying that the two words have the same sense in all contexts or independently of any context. In fact, as will be discussed in Chapter 4, it is erroneous to attach a sense or construal to a linguistic expression independently of any context. To employ Recanati's (1993: xiiff, 1995: 96) terms, linguistic modes of presentation must not be conflated with psychological modes of

---

38) „Wir können nun drei Stufen der Verschiedenheit von Wörtern, Ausdrücken und ganzen Sätzen erkennen. Entweder betrifft der Unterschied höchstens die Vorstellungen, oder den Sinn aber nicht die Bedeutung, oder endlich auch die Bedeutung. In Bezug auf die erste Stufe ist zu bemerken, dass, wegen der unsicheren Verbindung der Vorstellungen mit den Worten, für den einen eine Verschiedenheit bestehen kann, die der andere nicht findet. Der Unterschied der Übersetzung von der Urschrift soll eigentlich die erste Stufe nicht überschreiten. Zu den hier noch möglichen Unterschieden gehören die Färbungen und Beleuchtungen, welche Dichtkunst [und] Beredsamkeit dem Sinne zu geben suchen." (Frege 1892a: 30-31)

Chapter 3   Incomplete Understanding and Construal

presentation. Conventional linguistic meaning, as Burge (1990: 40/2007: 254) states, is "a complex idealization of conventional use and understanding". If sense and construal were context-independent entities uniquely attached to conventional linguistic signs, there could never be such divergence as observed between Adam and his doctor, each of whom uses the word 'arthritis' with his own construal attached to it. Returning to (36), a semantically competent person as understood here has the ability to grasp the sense expressed by each of the relevant terms in (36), in this particular context, clearly enough to see that one of the statements cannot be true without the other also being true. As Burge (1990: 45/2007: 259) points out, Frege held the view that "grasping a sense or thought is a matter of degree, and thoroughly grasping thoughts is an achievement worthy of some renown" as it typically occurs in mathematics (cf. Burge 2012: 60). On the other hand, "for successful communication and ordinary thinking", Burge (1990: 46/2007: 260) says, one can grasp senses "even though one lacks a 'clear' or 'thorough' 'grasp' of the sense". Semantic competence required for the application of Frege's Constraint should be understood in the latter context. A semantically competent person can fail to see the equivalence between (23a) and (23b), but not that between (35a)-(36a) and (35b)-(36b). Frege's Constraint thus fixes a lower bound on semantic competence. Incomplete understanding, properly understood, entails minimal semantic competence. A person ignorant of the equivalence between (23a) and (23b) can be credited with the concept of *the morning star* and *the evening star*, while a person ignorant of the equivalence between (35a)-(36a) and (35b)-(36b) cannot be credited with the public concepts expressed by 'horse', 'steed', 'in front of' and 'behind'.

Since Frege's Constraint merely sets a lower bound on semantic competence, one can freely set a higher standard as long as it is better suited for one's purpose. By stating that (35a) and (35b) differ in meaning, Langacker (2008: 75-76) proposes the notion of linguistic competence unobtainable from mere truth considerations. The standard Langacker sets is not independent of Frege's Constraint, since accepting the former implies accepting the latter. On the basis of the contrast between (35a) and (35b), Langacker (2008: 75) insists that "[t]he same objective situation can be observed and described from any number of different vantage points, resulting in different construals". For Langacker, a vantage point invoked by an expression is part of the meaning of that expression. Langacker's claim presupposes that (35a) and (35b) describe the same objective situation; otherwise it would be virtually useless to compare the vantage points invoked by 'X is in front of Y' and 'Y is behind X'. For this presupposition to hold, it must be the case that (35a) entails (35b), or vice versa[39]. To say that (35a) entails (35b) is to say that a semantically competent person cannot hold (35a) to be true without holding (35b) to be true. The same consequence is drawn by applying Frege's Constraint to (35). Langacker is implicitly committed to Frege's Constraint in his emphasis on the notion of vantage point. Langacker's view can be interpreted as suggesting that Frege's Constraint does not provide a sufficient condition for two statements to express the same thought. The constraint says that for two statements to express the same thought, it must be the case that competent speakers judge the two statements to have the same truth value. But it leaves open the possibility that two statements which are judged to be truth-conditionally equivalent nevertheless express different thoughts (Dummett 1991: 298, Burge 2012: 56). Thus, competent speakers must recognize the truth-conditional equivalence between (35a) and (35b). But this does not mean, for Langacker, that (35a) and (35b) express the same thought. Competent speakers are required to understand that (35a) and (35b) depict the same situation from different vantage points. In dealing with various construals imposed by grammatical constructions, Langacker sets a higher standard for semantic competence than Frege's Constraint suggests.

There is certainly a sense in which Frege's Constraint cannot be applied without begging the question. To determine whether (29) above constitutes a Frege case, for example, we must make sure that the speaker is semantically rational about the use of 'cilantro' and 'coriander'. To determine whether the speaker is semantically rational about the use of 'cilantro' and 'coriander', we must show that her attitudes toward (29) embody a genuine Frege case. Frege's Constraint on its own is of little use in determining whether (29a) and (29b) express two distinct thoughts or the speaker fails to recognize that they are dealing with a single thought. But this is not necessarily a defect of Frege's Constraint, because, in general, the final arbiter of linguistic competence is speakers' intuition (Langacker 1976: 356). When we understand Chomsky's (1965: 22) remark that (37a) and

---

39) Although (35a) and (35b) happen to entail each other, mutual entailment is in general not necessary. Recall that, as remarked in Section 3.3, (i) and (ii) can describe the same objective situation:

(i) Mary saw the glass with water in it.

(ii) Mary saw the container with liquid in it.

(i) entails (ii), but not vice versa. To say that two sentences can describe one and the same situation is not to say that the two sentences share the same truth condition.

180

(37b), but not (38a) and (38b), are cognitively synonymous, we trust Chomsky's linguistic competence in English:

(37) a. I expected a specialist to examine John.
    b. I expected John to be examined by a specialist.

((37a-b): Chomsky 1965: 22)

(38) a. I persuaded a specialist to examine John.
    b. I persuaded John to be examined by a specialist.

((38a-b): Chomsky 1965: 22)

Higginbotham (1998b) reports what happened in the Texas Linguistic Forum of 1959:

At the Texas Linguistic Forum of 1959 there was a panel discussion of Noam Chomsky's then novel theory of generative grammar, in the course of which Chomsky remarked by way of illustrating a general point that a certain expression of English – call it X – was not an English sentence. One of the panellists asked Chomsky how he knew that. Had he done a survey of speakers? Had he consulted a sufficiently large corpus, verifying that X and expressions like it did not occur? Chomsky replied, 'What do you mean, how do I know? I am a native speaker of the English language.' (Higginbotham 1998b: 429)

Our trust in Chomsky's competence derives partly from the fact that his judgment about (37)-(38) agrees with ours. Chomsky is rational because he makes the same judgment about (37)-(38) as we do, and he makes the same judgment about (37)-(38) as we do because he is rational. Chomsky's (1965: 3) assumption of 'an ideal speaker-listener' may enable one to close the loop, as far as the study of syntax is concerned. An ideal speaker-listener lives "in a completely homogeneous speech-community" and "knows its language perfectly and is unaffected by such grammatically irrelevant conditions as memory limitations, distractions, shifts of attention and interest, and errors (random or characteristic) in applying his knowledge of the language in actual performance" (ibid.). In the study of semantics, however, the loop cannot be closed, because speakers' intuitions vary to a considerable degree. Thus, as stated in Section 1.3.4, some people say that twater is not water and others say that twater is a kind of water. Likewise, as stated in Section 2.5.3, some say that cats are necessarily animals and others disagree. Such variations are related to the fact that understanding is a matter of degree. A person who knows the chemical makeup of water knows more about water than a person who does not. A person who believes that all cats are robots probably misunderstands something about cats, even if he is able to correctly identify cats. Semantic competence is not an all-or-nothing matter. If anyone proposes a method to unambiguously determine whether or not a person is semantically competent, it is most likely that the method is poorly conceived. By accepting Frege's Constraint, one is merely committed to the claim that there is a boundary between competence and non-competence and that competence does not entail full understanding. The boundary need not be sharp, and we need not fully understand a concept in order to be competent with the use of the word expressing that concept. It is therefore safe to conclude that Brown's (2003, 2004) and Wikforss's (2006) claim that Frege's Constraint cannot be combined with incomplete understanding is unwarranted. *Pace* Burge (2012: 60), Frege's Constraint presupposes the possibility for a semantically competent person to be ignorant of some aspects of the meaning of a linguistic expression.

A remaining question is how it is justified to credit Adam with the concept of *arthritis*. Assuming, following Burge (1979a/2007), that Adam is competent with the use of 'arthritis' despite his incomplete grasp of *arthritis*, it is possible to apply Frege's Constraint to Adam's case. Since Adam takes different attitudes toward (27a) and (27b) above, that is, he construes 'arthritis' in a different fashion from his fellows, it seems to follow that he attaches to the term 'arthritis' an idiosyncratic concept different from this community's concept of *arthritis*. In fact, this is the reason that Kimbrough (1998) insists that the notion of incomplete understanding is in conflict with Frege's Constraint (see also Elugardo 1993: 367-368). As said above, Wikforss (2006) suggests that incomplete understanding implies irrationality while Frege's Constraint presupposes rationality. Kimbrough stresses that Burge's notion of incomplete understanding is tied to what Kimbrough (1998: 472) calls "liberal criteria for possession of concepts", according to which "competent speakers typically possess the same concepts as their fellows despite ignorance of or mistakes about the conditions for making true applications of those concepts". Liberal criteria for possession of concepts are what makes it possible to ascribe to Adam the concept of *arthritis* despite his only partial understanding of the concept. However, Kimbrough (1998: 478, 480, 482) points out that this is the possibility denied by Frege's Constraint[40]. Given Frege's Constraint, the mere fact that Adam doubts the equivalence between (29a) and (29b) assumed in his

Chapter 3 Incomplete Understanding and Construal

community forces us to conclude that, unlike his fellows, he attaches different construals, and hence concepts, to 'arthritis' and 'a rheumatoid disease of the joints only' (Kimbrough 1998: 480, Wikforss 2015: 163). To avoid such conceptual fragmentation, the Fregean must, Kimbrough (1998: 481) suggests, "block the excessive application" of Frege's Constraint:

> The general strategy is to block the excessive application of DDT [= the differential dubitability test = Frege's Constraint] by calling into question apparent expressions of belief and doubt. A Fregean move of this requires fairly strict criteria of concept possession. For example, the Fregean may claim that understanding a concept consists in knowledge of the conditions for truly applying that concept. (Kimbrough 1998: 481)

But requiring "fairly strict criteria of concept possession" goes against the conception of semantic competence alluded to by Frege's Constraint. The question of how liberal criteria for possession of concepts are reconciled with the notion of construal will be addressed in Chapter 4.

3.6 Identity and Distinctness of Concepts

By saying that a minimally rational person may judge (23a) and (23b), but not (35a)-(36a) and (35b)-(36b), to have the same truth value, Frege partially defines what it is like for a person to be minimally rational. It is minimally rational to endorse (23a) without endorsing (23b), while it is not minimally rational to ascribe falsity to (35a)-(36a) but not to (35b)-(36b). It was only after a long period of scientific investigation that the identity between the morning star and the evening star was discovered. It is not difficult to imagine a community in which the identity discovered by astronomers long ago is still unfamiliar to the general public. The possible existence of such a community is sufficient to establish that the

---

40) In Kimbrough's account, Frege's Constraint also denies the possibility that Adam's community and Adam₂'s community may turn out to share one and the same concept, since the two communities construe 'arthritis' in mutually incompatible ways. Contrary to Kimbrough's view, Frege's Constraint on its own does not deny that possibility, because differing senses does not entail differing references. The denial of the possibility follows only on the assumption that sense determines reference, an assumption to which this chapter is not committed, as said in Section 3.4.

183

equivalence between (23a) and (23b) does not belong to the linguistic sphere. This can be rephrased with the help of the notion of (cognitive) synonymy. Depending on whether we conceive synonymy as an empirical fact or an *a priori* truth, we can say either that competent speakers do not have to know the synonymy between 'the morning star' and 'the evening star', or that the discovery that the morning star = the evening star does not make 'the morning star' and 'the evening star' (cognitively) synonymous. In his attempt to construct an internalist semantic theory, Katz (1972, 1978, 1997) held the view that knowledge of meaning includes knowledge of synonymy:

> We know sense properties and relations of expressions on the basis the speaker's *a priori* linguistic intuitions in clear cases. For example, our linguistic intuition tells us that "Sherlock Holmes loves his mother" is meaningful, that "The number seventeen loves its mother" is nonsense, that "Sherlock Holmes dusted the table" is ambiguous, that "sister" and "female sibling" are synonymous, that "open" and "closed" are antonymous, that "unmarried bachelor" is redundant," that "Squares are rectangles" is analytic, and that "Squares are circles" is contradictory. (Katz 1997: 22-23)

Since, as suggested in Chapter 1, the current semantic theories in linguists are mostly internalist, albeit by varying degrees, I shall opt for the internalist construal, saying that the discovery that the morning star = the evening star does not make 'the morning star' and 'the evening star' synonymous. In the standard internalist conception, synonymy is an *a priori* truth, that is, it is not something to be discovered and semantic rationality involves recognition of synonymy. By saying that 'sister' and 'female sibling' are synonymous, Katz (1997) commits himself to the claim that a linguistically competent person cannot take different attitudes toward (39a) and (39b) and that (40) is not something to be discovered:

(39) a. Mary has a sister.
    b. Mary has a female sibling.
(40) A sister is a female sibling.

For those who agree with Katz's judgment, holding only one of the statements in (39) to be true or denying (40) is not betraying an incomplete grasp of the concept of *sister*, but failing to grasp the concept of *sister*, that is, making a linguistic error

Chapter 3   Incomplete Understanding and Construal

about the word 'sister', in the sense defined in Chapter 2 (cf. Schwartz 1977: 38-39).

By contrast, a person who denies that the morning star is the evening star thereby does not make any linguistic error (Schwartz 1977: 25). Quine's (1943) remark confirms this point:

> To say that two names designate the same object is not to say that they are synonymous, that is, that they have the same meaning. To determine the synonymity of two names or other expressions it should be sufficient to understand the expressions; but to determine that two names designate the same object, it is commonly necessary to investigate the world. The names 'Evening Star' and 'Morning Star', for example, are not synonymous, having been applied each to a certain ball of matter according to a different criterion. But it appears from astronomical investigations that it is the same ball, the same planet, in both cases; that is, the names designate the same thing. The identity: (14) Evening Star = Morning Star is a truth of astronomy, not following merely from the words. (Quine 1943: 119)

Even Kripke, who, as remarked in Section 1.3.3, advanced the view that all identity statements were necessary if true in the actual world, acknowledged that the identity between the morning star (Phosphorus) and the evening star (Hesperus) was not *a priori*:

> [...] according to Mrs. Marcus, a dictionary should be able to tell you whether or not 'John' and 'Joe' are names of the same object. Of course, I do not know what ideal dictionaries should do, but ordinary proper names do not satisfy this requirement. You certainly *can*, in the case of ordinary proper names, make quite empirical discoveries that, let's say, Hesperus is Phosphorus, though we thought otherwise. [...] Even now, we could conceivably discover that we were wrong in supposing that Hesperus was Phosphorus. Maybe the astronomers made an error. (Kripke 1971/1993: 169-170)

This assertion also applies to general terms. Thus, Burge (1979a: 76/2007: 103) exploits Frege's Constraint to detect differences in sense between coextensive predicates such as 'water' and 'H_2O' as well as between coreferential singular terms (cf. Wikforss 2006: 167)[41]. A person who lacks the knowledge of the chemical

185

makeup of water would endorse (41a) without endorsing (41b):

(41) a. Water is not fit to drink.
      b. H_2O is not fit to drink. ((41a-b): Burge 1979a: 76/2007: 103)

In Burge's (1982/2007) 'water' thought experiment, it is hypothesized, following Putnam (1973, 1975), that "the scientific community on Earth has determined that the chemical structure of water is H_2O" and that "there are numerous scattered individuals on Earth [...] untouched by the scientific developments" (Burge 1982: 100-101/2007: 85). In Burge's view, even though the terms 'water' and 'H_2O' denote one and the same kind, *water* and *H_2O* are different concepts, in that "'[w]ater' may express or indicate one way of thinking of the kind – 'H_2O' another" (Burge 1982: 120, n. 15/2007: 94, n. 15). Consequently, ignorance of expert knowledge does not entail any incomplete linguistic understanding of 'water'. This position is highly compatible with Putnam's (1975):

> [...] when we said [...] that to be water something has to be H_2O we did not mean, as we made clear, that the speaker has to know this. It is only by confusing metaphysical necessity with epistemological necessity that one can conclude that, if the (metaphysically necessary) truth-condition for being water is being H_2O, then "water" must be synonymous with H_2O – in which case it is certainly a term of science. (Putnam 1975: 158)

Chomsky (2000: 189/2003b: 281) insists that English has no word 'H_2O', while chemistry has no word 'water' except in informal contexts, making it implausible to include the identity between 'water' and 'H_2O' in the knowledge of English required for linguistic competence. In Bromberger's (1997: 161-162) words, 'water' belongs to the native vocabulary, while 'H_2O' belongs to nomenclature.

To employ Place's (1956) terms, the verb 'is' in 'A sister is a female sibling' or 'A square is an equilateral rectangle' is an 'is' of definition, whereas 'is' in 'Water is H_2O' or 'Consciousness is a process in the brain' is an 'is' of composition:

> The all but universally accepted view that an assertion of identity between

---

41) As remarked in Section 1.3.3, Putnam (1992) is not committed to the idea that 'water' and 'H_2O' is coextensive. The relation between the two terms will be discussed in detail in Chapter 5.

consciousness and brain processes can be ruled out on logical grounds alone, derives, I suspect, from a failure to distinguish between what we may call the 'is' of definition and the 'is' of composition. The distinction I have in mind here is the difference between the function of the word 'is' in statements like 'a square is an equilateral rectangle', 'red is a colour', 'to understand an instruction is to be able to act appropriately under the appropriate circumstances', and its function in statements like 'his table is an old packing case', 'her hat is a bundle of straw tied together with string', 'a cloud is a mass of water droplets or other particles in suspension'. [...] Statements like 'a square is an equilateral rectangle' are necessary statements which are true by definition. Statements like 'his table is an old packing case', on the other hand, are contingent statements which have to be verified by observation. (Place 1956: 45)

Negating an 'is' of definition leads to a self-contradiction, whereas there is nothing self-contradictory about such statements as 'Water is not H_2O' or 'A cloud is composed not of tiny particles in suspension but of a dense mass of fibrous tissue' (ibid.: 46-47). Correspondingly, Burge states that (41a) expresses a different thought from (41b).

Note, incidentally, that, if the notion of sense is extended to cover both singular terms and predicates in this fashion, the similarity between Frege's and Langacker's conceptions of meaning becomes all the more evident. These considerations lend support to the view that sense or construal is part of a concept. The discovery that the morning star is the evening star is not the discovery that 'the morning star' and 'the evening star' are synonyms but the discovery that the two terms share the same conceptual content while being associated with different construals. Crucially, even after the discovery, the different construals remain attached to these terms. As Schroeter (2008: 126, n. 32) puts it in terms of 'mental files' (cf. Recanati 1993, 2016), "[i]f Lois Lane comes to believe that Clark Kent is Superman, it is not rationally incumbent on her to immediately change her mental filing system, reconnecting her standing CLARK and SUPERTMAN thoughts to a new SUPERMAN-CLARK file" (see also Bonardi 2019: 494, 496, 507, n. 44). Having two distinct files does "not *eo ipso* commit her to there being two distinct things represented" (Schroeter 2008: 131, n. 33).

Strawson (1974/2004: 43-46) emphasizes the peculiarity of identity statements of the form 'X is Y' in comparison to ordinary predications. That identity statements cannot be assimilated to ordinary predications is shown by a model in which a person's beliefs about individuals are represented by dots and lines. When the person learns (42a), the dot corresponding to Caesar is joined to the dot corresponding to Brutus:

(42) a. Caesar loved Brutus.
      b. Caesar loves himself.
      c. Tully is Cicero.

When the person learns (42b), a line emanating from the dot representing Caesar curls back on the dot of origin. Acquisition of further knowledge about individuals can thus be modeled by the addition of further lines. Strawson claims that this is not the case with identity statements like (42c):

But when it is an identity-statement containing two names from which he receives new information, he adds no further lines. He has at least enough lines already; at least enough lines and certainly one too many dots. So what he does is to eliminate one dot of two, at the same time transferring to the remaining one of the two all those lines and names which attach to the eliminated dot and are not already exactly reproduced at the surviving dot. (Strawson 1974/2004: 45-46)

Millikan (1997: 510) points out that this 'Strawson-model' yields "strikingly unFregean results". According to the Fregean view, even if two terms turn out to share the same conceptual content, the original two concepts expressed by the terms remain distinct:

The Fregean view assumes, on the contrary, that insertion of a sameness marker, hence change in the use of the marked terms, has no bearing on content. Placing a mental equals sign between <Cicero> and <Tully> has no effect on the representational value of either, even if Cicero is not in fact Tully. (Millikan 1997: 515)

[…] it is the introduction of this second way of marking identity, used for identities not known a priori to hold [e.g. Cicero is Tully.], that allows the Fregean thinker to identify referents without merging his thoughts of them. This second identity marker, we suppose, functions like a mental equals sign. It

188

Chapter 3   Incomplete Understanding and Construal

marks two thoughts as being thoughts of the same, not by merging or destroying either, but simply by flagging them for use together in mediate inference. (Millikan 1997: 513)

The terms 'the morning star' and 'the evening star' remain associated with different construals even after the discovery that the morning star is none other than the evening star. The same holds for 'water' and 'H₂O. We can perhaps say, following Putnam (1954: 118), that sentences of the form 'F is G' have a different logical structure from sentences of the form 'F is F', even for those who know that F and G corefer.

If construal were not part of the meaning or concept expressed by a word, the discovery that the reference of 'morning star' was identical with the reference of 'the morning star' would *ipso facto* make the two terms perfect synonyms. This conception would make it difficult to explain that Mary is considered semantically competent in (43a) but not in (43b):

(43) a. Mary believes that the morning star is more remote from the earth than the evening star.
      b. Mary believes that bachelors are taller than unmarried adult men.

It does not matter that some people may find no difference between (43a) and (43b). As said earlier, the standard for semantic competence, namely the boundary between linguistic error and incomplete understanding may vary from context to context. What matters is that there would be many people who say that in (43a) what Mary does not know is astronomy (Farkas 2006: 337) while in (43b) what Mary does not know is not marriage studies but English. By contrast, there would be few who say that in (43b) what Mary does not know is marriage studies while in (43a) what Mary does not know is not astronomy but English. To have minimal semantic competence, a speaker is required to know that 'the morning star' and 'the evening star' are associated with different construals, but is not required to know that the two terms share the same conceptual content. For full mastery of the concepts expressed by the terms, on the contrary, she is required to know that they share the same conceptual content, but the full mastery of the concepts is not required for semantic competence with the use of the terms. Incomplete understanding of a concept requires minimal semantic competence with the term which expresses the concept, but not full mastery of the concept.

189

As remarked in Section 3.3, Kimbrough (1998) and Wikforss's (2001, 2004) insist that the notion of incomplete understanding is inapplicable to Adam, because it may turn out that arthritis afflicts one's thigh and Adam may be as right as $Adam_2$ in thinking that he has what he refers to as 'arthritis' in his thigh. Burge's assumption that Adam's and $Adam_2$'s communities have different concepts expressed by 'arthritis', Wikforss argues, is unwarranted insofar as it is possible that experts, rather than Adam, are plagued with incomplete understanding:

'Arthritis afflicts the joints only' plays the role of a meaning-giving characterization – one on which the experts all agree and which is taken to be central to the meaning of 'arthritis'. However, since meaning-giving characterizations are revisable, it can no longer be concluded that the speaker who does not accept this characterization has an incomplete understanding of the concept of arthritis and makes a conceptual error when uttering 'I have arthritis in my thigh'. The experts would take him to have made a mistake, of course, but the experts themselves may be wrong. Consequently it cannot be concluded that 'arthritis' must express a different concept in the counterfactual community. The conclusion to be drawn is not that the counterfactual community has a different 'arthritis'-concept, but that one of the communities (ours or theirs) is mistaken in its 'meaning-giving characterizations'. (Wikforss 2001: 223-224)

Wikforss (2014: 2.1) echoes this point. Wikforss's claim conflicts with linguistic data, however. Suppose that $Adam_2$'s community's word 'arthritis' is translated as 'tharthritis in Adam's community's language, and that, as Wikforss imagines, it has finally been discovered that the two terms denote one and the same disease. Intuitively, unlike (44a), (44b) sounds informative even after the discovery.

(44) a. Arthritis is arthritis.
      b. Arthritis is thathritis.

(44a) is more like (45a), while (44b) is more like (45b):

(45) a. A bachelor is an unmarried adult man.
      b. A cloud is a mass of water droplets or other particles in suspension. (Place 1954: 45)

Chapter 3   Incomplete Understanding and Construal

This suggests that the discovery that the reference of 'arthritis' is identical with the reference of 'tharthritis' does not make the two terms perfect synonyms. The intuitive contrast between (44a) and (44b) stems from the fact that, before the relevant discovery, 'arthritis' and 'tharthritis' construed the same ailment in different manners, in the same way that 'the morning star' and 'the evening star' construed the same planet (or star) from different perspectives, as in (25). Competence with the use of 'the morning star' and 'the evening star' requires some awareness of the construals outlined in (25) even though they are erroneous. Likewise, speakers who are fully competent with the use of 'arthritis' and 'tharthritis' must associate these words with the construals in (46):

(46)   a. Arthritis is an inflammation of the joints only.
       b. Tharthritis is a rheumatoid ailment that may afflict a person's thigh.

Accordingly, in (47a), Adam is no more competent with the construals of *arthritis* and *tharthritis* than he is with the construals of *the morning star* and *the evening star* in (47b).

(47)   a. Adam believes that 'arthritis' and 'tharthritis' are perfect synonyms.
       b. Adam believes that 'the morning star' and 'the evening star' are perfect synonyms.

Adam can be qualified as fully competent with the conceptual content of *arthritis* and *tharthritis*, but not with the construals associated with the words. In (48), on the other hand, what Mary does not know is not English but the relevant discovery in medical sciences:

(48)   Mary believes that arthritis is more painful than tharthritis.

(48) is more like (43a) than (43b). Those who know that 'arthritis' and 'tharthritis' share the same conceptual content are more competent with the concepts expressed by these words than those who do not, but this knowledge is not required for minimal competence with the concepts.

To summarize, contrary to Wikforss's claim, Adam, who does not fully understand the generally accepted construal associated with 'arthritis', *ipso facto* understands the concept expressed by the word only incompletely, even if it may turn

191

out that his construal correctly determines the conceptual content expressed by the word. By contrast, experts, who believe that arthritis is found only in the joints, are *ipso facto* more competent with the use of 'arthritis' and with the concept expressed by the word, even if further scientific investigation may uncover their mistakes. They are possibly not fully competent, but this does not imply that they display an incomplete grasp of the concept. In saying that "it should be possible also for the *experts* to have an incomplete understanding of the concept they think with", Wikforss (2014: 2.1) trades upon the ambiguity of 'incomplete understanding'. Incomplete understanding is not a homogenous phenomenon (cf. Burge 2012: 65). Experts can only be plagued with incomplete understanding in the metaphysical sense, whereas laypeople like Adam suffer from incomplete understanding in the communal sense (and possibly from incomplete understanding in the metaphysical sense as well). Experts cannot have an incomplete grasp of *arthritis* in the communal sense insofar as the possible identity between *arthritis* and *tharthritis* is not part of semantic (and hence, conceptual) competence, that is, 'arthritis' and 'tharthritis' are not perfect synonyms. Even after the discovery, different construals remain attached to the words.

3.7 Minimal Semantic Competence

3.7.1 General Characterization of Minimal Semantic Competence with General Terms

I have so far argued that minimal semantic competence does not require that one be aware that 'the morning star' and 'the evening star', or 'arthritis' and 'tharthritis', share one and the same conceptual content. This is tied to the fact that the identity of the conceptual content of a concept can only be determined by empirical investigations. Construal, on the contrary, is part of conventional semantic value (Langacker 2008: 55). This suggests that semantic competence hinges more on understanding of construal than understanding of conceptual content. The foregoing discussion has demonstrated that understanding of conceptual content is often not part of semantic competence. Now, the question arises as to how much understanding of construal is required for minimal semantic competence. That we need not fully understand a concept for semantic and conceptual competence clearly does not imply that we need not understand anything at all. As noted earlier, Burge's notion of incomplete understanding rests on what Kimbrough (1998: 472) calls 'liberal criteria for possession of concepts', which allows one to say that "competent speakers typically possess the same concepts as their fellows despite ignorance of or mistakes about the conditions for making true applications of those concepts". Liberal criteria for possession of concepts, however, must not be so liberal as to credit a person who construes 'arthritis' as, say, a mountain or a castle with the concept of *arthritis* (Burge 1993: 325/2007: 306, Valente 2019: 320). Now, is Adam, who believes that arthritis can strike one's thigh, minimally competent with the construal attached to the public word 'arthritis'?

As stated in Section 3.5, semantic competence, though psychologically real, is not an all-or-nothing affair. It is not appropriate to unambiguously classify every speaker into either side, nor is it correct to say that there is no boundary between minimal competence and non-competence. Although, ultimately, the criteria for minimal semantic competence should be stated for each lexical item, some general remarks are in order. As far as general terms are concerned, minimal semantic competence can best be spelled out in terms of what Putnam (1970) called core facts, as in (49):

(49) A person S is minimally competent in the use of a general term X iff S understands most of the core facts about X.

As remarked in Section 2.4, Putnam (1970: 197ff) claimed that knowledge of some basic facts about words, namely, core facts, is necessary and approximately sufficient to be competent in the use of the words:

> [...] there are a few facts about "lemon" or "tiger" (I shall refer to them as core facts) such that one can convey the use of "lemon" or "tiger" by simply conveying those facts. More precisely, one can frequently convey the approximate use; and still more precisely, one cannot convey the approximate use unless one gets the core facts across. (Putnam 1970: 197)

3.7.2 One-criterion Terms

Since, as Putnam (1970: 201) states, the core fact about a one-criterion word such as 'bachelor' or 'vixen' is just the necessary and sufficient condition for the word to be correctly applied, misapplying a one-criterion word is equivalent to misunderstanding the unique core fact, necessarily failing to fulfill the condition outlined in (49). The utterer of (50a) or (50b) can thus be characterized as making a linguistic error, rather than partially understanding the concept of *bachelor* or *vixen*:

(50) a. I saw a married bachelor.
     b. I have a fear of male vixens.

The word forms 'bachelor' / 'vixen' in (50) do not express the concepts of *bachelor* / *vixen*, and some reinterpretation is called for[42]. As a consequence, there can be no incomplete understanding of one-criterion concepts. Combined with this characterization of one-criterion words, (49) gives rise to (51):

(51) A speaker S is not only minimally but also normally competent in the use of a one-criterion word X iff S understands the necessary and sufficient conditions for something to count as an X.

True, speakers are commonly supposed to know more about one-criterion words. As stated in Section 2.6.2, 'being small, old, fragile, etc." may constitute the prototype of 'grandmother at a given time and place (Peacocke 1992: 3) and 'being young, high spirited, living alone' may constitute the prototype of 'bachelor' at a given time and place (Putnam 1962a: 395). Fillmore (1982a: 34) points out that the word 'bachelor' can only be fully understood against the relevant social frame (see also Quine 1960: §11, n. 1). Taylor (2003) makes clear what is included in the

---

42) Burge (1978) argues that the occurrence of the one-criterion term 'fortnight' in (i) must be interpreted literally in accordance with the community norms, i.e. it must be taken to mean a period of fourteen days rather than a period of ten days (see also Liu 2002: 387-388).

(i)   For years I believed that a fortnight was ten days, not fourteen, though of course I never believed that fourteen days were ten days. (Burge 1978: 113)

If 'fortnight' in (i) were reinterpreted as 'a period of ten days' in accordance with the speaker's idiosyncratic construal, Burge (1978: 131) claims, "the speaker would never have made a mistake in *his* use of the word 'fortnight'; for the utterance, 'A fortnight is a period of ten days', would be analytically true". Burge concludes that "[a] rational believer may, despite reflection, *dis*believe simple analytic truth" (ibid.: 138). Although I shall not go into the details of Burge's (1978) argument, it may be noted that Burge (1978: 128) concedes that (i) is "probably about language" and can be paraphrased as (ii):

(ii)   For years I believed that 'fortnight' meant ten days, not fourteen, though of course I never believed that 'fourteen days' meant ten days.

The sentences in (50), by contrast, resist this kind of paraphrase. In such nonlinguistic contexts, it is more difficult to interpret occurrences of the relevant one-criterion terms as expressing the corresponding communal concepts.

frame invoked by 'bachelor' in addition to the simple notion of marriage:

> In the first place, what we might call the bachelor frame (as well as, *mutatis mutandis*, the spinster frame) includes the notion of a marriageable age. People who have passed this age are expected to have married; only those who fail to do so are normally referred to as bachelors (or spinsters, as the case may be). People below the marriageable age are not normally categorized in term of their unmarried status. [...] There are further ramifications of the frames activated by the words *bachelor* and *spinster*.[...] the frames attribute different motives to men and women who fail to marry. A man who does not marry does so from choice; he decides against the 'commitments' of marriage. A woman who does not marry does so from necessity. Thus eligible spinster is almost a contradiction, while eligible bachelor is a normal collocation. As Robin Lakoff put it, in her study of sexism in language, the spinster 'has had her chance, and been passed by'; she is 'old unwanted goods' (1975: 32f.). (Taylor 2003: 99)

This frame is highly simplified and leaves out of account Catholic priests or people who have long-term unmarried relationships (ibid., cf. Williamson 2007: 118). The word 'bachelor' is not readily applicable to the Pope (Fillmore 1982b: 34), to the extent that he is "not covered by the frame" (Taylor 2003: 99). On the basis of these facts, Fillmore applied the notion of frame originally elaborated in the field of artificial intelligence (Minsky 1974) to the study of semantics, resulting in a framework called 'frame semantics':

> Frame semantics offers a particular way of looking at word meanings [...] By the term 'frame' I have in mind any system of concepts related in such a way that to understand any one of them you have to understand the whole structure in which it fits; when one of the things in such a structure is introduced into a text, or into a conversation, all of the others are automatically made available. I intend the word 'frame' as used here to be a general cover term for the set of concepts variously known, in the literature on natural language understanding, as 'schema', 'script', 'scenario', 'ideational scaffolding', 'cognitive model', or 'folk theory'. (Fillmore 1982a: 111)

Virtually all cognitive linguists agree that word meanings are encyclopedic, unable to be characterized purely in linguistic terms. Thus, Lakoff (1987: 68) declares that the main thesis of his book is "that we organize our knowledge by means of structures called *idealized cognitive models*, or ICMs, and that category structures and prototype effects are by-product of that organization". This explains that cognitive linguists are often sympathetic with Putnam's notion of stereotype (Taylor 2003: 76, 90). Taylor (2003: 76) proposes to interpret the stereotype of a term as its folk definition as opposed to its expert definition. Before the rise of modern science, Taylor suggests, terms like 'water' and 'gold' were only endowed with folk definition and relied on "our knowledge of perceptual and interactional attributes of prototypical instances" (ibid.). As Kay (1983: 137) states, "a folk theory does not present a globally consistent whole the way a conscious, expert theory does". This coheres with the highly simplified or idealized character of stereotypes. Minsky's notion of frame, from which Fillmore's frame semantics originates, is defined in terms of stereotype:

Here is the essence of the theory: When one encounters a new situation (or makes a substantial change in one's view of the present problem) one selects from memory a structure called a *frame*. This is a remembered framework to be adapted to fit reality by changing details as necessary. A *frame* is a data-structure for representing a stereotyped situation, like being in a certain kind of living room, or going to a child's birthday party. Attached to each frame are several kinds of information. Some of this information is about how to use the frame. Some is about what one can expect to happen next. Some is about what to do if these expectations are not confirmed. (Minsky 1974: 1)

For this reason, Lakoff (1987: 117) remarks that "Putnam and Minsky deserve a great deal of credit for seeing early on that superficial prototype effects should be accounted for in terms of deviations from idealized cognitive models".

It would then be tempting to include in (51) much more information concerning the frame or ICM against which the one-criterion word is understood and in relation to which prototype effects are produced. As far as one-criterion concepts are concerned, however, there is good reason to believe that facts about prototypes and frames have no bearing upon the identity of concepts. Taylor (2003: 98) dismisses the question raised by Fillmore (1982a: 34) about whether the Pope can be considered a bachelor, as bizarre, because "the Pope is surely a very marginal instance of the category". If the sentence in (52a) is hedged with 'strictly speaking', which typically serves to remove the fuzziness from a category (ibid.: 80), it becomes much more acceptable, as in (52b):

(52) a. ?The Pope is a bachelor.
b. Strictly speaking, the Pope is a bachelor.
c. ??The Pope is a real bachelor. ((52a-c): Taylor 2003: 98)

This suggests that whether someone is a bachelor is ultimately determined with reference to its defining features, namely 'unmarried adult man'. The oddity of (52c) does not contradict the condition in (51), because 'a real X' generally does not express a one-criterion concept. Austin (1962: 76) remarks that "there are no criteria to be laid down *in general* for distinguishing the real from the not real" (emphasis in the original). Thus, Austin (1962: 70) observes that "'[a] real duck' differs from the simple 'a duck' only in that it is used to exclude various ways of being not a real duck", such as "a dummy, a toy, a picture, a decoy", and so on.

The irrelevance of prototypicality to the identity of a one-criterion concept becomes clearer when we compare *bachelor* with cluster concepts like *bird*. Suppose that birds in Adam$_2$'s community never fly. This is sufficient for us to doubt that the creatures are birds, making Adam's attitude reported in (53a) natural:

(53) a. Adam seriously doubts that 'birds' in Adam$_2$'s community are birds, even though they are feathered bipedal creatures.
b. Adam seriously doubts that 'bachelors' in Adam$_2$'s community are bachelors, even though they are unmarried adult men.
c. Adam thinks that bachelors in Adam$_2$'s community are low-spirited.

Suppose now that bachelors in Adam$_2$'s community are never high-spirited. Most of them live alone but seldom go out. This, on its own, is not sufficient for us to doubt that the people are bachelors, making (53b) less natural than (53c). Although the boundary between conceptual characterization and theorization is often not clear-cut, a person who does not know that typical birds fly is more likely to be regarded as less than competent with the concept of *bird*, while a person who does not know that typical bachelors are high-spirited is more likely to be regarded as holding a nonstandard theory about bachelors. As remarked in Section 2.6.2, the prototype of 'bachelor' or 'grandmother' fails to meet the condition of conceptual stability or content publicity proposed by Löhr (2020:

2183-2184). It is no more stable than, for instance, what Levinson (2000: 222-223) refers to as "our stereotypical assumptions about the sex of secretaries and bosses". Provided that word meaning is encyclopedic, knowledge about the standard theory is required for full competence with the use of the word 'bachelor', but not for minimal competence. That mastery of one-criterion concepts is mostly an all-or-nothing affair makes it difficult to apply the notion of incomplete understanding in the relevant sense to one-criterion concepts.

3.7.3 Nominal Kind Terms

As we have seen in Section 2.5.3, nominal kind terms such as 'pencil', 'lamp' and 'chair' and one-criterion terms have in common that they are associated with "an analytic specification in terms of form and function" (Schwartz 1978: 572). The nominal kind terms 'pencil' and 'sofa' are specified by the analytic statements in (54a) and (54b), respectively.

(54) a. Pencils are instruments for writing or drawing.
b. Sofas are pieces of furniture to be sat upon.

Nevertheless, nominal kind terms are distinguished from one-criterion words in that the core facts about nominal kind terms are not exhausted by the analytic specifications. Schwartz (1978: 571-572) argues that, appearances notwithstanding, the statements in (55) are not analytic, on the grounds that we may find out that pencils and sofas are organisms (cf. Putnam 1975: 161, Schwartz 1978: 570):

(55) a. Pencils are artifacts (with such-and-such superficial properties).
b. Sofas are artifacts (with such-and-such superficial properties).

Still, the characterizations in (55a) and (55b) are so central to 'pencil' and 'sofa' that we may hesitate to say that a person ignorant of these characterizations is normally competent with the concepts expressed by the words. Such a person might complain, for example, that biology textbooks do not deal with pencils and sofas. We would almost certainly be less sympathetic with his complaint that biologists are not interested in pencils than with his complaint that the pencil manufacturer does not strive to minimize the cost. The statements in (55) are stereotypical, though not analytic, descriptions of 'pencil' and 'sofa'. Combined with the observation that the analytic specifications in (54) and the stereotypical descriptions in (55)

Chapter 3   Incomplete Understanding and Construal

are both important for the understanding of *pencil* and *sofa*, (49) would be turned
into (56) for nominal kind terms:

(56)   A speaker S is minimally competent in the use of a nominal kind term X
       iff S understands most of the stereotypical descriptions associated with X,
       including the analytic specifications of X.

When Burge (1986a: 709/2007: 264) says, as seen in Section 2.4, that a person
who doubts (54b) "may be a sophisticate" and "need not lack linguistic understanding or be unapprised of expert or common opinion", he arguably assumes the standard articulated in (56) to be the standard for normal competence rather than
minimal competence. In general, when a subject understands the concept
expressed by X only incompletely, she is minimally competent with X but not normally competent with X. If (56) describes the standard for normal (rather than
minimal) competence with nominal kind terms, those who doubt (54b) do not *ipso*
facto betray incomplete understanding of *sofa*, provided that they understand the
stereotypical descriptions of sofas as given in (55b). When Wikforss (2004: 293)
objects that Burge (1986a/2007) and Sawyer (2003) implicitly assume that a person "who doubts that sofas are furnishings to be sat upon, *does* display an incomplete understanding of the concept of sofa", she is suggesting that, for Burge's
(1986a/2007) argument to go through, the standard for normal competence
should be set higher than Burge himself seems to assume. Presumably, what
Wikforss has in mind is something like (56)':

(56)' A speaker S is normally competent in the use of a nominal kind term X
       iff S understands both the analytic specifications of X and most of the
       stereotypical descriptions associated with X.

The higher standard for normal competence spelled out in (56)' might be motivated by Bloom's (2000: 162) observation that "[m]uch of the time the relationship
between appearance and intent is transparent" and that "[i]f something resembles
a typical chair, for instance, then it is highly likely that it was created with the
intent to be a chair", namely something to be sat upon. The stereotypical descriptions in (55) are not independent from the analytic descriptions in (54), except in
atypical situations (ibid.). In any case, the dispute between Wikforss (2001, 2004)
and Sawyer (2003) concerning whether Burge's (1986a/2007) 'sofa' thought

199

experiment features incomplete understanding or nonstandard theory partly stems from the variation in speakers' intuitions about semantic and conceptual competence[43].

3.7.4 Cluster Terms

As remarked in Section 2.5.3, cluster terms are distinguished from both one-criterion terms and nominal kind terms in that they have no analytic specifications (Putnam 1970: 189), except for trivial analytic statements such as 'every lemon is a lemon' (Schwartz 1978: 566). Typical cluster terms are natural kind terms such as 'lemon', 'water' and 'gold' and scientific terms such as 'multiple sclerosis' (Putnam 1962c/1975: 310-311) and 'energy' (Putnam 1962a: 379-380)[44]. Linguistic and conceptual competence with these terms requires knowledge of their stereotypes. Thus, speakers of English are expected to know that stereotypical tigers are striped (Putnam 1975: 168-169). The stereotype associated with a word 'X' "is a conventional (frequently malicious) idea (which may be wildly inaccurate) of what an X looks like or acts like or is" (Putnam 1975: 169), which may serve to identify a "normal member" of X (Putnam 1970: 198-199).

We have seen in Section 2.5.3 that 'mother' can be considered a cluster word involving a complex cognitive model consisting of the birth model, the genetic model, the nurturance model, the marital model and the genealogical model (Lakoff 1987: 74-76). Taylor (2003: 91) states that this complex cognitive model "is the structured whole" and calls it the "mother frame":

According to the mother frame, a mother is a woman who has sexual relations

---

43) As stated in Section 2.4, the point of Wikforss's (2004) argument is that Burge's (1986a/2007) and Sawyer's (2004) judgment is internally incoherent. On the one hand, Burge and Sawyer say that the 'sofa' thought experiment features nonstandard theorizing and not incomplete understanding (Burge 1986a: 709/2007: 264, Sawyer 2003: 271). In making this claim they seem to take the standard stated in (56) to be the standard for normal competence. On the other hand, they say that there are no sofas in Adam$_2$'s community (Burge 1986a: 708/2007: 263, Sawyer 2003: 268). Wikforss (2004: 293) indicates that this second remark appears to presuppose a higher standard than that suggested by (56). For the second remark to hold, nothing that fails to meet the analytic specifications in (54b) can count as a sofa.

44) Also included in this category are "artifactual terms ('carburator' [sic.], 'viola da gamba'), mathematical terms ('number', 'ellipse'), logical terms ('proof', 'validity', 'only if', 'or'), and even the terms of philosophy and psychology ('belief', 'thought', and, not to put too fine a point upon it, 'concept' itself)" (Rey 1983: 254, n. 18). Here I focus on typical cluster terms.

Chapter 3   Incomplete Understanding and Construal

with the father, falls pregnant, gives birth, and then for the following decade or so devotes much of her time to nurturing and raising the child, remaining all the while married to the father. In such a situation all five domains converge. Clearly, such a scenario is highly idealized, in that the frame abstracts away from its many untypical instantiations. [...] It is against background of the idealized scenario that we characterize a prototypical mother. [...] Ultimately, the frame embodies deeply held beliefs about the status and role of the family in society. (Taylor 2003: 91)

Taylor cautions that the idealized scenario is not immune to change and that the one he proposes may be "already outdated" (ibid.). This is to say that it is inappropriate to require nearly full mastery of the stereotype for minimal semantic and conceptual competence.

Adapted for cluster words, the condition in (49) would take the form articulated in (57):

(57)   A speaker S is minimally competent in the use of a cluster word X iff S understands most of the stereotypical descriptions associated with X.

Putnam (1975: 168) comments that there is not much point in talking about tigers with a person who, pointing to a snowball, asks, 'Is that a tiger?'. This is because the stereotype associated with 'snowball' has little in common with the stereotype associated with 'tiger'. A similar remark can be made for (58), discussed by Burge (1979a: 90-91/2007: 119-120):

(58)   I have been drinking orangutans for breakfast for the last few weeks.

As stated in Section 2.3, 'orangutan' in (58) should be reinterpreted as what the utterer calls 'orangutans', namely 'orange juice', in conformity with the principle of charity. The utterer of (58) is not talking about orangutans but about orange juice. There is no doubt that the stereotype associated with 'orangutan' includes the statement that an orangutan is an animal, which one cannot 'drink'. As discussed in Section 2.5.3, we may find out that cats are robots (Putnam 1962b, 1975, Donnellan 1962). There is nevertheless a sense in which a person who believes that that cats are robots is less competent with the concept of *cat* than a person who believes that cats are animals. That cats are animals is a central, though not

201

analytic, fact about cats. A person who believes that cats are something to drink is in a much worse position, because cats are to beverages what snowballs are to tigers. Robots can resemble animals, but beverages cannot. The belief that cats and orangutans are beverages surely distorts most of the stereotypical understanding of 'cat' and 'orangutan'. There is therefore no compelling reason to think that a person who believes that one can have the habit of drinking cats or orangutans is competent with the concept of *cat* or *orangutan*.

Returning to the 'arthritis' case, it must be noticed that 'arthritis' is a cluster word, since, as discussed earlier, even the most central definition in (28b) (Arthritis is a rheumatoid disease of the joints only.) may prove to be wrong (Kimbrough 1998, Wikforss 2001, 2004). In Burge's view, it is possible to ascribe to Adam the concept of *arthritis* even though he does not recognize that his belief in (27a) (Arthritis may occur in the thigh.) is as false as (27b) (A rheumatoid disease of the joints only may occur in the thigh.). Taken in isolation, Adam's belief that he has arthritis in his thigh evinces his misunderstanding of what arthritis is like and one may be tempted to think that he is not competent with *arthritis*. But to take in isolation Adam's belief that he has arthritis in his thigh is to misunderstand the upshot of the thought experiment. Recall that Burge (1979a/2007) depicts Adam as a person who has many correct beliefs about arthritis:

A given person has a large number of attitudes commonly attributed with content clauses containing 'arthritis' in oblique occurrence. For example, he thinks (correctly) that he has had arthritis for years; that his arthritis in his wrists and fingers is more painful than his arthritis in his ankles, that it is better to have arthritis than cancer of the liver, that stiffening joints is a symptom of arthritis, that certain sorts of aches are characteristic of arthritis, that there are various kinds of arthritis, and so forth. In short, he has a wide range of such attitudes. In addition to these unsurprising attitudes, he thinks falsely that he has developed arthritis in the thigh. (Burge 1979a: 77/2007: 104)

In retrospect, we can understand that this long description suggests that Adam satisfies the condition in (57), i.e. Adam understands most of the stereotypical descriptions of 'arthritis', making it possible for him to talk about arthritis with his doctor (cf. Valente 2019: 320). His use of 'arthritis' need not, and must not, be reinterpreted as, say, 'tharthritis' as is the case with 'orangutan' in (58). Adam is similar to a person who seriously asserts (59a) instead of (59b):

Chapter 3   Incomplete Understanding and Construal

(59)   a. Cats are robots remotely controlled from Mars. (Putnam 1975: 162)
       b. Cats are animals.

It may be revealed that (59a) is true in the same way that it may be revealed that arthritis can afflict one's thigh. However, this possibility does not rule out (59a) from the stereotypical descriptions of 'cat'. Adam is also similar to a person who seriously asserts (60a):

(60)   a. Microraptor is a four-legged bird.
       b. Birds are feathered bipedal creatures. (Hampton 2015: 131)

(60a) conflicts with the defining feature of birds given in (60b) in the same way that Adam's thought in (61a) is contradictory to the defining feature of arthritis laid down in (61b):

(61)   a. I have arthritis in my thigh.
       b. Arthritis is an inflammation of the joints only.

In most cases, the mere fact that a person assents to (60a) would not deprive her of semantic competence with the use of 'bird'. By parity of reasoning, we can reasonably say that the mere fact that Adam utters (61a) does not make him semantically irrational.

3.8 Incomplete Understanding as a Basis of Construal

The argument so far suggests that Frege's Constraint is not a primitive constraint but is derived from the fact that one can be semantically rational in the use of a linguistic expression E while being ignorant of something about the conceptual content of E. Such ignorance sometimes leads the subject to believe that there are two things even though, in fact, there is only one. This, however, is not a symptom of her irrationality, because, as Recanati (2016: 13) puts it, "reference is not epistemologically transparent" and "[s]ense is the level at which the subject's rationality can be assessed". Similarly, Chalmers (2006: 55) remarks that by proposing the notion of sense "Frege linked reason and meaning". Insofar as sense or construal is part of a concept, there can be two distinct concepts despite the identity

203

of the reference. If no one is aware of the identity of the reference, we have a case of incomplete understanding in the metaphysical sense. If, on the other hand, the discovery that the two senses or construals share the same reference or conceptual content spreads into lay communities to the point of being established as a core fact about the terms in question, people who, like Adam, remain ignorant of the discovery are considered to display an incomplete understanding of the relevant concepts in the communal sense.

Of particular importance is that externalism hinges on such ignorance on the part of the subject in question; Putnam's thought experiment makes use of the possibility for Oscar, a semantically rational person, to endorse (41a) while being totally unaware of (41b), and Burge's thought experiment presupposes that Adam, a semantically rational person, fails to recognize the truth-conditional equivalence between (27a) and (27b) (Wikforss 2006: 168-170). What is needed for the thought experiments in support of externalism is the assumption that one can be competent in the use of 'water' without knowing that water is H_2O, and that one can be competent in the use of 'arthritis' without knowing that arthritis afflicts the joints only[45]. That Adam has an incomplete grasp of the concept expressed by 'arthritis' does not deprive him of semantic rationality, provided that he understands most of the stereotypical descriptions associated with 'arthritis'. Wikforss (2006: 172) says following Brown (2003: 440-446) that a subject who endorses (29a) (Cilantro should be used sparingly.) but not (29b) (Coriander should be used sparingly.) would be held to have "a complete grasp of two distinct concepts (that happen to have the same extension in this world), the concept of *schmilantro* and *schmoliander* (say)". However, this is an abuse of Frege's Constraint. In effect, Frege's Constraint as construed here makes an implicit reference to the publicness of meaning and thought by alluding to semantic rationality. When applying Frege's Constraint to a person who accepts (62a) while rejecting (62b), one might draw the conclusion that the person has a complete grasp of the two distinct concepts expressed by 'bachelor' and 'unmarried adult man':

(62)   a. John is a bachelor.

b. John is an unmarried adult man.

---

45) Possible differences between physical externalism and social externalism will be addressed in Chapter 5.

This conclusion would make the person rational in the ordinary sense of the term (cf. Millikan 1993: 289, Boghossian 1994: 42), but would fail to make her semantically rational.

Which conclusion to draw from (29) ultimately depends on whether one can be competent with 'cilantro' and 'coriander' without recognizing that the two terms share the same conceptual content. If the equivalence is part of the grammar as is the case with the equivalence between 'bachelor' and 'unmarried adult man', then the two terms are synonyms, ignorance of which makes the subject less than minimally competent with 'cilantro' and 'coriander'. If, on the contrary, the equivalence is not part of the grammar as is the case with the equivalence between 'water' and 'H_2O', then the equivalence is to be discovered by people competent with 'cilantro' and 'coriander'. In any case, no definitive answer can be given without investigating the speakers' intuitions. Falvey and Owens (1994) appeal to the etymology of the two terms to argue for the first option:

> [...] these terms might just be synonyms ('coriander' and 'cilantro' are both derived from the Latin 'coriandrum', one by way of the French 'coriandre', the other by way of the Spanish 'culantro'), and this would tell strongly in favor of the claim that we simply have two expressions for the same thought. (Falvey and Owens 1994: 111, n. 3)

But arguments based on etymologies are generally not so strong as Falvey and Owens suggest, because it is well known that, as Lyons (1977: 552) states, "the native speaker is generally unaware of the etymology of the words that he uses and his interpretation of them is unaffected". The word form 'ball' in English, for instance, means either 'spherical object' or 'social event involving dancing' (Taylor 2012: 229). One may ask whether the single word 'ball' has two senses or if there happen to be two homonymous words both spelled 'ball'. History tells us that we should opt for the second view; 'ball' meaning 'spherical object' is a loanword from the Old Norse 'bǫllr' (ball), which goes back to the Proto-Indo-European *'bʰoln-' (round thing, bubble)[46], while 'ball' meaning 'social event involving dancing' derives from the Middle French 'baler' (to dance), which presumably goes back to

---

46) https://en.wiktionary.org/wiki/ball#Etymology_1
https://en.wiktionary.org/wiki/b%C7%ABllr#Old_Norse
Last accessed: 24/01/2024

the Proto-Indo-European "*gʷelH-' (to throw)[47]. Even though, from the historical perspective, the answer is evident, speakers' intuitions diverge; there are some speakers who feel that they are dealing with a single word which has two related senses (Taylor 2012: 229). These considerations cast doubt on "the very notion of 'a word', a stable, well-defined unit in the mental grammar" (ibid.: 233)[48]. Although Falvey and Owens bring historical evidence to bear on whether 'cilantro' and 'coriander' express the same sense or distinct senses, the argument is not conclusive and it remains possible that the two terms, despite their identity in etymology, express distinct senses which happen to determine the same reference. It is only through investigating speakers' intuitions that we can determine whether (63a) is akin to (63b) or to (63c):

(63) a. Cilantro is coriander.
      b. A bachelor is an unmarried adult man.
      c. Water is H_2O.

As a matter of fact, by appealing to historical evidence, Falvey and Owens (1994) agree with the basic point made here: Frege's Constraint can be applied to demonstrate that we are dealing with two concepts only when the subject is semantically competent. The identity in etymology between 'cilantro' and 'coriander' strongly suggests, according to Falvey and Owens, that the two terms express one and the same sense. If we are dealing with only one sense, that there is a person who takes different attitudes toward (29a) and (29b) suggests at best that the person fails to recognize that she is semantically irrational. Falvey and Owens assume, as I do here, that application of Frege's Constraint presupposes semantic competence, or what Brown (2004: 160, 165) refers to as 'transparency of sameness of content'. I only disagree with their claim that historical evidence can be brought to bear on the matter.

One may wonder whether Frege had in mind what is referred to here as semantic rationality. Unlike rationality per se, semantic rationality is a language-relative notion. A speaker of Japanese who knows little English would not

---

47) https://en.wiktionary.org/wiki/ball#Etymology_2
https://en.wiktionary.org/wiki/ballo#Latin
Last accessed: 24/01/2024
48) Taylor (2003: 106) offers a similar argument about 'eye' and 'ear'. See also Quine (1960: §27).

206

Chapter 3   Incomplete Understanding and Construal

recognize the truth-conditional equivalence between (35a) and (35b) above. But this does not make him an irrational person; he merely lacks semantic rationality relative to English. It may well be the case that Frege, as a logician, was as ambitious as Fodor, who said much later that "[i]n the long run – in the very long run – [...] we want a theory, not just of one rational process or other, but of rationality per se" (Fodor 1975: 195). The notion of semantic rationality would not allow us to achieve the goal Fodor aimed for. Still, given Frege's emphasis on the publicness of sense and thought, it is hardly conceivable that Frege's Constraint makes room for, or even justifies, purely private concepts and contents. To avoid such fragmentation of concepts, as Wikforss (2001) calls it, we must refrain from applying Frege's Constraint to such pairs as 'bachelor' vs. 'unmarried adult man'. To embrace internalism is not to embrace subjectivism. This point is substantiated by Langacker's (1987, 2008) emphasis on conventions. Langacker (1987: 51) states that "[s]peakers have the conceptual freedom to construe a given situation in many different ways, and we cannot predict in absolute terms which particular images might be chosen and conventionalized". Conceptualization in no way precludes conventionalization, because "[g]rammar (like lexicon) embodies conventional imagery" (Langacker 1987: 39; see also 1987: 138) and "meaning resides in hierarchies of conventional imagery" (ibid.: 40), where 'imagery' is equivalent to 'construal' (Langacker 2008: 43, n. 12). Incomplete understanding presupposes the publicness of meaning and thought, which is compatible with semantic internalism, according to which meaning consists of construal and conceptual content.

Incomplete understanding constitutes a basis for our ability to conceive one and the same object or situation in more than one way without appealing to the conventional apparatus provided by grammar. As seen above, Langacker defines construal as "our manifest ability to conceive and portray the same situation in alternate ways" (Langacker 2008: 43). It must be noticed, however, there are in fact two types of construals. When (35a) and (35b) describe the same situation from different vantage points (Langacker 2008: 75), competent speakers must know that the two sentences describe the same situation. The different construals evoked by (35a) and (35b) originate from the antonymy between 'in front of' and 'behind', which every speaker of English is supposed to know. When, on the contrary, (23a) and (23b) describe the same situation from different perspectives, competent speakers need not be aware that the two sentences describe the same situation. While the different construals attached to (35a) and (35b) draw on speakers' knowledge of the English grammar, the different construals attached to (23a) and

207

(23b) derive from speakers' possible lack of knowledge of astronomy. If speakers of English had been on Earth before the discovery that the morning star is the evening star, they could have been able to think of something as the morning star without being committed to any other construal. This underlies the fact that it is one thing to think of (23a) and another to think of (23b) (cf. Sainsbury and Tye 2012: 45, 53). In this sense, I submit, incomplete understanding provides another basis for our ability to construe the same situation in different fashions, even though Burge (2012: 61) cautions that counting various kinds of incomplete understanding as modes of presentation leads to postulating "modes of presentation of modes of presentation", undermining Frege's insightful view that "senses are thought contents"[49].

From a cognitive linguistic perspective, both grammar and incomplete understanding are naturally taken to constitute the two sides of the same coin. Far from incompatible with Frege's Constraint as argued by Kimbrough (1998), Brown (2003, 2004) and Wikforss (2006), the notion of incomplete understanding provides grounds for the notion of the mode of presentation or construal. On the one hand, a sheer ignorance of the concept(s) expressed by a pair of synonymous terms deprives the speaker of semantic competence, making Frege's Constraint inapplicable. Frege's Constraint does not allow us to say that 'bachelor' and 'unmarried adult man' express different concepts or that the equivalence between the two expressions is something to be discovered. On the other hand, a full mastery of the concept(s) expressed by a pair of non-synonymous terms strips the speaker of any possibility for her to take different attitudes toward two statements in which the terms occur. In this case, it is in principle possible to apply Frege's Constraint, but the result would be that, for example, 'arthritis' and 'rheumatoid disease of the joints only' express one and the same concept to the extent that the speaker judges that (27a) cannot be true without (27b) also being true. If the intuition that 'arthritis' and 'rheumatoid disease of the joints only' express different concepts deserves respect, we must grant that Frege's Constraint is applied to deviant speakers.

If, as claimed here, incomplete understanding underlies the construal, the real challenge posed for cognitive linguistics is to elucidate how incomplete

---

49) Burge (2012: 62) claims that "[i]n both incomplete- and full-understanding cases, the individual thinks the same sense through the same two expressions". This claim makes no room for incomplete understanding to constitute a sense in which a mode of presentation is contained.

understanding can be related to conceptual content. After all, if a speaker understands the meaning of a word only incompletely, there seems to be no means for her to correctly capture the conceptual content expressed by the word and understood by the community. How can Adam and his doctor, despite their contradicting construals, manage to talk about the same disease?

Chapter 4

Deferential Construal

This chapter specifies the condition for more than one sense or construal to be associated with one and the same form without communication being hindered, arguing that variations in individualistic construal have no bearing on the identity of a concept insofar as lay speakers defer to experts for the correct construal of the concept.

4.1 Different Construals vs. Same Concept

In Chapter 1, it has been suggested that the two social externalist assumptions in (1) (Burge 1979a/2007) seemingly pose challenges for cognitive linguistics, which identifies meaning with conceptualization (Langacker 2008):

(1)   a. Although Adam and Adam$_2$ conceptualize what is called 'arthritis' (or 'bird' discussed in Chapter 2) in exactly the same fashion, the meaning of 'arthritis' ('bird') and the thought content containing 'arthritis' ('bird') are different for them.

          b. Although Adam and his doctor conceptualize what is called 'arthritis' in a mutually incompatible way, the meaning of 'arthritis' and the thought content containing 'arthritis' are the same for them.

In Chapter 2, I have argued that (1a), which embodies what Fodor (1994: 23) calls a Twin case, is compatible with cognitive linguistics because an individual's conceptualization is more or less grounded in, or attuned to, her environment. It is possible that two individuals who have exactly the same intrinsic properties nevertheless have different conceptualizations due to their differing degrees of adaptation to their respective environments. Thus, Adam and Adam$_2$ are internally identical, but unlike Adam$_2$ Adam has an incomplete grasp of the community concept expressed by the word form 'arthritis'. As Loar (1988/2017: 154) states, "sameness

211

of conceptual role is not *sufficient* for sameness of content". What is needed for the social externalist assumption in (1a) is the notion of incomplete understanding without analyticity as opposed to linguistic error as well as non-standard theorizing. Since cluster words such as 'arthritis' have no analytic definition (Putnam 1970), the social externalist must show that one can have an incomplete understanding of *arthritis* without assuming any analytic definition of the concept. Wikforss (2001, 2004) insists that this is inconsistent, because, if 'arthritis' has no analytic definition, Adam's belief that he has arthritis in his thigh may prove to be true. In Wikforss's view, Burge's argument fails to demonstrate that Adam and Adam$_2$ have different concepts because Adam may well be merely developing a theory about arthritis which happens to be assessed as false by his contemporary community members. Burge's thought experiment does not preclude the possibility that Adam's community members are ignorant of the fact that their concept corresponding to the word 'arthritis' is in fact identical with Adam$_2$'s community's concept of *tharthritis*, which is also possessed by Adam. As Liu (2002: 391) puts it, it is possible that "the social environment *misrepresents* the physical environment" (emphasis in the original).

To rebut Wikforss's (2001, 2004) objection, I have argued in Chapter 3 that a concept consists of a conceptual content and its construal. Even though 'the morning star' and 'the evening star' share one and the same conceptual content, the two terms nevertheless express different concepts, insofar as speakers attach different construals to them. This is in line with Frege's Constraint, according to which a semantically competent person can be ignorant of some aspects of the meaning and concept expressed by the expression in question. Adam's community and Adam$_2$'s community have different concepts expressed by 'arthritis' to the extent that their construals of the relevant conceptual content are different. Falvey and Owens (1994), Kimbrough (1998), Brown (2003, 2004) and Wikforss (2006) suggest that the notion of incomplete understanding assumed by social externalism is incompatible with Frege's Constraint, on the grounds that the former implies that content may be opaque to the thinking subject, while the latter presupposes that content is transparent. It is conceivable that the experts in Adam's community are unable to recognize their irrationality in taking different attitudes toward their word 'arthritis' and the homonymous word employed in Adam$_2$'s community, i.e., that the identity of the concept is opaque to them. This objection loses sight of the fact that competence and transparency come in levels. To be minimally competent in English, we must know that 'X is in front of Y' and 'Y is behind X' depict the same situation, but we do not have to know that 'The morning star is remote from the sun' and 'The evening star is remote from the sun' represent the same state of affairs. The latter identity concerns not English but astronomy. This enables one to say, on the one hand, that, despite his deviant belief about arthritis, Adam is considered competent with the concept of *arthritis* provided that he understands most of the stereotypical descriptions associated with the word 'arthritis', and, on the other, that he has an incomplete grasp of *arthritis* to the extent that his construal of the concept deviates from the community practice. In saying that experts may have an incomplete understanding of a concept, Wikforss conflates two notions of incomplete understanding. Experts can only be plagued with incomplete understanding in the metaphysical sense, whereas lay people may suffer from incomplete understanding in the communal sense (and possibly from incomplete understanding in the physical sense as well). Experts cannot have an incomplete grasp of *arthritis* in the communal sense, because the possible identity between *arthritis* and *tharthritis* is no more part of semantic and conceptual competence than the identity between *the morning star* and *the evening star*. In other words, 'arthritis' and 'tharthritis' are not perfect synonyms just in the same way that 'the morning star' and 'the evening star' are not perfect synonyms.

As foreshadowed in Section 3.5, the remaining question is how we can credit Adam with the concept of *arthritis*. If a concept consists of a conceptual content and its construal and Adam construes the word 'arthritis' in a remarkably different way from his doctor, it seems to follow that the two subjects attach different concepts to the word. Burge's notion of incomplete understanding is tied to what Kimbrough (1998: 472) calls 'liberal criteria for possession of concepts', which makes it possible to ascribe to Adam the concept of *arthritis* despite his deviant conception of the concept. This apparently runs counter to the view that a concept is defined in terms of both conceptual content and construal. Adam misunderstands the doctor's "central belief" about arthritis, as Peacock (1992) puts it:

> It is possible for one and the same concept to receive different mental representations in different individuals. Again, what is in fact a relatively central belief for us, such as the belief that rain is water, can be informative to someone from a desert country who already possess the concept *water*. (Peacocke 1992: 3)

The cognitive linguistic assumption that meaning is conceptualization entails that any variation in central beliefs about a concept can only be described as a semantic variation. This makes it impossible to account for our intuition that lay people and experts can share the meaning of a word while conceptualizing its extension in different or even contradictory manners. As Loar (1988/2017: 154) states, "sameness of conceptual role is not *necessary* for sameness of psychological content". How can several contradictory conceptualizations be associated with one and the same subject matter? Thought contents are by definition both intentional in the sense of being about objects and events in the world and public in the sense of being able to be understood by others (Bilgrami 1992: 1, 4, 194, McGeer 1994: 431). To say simply that meaning is nothing but conceptualization is insufficient to accommodate the publicness of meaning and thought. Unlike (1a), (1b) remains a stark challenge for cognitive linguistics.

4.2 Frege Cases and *De Jure* Coreference

At first sight, (1b) may appear a simple Frege case, indicating that "concepts cannot be individuated by intentional content alone" (Prinz 2002: 6). In (1b), Adam, a person generally competent in English, believes both (2a) and (2b) even though these sentences represent contradictory broad contents.

(2) a. Arthritis may occur in the thigh.
     b. A rheumatoid disease of the joints cannot occur in the thigh.

As we have seen in Section 3.1, a Frege case is realized in a situation in which a rational person believes (3a) and (3b) simultaneously, despite their mutually incompatible broad contents:

(3) a. The morning star is remote from the sun.
     b. The evening star is not remote from the sun.

(2) and (3) are alike in suggesting that one can be competent in the use of a linguistic expression E while being ignorant of something about the meaning of E. In two-dimensional approaches to semantics including cognitive linguistics, it is quite easy to accommodate Frege cases, in contrast with, say, Fodor's (1994) theory. Although Langacker's theory and Fodor's theory are both internalist in the relevant sense, Frege cases pose no problem for cognitive linguistics, unlike for Fodor's theory. According to cognitive linguistics, meaning and conceptualization consist

Chapter 4 Deferential Construal

of conceptual content and its construal, whereas Fodor's semantics demands both that psychological processes be driven by computational mechanisms defined over syntactically structured objects (Fodor 1994: 8) and that meaning be reduced to information, namely, broad content defined in terms of truth and denotation (ibid.: 4, 7). Frege cases seem to seriously threaten the compatibility of Fodor's two assumptions (ibid.: 39), since Frege cases suggest that "more than one implementing mechanism (M1, M2) can correspond to the same intentional state (F1)" (ibid.: 23). Frege cases are so recalcitrant for Fodor that he seeks to explain them away (ibid.: 49). Langacker, by contrast, thinks that such cases are best explained in terms of the notion of construal. However, the optimism about (1b) should not be taken at face value, for it is not obvious whether (1b) really instantiates a Frege case. The analogy under consideration misses an important difference between typical Frege cases and what is depicted in (1b). (1b) amounts to saying (i) that both Adam and his doctor employ the word form 'arthritis', (ii) that Adam and his doctor construe the concept associated with the word form in mutually contradictory ways, and (iii) that despite (ii) they succeed in thinking and talking about the same disease. Contrary to (i), in a typical Frege case, a rational subject associates mutually exclusive senses with two different word forms. Thus, Adam may associate $sense_1$ with 'the morning star' and $sense_2$, a sense distinct from $sense_1$, with 'the evening star'. Unlike such a typical Frege case, (i) puts only one word form on the agenda, indicating that one and the same form can be tied to several different construals (or senses). (ii) also differs from typical Frege cases in making more than one protagonist appear on the scene. Finally, (iii) makes it clear that, in contrast to typical Frege cases, the difference in construal (or sense) does not prevent the protagonists from keeping track of one and the same broad content. In thinking and talking about the content expressed by (3a) and (3b), Adam is unlikely to be aware of thinking and talking about the same broad content; after all, the morning star is not the evening star for him. In thinking and talking about the content expressed by (2a) and (2b), by contrast, Adam fully understands that he and his doctor refer to the same ailment, resulting in the revision of his earlier view expressed by (2a).

As regards (i), Frege discussed several cases where one and the same linguistic form is associated with more than one sense (or thought, if the relevant linguistic form is a sentence). For instance, the sentence in (4) uttered in August 2024 is true if and only if the tree in front of the utterer is covered with green leaves in August 2024, while the same sentence uttered in February 1918 is true if and only if the tree in front of the utterer is covered with green leaves in February 1918:

215

(4)   The tree there is covered with green leaves.
(Dieser Baum ist grün belaubt.)   (Frege 1918-1919a: 76/1956: 309)

Since a difference in truth condition entails a difference in thought, this may be taken to suggest that the linguistic form in (4) is associated with more than one thought (Frege 1918-1919a: 76/1956: 309). But this interpretation arguably misrepresents Frege's idea about expressions of thought. For Frege, the expression of a thought includes not only the explicit linguistic form but also the time of utterance, the utterer, the pointing of fingers, hand movements and glances:

Therefore the time of utterance is part of the expression of the thought. If someone wants to say the same today as he expressed yesterday using the word "today", he must replace this word with "yesterday". Although the thought is the same its verbal expression must be different so that the sense, which would otherwise be affected by the differing times of utterance, is readjusted. The case is the same with words like "here" and "there". In all such cases the mere wording, as it is given in writing, is not the complete expression of the thought, but the knowledge of certain accompanying conditions of utterance, which are used as means of expressing the thought, are needed for its correct apprehension. The pointing of fingers, hand movements, glances may belong here too. The same utterance containing the word "I" will express different thoughts in the mouths of different men, of which some may be true, others false. (Frege 1918-1919a: 64/1956: 296)[1]

---

1) „Dann ist also die Zeit des Sprechens Teil des Gedankenausdrucks. Wenn jemand heute dasselbe sagen will, was er gestern das Wort ‚heute‘ gebrauchend ausgedrückt hat, so wird er dieses Wort durch „gestern" ersetzen. Obwohl der Gedanke derselbe ist, muss hierbei der Wortausdruck verschieden sein, um die Änderung des Sinnes wieder auszugleichen, die sonst durch den Zeitunterschied des Sprechens bewirkt würde. Ähnlich liegt die Sache bei den Wörtern wie ‚hier‘, ‚da‘. In allen solchen Fällen ist der bloße Wortlaut, wie er schriftlich festgehalten werden kann, nicht der vollständige Ausdruck des Gedankens, sondern man bedarf zu dessen richtiger Auffassung noch der Kenntnis gewisser das Sprechen begleitender Umstände, die dabei als Mittel des Gedankenausdrucks benutzt werden. Dazu können auch Fingerzeige, Handbewegungen, Blicke gehören. Der gleiche das Wort ‚ich‘ enthaltende Wortlaut wird im Munde verschiedener Menschen verschiedene Gedanken ausdrücken, von denen einige wahr, andere falsch sein können." (Frege 1918-1919a: 64)

Frege says here that the time of utterance is part of the expression of the thought rather than part of the thought per se, apparently endorsing the view that the expression of a thought consists of explicit verbal forms and facts accompanying the utterance. If we take this view at face value, we must think that the sentence in (4) uttered in August 2024 has a different form from (4) uttered in February 1918. This would not allow us to consider (4) a case in which one and the same form is associated with more than one sense. Genuine cases of one-to-many correspondence between form and sense can only be realized in statements for which the time of utterance, the utterer, etc. are definitively fixed. The statement in (5) is a case in point:

(5)   Dr. Lauben has been wounded.

Frege claims that (5) can express different thoughts depending on what the hearer understands by 'Dr. Lauben':

Now if both Leo Peter and Rudolph Lingens understand by "Dr. Lauben" the doctor who lives as the only doctor in a house known to both of them, then they both understand the sentence "Dr. Gustav Lauben has been wounded" in the same way, they associate the same thought with it. But it is also possible that Rudolph Lingens does not know Dr. Lauben personally and does not know that he is the very Dr. Lauben who recently said "I have been wounded". In this case Rudolph Lingens cannot know that the same thing is in question. I say, therefore, in this case: the thought which Leo Peter expresses is not the same as that which Dr. Lauben uttered. (Frege 1918-1919a: 65/1956: 297)[2]

This indicates that a Fregean sense cannot be equated with a mode of presentation

---

2)   „Wenn nun beide, Leo Peter und Rudolf Lingens, unter ‚Dr. Gustav Lauben' den Arzt verstehen, der in einer ihnen beiden bekannten Wohnung als der einzige Arzt wohnt, so verstehen beide den Satz ‚Dr. Gustav Lauben ist verwundet worden' in derselben Weise, sie verbinden mit ihm denselben Gedanken. Dabei ist es aber möglich, dass Rudolf Lingens den Dr. Lauben nicht persönlich kennt und nicht weiß, dass es eben der Dr. Lauben war, der neulich sagte: ‚Ich bin verwundet worden'. In diesem Falle kann Rudolf Lingens nicht wissen, dass es sich um dieselbe Sache handelt. Darum sage ich in diesem Falle: der Gedanke, den Leo Peter kundgibt, ist nicht derselbe, den Dr. Lauben ausgesprochen hat." (Frege 1918-1919a: 65)

conventionally attached to a linguistic form. If the expression of a thought consists of explicit verbal forms and facts accompanying the utterance, no utterance of (4) can correspond to any conventional verbal form. There can be an infinite number of utterances of (4) and hence an infinite number of facts accompanying the utterances, whereas the verbal form of (4) remains constant. In (5), on the contrary, there is a conventional verbal form to which various senses are attached, but the senses which Leo Peter and Rudolph Lingens attach to 'Dr. Lauben' are by no means conventional ways of thinking of Dr. Lauben. Millikan (1997: 507) states in a different context that "the very first job of [Fregean senses] was to correspond to shared meanings of words and sentences in public languages". The adjective 'first' cannot be omitted here. For Frege, the sense of an expression is not the conventional linguistic meaning of the expression, as stressed by Burge (1979b/2005, 1990/2005, 2012):

> It would be easy, though slovenly, to think of proper names and demonstrative expressions as special cases and to dismiss Frege's remarks about language getting in the way of thought as typical expressions of a logician interested in regimentation. But there is much more behind these remarks. They are symptoms of a radically epistemic conception of sense. (Burge 1990: 56/2005: 245, n. 5)

Loar (1976) offers an analogous example concerning the indexical 'he'. Loar points out that identifying who 'he' refers to in (6) does not suffice to understand the utterance:

(6)   He is a stockbroker.

Suppose that Smith and Jones are unaware that the man being interviewed on television is someone they see on the train every morning and about whom, in that latter role, they have just been talking. Smith says 'He is a stockbroker', intending to refer to the man on television; Jones takes Smith to be referring to the man on the train. Now Jones, as it happens, has correctly identified Smith's referent, since the man on television is the man on the train; but he has failed to understand Smith's utterance. It would seem that, as Frege held, some 'manner of presentation' of the referent is, even on referential uses, essential to what is being communicated. (Loar 1976: 357)

It is certainly a familiar point that the hearer must understand the sense of an expression as well as its reference (Valente 2019: 316-317, 326). What is novel with (6) is that the relevant sense is not conventionally tied to the expression under consideration. Neither 'the man on television' nor 'the man on the train' can be considered part of the conventional meaning, namely the 'character' (Kaplan's 1989a), of the indexical 'he'. Furthermore, there is no such concept as *he-ness* conventionally associated with the word 'he', in the same way that, as Fodor (2006: 15) states, there is no such concept as *this-ness* encoded in the demonstrative 'this'. Even if there were a concept which can be characterized as *he-ness*, it would have no specificity or stability enabling one to individuate and conceptualize the unique individual the utterer has in mind. Similar examples abound, as extensively discussed by Bezuidenhout (1997) and Pollock (2015). We must distinguish what Recanati's (1993: xiiff, 1995: 96) calls the linguistic mode of presentation of an expression, conventionally associated with the expression, from its psychological mode of presentation, which varies from context to context (ibid.: 69-76):

> The reference of 'I' is presented as being the speaker (linguistic mode of presentation). That linguistic mode of presentation is intersubjective, unlike the psychological mode of presentation which is subjective (i.e. the notion of *himself*, on the speaker's side, or the notion of *that man*, on the hearer's side) ; but the former may be construed as an aspect or part of the latter, an *aspect* (or *part*) which is *common* to the speaker's and the hearer's point of view. (Recanati 1993: 57)

As Recanati (2016: 116) makes clear, his proposal to distinguish the linguistic mode of presentation and the psychological mode of presentation is inspired by Frege's (1918-1919a/1956) distinction between the private sense and the public sense both associated with the indexical 'I' (ich)[3]:

> Now everyone is presented to himself in a particular and primitive way, in which he is presented to no-one else. So, when Dr. Lauben thinks that he has been wounded, he will probably take as a basis this primitive way in which he is presented to himself. And only Dr. Lauben himself can grasp thoughts

---

3) Recanati (1995: 97, 2016: 116) notes that he makes no claim that his interpretation is faithful to what Frege actually had in mind.

determined in this way. But now he may want to communicate with others. He cannot communicate a thought which he alone can grasp. Therefore, if he now says "I have been wounded". he must use the "I" in a sense which can be grasped by others, perhaps in the sense of "he who is speaking to you at this moment", by doing which he makes the associated conditions of his utterance serve for the expression of his thought. (Frege 1918-1919a: 66/1956: 298)[4]

Recanati (1993) holds that the private sense of 'I' cannot be its semantic content, because it is incompatible with the public character of semantic content:

The notion of semantic content must satisfy various constraints, and among the constraints there is one concerning *communicability*. The semantic content of an utterance must be a property of that utterance which can be recognized by both speaker and hearer and which remains stable in the process of communication. (Recanati 1993: 48, emphasis in the original)

According to Frege and Recanati, the thought involving the first-person pronoun 'I' (ich) systematically resists communication. This view is at odds with what Heck (2002) calls the Naïve Conception of Communication, according to which "what my words mean is precisely what I already believe and you come to believe: when you grasp the content of my assertion, you thereby grasp the very Thought I believe and am trying to communicate" (Heck 2002: 6)[5]. In this naïve view, "communication is the *replication* of thoughts: the thought the hearer entertains when

---

4) „Nun ist jeder sich selbst in einer besonderen und ursprünglichen Weise gegeben, wie er keinem anderen gegeben ist. Wenn nun Dr. Lauben denkt, dass er verwundet worden ist, wird er dabei wahrscheinlich diese ursprüngliche Weise, wie er sich selbst gegeben ist, zugrunde legen. Und den so bestimmten Gedanken kann nur Dr. Lauben selbst fassen. Nun aber wollte er anderen eine Mitteilung machen. Einen Gedanken, den nur er allein fassen kann, kann er nicht mitteilen. Wenn er nun also sagt: ‚Ich bin verwundet worden', muss er das ‚ich' in einem Sinn gebrauchen, der auch andern fassbar ist, etwa in dem Sinne von ‚derjenige, der in diesem Augenblicke zu euch spricht', wobei er die sein Sprechen begleitenden Umstände dem Gedankenausdrucke dienstbar macht." (Frege 1918-1919a: 66)
5) Despite what Frege (1918-1919a/1956) remarks about 'I', he seems to be committed to the Naïve Conception of Communication, if only because "when he started to think about communication, the Naïve Conception was just what came immediately to mind" (Heck 2002: 7). This makes Frege's (1918-1919a/1956) comment on 'I' "somewhat mysterious", as Recanati (2016: 114) puts it.

Chapter 4   Deferential Construal

he understands what the speaker is saying is the very thought which the speaker expressed" (Recanati 2016: 111, emphasis in the original). What Frege (1918-1919a/1956) states about 'I' in the above passage suggests rather that "one's placement in one's environment can affect the contents of the Thoughts one is capable of entertaining" (Heck 2002: 10). Such occasional senses as exemplified by the psychological mode of presentation associated in a given context with one and the same expression are what we are after in order to integrate into Frege cases the 'arthritis' case in which Adam and his doctor ascribe mutually incompatible properties to 'arthritis'. After all, it is reasonable to say that the difference between Adam's and his doctor's construals of *arthritis* is due to the difference of their placement in the environment in which they reside.

Nevertheless, there is a crucial difference between (5) and (6), on the one hand, and the 'arthritis' case, on the other. If two people, Herbert Garner and Leo Peter, understand completely different things by 'Dr. Lauben', Frege (1918-1919a: /1956: 297) argues, they "do not speak the same language" as far as the proper name 'Dr. Lauben' is concerned, even though they actually refer to the same person[6]. As Pollock (2015: 3237) states, "communication can fail *even if* the hearer grasps the very same wide-content as that expressed by the speaker". A similar picture may at first glance appear to hold for the 'arthritis' case, where Adam and his doctor understand 'arthritis' so differently that their beliefs contradict one another. The resulting pictures present a striking contrast, however; whereas Herbert Garner and Leo Peter are destined to fail to recognize that they are talking about the same person named 'Dr. Lauben', nothing hinders the communication between Adam and his doctor. This is the problem raised in (iii) above. As is evident from the formulation of Frege's Constraint, Frege's notion of sense is closely, if not essentially, tied to the possibility of failure of communication. Frege's Constraint says that $sense_1$ associated with linguistic expression E_1 is different from $sense_2$ associated with E_2 (possibly identical in form with E_1) if a rational person, S_1, can accept a statement in which E_1 occurs as true without yet endorsing another statement in which E_2 occurs, despite the identity of the broad content expressed by the two statements. This formulation implies that there can be disagreement between S_1 and another person, S_2. If S_2 accepts E_2 as true, it is possible that S_1 may agree with

---

6) „Dann sprechen Herbert Garner und Leo Peter, soweit der Eigenname ‚Dr. Gustav Lauben' in Betracht kommt, nicht dieselbe Sprache, obwohl sie in der Tat denselben Mann mit diesem Namen bezeichnen […]" (Frege 1918-1919a: 65)

E_1 but not with E_2 while S_2 may agree with E_2 but not with E_1. In such cases, the two subjects would not realize that they are talking about the same object or situation.

There is indeed a strong reason to believe that (1b) does not embody a genuine Frege case. Fine (2007: Ch. 2) contrasts cases in which the same word form occurs twice with cases in which two distinct coreferential expressions are used:

> The names 'Cicero' and 'Cicero' in the identity-sentence 'Cicero = Cicero' both represent the same object, as do the names 'Cicero' and 'Tully' in the identity 'Cicero = Tully'. But the first pair of names represents the object *as the same* whereas the second pair does not. In the first case, as opposed to the second, it is somehow part of how the names represent their objects that the objects should be the same. (Fine 2007: 39-40)

In (1b), Adam and his doctor employ the same word form 'arthritis', making their dialogue intuitively more akin to 'Cicero = Cicero' than 'Cicero = Tully'. This intuition is confirmed by the test proposed by Fine:

> [...] a good test of when an object is represented as the same is in terms of whether one might sensibly raise the question of whether it *is* the same. An object is represented as the same in a piece of discourse only if no one who understands the discourse can sensibly raise the question of whether it is the same. Suppose that you say 'Cicero is an orator' and later say 'Cicero was honest', intending to make the very same use of the name 'Cicero'. Then anyone who raises the question of whether the reference was the same would thereby betray his lack of understanding of what you meant." (Fine 2007: 40)

Anyone who, upon hearing the dialogue between Adam and his doctor, raises the question of whether the reference of 'arthritis' was the same would not be considered to have properly understood the dialogue. This suggests that the dialogue between Adam and his doctor represents the reference of their uses of 'arthritis' as the same. Fine points out that in order for objects to be represented as *being* the same it is essential that two coreferential expressions occur in a single sentence:

> The idea of representing objects as the same is to be distinguished from the idea of representing the objects as *being* the same. The sentences "Cicero =

Tully" and "Cicero = Cicero" both represent the objects as being the same but only the second represents them as the same. And, in general, one cannot informatively represent objects as being the same compatibly with representing them as the same. A further difference is that only a single sentence (such as "Cicero = Tully") can represent its objects as being the same but two different sentences (e.g., "Cicero is Roman," "Cicero is an orator") can represent their objects as the same. (Fine 2007: 40)

Obviously, any normal dialogue consists of more than one sentence. Thus, Adam's use of 'arthritis' and the doctor's use of 'arthritis' occur in different sentences, suggesting that understanding their dialogue is more similar to understanding the statement 'Cicero = Cicero' than to understanding the statement 'Cicero = Tully'. This decisively undermines the intuitive basis for assimilating (1b) to genuine Frege cases. Adam's and the doctor's uses of 'arthritis' represent the reference of the term as the same. In other words, the identity in reference is not to be discovered but is merely presupposed. This differs from typical Frege cases in which the audience is not required to understand that 'the morning star' and 'the evening star', for example, share the same reference. Frege's Constraint works only when the objects of the discourse are not represented as the same. As discussed in Section 3.6, the ability to understand that the objects of the discourse are represented as *being* the same does not belong to grammar. Competent speakers have the right to deny that (3a) and (3b) represent contradicting broad contents. By contrast, the ability to understand that the objects of the discourse are represented as the same seems to belong to grammar, as suggested by Pinillos (2011):

If I say in an ordinary context 'Bill is visiting. He is taking the train', then 'Bill' and 'he' in that discourse co-represent Bill in a way that makes that very fact evident to competent conversational participants who fully understand my speech. In roughly this sense, we say that co-representation or coreference (I may help myself to talk of 'reference' here) can be 'de jure'. If I say to you 'Hesperus is Phosphorus', the names corefer but this fact is not always evident: you may fully understand my speech while maintaining that the names refer to different planets. This would happen if you think that what I said is false. (Pinillos 2011: 301-302)

As Schroeter and Schroeter (2016: 197) put it, "[w]hen a subject consciously entertains a train of thought, certain elements *seem guaranteed* to pertain to the very same topic, simply in virtue of the way they are presented in thought" (emphasis in the original). In most (but not all) situations, competent speakers have no right to question the truthfulness of 'Cicero = Cicero' or to ask whether 'Bill' and 'he' corefer in 'Bill is visiting. He is taking the train'. As Pinillos remarks, the two occurrences of 'Cicero' in 'Cicero = Cicero' are coreferential *de jure*, and so are 'Bill' and 'he' in 'Bill is visiting. He is taking the train'. Likewise, there seems to be coreference *de jure* between Adam's use of 'arthritis' and his doctor's use of 'arthritis'.

Although (1b) is admittedly a case of coreference *de jure*, there is an obstacle to viewing (1b) as a typical case of such coreference. As has just been presented, typical cases of coreference *de jure* can be accounted for within the confines of grammar. Understanding of (1b), by contrast, cannot straightforwardly be reduced to understanding of the English grammar, insofar as Adam's construal of 'arthritis' is not conventionally encoded in the word and is more akin to what Recanati (1993) refers to as the psychological mode of presentation. Moreover, Adam's psychological mode of presentation of 'arthritis' is incompatible with its linguistic mode of presentation commonly understood by competent speakers. This is quite similar to (6), where the participants in the conversation, Smith and Jones, attach radically different psychological modes of presentation to one and the same word form 'he'. One might expect that, just as Smith and Jones cannot be sure that they are talking about the same person, Adam and his doctor grow skeptical of the identity of the subject matter. This is clearly not the case; Adam and his doctor are confident that they are talking about the same disease. We need therefore to consider why the 'arthritis' case behaves like cases of coreference *de jure* despite the radical divergence in construal between Adam and his doctor.

Unlike Frege's notion of sense, Langacker's notion of construal is defined without appealing to any possible disagreement between protagonists. For Langacker, construal is no more than "our manifest ability to conceive and portray the same situation in alternate ways" (Langacker 2008: 43). This definition is neutral about whether or when two speakers fail to recognize that they are talking about the same object or situation and to what extent their construals of the situation can be different without hindering their communication. But this neutrality does not help accommodate the case illustrated in (1b), chiefly because, unlike Frege's notion of sense, Langacker's notion of construal seems to be closely, if not essentially, tied to the notion of linguistic form, as confirmed by his repeated

Chapter 4   Deferential Construal

emphasis on the conventionality of construal (e.g. Langacker 2008: 55-57, 73, 96, 140, 143, 227-237, 458-462). In Langacker's framework, a difference in construal seems to entail a difference in form, and vice versa. What we are after in order to account for (1b) in terms of sense or construal is the condition for more than one sense or construal to be associated with one and the same form without communication being hindered. This issue has not been explicitly addressed in the cognitive linguistics literature. Let us refer to differences of construal which may lead to failure of communication as 'radical differences of construal', and differences in construal which have little risk of hindering mutual understanding between speakers as 'moderate differences of construal'. Typical cases of coreference *de jure* ensure moderate differences of construal, whereas Frege's Constraint discussed in Chapter 3 can now be held to define radical differences of construal.

In what follows I shall spell out in more detail the condition under which differences of construal remain moderate, taking as a starting point Fodor's (1994) assumption that "[h]aving a thought is being in a three place relation between a thinker, a (broad) content, and a mode of presentation" (Fodor 1994: 55) and that "[n]one of the three is dispensable if a propositional attitude is to be specified uniquely" (ibid.: 47)[7]. Assuming, following Fodor (1994), that a thought is defined by its broad content and its mode of presentation in addition to its thinker, it seems necessary for the speaker and the hearer to share the broad content and the mode of presentation in order that they communicate a thought with one another. But this is demanding too much. One may note that the sharing of the broad content is neither necessary nor sufficient. It is not sufficient because, in (6), Smith and Jones share the same broad content and yet there is a clear sense in which their communication is not successful. It is not necessary because, if Adam encounters $Adam_2$ and says, 'I have arthritis in my thigh', $Adam_2$ will have no difficulty understanding Adam's utterance. Those who accept social externalism would say that $Adam_2$ misunderstands Adam's thought, since their words spelled 'arthritis' are related to different diseases via their respective communities. But there is no reason to presuppose social externalism here, because Adam and $Adam_2$ are molecularly identical and nothing prevents them from talking about what they

---

7) A fundamental difference between cognitive linguistics and Fodor's (1994) assumption will be addressed in Section 4.3.2. Fodor's (1994) formulation is different from Fodor's (1975), according to which "having a propositional attitude is being in some *computational* relation to an internal representation" (Fodor 1975: 198). Fodor's original view did not take into account modes of presentation in individuating a thought (or propositional attitude).

225

consider to be the same disease. As far as communication between two people are concerned, what generally matters is the sharing of what they consider to be the same subject matter, rather than the sharing of the same subject matter (Pollock 2015: 3241). Whether the broad content is the same or not is extraneous to whether the communication is successful or not, insofar as the broad content is construed in similar fashions by the participants in the conversation. After all, as stated in Section 3.3, it is commonly (and implicitly) assumed in cognitive linguistics that there is no conceptual content independent of any construal. Since Adam and his doctor construe 'arthritis' in different fashions and yet succeed in communicating with one another, what is referred to here as the sharing of what they consider to be the same subject matter cannot be reduced to the sharing of one and the same mode of the presentation. To ask under what condition differing modes of presentation or construals do not lead to failure of communication is to ask under what condition the participants in a conversation are held to think about the same subject matter without assuming the complete identity of the mode of presentation or construal which each of the participants associates with the conceptual content. Since, in communication, a construal is often expressed by the choice of a particular linguistic expression, the sharing of construals may be facilitated by the use of one linguistic form rather than another. In the next section, I shall begin with a discussion on the relation between linguistic forms and construals.

4.3 Construal and Mutual Understanding

4.3.1 Identity in Form

Suppose that a construal$_1$ associated with a linguistic expression E_1 is different from construal$_2$ associated with another, non-pronominal linguistic expression E_2 which has the same conceptual content or broad content as E_1. In the definition spelled out above, the difference between construal$_1$ and construal$_2$ is radical if and only if, in a given context, a semantically competent person fails to recognize that E_1 and E_2 share the same conceptual content. One may note that the difference will be more likely to be radical when E_1 and E_2 have distinct forms than when E_1 and E_2 have the same form. When E_1 and E_2 differ in form, speakers must find out that E_1 and E_2 are coreferential *de facto* in order that the difference between construal$_1$ and construal$_2$ may remain moderate. As discussed in Section 3.6, Frege's Constraint rests on the fact that we often fail to take notice of the identity in reference or conceptual content between two expressions such as 'Tully' vs. 'Cicero', 'the morning star' vs. 'the evening star', and 'arthritis vs. 'inflammations of the joints'. Among the few exceptions are one-criterion terms, as illustrated by 'bachelor vs. unmarried man' and 'vixen vs. male fox'. Since, as argued in Section 3.7, any semantically rational speaker can by definition recognize the identity in reference between one-criterion terms, there can be no radical difference of construal concerning such terms. Recall that most of the terms we employ are cluster terms. It is often difficult to tell whether or not two cluster terms with distinct forms share the same conceptual content. When E_1 and E_2 are identical in form, on the contrary, speakers must assume, in order for the difference between construal$_1$ and construal$_2$ to be radical, that E_1 and E_2 are homonyms or that the single word E is polysemous between sense$_1$ corresponding to E_1 and sense$_2$ corresponding to E_2[8]. Language users usually do not assume homonymy or polysemy unless there is evidence to the contrary. For example, if, in a conversation about dogs, someone tells you something about what she calls a 'dog', you usually do not assume that there may be a word which is spelled 'dog' and yet means a different thing from your word 'dog', nor that she brusquely uses the word 'dog' in a completely different sense. In normal situations, both of you will continue to talk about dogs without being bothered by such troublesome possibility.

Bloomfield (1933: 396) states in this connection that sometimes "homonymy may lead to troubles of communication which result in disuse of a form". In Southwestern France, Latin [ll] as in 'bellus' ('pretty') changed into [t] as in [bɛt] (ibid.: 397). Curiously, however, nowhere in that district can we find the expected form [gat], deriving from Latin 'gallus' ('cock') (ibid.). As pointed out by Gilliéron and Roques (1912: 121ff), this gap probably has to do with the fact that, in the dialect in question, [gat] is homonymous with the word meaning 'cat', namely [gat],

---

8) In cognitive linguistics, a distinction is generally made between polysemy and homonymy, a distinction often blurred in philosophy and computational research (Hawthorne and Lepore 2011: 470-471, Haber and Poesio 2023: 3, 51). As Taylor (2002: 469) states, "[t]he distinction between polysemy and homonymy is usually drawn in terms of whether the different meanings associated with phonological form are related (as in polysemy) or whether they are unrelated (in which case we should speak of homonymy)". One may note that "relatedness of meaning appears to be a matter of degree" (Lyons 1977: 552) and that it is ultimately a subjective notion (Taylor 2003: 106, 2012: 229). This raises no theoretical difficulty, however, because "[w]hether a speaker perceives a word to be polysemous or homonymous probably has no consequences at all for their ability to use the word appropriately, in accordance with native speaker norms" (Taylor 2012: 230).

from Latin 'gattus'. Bloomfield (1933: 398) concludes, following Gilliéron and Roques, that the homonymic collision between the word meaning 'cock' and the word meaning 'cat' "must have caused trouble in practical life; therefore *[gat] 'cock' was avoided and replaced by makeshift words" such as [azā] ('pheasant') and [begej] ('farmer helper', 'handy man') (ibid. 397). This historical fact may provide indirect evidence that, other things being equal, mutual understanding is facilitated by the use of the same forms.

A caveat is in order regarding the notion of linguistic form. The identity or difference in form as mentioned here should not be interpreted in the strictly physical sense. Words like 'economics', 'either', 'schedule', and 'data' have allophones, i.e. alternative phonetic representations which do not affect the lexical identity of the word in question. Likewise, spelling variants like 'center/centre', 'realize/realise' and 'skeptic/sceptic' have no bearing upon the lexical identity of the word (Taylor 2012: 231, Sainsbury and Tye 2012: 41). Even if the speaker uses 'center' and the hearer understands it as 'centre', this does not count as a difference in form in the relevant sense. Kaplan (1990, 2011) proposes to explain the existence of allophones and spelling variants in terms of the notion of repetition. For Kaplan, "utterances and inscriptions are *stages* of words, which are *continuants* made up of these interpersonal stages along with some more mysterious *intra*personal stages" (Kaplan 1990: 98). Stages are linked by relations of repetition, that is, one's intention to use the very expression one has heard. In this conception, "[w]hat makes two utterances utterances of the same word is that they descend from a common ancestor" (Kaplan 2011: 509). Repetition should not be confused with imitation (Kaplan 1990: 103-104). No matter how poor the speaker's imitative ability may be, he may well be repeating the same expression. Kaplan (1990: 101) goes so far as to say that "the difference in phonographology, the difference in sound or shape or spelling, can be just about as great as you would like it to be"[9]. As Kaplan (2011: 509) puts it, the notion of repetition "no more requires them [= utterance of the same word] to resemble or replicate that ancestor than my children are required to resemble or replicate their parents in order to be members of my family". Millikan (1997) expresses a similar view:

[...] in English, contrasting pronunciations of "schedule" (s-k-e-dule versus sh-e-dule) count as tokens of the same word type while exactly the same contrast between the pronunciations of "skeet" and "sheet" or "skin" and "shin" produces different word types. And of course these practices may change over time. Surely the same should be true for mental word types. Whatever the individual mind/brain *treats* as the same mental word again *is* the same word again. Nor is there any reason why mental typing should not *evolve* in an individual mind or brain. In this particular respect, the situation is not like that of a public language, where there are typing conventions laid down in the public domain, prior to a particular person's use. For mental language, nothing corresponds to these conventions. (Millikan 1997: 514)

Such is the main origin of allophones and spelling variants[10]. When we say that, all else equal, mutual understanding is facilitated by the use of the same forms, 'the same forms' must be understood in Kaplan's (1990, 2011) sense. Adam's pronunciation of 'arthritis' may be somewhat different from his doctor's, but this does not make their utterances of 'arthritis' utterances of distinct words.

To summarize, one of the reasons why the 'arthritis' case exhibits a moderate difference of construal despite the radical divergence between Adam and his doctor is that they use the same word form to express their thoughts characterized by different construals. As Kamp (1985: 259) puts it, "[t]he term acts as intermediary, serving to connect the two elements of their respective minds". In other words, the use of the same form invokes the presumption of coreference *de jure*.

4.3.2 One-to-Many Correspondence Between Form and Construal

Attaching more than one construal to one and the same form departs from

---

9) Central to Kaplan's conception of words is what Hawthorne and Lepore (2011: 448) refer to as 'the constitutive authority of intentions'. Hawthorne and Lepore claim that this conception of words is too tolerant:

> If you see the word 'dog' for the first time and are ordered to rewrite it but proceed to write 'g' followed by 'o' followed by 'd', then you have failed to write the word you were asked to: your intentions, as a matter of fact, lack constitutive authority. (Hawthorne and Lepore 2011: 463)

Sainsbury and Tye (2012: 59, n. 3) comment that Kaplan's remark "is probably an exaggeration (as Lepore and Hawthorne [sic.] (2011) say, a grunt is not a repetition of a word, however it may be intended), but it shows that a high degree of similarity is not necessary". Stojnić (2022) argues that neither intention nor tolerance provides any criterion for determining which word a given utterance tokens. For Stojnić, the metaphysical question of which word is tokened is different from the epistemic question of how the hearer recognizes the word tokened.

10) This does not preclude that some allophones may be reinterpreted as distinct phonemes in the course of time, giving rise to a genuine phonological change in a particular language.

Langacker's (1987, 2008) initial proposal. Indeed, as stated in Section 3.3, the notion of construal was first introduced to account for the difference in meaning between two or more forms which nonetheless have the same conceptual content. It is fairly clear that Langacker has in mind a picture illustrated in Figure 4-1:

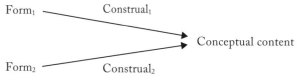

Figure 4-1: Different Forms - Different Construals

This 'different forms - different construals' picture is widely accepted in the cognitive linguistics literature, in accordance with the assumption that a particular construal is conventionally encoded in a particular linguistic expression (Langacker 1987: 47, 2008: 55). The 'arthritis' case, on the contrary, suggests the 'same form - different construals' picture illustrated in Figure 4-2, where construal$_1$ and construal$_2$ correspond to the ways in which Adam and his doctor construe the form 'arthritis'.

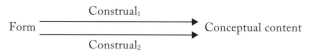

Figure 4-2: Same Form - Different Construals

Both speakers associate the same form with the same conceptual content, with the only difference residing in the way they do so. Since Adam's and his doctor's construals contradict one another, it cannot be the case that both construals are conventionally associated with the word form 'arthritis'. Cognitive linguists commonly lay emphasis on conventional connections between a particular form and a particular construal or meaning, as illustrated by Ziem's (2008) remark to the effect that slight differences in form can yield considerable differences in meaning (Ziem 2008: 10)[11], given that it is the phonological form of a linguistic expression that triggers the process of conceptualization of the content of that expression (ibid.:

---

11) „Kleine Unterschiede auf der Formseite können große Unterschiede auf der Inhaltsseite nach sich ziehen." (Ziem 2008: 10)

Chapter 4   Deferential Construal

12, 232)[12]. Although cognitive linguists are often reticent about whether the opposite holds, it seems reasonable to suppose that it does not, i.e., that a difference in construal does not entail a difference in form. Intuitively, the notion of construal pertains primarily to linguistic meaning rather than linguistic form, which would give a certain plausibility to the idea that the construal is, in principle, neutral about in which form(s) it is realized. Even though there are certainly cases in which a particular construal is conventionally associated with a particular form, there is no compelling reason to assume that every association between a form and a construal is conventional, or that, if the relevant association is conventional, there cannot be a single form which happen to be associated with more than one construal.

Non-conventional associations between forms and construals are so common that one may hardly notice that they exploit the same mechanism as involved in the 'morning star / evening star' case. Frege was very clear about this point. In fact, in (5) above, it was assumed that Leo Peter and Rudolph Lingens associated with 'Dr. Lauben' distinct construals, both of which are in no way conventional. Likewise, Fodor (1994) points out that we commonly associate with a concept a construal or mode of presentation which we know is not shared by others:

Suppose that I often think of water under the mode of presentation 'Granny's favorite drink' and suppose that you, not knowing Granny, don't. This sort of thing must happen all the time, and it can be perfectly innocuous. There's no reason why it should get you into trouble that you don't know that Granny likes water best; and there is also no reason why our water-directed behaviors shouldn't very largely overlap despite this presumed difference in our collateral information. (Fodor 1994: 51)

In total independence from the Fregean view, Ziem (2008) begins his introduction to cognitive linguistics with an episode of a Japanese passenger incapable of relating the English expression 'suicide bomb' to what happened on September 11, 2001 (Ziem 2008: 7-8). The passenger was arrested at Chicago airport for

---

12) „Die Formseite eines sprachlichen Zeichens bildet den Ausgangspunkt eines kognitiven Konzeptualisierungsprozesses der Inhaltsdimension desselben sprachlichen Zeichens." (Ziem 2008: 12)
„Es sind phonologische Einheiten, die derartige Aktivierungen schematischen Wissens motivieren." (Ziem 2008: 232)

231

carrying a notebook in which he had written 'suicide bomb'. It was later revealed that he had written down that expression in order to look it up in the dictionary after the flight. The current stereotype associated with 'suicide bomb' alludes to the September 11 attacks, and knowledge of this conventional association is required for full competence in English. Thus far, Ziem's introduction to cognitive linguistics is perfectly in line with Langacker's in that it highlights the importance of convention in form–construal correspondences. What is remarkable with Ziem's introduction is that the episode of the Japanese is immediately followed by another episode, in which a cannibal asks for a menu in a ship restaurant by saying, 'Could you please bring me the passenger list?' (Ziem 2008: 8)[13]. The waiter and the cannibal construe the word 'menu' ('Speisekarte') in partially (but not totally) different manners. While both think that the menu helps one decide what to eat and drink, the cannibal, unlike the waiter, expects the menu to include personal names. The cannibal's construal of 'menu' does not conform to the community convention which he is supposed to follow. This episode indicates that one and the same form can receive several construals, at least one of which is non-conventional.

In support of the view that one and the same form can receive several conventional construals is a hypothetical process described by Kaplan (1990: 114-115) whereby different construals come to be conventionally linked to the same form–reference pair:

[T]here can be distinct names which are phonographs [= both homophones and homographs] and which also have the same semantic value. [...] One evening, the mischievous Babylonian looked up and saw Venus, and he thought to himself "This one is just as beautiful as Phosphorus, so let's call it 'Phosphorus' too". [...] So he names, or perhaps we should say *renames*, Venus 'Phosphorus'. [...] Now that it seems clear that we have two common currency names. (Kaplan 1990: 114-115, emphasis in the original)

If this hypothetical process has an intuitive plausibility, that several linguistic expressions share the same phonological form and the same semantic value does not entail that they are conventionally associated with the same construal. A simi-

---

13) „Ein Kannibale sitzt im Restaurant eines Luxusdampfers. Der Kellner kommt und fragt, ob er die Speisekarte bringen soll. Der Kannibale entgegnet: Ja, bringen Sie mir doch bitte die Passagierliste.'" (Ziem 2008: 8)

lar remark was made by Evans (1982: 381):

A most vivid example of the second kind of case [= two name-using practices which concern the same individual] is found in R. L. Stevenson's *Dr. Jeckyll and Mr. Hyde*, in which two names, believed to refer to different persons, are in fact used of the same person. But the distinctness of the names is not essential for the distinctness of the practices: Stevenson could easily have told the story with the same name used in two distinct practices, with no one having the least idea that the nice Mr Hyde and the terrible Mr Hyde are one and the same person. So what is it for there to be one rather than two 'Hyde'-using practices? Intuitively, there exist two distinct practices involving the use of the name 'NN' if uses of the name can be associated with two distinct networks of communication in the community, such that information circulates through each network, but does not pass between the networks. (Evans 1982: 381)

Kaplan assumes that, in the situation described above, there are two homonymous words spelled 'Phosphorus'. This can admittedly be considered an alternative way of saying that there is a radical difference of construal involved in the two uses of the word form 'Phosphorus', in the same way that, in the above scenario depicted by Evans (1982: 381), the same name 'Hyde' receives two radically different construals. For the Babylonian who inadvertently renamed Venus 'Phosphorus', there are two distinct planets both called 'Phosphorus'. It follows that he can in principle accept 'Phosphorus is remote' as true while rejecting 'Phosphorus is remote', as long as he believes the two occurrences of 'Phosphorus' to denote different planets. This is tantamount to saying that there are two homonymous words spelled 'Phosphorus'. Whether the alleged same form embodies a single word or two distinct words therefore does not affect the validity of the overall picture in Figure 4-2.

The point just made should not be confused with the question of whether the putative homonymous words have different underlying syntactic structures or logical forms. As remarked earlier, Fodor (1994) maintains that "[h]aving a thought is being in a three place relation between a thinker, a (broad) content, and a mode of presentation" (Fodor 1994: 55) and that "[n]one of the three is dispensable if a propositional attitude is to be specified uniquely" (ibid.: 47). For instance, (7a) and (7b) have in common the thinker and the broad content, differing solely in the mode of presentation:

(7)   a. Oedipus wants to marry Jocasta.

          b. Oedipus wants to marry his mother.

This idea may at first sight appear equivalent to Frege's idea that there should be a distinction between sense and reference or Langacker's idea that conceptualization essentially consists of construal and conceptual content. Unlike Frege and Langacker, however, Fodor proposes to reduce differences of mode of presentation to syntactic differences of Mentalese (language of thought; LOT). For Fodor, "[t]he notion of a *Mentalese word* corresponds roughly to the intuitive notion of a *concept*" (Rescorla 2019: 1.3). The motivation for Fodor to postulate Mentalese is that natural languages are inapt to be the medium of thought:

> The obvious (and, I should have thought, sufficient) refutation of the claim that natural languages are the medium of thought is that there are nonverbal organisms that think. I don't propose to quibble about what's to count as thinking, so I shall make the point in terms of the examples discussed in Chapter 1. All three of the processes that we examined there – considered action, concept learning, and perceptual integration – are familiar achievements of infrahuman organisms and preverbal children. [...] the representational systems of preverbal and infrahuman organisms surely cannot be natural languages. So either we abandon such preverbal and infrahuman psychology as we have so far pieced together, or we admit that some thinking, at least, isn't done in English. (Fodor 1975: 56)

By combining his proposal of Mentalese with Frege's distinction between sense (mode of presentation) and reference, Fodor (1994: 47) claims that "modes of presentation are sentences of Mentalese" and that "sentences are individuated not just by their propositional content but also by their syntax" (cf. Heck 2012: 152). According to this syntactic conception of the mode of presentation, the difference in construal between (7a) and (7b) reduces to the difference of their syntax in Mentalese, just as the distinction between (8a) and (8b) is deemed purely syntactic:

(8)   a. John is a bachelor.

          b. John is an unmarried man.

Chapter 4   Deferential Construal

If this view is correct, the Babylonian who inadvertently renamed Venus 'Phosphorus' would be taken to associate, in Mentalese, two distinct syntactic structures to the surface word form 'Phosphorus'. This is not to say that the single word 'Phosphorus' is polysemous between two distinct construals, or that there are two homonymous words both spelled 'Phosphorus'. The notions of polysemy and homonymy presuppose the identity in phonological form. Thus, to say that the word 'port' is polysemous between 'harbor' and 'fortified wine' is to say that the two related senses are attached to the phonological form /pɔ.ɪt/ (Taylor 2002: 469)[14], and to say that there are two homonymous words both spelled 'bank' is to say that the two unrelated senses, 'river edge' and 'financial institution', are attached to the phonological form /bæŋk/. By the same token, assuming polysemy or homonymy for 'Phosphorus' requires that the polysemous word or the homonymous words can be defined phonologically. By contrast, reducing differences of mode of presentation to syntactic differences of Mentalese does not imply that the two Mentalese expressions corresponding to the modes of presentation are phonologically identical, because Mentalese has neither phonology nor morphology (Fodor 1994: 106, Rescorla 2019: 1.2).

The syntactic conception of modes of presentation is not without its disadvantages. As Braddon-Mitchell and Fitzpatrick (1990) point out, it is not clear at all whether the syntax of Mentalese can be in place without presupposing its semantics:

We have two related claims to make: first, that if you have a semantic interpretation and something to map it on to, then you can generate a trivial syntax; and second, that you can't have a syntax properly so described without a prior semantics of which it is the syntax. The LOT [= language of thought] requires that mental representations have syntactic structures realized in the brain. The problem here is what is going to count as syntactic structure. Syntax and semantics are intimately related. The practice of logicians to behave as though the syntax comes first and then an interpretation is applied puts the cart before the horse. A syntax is a simple, if not the simplest, description of a supposedly meaning-bearing system, given its intended meaning. A syntactic constituent of such a system is that which makes some uniform semantic contribution to

---

14) Taylor (2012: 229) observes that some speakers fail to see any connection between the two senses of 'port'.

235

that system. What this means is that a syntactic item is taken to be a syntactic item because it stands in a signifying relation to some semantic interpretation. (Braddon-Mitchell and Fitzpatrick 1990: 12)

The temptation then is to think that you have structure even if you jettison the semantic story which led to the taxonomy of those syntactic tokens. But in effect, we don't have any syntactic tokens in the absence of the semantic content. For a substantial syntactic account to be given, two factors are required: a semantics, to ensure that it really is a syntax that is being given rather than any other kind of description, and an independent motivation for the taxonomy of syntactic tokens, so as to avoid the merely trivial kind of syntax described above. (Braddon-Mitchell and Fitzpatrick 1990: 14)

Unless the relation between the syntax and semantics of Mentalese is not elucidated, it is difficult to determine whether its syntax can accommodate phenomena which are intuitively semantic in nature.

As stated earlier, Fodor (1994) maintains that (7a) and (7b) correspond to two different syntactic structures in Mentalese both of which represent the same broad content. This, Fodor argues, is no different from the relation between (8a) and (8b), since these two sentences also represent the same broad content, being distinguished merely at the syntactic level. The validity of the analogy between (7) and (8) is dubious, however, because knowing the equivalence between (8a) and (8b) but not knowing the equivalence between (7a) and (7b) constitutes semantic rationality as discussed in Chapter 3. Any competent speaker of English is supposed to know that a bachelor is an unmarried man, but not that Jocasta is Oedipus's mother. It is inconceivable that Fodor fails to notice this contrast between (7) and (8), for Fodor (1975: 124-125) ascribes the equivalence between (8a) and (8b) to the synonymy between 'bachelor' and 'unmarried man', an obviously semantic relation:

[...] 'He is a bachelor' and 'He is an unmarried man' receive identical representations at the message level assuming that 'bachelor' and 'unmarried man' are synonyms[15]. (Fodor 1975: 124)

---

15) Fodor (1975: 109) states that "messages are most plausibly construed as formulae in the language of thought".

Chapter 4 Deferential Construal

[...] one of the computational devices that mediate the relation between semantic representations and surface sentences is a dictionary and [...] one of the things that the dictionary says about English is that 'bachelor' corresponds to the metalinguistic formulae *unmarried man*. [...] In effect, the semantic level ignores the difference between 'bachelor' and 'unmarried man' but is sensitive to the fact that the latter has 'man' and 'unmarried' as constituents. If, therefore, a speaker wants to get 'bachelor' into a surface sentence, or if a hearer wants to get it out, they must do so via their knowledge of the dictionary. (Fodor 1975: 125)[16]

If 'bachelor' and 'unmarried man' were replaced by 'Jocasta' and 'Oedipus's mother' respectively, these passages (or at least the second one) would make little sense. It is far from clear whether the relation between (7a) and (7b) should be accommodated by the structural level of Mentalese that represents the equivalence between (8a) and (8b).

A more important point to be made for present purposes is that a syntactic difference in Mentalese, but not a semantic difference in sense or construal, seems to necessarily hinder communication. In a nutshell, Fodor's (1994) proposal is to reduce putative examples of the picture illustrated in Figure 4-2 to cases corresponding to Figure 4-1. In the statement in (6), the word form 'he' is construed either as 'the man on television' or 'the man on the train'. For Frege and Langacker, this difference belongs to semantics rather than phonology or morphology, as indicated by Figure 4-2. For Fodor, on the contrary, to say that the reference of 'he' is presented under two different modes of presentation is to say that there are two Mentalese expressions which differ in their syntactic structures. On this account, the ambiguity exhibited by the sentence of natural language in (6) is resolved in Mentalese. Thus, Smith would represent (6) as 'THE MAN ON TELEVISION IS A STOCKBROKER' in his Mentalese and Jones 'THE MAN ON THE TRAIN IS A STOCKBROKER'. As remarked earlier, other things being equal, mutual understanding is facilitated by the use of the same forms. It seems that any syntactic difference arising from the two modes of presentation of (6) would work in the other direction, leaving little chance for Smith and Jones to believe that they are talking about the same man. For the same reason, the syntactic conception of

16) Fodor (1975: 125) attributes the view presented in the passage to Katz and Fodor (1963).

237

the mode of presentation would cause detrimental effects on the conversation between Adam and his doctor. Whatever sentence of Mentalese may correspond to Adam's utterance of the sentence of English 'I have arthritis in my thigh', the resulting sentence of Mentalese should entail for Adam that ADAM HAS IN ADAM'S THIGH INFLAMMATIONS THAT MAY AFFECT A PERSON'S THIGH, and for the doctor that ADAM HAS IN ADAM'S THIGH INFLAMMATIONS THAT CANNOT AFFECT A PERSON'S THIGH. If Adam and his doctor think in their respective Mentalese, there seems to be no hope for them to notice that they are thinking and talking about the same disease.

As it stands, the argument so far is not decisive for two reasons. First, it must be borne in mind that "Mentalese is not an instrument of communication" (Rescorla 2019: 6.2) but "the medium of thought" (Fodor 1975: 56). This characterization of Mentalese is bolstered by the observation that preverbal children apparently engage in thinking but not in verbal communication. Consequently, we cannot suppose that the success of communication between Adam and his doctor should be accounted for in terms of the structure of their Mentalese. In effect, we know as little about the relation between language of thought and language of communication (English, for example) as when Fodor (1975: 127) remarked several decades ago that "if [...] the language of thought is a system distinct from natural languages, then correspondences between their structure should be thought of as *surprising* facts, facts to be explained" (emphasis in the original).

The second reason that the above argument is not decisive is that, as Ludlow (2003b) argues, Mentalese may possibly be sensitive to the environment in which it is tokened, without necessarily preventing subjects living in different environments from communicating with each other. Ludlow (2003b: 407ff) considers a hypothetical scenario in which on Twin Earth, but not on Earth, Socrates was an invention of Plato. It now follows that an Earthian (like Oscar) and his twin (like Oscar$_2$) associate different logical forms to the same utterance of (9):

(9)   Socrates was a philosopher.

When Oscar employs the expression 'Socrates', he succeeds in referring to a particular individual, while Oscar$_2$'s use of 'Socrates' fails to refer. If Oscar$_2$'s use of the expression is to be meaningful, it must be interpreted as a description in disguise, say, 'the teacher of Plato who drank hemlock' (Ludlow 2003b: 412), just as 'Santa Claus' is deemed equivalent to a description like 'the fat jolly elf who lives at the

Chapter 4   Deferential Construal

North Pole' (ibid.: 404). Even though Oscar and Oscar$_2$ are intrinsically identical, the form and content of their thoughts are different insofar as thoughts are represented in logical forms:

> In the version of externalism I have in mind, my twin – a molecular duplicate of me – has thoughts that not only differ in content from mine, but also differ in form. So, for example, my thought that I express as 'Socrates was a philosopher' is a singular proposition containing Socrates as a constituent. The thought that my twin expresses as 'Socrates was a philosopher' is a general proposition. More, the linguistic expressions of our thoughts will differ in ways correlative to the ways in which the thoughts differ in form. (Ludlow 2003b: 407)

The differences in question may not prevent Oscar and Oscar$_2$ from talking about what they call 'Socrates', because they are not aware that they think with different Mentalese expressions. Similarly, even if Adam and the doctor think with different Mentalese words because of the difference of their placement in the environment in which they reside, it remains possible for them to talk about the same topic.

It is important, however, to realize that the syntactic conception of the mode of presentation proposed by Fodor fails to offer an account of how Adam and his doctor, who construe the word form 'arthritis' in mutually incompatible ways, succeeds in referring to the same disease by employing that word form. Unlike in the 'Socrates' case, the doctor is cognizant of Adam's deviant construal of 'arthritis'. We need an apparatus which helps explain why two people who entertain thoughts that differ in form and content and to whom the divergence is mutually manifest still succeed in communicating with each other.

4.3.3 Similarity in Construal[17]

In general, the participants in the conversation need not share exactly the same construal, as a consequence of (10) proposed in Section 3.7:

> (10) A speaker S is minimally competent in the use of a cluster word X iff S understands most of the stereotypical descriptions associated with X.

---

17) Section 4.2.3 is based on Sakai (2018) and (Sakai 2023b: Sections 3 and 4).

239

As described by Burge (1979a/2007), Adam has may correct beliefs about arthritis. He understands most of the stereotypical descriptions of 'arthritis', making it possible for him to talk about arthritis with his doctor. The use of the same form is expected, unless there is evidence to the contrary, to evoke similar construals, in the minds of the participants in the conversation.

Nevertheless, it has widely been assumed that, when communication is successful, some thought or proposition, including its construal, must be shared between the speaker and the hearer. If John successfully communicates to Mary the thought expressed by the utterance of (11), Mary comes to entertain the same thought expressed by (11):

(11) It is raining in Stockholm.

Although this may appear self-evident, it is often not the case that the same construal is shared by the speaker and the hearer. One may note, first of all, that it is one thing to say that some thought must be shared between speaker and hearer in successful communication, and it is another to say that the very thought expressed by the speaker must be shared by the hearer. Suppose that John utters (12) to Mary:

(12) I am hungry.

It is evident that communication fails if Mary comes to entertain, on her part, the thought expressed by John's utterance of (12), because this would make it the case that Mary now thinks that she rather than John is hungry (Recanati 2016: 111). The shared belief must be 'John is hungry', not 'I am hungry'. In John's thought, John is presented as 'I', namely in the first-person. But this mode of presentation must not be shared by Mary, who is expected to understand John's first-person utterance 'I am hungry' as expressing the third-person thought that John (or he) is hungry. If, as assumed here, thoughts contain construals, 'I am hungry' is a different thought from 'He is hungry'.

Even in this case, however, it might be said that something must be shared between speaker and hearer in order for communication to be successful. For some philosophers, this something is a singular proposition, namely a proposition about one or several individuals. Even though a referring expression contains descriptive content, the descriptive content serves exclusively to pick out the reference and is

240

not part of the singular proposition in which the expression occurs (Kamp 1985: 251, Recanati 1993: 283). If (12) expresses a singular proposition, the descriptive content of 'I', whatever it may be, does not go into the proposition. The singular proposition expressed by (12) is something like (13), in which '*a*' represents the individual picked out by the descriptive content of 'I':

(13)   *a* is hungry.

The proposition in (13) contains no mode of presentation of *a*. This is to say that, when someone believes (13), the belief attribution is *de re* (as opposed to *de dicto*)[18]. This is the result of the directly referential character of 'I'. Although the expression 'I' is associated with a particular mode of presentation, that mode of presentation does not go into the proposition in which 'I' occurs. Such is the gist of the notion of direct reference, as Recanati (1993) expounds:

> The meaning of a directly referential expression includes a particular semantic feature, REF, and in quite the same way there is an intrinsic feature of de re concepts – the thought-constituents corresponding to directly referential expressions – which distinguishes them from 'descriptive' concepts; what renders direct reference direct is not the alleged fact that no mode of presentation occurs but the fact that the modes of presentation that occur are filtered out and made truth-conditionally irrelevant by virtue of the features in question. (Recanati 1993: xii)

The thought corresponding to (15) can therefore be shared by both John and Mary, unlike the first-person thought only John entertains. This coheres with Perry's (1988: 5/1993: 231) view that "[o]ne reason we need singular propositions is to get at what we seek to preserve when we communicate with those who are in different contexts".

It turns out, however, that the requirement Perry suggests is still too stringent. Which proposition must be shared when the speaker utters (14a) or (14b) to the hearer?:

---

18) *De re* and *de dicto* are defined as follows:
   A sentence is *semantically de re* just in case it permits substitution of co-designating terms *salva veritate*. Otherwise, it is *semantically de dicto*. (Nelson 2023)

(14) a. Superman leaps more tall buildings than Clark Kent. (Braun and Saul, 2002: 1)

b. Romain Gary won the Prix Goncourt earlier than Émile Ajar. (Sakai 2023b: 248)

The trouble with Perry's view is that some people know the identity in (15) while others do not:

(15) a. Superman is Clark Kent.

b. Romain Gary is Émile Ajar.

Braun and Saul (2002: 7ff) call those who know the identity in (15) 'enlightened speakers' and those who do not 'unenlightened speakers'. For unenlightened speakers, (14a) expresses a singular proposition about two individuals represented by the names 'Superman' and 'Clark Kent. That is, unenlightened speakers construe (14a) as meaning that individual X leaps more tall buildings than individual Y. This construal is not shared by enlightened speakers. Enlightened speakers construe (14a) as saying that individual Z leaps more tall buildings when Z is X than Z does when Z is Y. This is not a singular proposition about two individuals but a proposition about two different aspects of one and the same individual. Enlightened speakers and unenlightened speakers disagree about whether (14a) expresses a singular proposition or not due to the fact that they stand in different epistemic relations to Superman and Clark Kent. Their different epistemic states give rise to their different construals of the relevant objects, i.e., objects *qua* aspects and objects *qua* individuals, respectively. Nevertheless, they agree that (14a) is a true statement about Superman and Clark Kent. Their commitment to different ontologies does not hinder communication. A similar remark can be made about (14b). This suggests that the participants in the conversation need not share any singular proposition to understand each other . A weaker condition is proposed by Heck (1995) in a different context:

Now, it may be correct that a given sentence can have different cognitive values for different speakers all of whom understand it, but how different can these be? At the very least, the different beliefs speakers would form, were they to accept the truth of a sentence they all understand, surely must concern the same objects: they must at least get the *references* of the names in the sentence correct. (Heck 1995: 88, emphasis in the original)

The communication of the proposition expressed by (14) can succeed if the speaker and the hearer get the references of the terms correct, whether they be construed as individuals or aspects.

There need not even be reference. As stated earlier, there may be no communication failure between Oscar, who construes 'Socrates' as the name of an individual as we do, and Oscar$_2$, who believes that, as Ludlow (2003b) imagines, Socrates is a mere invention of Plato, construing 'Socrates' as an abbreviation of the description 'the teacher of Plato who drank hemlock' (Ludlow 2003b: 412). Likewise, there is usually no communication failure between adults who do not believe in Santa Claus and children who do. The fact that children construe 'Santa Clause' as a name while adults construe it as a description which cannot be satisfied by anything does not prevent them from talking with one another about Santa Clause. In such cases, participants in the communication do not even agree on the reference of the term. Positing two different construals for one and the same sentence thus provides no obstacle for communicative interactions in which the sentence occurs. As Bezuidenhout (1997: 217) remarks, "[t]he conception the speaker has of the name-bearer doesn't have to be shared by the audience to any great degree". If, as assumed here, a though and a concept consist of both construal and conceptual content, there needs be no such thing as *the* thought that all subjects, enlightened or not, must entertain in order to properly understand an utterance:

[I]t is not necessary in addition to the speaker-relative content and the listener-relative content to posit some non-relative notion of utterance content in order to account for successful communication. Successful communication requires only a contextually determined degree of similarity between speaker-relative and listener-relative content. (Bezuidenhout 1997: 222; see also Recanati 1995, 2016: 119)

There is a sense in which enlightened speakers and unenlightened speakers mean different things by uttering (14a-b) and attach distinct concepts to the word forms 'Superman', 'Clark Kent', 'Romain Gary' and 'Émile Ajar', in conformity with what Weiskopf (2009: 157-158) refers to as 'representational pluralism'. There is no such thing as *the* concept of Superman, consisting of one and the same conceptual content and one and the same construal. This does not mean, however, that they talk at cross-purposes. There is also a sense in which enlightened speakers and unenlightened speakers share the same concepts. As Onofri (2016) argues, there are two conceptions of concept which are seemingly incompatible, one corresponding to the FC and the other corresponding to PUB:

> **The Fregean Constraint (FC):** If a subject S is involved in a Frege case with respect to a certain object x, then S has two concepts C_1-C_2 such that C_1-C_2 refer to x and *C_1 is a different concept from C_2*. (Onofri 2016: 6; see also Valente 2019: 327)

> **Publicity (PUB):** Whenever a group of subjects communicates successfully, genuinely agrees, or is covered by the same intentional generalization, then those subjects must share the corresponding concepts. (Onofri 2016: 5; see also Valente 2019: 316)

True, competent speakers are not required to share the mode of presentation of the object(s) talked about:

> It is often said that proper names are associated with no particular way of thinking of their reference. [...] [This claim] means that there is no unique mode of presentation (or unique sort of mode of presentation) such that, whenever a proper name is used, its reference is thought of under this mode of presentation (or under a mode of presentation of this sort). This is consistent with the view that, whenever a proper name is used, *there is* a mode of presentation, although not always the same one, under which its reference is thought of. (Recanati 1993: 169, emphasis in the original)

Bloom (2000: 19) is right to claim that "[w]e are comfortable translating a word from an ancient Greek text into the English word *star*, even though the ancient Greeks believed that stars were holes in the sky". But this observation does not make the mode of presentation useless. It merely suggests that, as Valente (2019: Section 6) claims, PUB must suitably be weakened. As discussed in Section 3.7, minimally competent speakers are required to understand most of the stereotypical descriptions associated with the term in question. Thus, a person who takes 'Superman' to be the name of an aspect of a planet just like 'the morning star', or

'Émile Ajar' to be the name of a chair, would not be considered to have correctly understood the sentences in (14). Competent speakers are supposed to understand what Braun and Saul (2002) call 'accuracy conditions' for the application of terms:

We also associate different images, and imaging routines, with the names 'Superman' and 'Clark'. If asked 'Does Superman wear red boots?', we form an image of a man wearing a cape, not an image of a man in glasses and a business suit. When we read in a newspaper the sentence 'Superman saved a person who fell off a cliff', we generate an image of a man with a red cape, flying and catching a person in mid-air, and not an image of a man in glasses catching a person. One reason that it's reasonable for us to associate different sorts of image with the two names is that the two sorts of image differ in their *accuracy conditions*. For example, the former image is accurate only if a man, while wearing a red cape, caught a person in mid-air. This image is likely to be accurate. The second image is accurate only if a man, while wearing glasses and a business suit, caught a person. It is likely to be *in*accurate. If we were just as likely to form a 'glasses' image as a 'caped' image when we heard a 'Superman' sentence, many more of our images would be inaccurate. (Braun and Saul 2002: 20)

The ancient Greeks and we would agree that there are numerous stars shining in the sky. That the ancient Greeks and we have distinct construals of 'star' does not entail that we share no construal. Competence with the term 'star' requires approximate understanding of the accuracy conditions for something to count as a star. Bloom (2000: 19) is mistaken to claim that "[i]t is enough that we all use the word to refer to the same things; further cognitive overlap is not necessary". On the one hand, speakers competent with 'Superman' and 'Clark Kent' need not understand that the two terms are coreferential. This makes it possible for unenlightened speakers to talk about Superman and Clark Kent with enlightened speakers. Unenlightened speakers are equally competent with these terms. On the other hand, speakers competent with 'Superman' and 'Clark Kent' must understand that the two terms are associated with distinct accuracy conditions. A person who takes 'Superman' and 'Clark Kent' to be mere synonyms is not qualified as competent with these terms. Similarity in the construal is both necessary and sufficient for successful communication (Pollock 2015: 3239). This admittedly is the key to understanding (1b), an apparent challenge for cognitive linguistics.

245

To summarize the argument so far, if the speaker and the hearer use the same forms, and both of them are competent with the relevant terms, the difference of construal, if any, is likely to remain moderate. In a sense, enlightened and unenlightened speakers do not share the same concept of *Superman* since they do not construe it in exactly the same fashion. In another sense, however, they share the same concept of *Superman* since they construe one and the same conceptual content in relevantly similar fashions. For the same reason, it seems reasonable to assume that Adam, who is minimally competent with 'arthritis', can talk about arthritis with his doctor, despite their different construals of the concept. There remains a problem, however. Enlightened speakers and unenlightened speakers agree that (14a) is a true statement as long as their differing construals of 'Superman' and 'Clark Kent' pose no difficulty in identifying Superman and Clark Kent. In the 'arthritis' case, by contrast, Adam makes a conceptual error in construing arthritis as possibly afflicting one's thigh. Adam's construal of 'arthritis' is contradictory to the doctor's construal. How can two expressions with obviously contradictory construals be coreferential *de jure*?

4.4 Deference[19)]

4.4.1 Division of Linguistic Labor

Even though Adam's and his doctor's construals of 'arthritis' contradict each other, their construals are not on the same level, since Adam is a layperson while the doctor is an expert. We are here dealing with what Putnam (1973: 703-706, 1975: 144-146) famously called the 'division of linguistic labor':

> Every linguistic community exemplifies the sort of division of linguistic labor [...], that is, possesses at least some terms whose associated "criteria" are known only to a subset of the speakers who acquire the terms, and whose use by the other speakers depends upon a structured cooperation between them and the speakers in the relevant subsets. [...] Whenever a term is subject to the division of linguistic labor, [...] it is only the sociolinguistic state of the collective linguistic body to which the speaker belongs that fixes the extension. (Putnam 1975: 146)

---

19) Section 4.3 is an elaboration of Sakai (2022a: Sections 1 and 4) and Sakai (2022b: Section 5).

Chapter 4   Deferential Construal

Putnam (1975: 146) suggests that the division of linguistic labor is "a fundamental trait of our species". We have the categories of elm and beech not because each of us can distinguish elm trees from beech trees, but because there are experts in our community who are competent to identify them (Fodor 1994: 33, Aydene 1997: 435-436). Crucially, individual speakers, whether they be experts or not, are supposed to know that there is a division of linguistic labor in their community, i.e., they are supposed to know that (as opposed to how) the meanings of linguistic expressions may be determined non-individualistically or socially. The division of linguistic labor thus construed ascribes the ability to categorize gold to the speech community as a whole as opposed to its individual members. We can use words we incompletely understand precisely because, "as Putnam suggests, we rely on a belief that somewhere there are experts who do have such knowledge and can tell the difference between different species of tree" (Saeed 2016: 34).

Lay speakers' reliance on experts is known as linguistic or semantic deference. As Chalmers (2012: 280) states, when an expression is used deferentially, "the referent of the speaker's use of the expression depends on how others in the linguistic community use the expression". Marconi (1997) emphasizes that it is very common that we defer to experts in the use of words:

> The phenomenon of *semantic deference* is real enough: we are all prepared to acknowledge that some speakers are more competent than we are on this or that word or family of words, and even that there may be speakers, for example, lexicographers, who are more competent than we are on many, perhaps most, words. Therefore, we are prepared to accept corrections to our semantic habits, both referential and inferential. The phenomenon concerns most words, certainly including natural kind words. (Marconi 1997: 90)

The findings of externalism can largely, if not wholly, be accommodated by internalist frameworks, provided that these frameworks take into account the phenomenon of semantic deference. As De Brabanter et al. (2005) suggest, the notion of semantic deference, when properly understood, can help reconcile externalism and internalism:

> Two intuitions are at conflict here. On the one hand, we do not master all the concepts that we use. Still, we would not want to say that it is impossible for us

247

to have or express thoughts about, say, rockets, aluminum or contracts just because our understanding of those concepts is incomplete. On the other hand, it is not clear how we manage to say anything true or false when we don't master the concepts associated with the words we are using. Talking nonsense is not the same as saying something false. The idea of semantic deference was introduced precisely in an attempt to reconcile these conflicting intuitions. Its rationale is that we can meaningfully use concepts that we do not master because we defer to the public language, whose rules are fixed by our linguistic community. (De Brabanter et al. 2005: 2)

It is because Adam defers to his doctor in the use of 'arthritis' that they can be considered to share the concept expressed by the word even though they hold contradictory beliefs. Even Chomsky, a radical internalist in Segal's (2000: 27) sense, concedes that the lexicon of a person's I-language makes reference to the division of linguistic labor and semantic deference:

[…] the study of language and UG, conducted within the framework of individual psychology, allows for the possibility that the state of knowledge attained may itself include some kind of reference to the social nature of language. Consider, for example, what Putnam (1975) has called "the division of linguistic labor". In the language of a given individual, many words are semantically indeterminate in a special sense: The person will defer to 'experts' to sharpen or fix their reference. […] In the lexicon of this person's language, the entries […] will be specified to the extent of his or her knowledge, with an indication that details are to be filled in by others, an idea that can be made precise in various ways but without going beyond the study of the system of knowledge of language of a particular individual. (Chomsky 1986: 18)

Although in this passage Chomsky says merely that "details are to be filled in by others", speakers sometimes possess inaccurate pieces of information. As a competent speaker, Adam is prepared to discard his beliefs about arthritis if it turns out that they are out of line with what the doctor says. As Schroeter and Schroeter (2016: 195) suggest, on the standard conception of deference, "[t]he very fact that subjects take themselves to stand corrected by expert opinion reveals that deference to experts (or some other social factor) is part of their ultimate criterion for identifying the reference" (cf. Greenberg 2014: 162).

Burge's 'arthritis' case is so well known that it is sometimes thought that assuming contradictory beliefs is a necessary condition to substantiate externalism. As Hunter (2003: 736-737) remarks, however, the externalism does not hinge on the assumption of contradictory beliefs, since it equally follows from cases, as discussed by Putnam (1975: 143-144, 165, 168-169), where laypeople, unlike experts, know little about the distinction between elm trees and beach trees. The same applies to the 'water' case, in which the experts' conceptualization of water subsumes (and in no way contradicts) Oscar's. Such cases are admittedly what Chomsky (1986) has in mind. The challenge posed for internalism is to spell out how such a division of linguistic labor or semantic deference is represented in an individual's mind.

4.4.2 Recanati's (1997) Deferential Operator

Recanati (1997: 96) construes semantic deference as the mental counterpart of quotation marks or quasi-quoting in public language (cf. Woodfield 2000: 443, Recanati 2000: 458). Suppose that a student utters (16a) without fully understanding the term 'synecdoche:

(16) a. Cicero's prose is full of synecdoches. (Recanati 1997: 85)
      b. Cicero's prose is full of 'synecdoches'. (ibid.: 86)
      c. Cicero's prose is full of R_x (synecdoches).

Since, in the speaker's lexicon, the term 'synecdoche' is not fully defined, the proper way to express her utterance is (16b), where the term is quasi-quoted. Recanati's point is that (16b) is represented in her Mentalese as (16c), where R_x represents what Recanati (1997, 2006) dubs the 'deferential operator'. It is generally assumed that Mentalese cannot contain any uninterpreted symbols, since "all mental entertaining is 'interpretation'" (Recanati 1997: 91). Recanati (2000: 461) calls this the 'Interpretation Principle':

> **Interpretation Principle:** If a mental sentence is well-formed, it must possess a definite meaning – a character – even if it falls short of expressing a definite content. (Recanati 1997: 91, 2000: 461)

The Interpretation Principle prohibits the public word 'synecdoche' from going into the speaker's Mentalese unless it has a definite meaning. This is where the deferential operator R_x comes into play. The deferential operator serves to turn the empty symbol σ into the deferential concept $R_x\,(\sigma)$, which, unlike σ, is conceptually available to the speaker who has only a vague idea of σ. In a nutshell, "[t]he deferential operator makes a concept out of an empty symbol" (Recanati 1997: 95), in the same way that quotation marks in public language turn nonwords into words. The deferential operator is defined as in (17):

(17) The deferential operator R_x ( ) applies to a symbol σ and yields a complex expression $R_x\,(\sigma)$ whose character is distinct from that of σ (if σ has one). The character of $R_x\,(\sigma)$ takes us from a context in which the speaker tacitly refers to a certain cognitive agent x (which can be an individual or a community of users) to a certain content, namely the content which σ has for x, given the character which x attaches to σ. (Recanati 1997: 91-92)

The formulation of the deferential operator in (17) draws on Kaplan's (1989a, 1989b) distinction between character and content presented in Section 1.3.3. The indexical 'I' is associated with the conventional meaning 'the utterer', independent of the context of use, which determines the reference in each context of use. Kaplan (1989a: 505ff, 1989b: 574) refers to the constant linguistic meaning as the 'character' and the reference determined in context as the 'content'. Competent speakers know the character of 'I' but not its content, which is only determined with respect to the context in which 'I' is tokened. Recanati (1997) applies the same picture to the interpretation of symbols incompletely understood. The speaker who has only a vague idea of what σ is like does not understand the character of the expression 'σ'. The deferential operator serves to provide a character to an expression containing 'σ' by converting the uninterpreted symbol 'σ' into the complex symbol '$R_x\,(\sigma)$'. The speaker does understand the character of '$R_x\,(\sigma)$' in contrast to the character of 'σ'. Just as the character of 'I' takes us from a context in which 'I' is used to a definite content, the character of '$R_x\,(\sigma)$' takes us from a context in which the ignorant student relies on some cognitive agent, say, his teacher who knows better about σ, to the content which the expression 'σ' has for the teacher[20]. The student only understands the character of '$R_x\,(\sigma)$' while the teacher understand the character of 'σ *tout court*. This makes the student's mental representation of (16a) a deferential representation, namely a representation containing the deferential operator (Recanati 1997: 93), as illustrated in (16c). Despite this

Chapter 4   Deferential Construal

difference, the characters of 'R$_x$ (σ)' and 'σ' both determine the same content, due to the epistemological dependence of 'R$_x$ (σ)' vis-à-vis 'σ'. Although the deferential representation (16c) entertained by the student is epistemically indeterminate, it is semantically determinate (Recanati 1997: 87). This enables the student to talk about synecdoche, despite his only partial grasp of the concept (Recanati 2006: 253). Now, Recanati (1997: 91-92) is explicit that Burge's 'arthritis' case can also be analyzed with the help of the deferential operator. According to Recanati (1997: 92), "the speaker who utters [(18a)] expresses the proposition that she has arthritis in the thigh, even if she does not know what arthritis is":

(18) a. I have arthritis in my thigh.
      b. I have 'arthritis' in my thigh.
      c. I have R$_x$ (arthritis) in my thigh.

The use of 'arthritis' in (18a) is deferential (ibid.), which is expressed as in (18b) in public language and represented as in (18c) in the speaker's Mentalese.

The trouble with Recanati's (1997) deferential operator is that it works too well. Since quotation marks can be used for any kind of word or even nonword, there is nothing that prevents the deferential operator, the mental equivalent of quotation marks, from applying one-criterion words like 'bachelor' and nominal kind terms like 'sofa', as in (19)-(20):

(19) a. Mary met an eligible bachelor.
      b. Mary met an eligible 'bachelor'.
      c. Mary met an eligible R$_x$ (bachelor).
(20) a. My teacher has a sofa in her office.
      b. My teacher has a 'sofa' in her office.
      c. My teacher has R$_x$ (sofa) in her office.

According to Recanati's account, by uttering (19a), a person who does not know

---

20) The definition of the deferential operator in (17) mentions the speaker's tacit reference to a certain cognitive agent. This indicates, in Recanati's view, that the speaker may defer to others unwittingly (Woodfield 2000: 446). Kay (1983: 136) construes Putnam's notion of the division of linguistic labor as suggesting our "unconscious recourse" to experts' concept. This casts doubt on Recanati's proposal to characterize deference by analogy with quasi-quoting, because quasi-quoting is normally a conscious act. This issue will be raised in Section 4.4.3.

what 'bachelor' means can nevertheless express the proposition that Mary met an eligible bachelor. Likewise, by uttering (20a), a person totally ignorant of what sofas are like can express the proposition that his teacher has a sofa in her room. This would undermine the very point of Burge's 'arthritis' thought experiment, in which Adam is described as a person minimally competent in the use of the term 'arthritis'. Adam's minimal competence with the term enables us to ascribe to him the concept of *arthritis* despite his deviant understanding of the concept. Intuitively, a person who has an incomplete grasp of *arthritis* can be credited with *arthritis*, whereas a person who does not understand at all what arthritis is can hardly be credited with the concept. As Woodfield (2000) points out, Recanati's proposal obscures the distinction between incomplete understanding and non-competence, a distinction vital to social externalism:

Note that, for Burge, speakers who utter a word which they do not understand *at all* are not credited with the concept expressed by the word, but *partial* understanders may be said to possess the concept. Recanati, on the other hand, assimilates Burgean cases to indexical beliefs. The contents are externally individuated, but social factors (other people and their utterances) come in only as elements of the subject's context of utterance. The context helps to fix a referent, and the referent itself is a constituent of the content. It does not matter whether the subject partly understands the word or completely fails to understand it. The mechanism of reference-fixation is the same in either case. (Woodfield 2000: 447, emphases in the original)

Given that, in Recanati's (1997) view, an expression either is accompanied by the deferential operator or stands alone, it falls short of capturing the obvious fact that competence comes in degrees (Quine 1960: 13, Dupré 1981: 70, Burge 1986a/2007: 713, 718, Dummett 1991: 321, Wiggins 1995: 71-72, Millikan 1997: 514, Recanati 1997: 88, 94, Stanley 1999: 17-18, Woodfield 2000: 447-448, De Brabanter et al. 2005: 27, 2007: 15-16, Boyd 2013: 206, 209-211, 214-215, Wikforss 2014: Section 2.1). Recanati's (1997) position on the issue seems inconsistent. On the one hand, he acknowledges that "deferentiality is a matter of degree" (ibid.: 94) and that "[w]e start by accepting a representation without understanding it; this attitude of acceptance leads us to use the representation in a certain way; and by so using the representation we end up understanding it" (ibid.: 89). On the other hand, he states that "[e]ven when they have both a character and a content, deferential representations, though semantically determinate, are *epistemically* indeterminate: the quasi-believer does not know which proposition the deferential sentence she accepts expresses" (ibid.: 93). This misrepresents Burge's (1979a/2007) point. It is not the case that Adam does not know which proposition he expresses with the sentence 'I have arthritis in my thigh'. Adam is adamant that he thereby expresses the belief that he has arthritis in his thigh. It is merely the case that he is less competent with *arthritis* than the experts in his community. As pointed out by Woodfield (2000) and Wikforss (2014: 2.1), such graded understanding is not possible if, as described by Recanati, concept acquisition is nothing but the removal of the deferential operator:

> It seems impossible that there could be a *gradual* process of moving out of quasi-quotes. It's clearly not a process of bit-by-bit removal (like taking one's clothes off), nor is it a process of decay (like quotation marks fading away on a page as the ink loses its colour). The learner starts off using mental symbols like Rx(*'synecdoches'*) and Rx (*'kachna'*) and ends up using completely distinct symbols like *synecdoches* and *duck*. Prima facie, there has to be a saltation – a switch of symbol-type – at some point. (Woodfield 2000: 447)

The all-or-nothing character of the deferential operator admittedly has to do with the fact that the notion is modeled on the interpretation of indexicals such as 'I'. As stated in Section 4.3.2, the indexical 'I' is a directly referential expression in the sense that the mode of presentation associated with the expression is "filtered out and made truth-conditionally irrelevant" (Recanati 1993: xii). What matters is who 'I' refers to, not how the referent is construed. If the deferential representation $R_x (\sigma)$ is interpreted in a fashion similar to 'I', it is to be expected that what matters is what '$R_x (\sigma)$' refers to, not how the reference is construed. Indeed, Recanati (1997: 96) states that deferential symbols are directly referential. However, as Woodfield (2000) makes clear, the point of Burge's (1979a/2007) argument lies in the fact that Adam is taken to think of arthritis as *arthritis*, rather than as *what people call 'arthritis'*, despite his incomplete understanding of the concept:

> According to Recanati, the boy who thinks [(16c)] has a directly referential belief about synecdoches, which he thinks of, in context, as *Those*. That is how Alf thinks of them, if Alf's mental representation is [(16c)]. But on Burge's view, this is not how Alf thinks of them. He thinks of them *as synecdoches*. In

the thought-experiments, the belief-attributions are supposed to be true when construed opaquely, as specifying the subject's conceptual mode of presentation. The attributions are not to be taken *de re*. (Woodfield 2000: 447)

Recanati's notion of the deferential operator obscures the notion of conceptual competence in yet another sense. Competent speakers are supposed to know that they can defer to experts for the use of terms such as 'synecdoche' and 'arthritis', but not for the use of terms such as 'bachelor' (Cohnitz and Haukioja 2013: 489, Haukioja 2015: 2147) and 'sofa':

And some words do not exhibit any division of linguistic labor: "chair;" for example. But with the increase of division of labor in the society and the rise of science, more and more words begin to exhibit this kind of division of labor. "Water," for example, did not exhibit it at all prior to the rise of chemistry. Today it is obviously necessary for every speaker to be able to recognize water (reliably under normal conditions), and probably every adult speaker even knows the necessary and sufficient condition "water is H_2O," but only a few adult speakers could distinguish water from liquids which superficially resembled water. In case of doubt, other speakers would rely on the judgment of these "expert" speakers. Thus the way of recognizing possessed by these "expert" speakers is also, through them, possessed by the collective linguistic body, even though it is not possessed by each individual member of the body, and in, this way the most recherché fact about water may become part of the *social* meaning of the word while being unknown to almost all speakers who acquire the word. (Putnam 1975: 145)

Competent speakers are meta-internalists in Cohnitz and Haukioja's (2013) and Haukioja's (2015: 2146-2147) sense, i.e., they have the ability to judge whether or not a given word is subject to a division of linguistic labor[21]. White (1982: 352) contrasts words like 'elm' with words like 'chair', stating that "speakers who cannot associate even such common words as 'chair' with certain typical examples in their environment picked out ostensively will not ordinarily count as speakers of English". Competent speakers tacitly know that, in general, only cluster words as opposed to one-criterion words and nominal kind words necessitate a division of linguistic labor. This indicates that, appearances notwithstanding (cf. Bilgrami 1992: 258, n. 13), Putnam's notion of division of linguistic labor involves an

Chapter 4 Deferential Construal

essentially internalist or individualistic conception of concepts, which is in tension with Burge's social externalism or anti-individualism.

As Bilgrami (1992) makes clear, the social externalist is committed to the thesis that "an individual's concepts (such as that of arthritis) are often determined by the experts in his or her society" (ibid.: 24), whereas the notion of division of linguistic labor highlights "the individual's own beliefs rather than the expert's as determining what concepts are to be attributed to him" (ibid.: 23). As outlined in (1b), social externalism ascribes to Adam and his doctor exactly the same concept of *arthritis*, despite their divergent construals of the term 'arthritis'. Likewise, social externalism holds that individuals unable to discern elm trees from beech trees are nevertheless credited with the experts' concepts of *elm* and *beech*. By contrast, the thesis of the division of linguistic labor draws a distinction "between the concepts of an elm tree that the relying agent has and the relied upon experts have" (ibid.: 23). Indeed, as Liu (2002: 388) points out, contrary to Burge (1979a/2007, 1986a/2007, 1993/2007), Putnam held the view that concepts are in the individual's head, whereas meanings can be unknown even to the most competent speakers in the linguistic community. This is to say that laypeople and experts construe the putative conceptual content in different ways. If so, the natural strategy to reconcile (1b) with the internal conception of concepts is to posit two different concepts of *arthritis*, which are coreferential *de jure*. This is a line of thought pursued by Recanati (2000), in response to Woodfield's (2000) criticism of Recanati's (1997) deferential operator. Since, as stated above, laypeople know when to defer to experts, laypeople's concept of *arthritis* should allude to the presence of experts who know better about the conceptual content.

4.4.3 Deferential Construal

As discussed in the previous section, the problem with Recanati's (1997)

---

21) Meta-internalism is defined as follows:

> *Meta-Internalism*: How a linguistic expression E in an utterance U by a speaker S refers and which theory of reference is true of E is determined by individual psychological states of S at the time of U. (Cohnitz and Haukoja 2013: 482)

Meta-internalism must be distinguished from the First-Order internalism, to which the notion of semantic deference is irrelevant:

> *First-Order Internalism*: The reference of any linguistic expression used by a speaker S is determined by the individual psychological states of S. (Cohnitz and Haukioja 2013: 476)

255

deferential operator is that it deprives the term in question of any construal of its conceptual content, which is indispensable to one's conceptual competence. The desideratum is to reinterpret R_x (σ) as a construal of σ, which is linked to the experts' construal of the same conceptual content. Fodor (1994: 33) characterizes R_x (σ) as the deferential concept of σ. Deferential concepts are defined as "concepts whose semantics are said to depend on the knowledge of experts in the linguistic community" (Aydene 1997: 434). This does not mean that deferential concepts work in total independence of the possessor's internal state. As Fodor (1994: 36) puts it, semantic deference is best seen as *"the use of experts as instruments"*[22]. We defer to the experts when we cannot tell elms from beeches just as we defer to the litmus paper when we cannot tell acids from bases (ibid.: 34)[23]. This is so fundamental a fact that it is naturally taken to be a built-in feature of concept acquisition. In line with this conception of deferential concepts, Recanati (2000) defends the view that when we acquire a public word W, we automatically acquire a deferential concept R_x (W). We do not attach the deferential operator to W, since such a process would presuppose that our Mentalese contains an uninterpreted word W, violating the Interpretation Principle mentioned earlier, according to which our Mentalese consist exclusively of symbols with a definite meaning (Woodfield 2000: 447-448). Any public word is accompanied, from the very start, by a deferential concept whose "content is determined via the users whom we get the word from (or via the community in general)" (Recanati 2000: 461-462). Recanati's (2000) view is congenial to Kaplan's (1989b) Consumerist Semantics, according to which "[w]ords come to us prepackeged with a semantic value" and "[i]f we are to use *those words*, the words we have received, the words of our linguistic community, then we must defer to *their* meaning" (Kaplan 1989b: 602, emphases in the original).

---

22) Greenberg (2014: 160, n. 25) even talks about 'deference to the world' for the determination of the meaning of a natural kind term. It may also be noted, incidentally, that Braddon-Mitchell (2004) denies that deference exclusively relates a thinking subject to something outside the subject:

> [...] There is deference going on here, but it is deference to internal processes rather than external experts. Both are defeasible, and if we grant that external deference is possible, I don't see why bringing it inside the (sub-personal) mind makes it any different, for both the expert and the internal module are from the personal perspective mere black boxes. (Braddon-Mitchell 2004: 142)

23) Recanati (1997, 2000) does not explicitly mention Fodor's (1994) view of deferential concepts.

Chapter 4   Deferential Construal

As stated in Section 4.4.2, in his earlier work (Recanati 1997: 96) Recanati held semantic deference to be the mental equivalent of overt quotation in written speech (Recanati 2000: 458). This analogy overlooks the fact that, unlike overtly quoting someone's remark, semantically deferring to others is not an intentional speech act on par with the other canonical speech acts (Austin 1962/1975) such as promising, ordering, asserting, and so on. Although to put an expression in scare-quotes is a less typical speech act, it nevertheless has an effect of making it manifest that the speaker "signals that he distances himself from the expression in some way and that it is not functioning normally" (Woodfield 2000: 448), as when Putnam put the term 'essence' in scare-quotes (Hacking 2007a: 11-12, 2007b: 228). As pointed out by De Brabanter et al. (2007: 2, 7), the speaker often has no intention to make his intention to defer manifest to the hearer, and the hearer need not recognize the speaker's intention to defer[24]. Semantic deference is done by default, in contrast to quasi-quoting (ibid.). This suggests that semantic deference should be couched not in terms of communicative intention à la Grice (1957/1989) but in terms of semantic and conceptual competence discussed in Chapter 3. Just as the use of the word 'roe' automatically evokes the reproductive cycle of fish (Langacker 1987: 164) regardless of the utterer's communicative intention, so the use of a cluster term such as 'arthritis' and 'water' automatically activates the deferential concept associated with the term, insofar as the term is stored in the speaker's mental lexicon[25]. In his formulation of the deferential operator, Recanati (1997: 91-92) mentions the speaker's tacit reference to a cognitive agent. But the speaker's intention to tacitly refer to an indefinite cognitive agent can hardly be made manifest to the audience. Recanati's (2000) endorsement

---

24) De Brabanter et al. (2005: 4, 28, 2007: 2, 7) say simply that the speaker defers without intending to defer. This goes against Fodor's (1994: 36) idea mentioned above that semantic deference is nothing but the use of experts as instruments, since the use of an instrument is usually an intentional act. Brabanter et al. seem to acknowledge that deference is an intentional act, as illustrated by their comment that "[o]f course, whenever we engage in communication, we implicitly intend to conform to the rules of language use" (De Brabanter 2005: 4, n. 4). Brabanter et al.'s (2005: 4, 2007: 2, 7) remarks in question should presumably be interpreted as suggesting that the speaker's intention to defer is not a communicative intention as originally advertised by Grice (1957/1989). In effect, the authors mention (recognition of) communicative intention elsewhere to distinguish default deference and deliberate deference (De Brabanter et al. 2005: 1, 5, 21-22, 2007: 10-11). Relevant to the present discussion is default deference (De Brabanter et al. 2005: 4), which is made without overt communicative intention.

257

of the consumerist semantic conception of concepts enables one to avoid the problem. Semantic deference is a built-in feature of certain cluster terms, which enables the lay speaker to access the corresponding public conceptual content.

It is worth mentioning that, as De Brabanter et al. (2005, 2007) point out, there is another type of deference which is made with overt communicative intention. In this type of deference, which de Breabanter et al. dub 'deliberate deference', the speaker makes it manifest that she has the intention to allude to someone's use of the relevant term. Suppose that Adam keeps saying (21a) to his doctor and that the doctor, feeling pain in her calves, utters (21b) to her colleague:

(21) a. I have arthritis in my calves.
      b. My calves really hurt. It must be arthritis. (De Brabanter et al. 2005: 5)
      c. My calves really hurt. It must be 'arthritis'.

It is mutually manifest to the doctor and her colleague that the doctor does not believe that she is suffering from arthritis, since it is a common knowledge among experts that arthritis cannot strike one's calves. The doctor alludes to Adam's mistaken use of 'arthritis' and wants her intention to do so to be recognized by her colleague. In written speech, her utterance of (21b) would be represented as the sentence in scare-quotes in (21c). This is analogous to (22) discussed by Recanati (2001: 667-668, 2010: 250, 279):

(22) a. Paul says he's due to present his work in the paper session.
      b. Paul says he's due to present his work in the 'paper session'.
      c. Paul says he's due to present his work in the poster session.

The utterer of (22a) is mimicking Paul's deviant use of the term 'paper session' by which he intends to mean 'poster session'. In written speech, (22a) would be

---

25) If the speaker has not acquired the term yet, the deferential concept is not evoked, because she has no such concept in her lexicon. This is the reason that, as stated in 2.3 and 3.7, (i) is not literally interpreted but reinterpreted as meaning (ii):
(i)   I have been drinking orangutan for breakfast for the last few weeks.
(ii) I have been drinking orange juice for breakfast for the last few weeks.
The utterer of (i) has not yet acquired the word 'orangutan', failing to defer to the community. This is to say that her use of the word form 'orangutan' is not linked to the public word 'orangutan', and hence to the public concept of *orangutan*.

Chapter 4   Deferential Construal

represented as in (22b), in which Paul's deviant use of the term is put in scare-quotes. The communication fails if the hearer does not recognize the utterer's intention to convey (22c) by alluding to Paul's utterance. In such cases, the analogy between deference and overt quotation goes through. De Brabanter et al. (2005, 2007) emphasize that we must not confuse deliberate deference as illustrated by the doctor's utterance of (21b) and default deference as illustrated by Adam's utterance of (21a). Unlike deliberate deference, default deference takes place in any act of verbal communication (De Brabanter et al. 2005: 6, 2007: 10).

Returning to the main issue, another difficulty raised by Recanati's (1997) deferential operator was that it made the occurrence of the term in question directly referential. Thus, we are forced to say that when Adam thinks of arthritis deferentially, he thinks of it as, say, *that thing* rather than as *arthritis*. Now that semantic deference is considered a way to think of public conceptual content, it is possible to say that Adam thinks of arthritis in a deferential manner, which guarantees that he thinks of the same conceptual content as his doctor, who thinks of arthritis in a non-deferential manner. Both Adam and his doctor think of arthritis as *arthritis*; it is just that there is more than one way to construe arthritis as *arthritis*:

If I am right, the difference between the doctor's concept of arthritis and [Adam]'s is similar to that between 'I' and 'you' in their respective utterances 'You have arthritis' and 'I have arthritis': 'I' and 'you' refer to [Adam] under different modes of presentation. Similarly, the doctor's concept of arthritis and [Adam]'s deferential concept R_{doctor} (*arthritis*) both refer to arthritis, under different modes of presentation. (Recanati 2000: 459)

Even though this proposal brings some amendments to the problem posed by Recanati's (1997) conception of the deferential operator, it is still unsatisfactory. Recanati assimilates the contrast between Adam's construal of 'arthritis' and the doctor's construal of 'arthritis' to the contrast between the two indexical expressions 'I' and 'you' which, in the relevant context, share the same content. Recall that the mode of presentation associated with an indexical is filtered out and hence is not included in the truth-conditional content expressed by the sentence in which the expression occurs (Recanati 1993: xii). Even though the thought expressed by Adam's utterance of (23a) and the doctor's utterance of (23b) express different thoughts, the difference is filtered out and the two subjects come to entertain the *de re* belief that *a* has *b*, where *a* and *b* represent Adam and arthritis, respectively,

259

independently from any construal:

(23) a. I have arthritis.
      b. You have arthritis.

But this obscures the fact, emphasized by social externalism, that Adam thinks of arthritis as *arthritis* despite his deviant construal. It is erroneous to bring the point of Burge's thought experiments to bear only on the *de re* aspect of the subject's mental state (Burge 2007: 159). Focusing on *de re* attitudes is also detrimental to the cognitive linguistic conception of meaning, since, if the modes of presentation are filtered out, (24a) and (24b) express the same proposition:

(24) a. Superman flies.
      b. Clark Kent flies. ((24a-b): Heck 2002: 2)

Such coarse-grained individuation of content is out of place for the two-dimensional view that a concept consists of conceptual content and its construal. It is not legitimate to suppose that Adam's and the doctor's uses of 'arthritis' are directly referential.

Recall, however, that, as remarked in Section 4.1, the contrast between Adam's construal of 'arthritis' and the doctor's construal of 'arthritis' cannot be assimilated to the contrast between two non-indexical expressions illustrated by the contrast between 'Superman' and 'Clark Kent'. We are certainly not compelled to say that the terms 'Superman' and 'Clark Kent' are directly referential, as demonstrated by the intuitive non-equivalence between (24a) and (24b). Another problem with the analogy between (23) and (24) is that it falls short of capturing the fact that Adam's use of 'arthritis' and the doctors use of 'arthritis' are coreferential *de jure*. The subject nominals of (23a) and (23b) are coreferential *de jure*, while those of (24a) and (24b) are merely coreferential *de facto*. That is, a person who does not understand that (23a) and (23b) express the same thing is clearly considered not to understand the conversation between the utterer of (23a) and the utterer of (23b), whereas minimal competence with English does not require the ability to understand the equivalence between (24a) and (24b). The fact that Lois Lane is an unenlightened speaker does not *ipso facto* deprive her of competence in English. The relation between Adam's use of 'arthritis' and the doctors use of 'arthritis' is more akin to the relation between Adam's use of 'I' and the doctors use of 'you'

260

than to the relation between 'Superman' and 'Clark Kent'. In this respect, Recanati's idea that the difference between the doctor's concept of *arthritis* and Adam's resembles the difference between 'I' and 'you' seems to be on the right track. What is wanting is that which guarantees the coreference *de jure* between Adam's and the doctor's concept of *arthritis* without making their utterances directly referential.

The answer to this problem is tied to how we should understand the gradual nature of concept acquisition, a phenomenon difficult to describe within the framework defended by Recanati (1997). Fodor (1998a) suggests that colloquial concepts can be replaced by corresponding scientific concepts:

> Anyhow, it seems just obvious that concepts like STAR in, as one says, the 'technical sense' – the concept of stars that is prepared to defer about the Sun and black dwarfs on the one hand and meteors and comets on the other – come after, and sometimes come to replace their colloquial counterparts. (Fodor 1998a: 154)

Applied to the 'arthritis' case, this picture amounts to saying that Adam, who initially possesses the deferential concept of *arthritis$_1$*, comes to possess the medical concept of *arthritis$_2$* instead of the deferential concept. The trouble with this picture is that it is difficult to understand how the replacement occurs gradually. It seems that Recanati's (1997) and Fodor's (1998a) suggestions have difficulty accommodating the obvious fact that, as Stanley (1999) states, there is an array of levels of understanding between minimal competence and full understanding:

> Understanding comes in levels. At the bottom, there is minimal linguistic competence. At the top, there is full understanding, that is, the sort of understanding one must have to discourse competently with experts. Between minimal linguistic competence and full understanding, there is an array of levels of understanding, suitable for different communicative contexts. (Stanley 1999: 17-18)

As Wiggins (1995: 71-72) remarks, rudimentary understanding could advance through different stages to become the capacity of an expert. Recanati (2016: 128) states that semantic deference, which is a symptom of rudimentary understanding, "is only a *stage* in the development of a full-fledged encyclopedia entry" (emphasis in the original). Pursuing this line of thought, Recanati (2000) proposes an account of the gradual character of concept acquisition in terms of a merge of the deferential concept and the non-deferential concept:

[...] when a deferential concept – for example, Putnam's concept of an elm – gets associated with a concept (e.g. the demonstrative concept 'that type of tree'), and that association stabilizes, a new concept results, with a distinct character. How is the merging process to be properly described? I do not know, but I have no doubt that it can be gradual, and that is all that matters for us. (Recanati 2000: 462-463)

The putative merging process may certainly be a gradual one. But Recanati's (2000) new account, as well as his earlier account, seems to entail that the deferential concept is replaced by some other concept at the final stage of concept acquisition. This picture conflicts with Woodfield's (2000) observation that even experts are prepared to defer to still more competent experts:

Every rational speaker should be disposed to accept semantic corrections from those who are more knowledgeable. Since experts are rational speakers, they too have the same conditional willingness to defer. There is a sense in which the pressure to defer never goes away. (Woodfield 2000: 436)

Even if Adam's doctor happens to believe that arthritis can afflict one's thigh, his use of 'arthritis' means *arthritis* as do the other specialists' uses of the term. This indicates that Adam's doctor is prepared to defer to others for the use of the term in question. Of course, one could say that experts who are prepared to defer to others are not at the final stage of concept acquisition, failing to be qualified as genuine experts. But this idea is at odds with the fact that, as Burge (1986a: 714/2007: 268) says, "[t]he consensus of the most competent speakers can be challenged". As we have seen in Section 3.3, this has led Rey (1983: 255) to propose the Hypothesis of External Definitions, according to which "the correct definition of a concept is provided by the optimal account of it, which need not be known by the concept's competent users". There is no ground for denying Rey's hypothesis, which is embraced by a number of researchers (Frege 1969/1979, Burge 1986a/2007, 1990/2007, 1993/2007, 2012, Higginbotham 1998a, De Brabanter et al. 2005: 27, 2007: 15-16). This points to the idea that the deferential

262

Chapter 4   Deferential Construal

concept remains attached to the word at every stage of development.

In Section 3.7, I have proposed the condition for competence with cluster words outlined in (25):

(25)   A speaker S is minimally competent in the use of a cluster word X iff S understands most of the stereotypical descriptions associated with X.

On the basis of the foregoing argument, I now propose to interpret (25) as an individualistic construal of X, which should be supplemented with its deferential construal:

(26)   A speaker S is minimally competent in the use of a cluster word X iff (i) S understands most of the stereotypical descriptions associated with X, which constitutes S's individualistic construal of X, and (ii) S attaches to X a deferential construal.

In fact, (ii) is not independent of (i), because, as suggested earlier, (i) automatically activates (ii). As a result, every cluster word is associated with both an individualistic construal and a deferential construal. This account is compatible with the gradual character of concept acquisition described by Woodfield (2000):

Communication-based learning typically proceeds as follows: somebody tells you something, you understand what they are saying, you believe them, you add the knowledge to your store, and if necessary you delete previously held beliefs that are incompatible. This is also what goes on in ordinary cases of deferring. For the learning to work, you must already possess the concepts (in order to understand), and they must be the same concepts that the teacher or expert is employing (otherwise there is communication-failure). (Woodfield 2000: 447-448)

When we acquire a word, we attach to the word a deferential construal in addition to an individualistic construal. The deferential construal serves to connect us to more competent speakers in the community, making our use of 'arthritis' and an expert's use of 'arthritis', for instance, two occurrences of the same word 'arthritis' rather than two homonymous words, even though our individualistic construal is poorer than, or even contradictory to, the expert's. More specifically, our deferential

263

construal of *arthritis* is dependent on the expert's individualistic construal of *arthritis*, which is on its own sufficiently rich to determine the corresponding conceptual content. Incomplete understanding, as opposed to both non-competence and full mastery, activates the deferential construal. In our mental lexicon, the deferential construal works prominently, while in the expert's lexicon, the individualistic construal is activated to a greater degree than the deferential construal. Our deferential construal of *arthritis* is one way to construe *arthritis*, and the expert's individualistic construal of *arthritis* is another. Both construe arthritis as *arthritis*, making the notion of direct reference irrelevant. This embodies the 'same form different construals' picture illustrated in Figure 4-2. By virtue of the link between speakers established by the deferential construal, what more competent speakers tell you about a concept is added to your individualistic construal of the concept.

As Jackman (2005: 374) points out, "when we defer to a person we take to be authoritative, we defer to what she *believes* or *claims* about the world, not just her usage" (emphases in the original)[26]. The experts' usage of a word reflects what they believe to be true of the reference. It is to such beliefs that lay speakers defer (ibid.: 375). Thus, if our individualistic construal of the concept contains a piece of information incompatible with the information deriving from interaction with experts, that piece of information is deleted from the individualistic construal (cf. Greenberg 2014: 162, Valente 2019: 324). The deferential construal has an effect of making information stored in the individualistic construal inert if it contradicts what experts tell you. This process prevents what Wikforss (2001: 218) calls a fragmentation of concept. If what an individual had in mind entirely determined what concept she had, there would be as many concepts of *arthritis*, *sofas*, *bird*, etc. as individual speakers, with no possibility of conceptual errors[27]. Such a conceptual fragmentation is as much a non-starter for cognitive linguists as for other theorists. As Taylor (2003: 86) cautions, "[t]o say that the dictionary is encyclopaedic is not equivalent to saying that the dictionary *is* an encyclopaedia". Even in cognitive linguistics, commonly assumed to be an internalist framework, convention plays an

---

26) If an American uses the word 'lift' in Australia to refer to an elevator, she defers to Australians' usage of the word. Jackman (2005: 374-375) emphasizes that one fails to recognize the implications of the notion of deference for the study of mental states if one takes this kind of deference to be what deference is all about.

27) Davidson (1987: 449) puts forward the view that 'Carl has arthritis' expresses different thoughts, depending on what the subject thinks causes the disease. Wikforss (2001: 227) worries that this view will lead to conceptual fragmentation.

essential part. This is illustrated in Taylor's (2003: 86) remark that "the relevant background information for the characterization of word meanings [is] a network of shared, conventionalized, and to some extent perhaps idealized knowledge, embedded in a pattern for cultural beliefs and practices" as well as in Langacker's remark that "[a]t a given time, at a given speech community, a large body of conventions are firmly enough established that speakers invoke them as the basis for apprehending expressions" (Langacker 2008: 227). In the latter remark, "speakers invoke" should be interpreted normatively as well as factually, to the extent that "[s]peakers must have some preconception of what the words they use are normally expected to mean" (ibid.: 30).

The notion of deferential construal enables one to respond to Rey's (1983) objection to the internalist conception of concept. Rey (1983: 249) states that "not just any change in a belief about how you *tell* whether something satisfies a concept ought to count as a change in that concept". Beliefs about how you tell whether something satisfies a concept are none other than individualistic construals of the conceptual content. Changes in individualistic construal do not affect the identity of a concept, insofar as lay speakers defer to experts for the correct construal of the concept. This provides the answer to the question in (1b) raised at the beginning of this chapter. Adam's deferential construal of 'arthritis' is linked to the doctor's individualistic construal of 'arthritis'. This makes their uses of the term coreferential *de jure*, enabling them to talk about the same ailment. Although Adam and his doctor conceptualize arthritis in mutually incompatible ways, Adam is prepared to discard his beliefs about arthritis if they are incompatible with what his doctor tells him, due to his deferential construal of 'arthritis' stored in his mental lexicon. Through the process of revision, Adam's individualistic construal becomes more and more similar to the doctor's. Note that the deferential construal does not work in the other direction. The doctor does not jettison his beliefs about arthritis unless he recognizes Adam as more competent with the concept.

This view is consonant with Valente's (2019):

Deferential concepts, then, allow their users to guarantee co-reference with the thinkers they defer to regardless of there not being any relation between the deferential concept's rule and that of the concept expressed by the deferred party. In other words, by employing a deferential concept we manage to communicate successfully (and even genuinely agree) with people whose concepts we can be completely ignorant about. It is truly an ingenious representational mechanism in that it allows people coming from very different epistemic standpoints to hook onto the same subject matter. (Valente 2019: 328)

There is, however, a major difference between Valente's view and the one defended here. In the passage quoted, Valente talks about concepts instead of construals. He rejects the view that Adam and the doctor share one and the same concept on the grounds that, if one posits another way to express the relevant concept, in addition to the non-deferential way, the concept must be defined in terms of the disjunction of different rules: either one associates the concept with non-deferential rules or one defers to someone who knows such rules[28]:

However, what was most interesting about Internalism was how neatly it accounted for expressing a concept in terms of the personal-level cognitive mechanisms that thinkers employed (i.e., the rules they followed and the explanations they could give of their uses of a representation). This virtue is evidently lost when one adds a proviso to Internalism allowing that, on top of the usual way of expressing a concept, one gets to achieve the same feat by doing something completely different [...] (Valente 2019: 325; see also Greenberg 2014: 163)

The point Valentes makes here seems akin to Schroeter and Schroeter's (2016: 203) remark that the notion of deference "makes concepts unstable across differences in reference-fixing criteria within a single representational tradition". It must be noticed, however, that, on the view advocated here, the non-deferential construal of the concept is by no means 'usual'. Every individual's lexicon retains both deferential and non-deferential construals at every stage. Nobody is born as an expert; every expert was initially a layperson whose individualistic construal contained a minimum amount of information or even misinformation. No expert is omniscient; any expert is prepared, in case of doubt, to defer to more competent members of the community (De Brabanter 2007: 16, Schroeter and Schroeter 2016: 200). In any mental lexicon, both construals are more or less activated. This is a natural consequence of "our manifest ability to conceive and portray the same situation in alternate ways" (Langacker 2008: 43). It is erroneous to think that

---

28) It also seems that Valtente's rejection of the view that Adam and the doctor share one and the same concept is not conclusive. See Valente (2019: 329-330).

some speakers have (usual) non-deferential concepts while others have (unusual) deferential ones.

Pollock (2015) insists that social externalism is incompatible with the view that coordination of understanding is necessary and sufficient for communicative success, because social externalism divorces content from understanding, allowing for the possibility that the same content is shared by the speaker and the hearer without much understanding being shared. This claim seems to overlook the fact that understanding involves deferential construal, due to which lay uses of a word get closer to the communal uses. Pollock (2015: 3239) is certainly right in defending the principle that "[a] communicative attempt will succeed only if the hearer's understanding of the content she grasps is similar to the speaker's understanding of the content she expressed" (see also Bezuidenhout 1997: 222, Recanati 2016: 119). But this principle does not necessarily conflict with social externalism, provided that the similarity of understanding can be attained through interactions between speakers with varying degrees of understanding.

4.4.4 Deferential Construal and Identity of a Concept

Grayling (1995: 82) states that, since language is a means of communication, "at the very least the great majority of speakers understand the same thing by the same expression at the same time", arguing for the necessity of the stabilized or authoritative Fregean sense agreed upon by speakers. Several authors have taken social externalism to presuppose the authoritative sense or the like. Thus, Hunter (2003: 734) assumes that social externalism relies on the thesis in (27a)[29], and Wikforss (2014) attributes the thesis in (27b) to Burge:

(27) a. (T) If the experts in S's community use a word, W, to express concept C, and S is minimally competent with W and defers to the experts in its use, then S has C too. (Hunter 2003: 734)

b. (ICU) S may think thoughts containing concept C, even if S has an incomplete understanding of C. (Wikforss 2014)

The thesis in (27a) entails that Adam has exactly the same concept of *arthritis* as his doctor insofar as he defers to the doctor for the use of the word 'arthritis'. The

---

29) Hunter (2003: 744, n. 18) notes that (27a) is his formulation of Segal's (2000) interpretation of social externalism.

thesis in (27b) points to the same conclusion, because, according to (27b), Adam's incomplete grasp of the concept does not affect the identity of the concept. It is one thing to have a concept and it is another to fully understand it. The theses in (27), however, do not seem to be fully in accord with the two-dimensional view of concepts advocated here. If the construal is part of a concept on a par with its conceptual content and semantic deference is a form of construal, it follows that Adam has a different concept of *arthritis* as his doctor as long as Adam construes *arthritis* deferentially while his doctor does not. Indeed, Wikforss maintains that the notion of deferential concept is orthogonal to the central thesis of social externalism outlined in (27b):

At the same time, the appeal to special deferential concepts does not support thesis ICU, since it does not support the distinction between having a concept and fully understanding it. For this reason it is also doubtful that Recanati's deferential concepts can be fitted into Burge's framework. (Wikforss 2014: 2.1)

Similarly, Greenberg (2014: 161) claims that the notion of deferential concept "rejects the possibility of incomplete understanding, rather than accounts for it", because it allows the putative deviant speaker to possess another concept for which she has a canonical understanding. To reconcile the social externalist theses in (27) with the two-dimensional conception of concepts, I propose the criterion in (28):

(28) If S_1's use of a word W and S_2's use of W are coreferential *de jure*, then S_1 and S_2 share the same concept C expressed by W.

In the dialogue between Adam and his doctor, their uses of 'arthritis' are coreferential *de jure*. That is, a person who does not understand that Adam and his doctor talk about the same ailment must be considered not to understand the dialogue. The coreference *de jure* between Adam's and his doctor's uses of 'arthritis' buttresses our intuition that Adam's utterance 'I have arthritis in my thigh' is false. By 'arthritis' he means not a peculiar disease that may strike one's thigh but what his fellows normally understand by the term.

This suggests that the sharing of a concept does not require that both parties construe its conceptual content in exactly the same fashion. There need therefore be no such thing as the authoritative sense. This view is not new. Thus, Recanati's

(2016) 'mental file' framework is driven by the idea that "[t]he identity of a container is independent of that of its contents" (Recanati 2016: vii; see also Schroeter 2008: 114-121). The contents of a concept are open-ended and hence, as De Brabanter et al. (2005: 27) state, "it is not obvious that anyone ever achieves perfect mastery". If so, the identity of a concept can and must be secured without appealing to the putative authoritative sense. What is needed instead for our purpose is the condition for two uses of a word to be coreferential *de jure*. Even though Recanati (2016) also attempts to generally define the notion of coreference *de jure*, a notion "that looms large in [his] book" (ibid.: x), we rather need a condition for coreference *de jure* specifically designed to reconcile the social externalist theses in (27) with the two-dimensional conception of concepts. To this end, it is not necessary to define coreference *de jure* in terms of an 'iff' relation as does Recanati (2016: Ch. 2). It is enough to state an 'if' relation as in (29):

(29) A lay speaker S_1's use of a word W and an expert S_2's use of W are coreferential *de jure*, if (i) both uses have the same form, (ii) both uses are associated with minimally similar individualistic construals, and (iii) S_1' use is associated with a deferential construal which refers to S_2's individualistic construal of W.

The clause in (ii) is automatically guaranteed if S_1 is minimally competent with W, because, given (25) above, S_1 thereby understands most of the stereotypical descriptions associated with W. The clause in (iii) is also automatically guaranteed if S_1 is minimally competent with W, because being minimally competent with W entails associating to W an appropriate deferential construal. (29) can easily be adapted to apply to dialogues between two lay speakers:

(30) A lay speaker S_1's use of a word W and a lay speaker S_2's use of W are coreferential *de jure*, if (i) both uses have the same form, (ii) both uses are associated with minimally similar individualistic construals, and (iii) both uses are associated with a deferential construal which refers to the individualistic construals which experts in S_1's and S_2's community associate with W.

In short, when two people minimally competent with W employ W without modifying the word form, then their uses of W are coreferential *de jure*, which, given

(28), entails that the two people have the same concept expressed by W.

The foregoing discussion paves the way for integrating Schroeter and Schroeter's (2016) observation into the cognitive linguistic framework:

The appearance of *de jure* sameness is not confined to co-conscious thoughts within a given individual: it extends to past thoughts and to thoughts linguistically expressed by others. When Bert remembers glimpsing Cate Blanchett at the airport, Bert's occurrent memory seems to present the content of his past thoughts as *de jure* pertaining to the same topic as his current beliefs about the star. And when he hears others using the term "arthritis," he understands their claims as pertaining *de jure* to the same topic as he himself associates with that term. In such cases, the appearance of *de jure* sameness does not seem to depend on a precise match in reference-fixing criteria. [...] it seems possible to coherently reject virtually any particular substantive claim about "arthritis" without threatening the appearance of *de jure* sameness. When Bert's doctor says "Arthritis is a disease of the joints," or when his guru says "Doctors are not experts on arthritis," Bert will automatically hear both claims as pertaining *de jure* to the same topic as his own "arthritis" thought. [...] Concept identity should not be tied too closely to topic-specific assumptions (criteria of application, epistemic methods for self-correction, and so on) if we want to allow for the possibility of conceptual stability through open-ended inquiry, debate, and disagreement. [...] sameness of concept does not depend on accepting any particular set of substantive commitments about the reference (Schroeter and Schroeter 2016: 205-206)

Even under the two-dimensional conception of concepts, it is possible to say that Adam's incomplete understanding of 'arthritis' does not prevent him from having the same concept as his doctor, in conformity with (27a) and (27b). Having the same concept does not entail having the same individualistic construal. As Marconi (1997: 87) states, successful communication only requires "some degree of *convergence* of the referential abilities and practices of the speakers" (emphasis in the original). How much convergence is required varies from term to term, as suggested by (26). We have seen in 1.3.3 that you can be competent with 'molybdenum' if you know that molybdenum is a metal (Goosens 1977: 151), but you cannot be competent with 'tiger' if all you know about tigers is that they are animals (Putnam 1975: 169). Valente (2019: 324) suggests that different kinds of deference are at

Chapter 4   Deferential Construal

work in the case of *arthritis* and in the case of *black hole*, as illustrated by the fact that a lay person's grasp of *arthritis* has "some life of its own" (ibid.), while she knows virtually nothing about black holes other than the fact that "they are something physicists talk about" (ibid.). Contrary to Valente's suggestion, however, the difference between *arthritis* and *black hole* should be attributed to the different amount of knowledge required for minimal competence with these terms (i.e. (30ii)), rather than to the putative different kinds of deference (i.e. (30iii)). The less amount of the non-deferential construal is required, the more role the deferential construal has to play. (30ii) sets a lower bound on the amount of the non-deferential construal, ruling out cases where the speaker knows nothing about what the term expresses (cf. Valente 2019: 334). This substantiates Quine's (1960: 8) remark that "[t]he uniformity that unites us in communication and belief is a uniformity of resultant patterns overlying a chaotic subjective diversity of connections between words and experience".

Conversely, having the same individualistic construal does not entail having the same concept. This is because the deferential construal associated with a term is indexical in the sense that it tacitly refers to the public language to which the term belongs, namely what De Brabanter et al. (2005: 6ff) call 'source language', and that the deferrer does not have to "know which source language is contextually selected" (ibid.: 28). The indexical expression 'in eighty-four days', for instance, tacitly refers to the time of utterance, with respect to which the reference of the expression 'in eighty-four days' is determined, and the utterer need not know exactly which date the expression refers to. Similarly, Adam and Adam$_2$ tacitly refer to their respective source languages spoken in different communities without necessarily recognizing the identity of the linguistic community they defer to. As De Brabanter et al. (2005: 1, 6, 21-22) point out, in semantic deference, the language parameter is in an individual's mind, while the value for the parameter is contextually supplied. This analysis can be considered an elaboration of White's (1982) suggestion:

> Speakers of the language must have a general commitment to use the language in the same way it is used in the community, and these commitments will be represented by the intentions with which speakers engage in linguistic activity. These intentions (or at least some important aspects of them) will be in the head in Putnam's sense and will help determine the extensions of the speakers' concepts. (White 1982: 351)

Since the source language constitutes part of the deferential construal of a given term, it follows that Adam and Adam$_2$ have different concepts corresponding to the word form 'arthritis', despite the fact that their individualistic construal of 'arthritis' is identical.

Segal (2003: 416-418) offers an argument against the social externalist thesis in (27a) with the help of a variant of Burge's (1979a/2007) 'arthritis' thought experiment. Suppose that Adam, who believes that he has arthritis in his thigh, goes to live in France instead of consulting his doctor in his hometown. In France, he becomes an expert in the use of the French word 'arthrite' without yet realizing that it is synonymous with the English word 'arthritis'. Adam now believes both (31a) and (31b), the latter entailing the negation of (31c):

(31) a. Arthritis is an inflammation that may afflict one's thigh.
      b. Arthrite is an inflammation of the joints only.
      c. Arthrite is an inflammation that may afflict one's thigh.

Frege's Constraint enables us to conclude, Segal argues, that (31a) and (31c) express different thoughts for Adam and, equivalently, that 'arthritis' and 'arthrite' express different concepts[30]. Adam relates the two concepts as in (32):

(32) a. Not all arthritis is arthrite.
      b. All arthrite is arthritis.

Now, the experts in Adam's hometown use the term 'arthritis' as Adam uses the term 'arthrite'. Since for Adam 'arthritis' and 'arthrite' express different concepts, his concept corresponding to 'arthritis' is different from the experts'. This runs counter to Burge's assumption that Adam and his doctor mean the same thing by 'arthritis'. Contrary to the thesis in (27a), Segal claims, Adam does not possess the community concept of *arthritis*, or at least, he has, in addition to the social concept of *arthritis*, another concept expressed by 'arthritis', which is individuated inde-

---

30) Segal (2003: 417) formulates Frege's Constraint as follows:

(FD) [= Fregean principle of difference] If a subject, s, rationally assents to P(t1) and dissents from or abstains on the truth value of P(t2) (P(x) an extensional context), then t1 and t2 have different meanings in s's idiolect and s associates different concepts with them.

Chapter 4 Deferential Construal

pendently from any social factors[31].

Segal's argument is flawed, however, in not taking into consideration the fact that Adam defers to different linguistic communities when he uses the French word 'arthrite' and the English word 'arthritis'. In employing 'arthrite', Adam seems to defer to the French-speaking community, which determines the concept of *arthrite*. In employing 'arthritis', on the contrary, Adam seems to defer to the English-speaking community, which determines the concept of *arthritis*. This on its own in no way establishes that Adam has a different concept from *arthritis*. The validity of Segal's argument depends entirely on the possible application of Frege's Constraint to (31a) and (31c), to which Adam takes different attitudes. The question of how to make sense of Adam's different attitudes toward (31a) and (31c) is similar to the question raised by (33), discussed in Chapter 3:

(33) a. Cilantro should be used sparingly.
      b. Coriander should be used sparingly.

((33a-b): Falvey and Owens 1994: 110)

I have said in Section 3.8 that 'cilantro' and 'coriander' are synonyms if their equivalence is part of the grammar, as is the case with 'vixen' and 'female fox'. If the two terms are grammatically equivalent, ignorance of the equivalence makes the subject less than minimally competent with 'cilantro' and 'coriander' and Frege's Constraint does not enable us to establish that there are two distinct concepts expressed by the two terms. The subject is merely ignorant of her semantic irrationality. If, on the contrary, the equivalence is not part of the grammar, as is the case with the equivalence between 'the morning star' and 'the evening star', then the equivalence is to be discovered by people who are competent with both terms.

---

31) Kimbrough (1998) offers a similar argument to demonstrate that Frege's Constraint is incompatible with social externalism:

The *prima facie* problem for Fregeans is this: application imply a negative answer to the question of sameness that question is asked. To illustrate, let us suppose as well as English. As a speaker of French, he is competent term '*arthrite*', but he is unaware that '*arthrite*' is the French translation of '*arthritis*'. Suppose further that, despite believing that he has arthritis in his thigh, Bert doubts that he has arthrite in his thigh. Just by *having* such doubts, Bert apparently forces Fregean proponents of DDT [= Frege's Constraint] to distinguish the contents of the beliefs he expresses using the terms '*arthritis*' and '*arthrite*'. And Bert's case is not extraordinary: similar examples can be constructed using any other pair of inter-translatable terms. (Kimbrough 1998: 480)

273

Complicating the matter is that, regarding (31)-(32), it does not make sense to talk about *the* grammar. It is commonly assumed that French and English are different languages and hence that competence in French is different from competence in English. Not only is it off the mark to talk about *the* grammar relevant to both French and English but many of us do not know what it is like to be simultaneously competent with French and English. It is therefore far more difficult to determine whether it is possible to apply Frege's Constraint to (31a) and (31c) than it is in the case of (33). Neither monolingual speakers of French nor monolingual speakers of English can judge with confidence whether Adam is competent with both 'arthrite' and 'arthritis'. If Adam is not competent with these terms, it is not possible to apply Frege's Constraint to (31a) and (31c).

If, as Segal assumes, Adam is competent with both terms, Frege's Constraint does allow us to say that he possesses a concept expressed by 'arthrite' and another concept expressed by 'arthritis'. Even though it is difficult to assess whether Adam is competent with the two terms, we can assume for the sake of the argument that he is. This assumption does not seem incompatible with (26), which dictates that a competent speaker is required to understand most of the stereotypical descriptions associated with the term in question. Since the stereotypical descriptions associated with an English word generally make no reference to any French word (unless it is a loanword) and vice versa, competence in neither language requires recognition of the synonymy between 'arthrite' and 'arthritis'. Adam's competence with the two terms thus construed entails that he attaches to each of the terms a deferential construal, which allows us to say that he has the communal concepts of *arthrite* and *arthritis*. However, this demonstrates at best that Adam has an individualistic construal of *arthritis* incompatible with the experts' construal, not that he has an idiosyncratic concept. As stated earlier, a lay speaker's individualistic construal on its own has no ability to identify the concept to which it is related. The lay speaker's deferential construal, which tacitly refers to the experts' individualistic construal, needs to be activated to identify the concept. Due to Adam's deferential construals of 'arthrite' and 'arthritis', Adam is related to the communal concepts of *arthrite* and *arthritis*. Whether Frege's Constraint may be applicable or not, it does not follow from Adam's different attitudes toward (31a) and (31c) that Adam has an idiosyncratic concept distinct from the public concept *arthritis* possessed by the English-speaking community to which Adam defers. To borrow Quine's metaphor, Adam and the experts trim bushes differently to obtain the same shape of an elephant:

Different persons growing up in the same language are like different bushes trimmed and trained to take the shape of identical elephants. The anatomical details of twigs and branches will fulfill the elephantine form differently from bush to bush, but the overall outward results are alike. (Quine 1960: 8)

In conclusion, Segal's argument does not succeed in rejecting the social externalist thesis in (27a).

Chapter 5

Physical Externalism and Polysemy

After examining what conception of reality underlies physical externalism, a position clearly incompatible not only with cognitive linguistics but also with biology, chemistry and the philosophy of science, this chapter shows that the physical externalist intuition derives from our quintessentialist bias, our deference to future usage and our strong inclination to raise the degree of discourse coherence.

5.1 Social Externalism vs. Physical Externalism

So far, I have argued that the cognitive linguistic assumption in (1) is compatible with both (2a) and (2b):

(1)   Meaning is conceptualization.
(2)   a. Although Adam and Adam$_2$ conceptualize what is called 'arthritis' (or 'bird' discussed in Chapter 2) in exactly the same fashion, the meaning of 'arthritis' ('bird') and the thought content containing 'arthritis' ('bird') are different for them.
       b. Although Adam and his doctor conceptualize what is called 'arthritis' in a mutually incompatible way, the meaning of 'arthritis' and the thought content containing 'arthritis' are the same for them.

As stated in Chapter 2, an individual's conceptualization is more or less grounded in, or attuned to, her environment. Although Adam and Adam$_2$ are internally identical, Adam unlike Adam$_2$ has an incomplete grasp of the community concept expressed by the word form 'arthritis', due to the lesser degree to which he is attuned to his environment. I have argued in Chapter 3 that a concept consists of conceptual content and its construal. Insofar as 'the morning star' and 'the evening star' correspond to differing construals of the same conceptual content, these two terms express different concepts. Adam's community and Adam$_2$'s community

277

attach different concepts to the same word form 'arthritis', because their construals of the relevant conceptual content are duly different.

Chapter 4 has demonstrated that Adam's incomplete understanding does not prevent his possessing the communal concept of *arthritis*. Competence comes in levels. Adam can be considered competent with the concept of *arthritis* provided that he understands most of the stereotypical descriptions associated with the word 'arthritis'. Adam's minimal competence seems insufficient, however, to credit him with the communal concept of *arthritis*, to the extent that his construal of the concept contradicts the community standards. The cognitive linguistic assumption in (1) apparently entails that any variation in construal can only be described as a semantic variation, which makes it impossible to account for (2b). This tension is dissolved, however, if the construal of a concept includes its deferential construal in addition to its individualistic construal. Adam's competence with *arthritis* entails that he construes the concept both individualistically and deferentially. Even though his individualistic construal of *arthritis* is incompatible with his doctor's, the deferential construal associated with the term 'arthritis' links his mental lexicon to the experts' individualistic construal of the term. Due to the link established between Adam's mental lexicon and the experts', Adam is prepared to jettison his beliefs about arthritis if they are incompatible with the community standards. In other words, Adam's deferential construal of 'arthritis' makes his misbeliefs about the disease inert, making Oscar's use of 'arthritis' and the experts' use of 'arthritis' two occurrences of the same public word 'arthritis'.

Despite the remarkable difference in construal, Adam's and the experts' uses of 'arthritis' are coreferential *de jure*. Oscar's deferential construal of *arthritis* is one way to construe *arthritis* and the experts' individualistic construal of *arthritis* is another. This embodies "our manifest ability to conceive and portray the same situation in alternate ways" (Langacker 2008: 43). (1) is therefore compatible with (2b). In semantic deference, Adam and Adam$_2$ tacitly refer to their respective source languages spoken in different communities. Since the deferential construal of a term is defined in relation to the source language to which the term belongs, it follows that Adam and Adam$_2$ have different concepts corresponding to the word form 'arthritis', despite the fact that their individualistic construal of 'arthritis' is identical. (1) is therefore compatible with (2a) as well.

One may be inclined to think that the same argument applies to the 'water' case discussed in Chapter 1, if only 'arthritis' is replaced by 'water'. In effect, we can rehearse exactly the same argument for the 'water' case, assuming that the experts

Chapter 5   Physical Externalism and Polysemy

on Earth agree that water is H_2O while the experts on Twin Earth agree that twater is XYZ and that both Oscar on Earth and $Oscar_2$ on Twin Earth are ignorant of chemistry. This is exactly what Burge (1982/2007) does:

In 'Individualism and the Mental' [...] I presented a thought experiment in which one fixed non-intentional, individualistic descriptions of the physical, behavioral, phenomenalistic, and (on most formulations) functional histories of an individual. By varying the *uses of words* in his linguistic community, I found that the contents of his propositional attitudes varied. I shall draw a parallel conclusion from Putnam's twin-earth thought experiment: We can fix an individual's physical, behavioral, phenomenalistic, and (on some formulations) functional histories; by varying the *physical environment*, one finds that the contents of his propositional attitudes vary. (Burge 1982: 99/2007: 84-85, emphases in the original)

The analogy between the 'arthritis' case and the 'water' case fails, however, because considerations of physical environments are essentially different from considerations of social environments. Burge reduces the former to the latter when he omits one of Putnam's basic assumptions about the Twin Earth thought experiment:

I am omitting a significant extension of Putnam's ideas. Putnam considers "rolling back the clock" to a time when everyone in each community would be as ignorant of the structure of water and twater as Adam and $Adam_{te}$ are now. I omit this element from the thought experiment, partly because arriving at a reasonable interpretation of this case is more complicated and partly because it is not necessary for my primary purposes. Thus, as far as we are concerned, one is free to see differences in Adam's and $Adam_{te}$'s mental states as deriving necessarily from differences in the actions and attitudes of other members in their respective communities." (Burge 1982: 119/2007: 86, n. 8)

But what Burge omits is essential for physical externalism. According to physical externalism, meaning and mental content are individuated only in relation to the physical environment the speaker inhabits. Social externalism, on the contrary, holds that it is our conventional usage of the term in question that determines what the term means (Liu 2002: 395). Although physical externalism and social

279

externalism have in common that they reject the idea that meaning and mental content supervene on the speaker's intrinsic properties, they deliver different results in scenarios where nearly everyone is infected with incomplete understanding. Following Liu (2002: 390), let us imagine a counterfactual situation in which the experts on Earth have misidentified the chemical makeup of what they call 'water' as XYZ instead of H_2O. The prevalent view on Earth is that water is XYZ. Oscar, ignorant of the prevalent view, has found out on his own that water is H_2O. In this case, the social externalist would say that Oscar's utterance of (3) evinces his incomplete grasp of the communal concept of *water*.

(3)   Water is composed of hydrogen and oxygen.

Still, Oscar's use of 'water' expresses the communal concept of *water* via his deferential construal associated with the word, making his utterance of (3) false. By contrast, physical externalism holds that the meaning of a natural kind term is determined by the nature of the physical environment, even if the nature is unknown to the inhabitants of the environment. Importantly, in Putnam's account, the meaning of a natural kind term is not determined by the presently known underlying structure of the kind (Liu 2002: 394). As Abbott (1989: 272) remarks, each natural kind term has "a variable standing for an unknown quality, which nature has been allowed to fill in in whatever way suits her". Similarly, Haukioja (2015: 2147) states that the meaning of a natural kind term includes "a placeholder to be filled in by the actual world". In the situation we are imagining, although no one except Oscar is aware, the nature of water lies in being composed of hydrogen and oxygen, which makes Oscar's utterance of (3) true.

Now, suppose that the experts in Oscar's community realize their error and come to believe that water is H_2O. Their recognition may lead to a change in the relevant linguistic convention. The social externalist would say that the word 'water' underwent a semantic change; 'water', which used to denote XYZ, now denotes H_2O. The physical externalist would rather say that the experts have discovered the correct meaning of the word determined by the nature of the environment (Liu 2002: 390-391). For the physical externalist, the meaning of 'water' has been H_2O all along, whether or not it be known to anyone (Putnam 1973: 702, 1975: 141, Linsky 1977: 821). The same applies to biological species such as the tiger and the lemon. Kripke (1980: 138) claims that "scientific discoveries of species essence do not constitute a 'change of meaning'; the possibility of such discoveries was part of

Chapter 5   Physical Externalism and Polysemy

the original enterprise". Although Putnam seldom talked about essence without scare-quotes (Hacking 2007a: 11-12, 2007b: 228), Putnam's and Kripke's views are commonly referred to as 'Kripke/Putnam essentialism' (Leslie 2013: 125, n. 12), or more simply as 'the KP-thesis' (Häggqvist and Wikforss 2018: 912ff).

As Liu (2002: 391) remarks, it is possible that "the social environment *misrepresents* the physical environment". The independence of the physical environment from the social environment is also pointed out by Burge (1986a/2007):

> [...] social practices are not the only or ultimate nonindividualistic factor in individuating mental states and events. I have elsewhere argued for this view on other grounds. Some mental states (for example, some perceptual states) depend for their identity on the nature of the physical environment, in complete independence of social practices. What I want to show here is that, even where social practices are deeply involved in individuating mental states, they are often not the final arbiter. This is because the sort of agreement that fixes a communal meaning and norms for understanding is itself, in principle, open to challenge. The argument that follows articulates this fact. (Burge 1986a: 707/2007: 262-263)

It is generally considered that Burge's (1979a/2007) 'arthritis' thought experiment is designed to establish social externalism, whereas Burge's (1986a/2007) 'sofa' experiment presented in Chapter 2 attempts to defend physical externalism (Sawyer 2003: 272-273, Wikforss 2004: 289-290). From the social externalist perspective, in uttering (3), Oscar displays his incomplete grasp of the communal concept of *water*. From the physical externalist perspective, on the contrary, Oscar challenges what Burge (1986a: 703/2007: 259) refers to as the 'normative characterization' of water. To doubt the normative characterization of a concept is not necessarily a sign of incomplete understanding:

> There is a potential gap between even the best understanding of accepted usage and belief. The consensus of the most competent speakers can be challenged. Usually such challenges stem from incomplete understanding. But, as our arguments [...] indicate, they need not. One may always ask whether the most competent speakers' characterizations of examples (or one's own best characterizations) are *correct* [...] (Burge 1986a: 714/2007: 268-269)

281

As Dupré (1981: 70) states, the difference between expert knowledge and lay knowledge is a matter of degree rather than a matter of kind. It is because the final arbiter for the identity of a concept is the nature of the physical environment that one can rationally ask whether the current normative characterization of the concept is correct. As stated in Chapter 1, while social externalism hinges upon the fact that other people know better about the extension of the relevant word, physical externalism can be established even when no one is aware of the nature of the environment. As Malt (1994: 42) summarizes, "Putnam's approach takes as fundamental the idea that word meanings are not a matter of mental representation; they are a matter of truths about the world". The challenge set for the cognitive linguistic assumption in (1) can therefore be stated as in (4):

(4) a. Although Oscar and $Oscar_2$ conceptualize what is called 'water' in exactly the same fashion, the meaning of 'water' and the thought content containing 'water' are different for them.
     b. Even when no one, including experts, knows the underlying structure of water which distinguishes it from twater, Oscar's utterance of 'water' and his thought about 'water' refer to water but not twater.

As Liu (2002: 392, 396) points out, physical externalism and social externalism are in disagreement only about the treatment of natural kind terms. In the same way that, as discussed in Chapter 2, physical externalism is unsuited to the semantic description of nominal kind terms such as 'sofa' and 'pencil'[1], social externalism can hardly accommodate intuitions about natural kind terms (Liu 2002: 399). Burge's (1982/2007) discussion of 'water' provides only partial descriptions of the term.

A caveat is in order regarding the definition of natural kind terms and natural kinds. Bromberger (1997: 149) states that "[t]he term *natural kind* is a philosopher's term". Accordingly, the term has acquired a special sense which is not necessarily accessible to ordinary speakers, as Abbott (1997) cautions:

However this phrase (and correspondingly "natural kind term") has acquired a

---

1) In Section 2.4, we have seen that, *pace* Burge (1986a/2007), it is difficult to rationally doubt the nature of sofas. Section 2.5.3 has presented problems with Putnam's (1975) attempt to extend physical externalism to the meaning of 'pencil'.

special use following Putnam (1975) and Kripke [(1980)]. In the latter use it does not apply to all kinds of things found in nature, but rather to species of plants and animals, well-defined substances such as gold and molybdenum, and natural phenomena like heat and lightning. These are things whose names (natural kind terms) were argued by Kripke to be nondescriptional. So although mud and bugs exist in nature, they are not natural kinds in the technical sense, and the words "mud" and "bug" are not natural kind terms in this sense. When Malt [(1994)] is considering whether the meanings of natural kind terms are in fact more similar to those of artifact terms than is commonly assumed, she points to examples like trees and vegetables (pp. 67f); but these also are not natural kinds (and "tree" and "vegetable" are not natural kind terms) in the technical sense that is relevant to issues of word meaning. (Abbott 1997: 312)

Natural kinds are "kinds that are individuated by nature" (Liu 2002: 392). There is a natural boundary between one natural kind and another. The boundary is there even if no one has enough information to find out where the boundary lies. What constitutes the natural boundary is the underlying nature or hidden structure of the kind in question, which is held to be causally responsible for its superficial characteristics available to laypeople (Fodor 1998a: 154-155, Leslie 2013: 112). The underlying structure or hidden structure carves nature at its joints without any human intervention (Bromberger 1997: 151, Leslie 2013: 111-112). Even if water is superficially similar to the hypothetical substance denoted by the Twin Earthian word 'water' (i.e. twater), the two substances are distinguished by their microstructures. Likewise, Putnam (1975: 153) maintains that the extension of the Ancient Greek term χλωρός (khlōrós) employed by Archimedes is the same as the modern English word 'gold', even though Archimedes had no method to distinguish gold from superficially similar substances such as iron pyrites. According to Putnam (1973: 702-703, 1975: 142) and Kripke (1980: 119), what has changed since the ancient times is not the meanings of the term 'water' and 'gold' but our theories about water and gold. The meanings of 'water' and 'gold' have always been present. As Liu (2002: 395) points out, the word 'arthritis', which figures prominently in the externalist debate, is presumably not a natural kind term in the relevant sense (cf. Wikforss 2001: 226):

Presently the term is defined through the symptom (the inflammation of the joints) of the disease. If it is discovered that arthritis is caused by a certain virus, then whenever the inflammation is caused by this virus, it is a case of arthritis. 'Arthritis' would then be a natural-kind term. (Liu 2002: 402, n. 25)

In order not to confound physical externalism with social externalism, we must consider genuine natural kind terms whose true meaning has not been uncovered by anyone. The word 'water' before 1750 discussed by Putnam (1975) is a case in point.

5.2 Deference and Physical Externalism

In Section 4.4.4, we have seen that what allows us to say that a lay speaker and an expert share the same communal concept C is the deferential construal which the lay speaker attaches to the term expressing C and which tacitly refers to the expert's individualistic construal:

(5) S_1's use of a word W and S_2's use of W are coreferential *de jure*, then S_1 and S_2 share the same concept C expressed by W.

(6)   A lay speaker S_1's use of a word W and an expert S_2's use of W are coreferential *de jure*, if (i) both uses have the same form, (ii) both uses are associated with minimally similar individualistic construals, and (iii) S_1' use is associated with a deferential construal which refers to S_2's individualistic construal of W.

(7)   A lay speaker S_1's use of a word W and a lay speaker S_2's use of W are coreferential *de jure*, if (i) both uses have the same form, (ii) both uses are associated with minimally similar individualistic construals, and (iii) both uses are associated with a deferential construal which refers to the individualistic construals which experts in S_1's and S_2's community associate with W.

This conception of meaning and concept presupposes that the expert's individualistic construal attached to W is sufficiently rich to determine the concept expressed by W. White (1982) states:

Thin stereotypes work because of the division of linguistic labor, but for every meaningful expression some members of the community, the experts, must have thick stereotypes if the expressions are to have an appropriate connection with the world. (White 1982: 352)

Similarly, Fodor states that "deference has to stop somewhere; if *my* ELM concept is deferential, that's because the *botanist's* isn't". As Schroeter and Schroeter (2016: 200) remark, the notion of deference requires that social deference criteria depend for their reference on other subjects' non-social criteria. This is captured by Recanati's (2000) Groundedness Thesis:

Groundedness Thesis: A deferential use is *grounded* only if someone at the other end of the deferential chain uses the expression in a non-deferential manner. (Recanati 2000: 452; see also Recanati 2006: 253)

A layperson's deference is vacuous unless there are reliable experts in the community (McKay and Stern 1979: 32).

The problem posed by physical externalism is that no one may attach such a rich construal to W. In the case of 'arthritis', we can assume that there is a coordination between lay speakers and far more competent speakers. Similarly, the distinction between 'elm' and 'beech' can be secured by our deference to experts. As regards the term 'water' before 1750, however, there can be no such coordination, making semantic deference incapable of determining the conceptual content of the term. This resembles Lacanians' belief in (8a) discussed by Recanati (1997), which is interpreted deferentially as in (8b):

(8) a. The unconscious is structure like language.
  b. R_x (the unconscious is structured like language)

Lacanians believe (8a) to be true simply because Lacan said so. According to Recanati (1997: 92), however, no cognitive agent x has the cognitive resource to determine the content of (8a). Since no individualistic construal of (8a) is sufficiently rich to determine its content, the deferential construal in (8b) is vacuous. What distinguishes natural kind terms from the case of the Lacanians is that the meanings of natural kind terms are provided by the physical environment. If there is a coordination in the use of natural kind terms, it holds between humans and the world. People defer to the nature of the environment for the use of 'water' (Greenberg 2014: 160, n. 25). But, as De Brabanter and Leclercq (2019: 5) remark, this is only a metaphorical way to say that semantic deference is of no use for physical externalism, according to which, as Liu (2002: 390) states, we may be as ignorant of the meaning of a term as of the physical environment in which the reference of the term is embedded.

As stated in Section 4.4.1, semantic deference hinges on our knowledge of the division of linguistic labor. Putnam (1973: 705, 1975: 145) points out that the division of linguistic labor in turn rests on the division of non-linguistic labor. By the 'division of non-linguistic labor' Putnam means the labor of scientists (Liu 2002: 389). Accordingly, "[w]hat the essential nature is is not a matter of language analysis but of scientific theory construction" (Putnam 1970: 188; see also Schwartz 1977: 27, 31). This leaves open the possibility for scientists to misidentify the meaning of the relevant term (Putnam 1975: 142, Liu 2002: 389, Gasparri and Marconi 2021: Section 3). True, as LaPorte (2004: 31-32) states, we commonly defer to biologists or zoologists for the proper meaning of terms like 'bear'. Although we sometimes use the expression 'koala bear', that is, we include 'bear' in the stereotype of 'koala' (Poncinie 1985: 424), we are ready to accept the experts' opinion that, strictly speaking, koalas are not bears. After all, as Jackman (2005: 376) says, "experts typically *do* know more about (the relevant portions of) the world than we do". But 'typically' does not entail 'always', nor does 'more' entail 'perfectly'. It happens that experts disagree about whether a given animal belongs to the kind of bear, for instance. The giant panda was first described in 1869 by Père Armand David, a French missionary, and since then zoologists disputed whether the giant panda was a bear (ursid) or a racoon (procyonid) for one hundred years (Sarich 1973, O'Brien 1987). Such uncertainty provides evidence against the descriptivist claim that a speaker's psychological state determines the meaning of a term the speaker understands (Putnam 1973: 700, 1975: 135-136).

Understanding a natural kind term does not require knowing its intension, an entity which determines the extension of the term (Schwartz 1977: 13, Liu 2002: 386). Even though Putnam cannot tell elm trees from beech trees (Putnam 1973: 704, 1975: 143), he is considered to understand the terms 'elm' and 'beech' insofar as he associates the stereotype 'common deciduous tree' with both terms (Putnam 1975: 147). Stanley (1999) objects that Putnam's conception of understanding overlooks the fact that "understanding comes in levels" (ibid.: 17) and that "whether or not someone understands a term depends upon context" (ibid.: 16). Putnam can certainly be deemed competent with 'elm' and 'beech' relative to contexts in which the level of understanding required is low, but there are contexts relative to which

Chapter 5   Physical Externalism and Polysemy

he is considered not to understand the terms. Descriptivism is right if it is interpreted as claiming that a speaker's full understanding of a term determines the
intension of the term (ibid.: 17). In Stanley's (ibid.) view, full understanding is "the
sort of understanding one must have to discourse competently with experts".
Stanley's argument misses its target, however, because it merely rehearses Putnam's
(1973: 705, 1975: 145) view that semantic competence with certain terms belongs
not to individual speakers but to the linguistic community considered as a collective body. It is a mistake to think, as Stanley (1999) does, that this picture is valid
for all natural kind terms. History tells us that even experts are not fully competent
with the technical terms they understand:

> The history of scientific change indicates that current expert belief may well be
> mistaken, and the history of scientific disagreement indicates that current
> expert belief may well be divided. This shows that it is false that for every nat-
> ural kind term there is a true proposition that formulates a non-trivial uniquely
> identifying truth about its referent that is believed, let alone known, by all
> experts in the field. (Hunter 2001: 544) "

As Hunter (1999: 544) points out, "Lavoisier competently discoursed with experts
using the term 'phlogiston'". If Stanley is right, this implies that Lavoisier's and the
experts' psychological states determine the same intension of 'phlogiston'[2]. But
Lavoisier did not believe in phlogiston contrary to the experts' opinion and it is
generally agreed today that 'phlogiston' is an empty name which has no reference
(Devitt and Sterelney 1999: 227, Sainsbury and Tye 2012: 65). This strongly suggests that a speaker's full understanding of a term may be extraneous to the question of what intension, if any, the term possesses (see also Burge 2012: 60-61).
Hunter (2001: 545) concludes that "Stanley's attempt to revive the description
theory of reference for natural kind terms by appealing to expert knowledge fails".

The situation for the term 'water' before 1750 was much worse. Those who may
be called 'scientists' today were even not aware that the term necessitated a division
of linguistic labor (Putnam 1973: 705, 1975: 145). Fodor (1998a: 154) attributes
to Putnam (1973, 1975) the view that "natural kind concepts thrive best – maybe

---

2) Some might say that 'phlogiston' is not a natural kind term. In response to this objection,
Hunter (2001: 544) remarks that "[t]he fact that it is an empty term no more prevents its
being a natural kind term than the emptiness of 'Sherlock Holmes' prevents its being a proper
name".

only – in an environment where conventions of deference to experts are in place". Natural kind concepts in this sense are only recent achievements:

> If it's easy to miss the extent to which natural kind concepts are sophisticated achievements, that's perhaps because of a nasty ambiguity in the term. [...] Consider this dialectic:
> – *Did Homer have natural kind concepts?*
> Sure, he had the concept of WATER (and the like), and water is a natural kind.
> But also:
> – *Did Homer have natural kind concepts?*
> Of course not. He had no disposition to defer to experts about water (and the like); I expect the notion of an expert about water would have struck him as bizarre. And, *of course* Homer had no notion that water has a hidden essence, or a characteristic microstructure (or anything else does); a fortiori, he had no notion that the hidden essence of water is causally responsible for its phenomenal properties. (Fodor 1998a: 155)

The absence of any division of nonlinguistic labor concerning water would make any division of linguist labor concerning 'water' vacuous, failing to associate the meaning of 'water' with the concepts of *hydrogen* and *oxygen*. Still, Putnam insists that the Earthian word 'water' has always meant water as distinct from twater. It follows that the meaning of 'water' is determined not by any mental representations but by the nature of the physical environment itself.

Thus construed, physical externalism is clearly incompatible with any internal conception of meaning and concept. Before 1750, no one construed water as a compound consisting of hydrogen and oxygen. In Ancient Greece, water was considered one of the elements, on a par with air, fire and earth. It was only at the end of the eighteenth century that this theory was completely overthrown (Edelstein 1948: 124). We cannot have the concept of H_2O without having the concept of *hydrogen* and *oxygen* (Fodor 1998a: 105). It is generally considered that Cavendish discovered hydrogen in 1766 (Edelstein 1948: 124). It was in 1774, just before the American Revolution, that oxygen was discovered by Priestley, but Priestly called the gas 'dephlogisticated air'[3], clinging to the now-obsolete phlogiston theory (Porter 1975: 95). If Earthians had encountered twater before the rise of modern chemistry, they would have no hesitation to apply the term 'water' to twater

288

Chapter 5   Physical Externalism and Polysemy

(Marconi 1997: 89-90). Nevertheless, in Putnam's assumption, water has always been distinguished from twater by its underlying molecular structure, which exclusively defines the meaning of 'water'. This implies that the meaning of 'water' is independent of any construal which language users associate with the term. This obviously conflicts with the cognitive linguistic thesis presented in (1).

In what follows, I shall argue that, even though physical externalism per se is incompatible not only with cognitive linguistics but also with the philosophy of science, the externalist intuition elicited by Putnam's Twin Earth thought experiment can largely be accommodated by the cognitive linguistic conception of meaning and concept. As Leslie (2013: 108) states, philosophers appeal to intuitions to establish a conclusion about the nature of the subject matter. To the extent that the conclusion must be epistemologically justified, the intuitions must be free from any bias:

It is common practice in philosophy to "rely on intuitions" in the course of an argument, or sometimes simply to establish a conclusion. One question that is therefore important to settle is: what is the source of these intuitions? Correspondingly: what is their epistemological status? Philosophical discussion often proceeds as though these intuitions stem from insight into the nature of thing – as though they are born of rational reflection and judicious discernment. If these intuitions do not have some such status, then their role in philosophical theorizing rapidly becomes suspect. We would not, for example, wish to place philosophical weight on intuitions that are in effect the unreflective articulation of inchoate cognitive biases. (Leslie 2013: 108)

In cognitive linguistics, on the contrary, researchers appeal to intuitions to elucidate how speakers construe the relevant conceptual content. As stated in Section 3.3, veracity is orthogonal to construal. Thus, fictive motion constitutes one of the ways in which speakers construe static state of affairs, even if they know that it distorts reality (Talmy, 1983, 1996/2000, Langacker 1987: 170-174, 2008: 528-530, Fauconnier 1997: 177-181). In a similar vein, as Gelman and Hirschfeld (1999: 45) state, the physical externalist intuition may "yield insights on how the

---

3) In the eighteenth century, 'inflammable air', 'dephlogisticated air' and 'phlogisticated air' meant what we call today 'hydrogen', 'oxygen' and 'nitrogen', respectively (Edelstein 1948: 125).

289

human mind construes reality". The purpose of the following argument is to reveal on what conception of reality physical externalism is based.

5.3 The (Un)importance of the Putative Underlying Structure

5.3.1 Physical Externalist Metasemantics vs. Philosophy of Science
5.3.1.1 The Physical Externalist Metasemantics

Natural kinds and natural kind terms provide topics situated at the interface between philosophy of language and philosophy of science (Dupré 2004). While physical externalism has been accepted enthusiastically in the philosophy of language, it has recently come under attack in the philosophy of science. According to physical externalism, the reference of the word 'water' is water as distinct from twater. This is claimed to be a semantic fact about English. As Kaplan (1989a: 573-574) points out, this claim must be distinguished from a claim about what makes 'water' refer to water. The reason why 'water' refers to water is not a semantic fact about English. Such a question, Kaplan says, belongs to the metasemantics of English (see also Stanley 1999: 14-15, Burgess and Sherman (eds.) 2014). Häggqvist and Wikforss (2015: 112) point out that "metasemantic theories are more theoretically committed than descriptive semantics". In particular, the metasemantics of natural kind terms advocated by physical externalism is in tension with the general consensus of philosophers of science (Leslie 2013, Häggqvist and Wikforss 2018, 2020). Häggqvist and Wikforss (2018: 912) comment that "we have a strange situation where philosophers of language take the KP-thesis to be beyond dispute, even though it depends on a theory of natural kinds that is widely rejected among philosophers of science".

Putnam's (1973, 1975) answer to the metasemantic question about natural kind terms involves the notion of 'ostensive definition':

Suppose I point to a glass of water and say "this liquid is called water." My "ostensive definition" of water has the following empirical presupposition: that the body of liquid I am pointing to bears a certain sameness relation (say, x is *the same liquid as y*, or *x is the same_L as y*) to most of the stuff I and other speakers in my linguistic community have on other occasions called "water." (Putnam 1973: 702 1975: 141-142)

The speaker's ostension identifies a local paradigm of the natural kind, and the

Chapter 5   Physical Externalism and Polysemy

relevant sameness relation picks out all items belonging to the same kind. This suggests that, as Ambrus (1999: 4) puts it, "the meaning of a term is determined for Putnam only by the introducing event and the structure of reality - independently of the speaker's state of knowledge. Putnam's (1973, 1975) notion of ostension is virtually equivalent to Kripke's (1980) notion of baptism, initially introduced for the metasemantics of proper names like 'Napoleon' or 'Nixon' (Ambrus 1999: 12, n. 17):

> A rough statement of a theory might be the following : An initial 'baptism' takes place. Here the object may be named by ostension, or the reference of the name may be fixed by a description. When the name is 'passed from link to link', the receiver of the name must, I think, intend when he learns it to use it with the same reference as the man from whom he heard it. (Kripke 1980: 96)

In the initial baptism, the object in question is fixed through either an act of ostension or a description. Even when it is fixed by a description, the descriptive content is not included in the meaning of the name. The description merely serves to fix the object, which is the meaning of the name across all possible worlds (Schwartz 1977: 27, Wikforss 2013: 250). For instance, the description 'the President of the United States in 1970' serves to identify Nixon, but someone else might have been the President of the United States in 1970, suggesting that the name 'Nixon' is not synonymous with the description 'the President of the United States in 1970', or with any other description (Kripke 1980: 49). The name 'Nixon' picks out the same individual as the actual Nixon in all possible worlds. In some possible worlds, Nixon was not the U.S President in 1970. In such worlds, it is a mistake to identify the individual who was the U.S. President in 1970 as Nixon. The same argument can be made for any other description. A name cannot be synonymous with any description because a name is a rigid designator, namely "a term that designates the same object in all possible worlds" (Kripke 1971/1993: 172), while a description is a nonrigid designator (Kripke 1971/1993: 171, 1980: 48)[4].

Kripke (1980: 135) extends this idea to the metasemantics of natural kind terms such as 'gold' or 'water'. The resulting picture is essentially the same as Putnam's (1973, 1980). An act of ostension or a description helps fix a local

---

4) For a succinct review of Kripke's doctrine of rigidity, see Geelen (2011: Ch. 2).

291

paradigm of water, for instance, and the relation $same_L$ determines the extension of the term across all possible worlds. Even though descriptions of the superficial characteristics of water, such as a 'liquid which is colorless, transparent, tasteless, thirst-quenching, found in lakes, etc.' (Putnam 1975: 191) serve to identify a local paradigm of water, these descriptions in no way define the meaning of 'water', just as the description 'the U.S President in 1970' is external to the meaning of 'Nixon'. The extension of 'water' is determined solely by virtue of the relation $same_L$ concerning the hidden underlying structure of water. In some possible worlds, water is not a colorless, transparent or tasteless liquid, and a colorless, transparent and tasteless liquid is not water. In such worlds, we cannot identify the colorless, transparent and tasteless liquid as water. This, Putnam (1973, 1975) claims, vindicates the idea that twater (XYZ) is not included in the extension of the Earthian word 'water'. The relevant sameness relation is uncovered by an indeterminate amount of scientific investigation:

The key point is that the relation $same_L$ is a *theoretical* relation: whether something is or is not the same liquid as *this* may take an indeterminate amount of scientific investigation to determine. [...] Thus, the fact that an English speaker in 1750 might have called XYZ "water," while he or his successors would not have called XYZ water in 1800 or 1850 does not mean that the "meaning" of "water" changed for the average speaker in the interval. [...] What changed was that in 1750 we would have mistakenly thought that XYZ bore the relation $same_L$ to the liquid in Lake Michigan, while in 1800 or 1850 we would have known that it did not [...] (Putnam 1973: 702-703, 1975: 142)

Putnam's view resurrects Locke's (1690) distinction between nominal essence and real essence (Dupré 1981, 1993: 21-22). The nominal essence of a substance "usually consist[s] of a few obvious qualities observed" in the substance (Locke 1690: Book III, Ch. VI, 29). The real essence of a substance, by contrast, is "that real constitution of anything, which is the foundation of all those properties that are combined in, and are constantly found to co-exist with the nominal essence" (Locke 1690: Book III, Ch. VI, 6). In a nutshell, the nominal essence observed by us flows from, or is caused by, the real essence unknown to us (ibid.: Book II, Ch. XXII, 3; Book II, Ch. XI, 6; Book II, Ch. XXXI, 13; Book III, Ch. VI, 11):

[...] the nominal essence of gold is that complex idea the word gold stands for,

Chapter 5 Physical Externalism and Polysemy

let it be, for instance, a body yellow, of a certain weight, malleable, fusible, and fixed. But the real essence is the constitution of the insensible parts of that body, on which those qualities and all the other properties of gold depend. How far these two are different, though they are both called essence, is obvious at first sight to discover. (Lock 1690: Book III, Ch. VI, 2; see also Hanna 1998)

Even though the nominal essence is "inseparably annexed" to the real essence (ibid.: Book III, Ch. III, 18), we can only know the nominal essence (ibid.: Book III, Ch. VI, 9; Book III, Ch. IX). As Dupré (1981: 67, 1993: 22) remarks, "Locke's skepticism was premature". Fortunately, Putnam (1973: 705, 1975: 145) says, we know today that the necessary and sufficient condition for something to count as water is provided by the statement that water is H_2O. Similarly, the hidden underlying structure of a lemon is provided by its genetic code (Putnam 1975: 158), and gold essentially has the atomic number 79 (Kripke 1980: 125, Rey 1983: 253). Locke's real essence is nothing but Putnam's sameness relation which scientists endeavor to discover (Dupré 1981: 70, 1993: 23), while Locke's nominal essence roughly corresponds to Putnam's stereotype (Dupré 1981: 69, 1993: 23).

Kripke (1980: 128) expresses his optimism about whether science will uncover the relevant underlying structures of natural kinds such as 'cow' and 'tiger'. In Kripke's account, natural kind terms are rigid designators on a par with proper names. Thus, Kripke (1971/1993: 187) states that 'heat' and 'the motion of molecules' are both rigid designators representing certain external phenomena. Since heat is the motion of molecules in the actual world, there is no possible world in which the two terms pick out different phenomena, making (9a) a necessary statement which is true in all possible worlds:

(9)   a. Heat is the motion of molecules.
        b. Water is H_2O.

For the same reason, (9b) is a necessary statement if 'water' and 'H_2O' are both rigid designators[5]. Steward (1990: 389) schematizes Kripke's 'water argument' as follows. For any rigid designators x and y, if x = y, then it is necessary that x = y. In the actual world, it is true that water = H_2O. Since 'water' and 'H_2O' are rigid designators, it follows that it is necessary that water = H_2O.

293

5.3.1.2 The *Qua* Problem

A great number of researchers from various scientific fields mount attacks against the metasemantic picture advertised by Putnam and Kripke. The trouble with the picture is that, as Häggqvist and Wikforss (2020: 338) put it, "the world doesn't supply a unique referent/extension". Although, as we have seen in Section 1.3.3, physical externalism holds that the meaning of a natural kind term depends on its extension initially determined, it remains unclear how 'depends on' can be turned into 'is determined by'. Bromberger (1997: 153) states that Putnam's and Kripke's metasemantics of natural kind terms comes "only at the price of a new problem, namely, that of determining what constitutes *being the same substance*, or in the case of animals, *being of the same species*" (see also Boyd 2013: 209). This is what Devitt and Sterelney (1999: 90-93) famously call the '*qua* problem'. Putnam says that an act of ostension serves to fix a local paradigm of the natural kind in question. But the local paradigm can instantiate any number of kinds, only one of which is the relevant natural kind (McKay and Stern 1979: 27-29). As Rey (1992: 326) states, "a token caused by a cat is a token caused by a mammal, an animal, a material object, portions of the cat's fur, etc." Suppose, following Leslie (2013: 129), that a baptizer points to a Bengal tiger, intending to define the natural kind *tiger*. How can we recognize her intention without appealing to the word 'tiger', undefined at the time of the baptism? The local paradigm demonstrated are simultaneously samples of *Bengal tiger, Sumatran tiger, Siberian tiger, Felidae*, and so on and so forth. The local paradigm also instantiates any number of non-natural kinds, such as kinds that include Bengal tigers, lions and panthers.

Leslie (2013: 129) suggests that the *qua* problem can be avoided if we add the assumption that "novel terms name basic level categories". According to Rosch et al. (1976: 385), basic level objects occupy the privileged level of the taxonomic tree

---

5) Kripke (1971/1993: 162) offers a formal proof of the necessity of 'x = y', where x and y are both rigid designators. The proof uses (i) and (ii) as premises:

(i) $\forall x \, \forall y \, ((x = y) \rightarrow (F(x) \rightarrow F(y)))$

(ii) $\forall x \, \Box(x = x)$

By substituting the predicate $\Box(x = \;)$ for F in (i), we obtain (iii):

(iii) $\forall x \, \forall y \, ((x = y) \rightarrow (\Box(x = x) \rightarrow \Box(x = y)))$

Since we know that (ii) is true, the condition '$\Box(x = x)$' in (iii) can be omitted, as in (iv):

(iv) $\forall x \, \forall y \, (x = y \rightarrow \Box \, x = y)]$

(iv) says that 'x = y' is necessarily true, if true. This theorem is anticipated by Barcan Marcus (1961: 307), to whom Kripke (1971/1993: 167-168) credits his view about identity statements.

Chapter 5   Physical Externalism and Polysemy

"at which there are attributes common to all or most members of the category" (see also Rosch and Mervis 1975: 586, Rosch 1977: 31, Rosch 1978: 30-31, Burge 1986b: 6/2007: 223). Thus, chairs are basic level objects in relation to both superordinate level items like furniture and subordinate level items like kitchen chairs (Rosch et al. 1976: 388). Likewise, peaches are basic level objects in relation to both superordinate level items like fruit and subordinate level items like freestone peaches (ibid.). As Taylor (2003: 52) summarizes, basic level categories simultaneously "maximize the number of attributes shared by members of the category" and "minimize the number of attributes shared with members of other categories". In comparison to different kinds of chairs, different pieces of furniture share fewer attributes. Conversely, even though kitchen chairs share a number of attributes, many of these attributes are also shared by dining-room chairs. In Leslie's (2013: 111) words, the basic level is "a 'sweet spot' in this trade-off between within-kind variation in quintessence, and cross-kind quintessential distinctness". Now, tigers can plausibly be taken to be basic level objects in relation to both superordinate level items like Felidae and subordinate level items like Bengal tigers. Assuming that novel terms name basic level categories, we can interpret the baptizer's act of ostension as defining the meaning of 'tiger' rather than 'Felidae' and 'Bengal tiger'. This solution cannot be generalized, however. One may suppose that 'beetle', for instance, is a basic level term, given the numerous readily recognizable features exhibited by beetles. As Dupré (1981: 76, 1993: 30) points out, these features are far from sufficient to choose a unique species from the 290,000 species so far identified. Basic level categories fail to correspond neatly to recognized species (Leslie 2013: 139). Moreover, Dupré (1981: 73, 1993: 27) notes that "it is far from universally the case that the preanalytic extension of a term of ordinary language corresponds to *any* recognized biological taxon", as illustrated by such pairs as 'moth' and 'butterfly' (Abbott 1989: 274-275). This provides a basis for understanding why languages differ significantly in their classification of natural kinds. Thus, both snails and slugs are called 'Schnecke' in German, and both mice and rats are called 'topo' in Italian (Taylor 2012: 198). Taylor states that natural kinds "are not simply 'in the world'" (ibid.).

The problem runs deeper. Häggqvist and Wikforss (2018: 915) remark that "the *qua* problem has not been taken sufficiently seriously". The notion of the basic-level category presupposes that categories are arranged in a taxonomic hierarchy, as originally conceived by Linnaeus[6]. But there exist crosscutting categories in nature (Tobin 2010). Thus, arsenic is both a kind of mineral and a kind of

295

poison, and hemlock is both a kind of poison and a kind of vegetable (Hacking 1993: 286, 299). Poisons overlap, but do not subsume, minerals and vegetables. In response to the possible objection that poison is not a genuine scientific kind, Hacking (1993: 299) remarks that "we have a veritable science of poisons, toxicology". Hacking (1993: 299-300) appeals to Mill's (1843: Book I, Ch. VII) notion of real kind to exclude putative counterexamples to the taxonomic hierarchy of natural kinds. A real kind "is distinguished from all other classes by an indeterminate multitude of properties not derivable from one another" (Mill 1843: 99). Based on this definition, we can say that sulphur, for instance, is a real kind, whereas white is not:

> Some classes have little or nothing in common to characterize them by, except precisely what is connoted by the name: white things, for example, are not distinguished by any common properties except whiteness; or if they are, it is only by such as are in some way dependent on, or connected with, whiteness. But a hundred generations have not exhausted the common properties of animals or of plants, of sulphur or of phosphorus; nor do we suppose them to be exhaustible, but proceed to new observations and experiments, in the full confidence of discovering new properties which were by no means implied in those we previously knew. (Mill 1843: 97)

By the same reasoning, Hacking (1993: 300) concludes that arsenic, but not poison, is a real kind. While the common properties of arsenic are hardly exhaustible, "[t]here is nothing much common to poisons except what puts them in the class in the first place, namely the potential for killing people after being ingested" (ibid.). On the assumption that scientific kinds are real kinds, poison does not count as a scientific kind.

Hacking (1993: 301) acknowledges that this argument does not prove the impossibility of nontaxonomic scientific kinds, given the indefiniteness surrounding Mill's characterization of real kinds. Indeed, as Khalidi (1998: 39-41) points out, there are scientific crosscutting categories. Thus, fleas are simultaneously insects and parasites. Since there are insects that are not parasites, such as flies, and there are also parasites that are not insects, such as tapeworms, the category *insect*

---

6) Hacking (2007b: 210) points out that, although Aristotle talked about genera and species, he did not intend to arrange them in a taxonomic hierarchy.

Chapter 5   Physical Externalism and Polysemy

does not subsume the category *parasite* or vice versa; the category *parasite* crosscuts the taxonomic tree. The category *parasite* is a real kind in light of Mill's definition, because biologists have discovered a number of properties which are common to all parasites but are not among the properties that were associated with the category as initially understood. Similar categories abound:

> The same could be said for the entomological categories – *larva, pupa,* and *imago* – that cut across the Linnaean species categories, or of the phase categories – *solid, liquid, gas* – that cut across the categories of the periodic table. Or, for that matter, the chemical categories – *acid* and *base* – that crosscut the categories *organic* and *inorganic.* All of these categories are real kinds in the sense that we discovered things about them which were by no means implied when they were first introduced. (Khalidi 1998: 41-42)

Khalidi (1998: 50) concludes that "there is no hope for the dream of a single overarching taxonomic hierarchy for the whole of nature". This conclusion is also confirmed by 'the lateral genetic transfer' observed in unicellular organisms, the majority of the population on Earth all through history (Dupré 2004).

5.3.1.3 The Vacuity of the Sameness Relation

There are further problems with Putnam's and Kripke's metasemantics of natural kind terms. Even when we are dealing with a taxonomic hierarchy and the baptizer's intention to name a basic level object is manifest to the audience, the alleged sameness relation can fail to hold. Thus, although Putnam (1975: 158) assumes that "to be a lemon something has to have the genetic code of a lemon", philosophers of biology agree that there is no such thing as the genetic code of a lemon:

> On the question of whether species have these sorts of essences, there is a degree of consensus among philosophers of biology (and indeed biologists) that is almost unprecedented in philosophy at large (e.g. Dupré, 1981, 1993; Ghiselin, 1987; Hull, 1965; Laporte, 1997, 2004; Mayr, 1982, 1988, 1991; Okasha, 2002; Sterelny and Griffiths, 1999, and many others.). There is no such thing as "lemon DNA," no common genetic code that makes for membership in the kind *Panthera tigris.* To a first approximation, most biologists subscribe to the notion that a species is delineated by the boundaries of an

297

ecological niche, or by the boundaries of a reproductive community. Within such bounds, considerable genetic variation is possible, and conversely, it is possible for there to be *less* genetic variation *across* such boundaries. (Leslie 2013: 132)

Unlike 'bachelor' or 'sibling' (Quine 1960: §12), for example, the names of biological taxa can hardly be associated with any necessary and sufficient conditions (Hull 1965: 323). It is difficult to make sense of Garrett's (1983: 79) claim that internal structural correspondence is a necessary condition for membership of a kind. There is simply no privileged sameness relation that unambiguously defines the extension of biological kinds (Dupré 1981: 78, 88-90, Sainsbury 1990/1996/2002: 83), that is, as Hacking (2007b: 234) remarks, "[t]here are no necessary and sufficient conditions for being a tiger or a lemon". There is no more a 'tiger DNA' than there is a 'black DNA' (Leslie 2013: 130). Scientific findings tell us that "the genetic variability *within* a racial group is just as high as the degree of variability *across* racial groups" (Leslie 2013: 122, emphases in the original). The same bias that causes a person to believe in the 'black DNA' underlies Putnam's assumption that lemons and tigers each have a determinate genetic code. As a matter of fact, "there is no such thing as the 'species' genotype" (Leslie 2013: 124). The baptizer's intention to name lemons or tigers is bound to fail, insofar as her intention relies on the presence of a unique hidden underlying structure of the kind.

Several attempts have been made to state necessary and sufficient conditions for belonging to a kind (Okasha 2002, LaPorte 2004), but none of the attempts exclusively refers to the intrinsic, namely, non-relational properties of the local paradigm. Thus, Okasha (2002) proposes to replace Putnam's 'hidden structure' with relational properties which determine species membership. This may salvage Kripke's notion of kind essence, insofar as having such relational properties can be considered essential for kind membership. But substituting 'relational property' for 'hidden underlying structure' may yield a disastrous result for the KP-thesis:

On all modern species concepts (except the phenetic), the property in virtue of which a particular organism belongs to one species rather than another is a relational rather than an intrinsic property of that organism. On the interbreeding concept, the property is "being able to interbreed successfully with one group of organisms and not another"; on the ecological concept the property is "occupying a particular ecological niche"; on the phylogenetic concept the property is "being a member of a particular segment of the genealogical nexus". Clearly none of these properties is intrinsic to the organisms possessing them, nor supervenes on any of their intrinsic properties. Two molecule-for-molecule identical organisms could in principle be members of different species, on all of these species concepts. (Okasha 2002: 201)

If the molecular structure of an organism falls short of defining the species to which it belongs and we need to take into consideration the relation between the organism and its environment, Kripke's claim that natural kind terms are rigid designators loses all its plausibility. It is no longer evident that an act of ostension which takes place in the actual world determines the extension of the term in all possible worlds, because in other possible worlds the organism the baptizer points to may stand in different relations to the environment. Moreover, if, by parity of reasoning, two molecule-for-molecule identical samples of water can belong to different substances, Putnam's claim that the Earthian word 'water' has always meant water as distinct from twater loses ground, since his claim rests entirely on the assumption that water is defined by its molecular structure. Leslie (2013: 142) concludes that "Kripke/Putnam essentialism about biological kinds looks to be untenable, even if one attempts to reconstruct it in the most charitable of ways".

It might be said that the KP-thesis about chemical kinds (as opposed to biological species) is tenable. Indeed, the identity statement in (9b), 'Water is H_2O', "survived widespread acknowledgement that biological species do not have intrinsic essences" (Häggqvist and Wikforss 2020: 337). While Bird (2009: 134) disputes the view that biological kinds are defined in terms of micro-constitution, he still endorses microessentialism about chemical kinds by merely replacing Putnam's 'relation $same_L$' by 'same-kind relation', on the grounds that "a phase difference does not imply a kind difference" (Bird 2009: 134, n. 4; see also Leslie 2013: 142, n. 27). Nevertheless, the idea that water is defined by its being H_2O is riddled with as many problems as the idea that the extension of 'tiger' is fully determined by the intrinsic properties of tigers. First of all, it is erroneous to construe 'H_2O' as the structural description of water. 'H_2O' is merely a compositional formula which expresses the proportion of hydrogen to oxygen (Needham 2000: 13-14, 2002: 211-212, 2007: 46). As long as 'H_2O' is meant as a compositional formula, Needham (2007: 46) states, it can in principle be also written as 'OH_2', "since the compositional formula says nothing about structure, but merely states that hydrogen and oxygen are combined in the proportion of two chemical equivalents to one". Since the 1820s it has been recognized that composition is not sufficient to determine a unique kind, because there can be different substances which share one and the same composition (Needham 2002: 212, 223, 2011: 15). Berzelius coined the term 'isomerism' for this phenomenon (Needham 2011: 15). Thus, the compositional formula C_2H_6O is common to ethyl alcohol and dimethyl ether (Needham 2000: 14). But ethyl alcohol and dimethyl ether are indisputably different substances, as evidenced by their different boiling points. Substances which have the same composition but different chemical or physical properties such as melting points and densities are called isomers (Needham 2000: 14, 2007: 46, 2002: 212). To distinguish isomers, we need structural formulae rather than compositional formulae (Needham 2011: 11). The structures of ethyl alcohol and dimethyl ether are represented by C_2H_5OH and $(CH_3)_2O$, respectively (ibid.:9). Since "[t]he notion of a structural formula was elaborated throughout the 19th century" (Needham 2002: 212), the discovery that water is H_2O in the second half of the 18th century cannot be characterized as the discovery of the microstructure of water (ibid.: 211-212).

True, water has no isomer and hence is uniquely determined by the compositional formula H_2O (Needham 2000: 14, 2007: 46). But this is at best fortuitous. By the law of constant proportion, a compositional formula merely provides a necessary condition for something to belong to the kind in question (Needham 2002: 223). If substances were identified solely by their compositions, it would not even be possible to distinguish diamond from graphite, a substance typically used for pencils. Although, unlike graphite, diamond may appear to be composed of rare elements, diamond and graphite are both allotropes of carbon. As LaPorte (1996: 127) tells us, chemists were surprised to discover that "diamond's chemical composition was [...] *exactly the same* as that of *charcoal*". What distinguishes diamond and graphite is their crystal structures, suggesting that the identity of a substance depends on both chemical composition and crystal structure (LaPorte 1996: 126-127)[7]. To vindicate the KP-thesis, we must therefore seek for the microstructure (as opposed to the chemical composition) of water.

The enterprise to identify the microstructure of water, however, is clouded by the fact that, as Needham (2011: 11) puts it, "[w]hatever water's microstructure is,

---

7) LaPorte (1996: 127) states that chemists have not determined that diamond and charcoal are two varieties of a single species. Needham (2002: 209) points out, however, that this interpretation is not correct, because it is generally agreed that diamond and graphite are two varieties of the same species, namely, carbon.

Chapter 5   Physical Externalism and Polysemy

it is very complicated". Let us represent the structure of typical water molecules as 'H-O-H', where the bond angle is 104.5° (Needham 2011: 17-18, Leslie 2013: 145). The problem with the idea that water has the microstructure of H-O-H is that "[w]ater [...] is not molecular, except under certain conditions in the gas phase" (Needham 2011: 16) and that "water in the form of ice has a very different microstructure from water in the form of a liquid, and again a very different microstructure from water in the gas phase" (ibid.: 9). According to Leslie (2013: 145), ice has at least fifteen different forms, in one of which there is no molecular structure at all, even though the proportion of hydrogen to oxygen remains 2:1. In the liquid phase, some H-O-H molecules dissociate into H+ and OH- ions, some of which attach to H-O-H molecules, forming complex ions such as H_3O+ and $(H_2O)OH-$. Hence, if we nevertheless maintain that water essentially has the microstructure of H-O-H, we are forced to say that water is essentially steam or gas (Leslie 2013: 146, 152). As Needham (2002: 207) states, "[w]hereas the composition of water was settled long ago, any talk of having discovered *the* microstructure of water would be premature" (emphasis in the original).

It might be tempting to return to the definition of water exclusively by virtue of the compositional formula H_2O since, fortunately, water happens to have no isomer and thus the compositional formula is necessary and sufficient to identify water. But this move is disastrous for several reasons. First, the compositional structure H_2O alone cannot account for "[w]ater's relatively high freezing and boiling points, in relation to other substances of comparable molecular weight" (Needham 2000: 19). As Leslie (2013: 145) remarks, this characteristic of water, which ensures that we can drink water at normal temperatures, derives from the fact that "liquid and solid water do not simply consist of H-O-H molecules". Secondly, H_2O has a variety written as D_2O or D-O-D. D_2O is commonly known as 'heavy water', because its two hydrogen nuclei each contain a neutron, while in typical 'light water', the hydrogen nuclei contain no neutron, consisting solely of a single proton[8]. A typical light hydrogen atom with one proton and no neutron is called protium and a heavy hydrogen atom with one proton and one neutron is called deuterium (LaPorte 1996: 118, Leslie 2013: 150). There is also a heavy hydrogen atom with one proton and two neutrons, known as tritium (Soames 2002: 286, Leslie 2013: 150). Protium, deuterium and tritium are isotopes of

---

8) There is also semiheavy water HDO (H-O-D), where one of the two hydrogen nuclei contains a neutron.

hydrogen distinguished solely by the number of neutrons they contain. In most cases, isotopes have almost the same chemical properties and the differences, if any, are negligible. Thus, as Leslie (2013: 150) states, "if the most common variant of an element enters into a given chemical reaction, so will its isotopes". Due to its low mass, however, hydrogen is an important exception to this tendency. Since deuterium has twice the mass of protium, heavy water, which contains deuterium in place of protium, exhibits remarkably different chemical properties from light water (ibid.: 151), even though heavy water is often counted as a kind of water (Soames 2002: 286; see also Kripke 1980: 128-29). As a result, if you continue to drink heavy water instead of light water, you will die after suffering from sterility and neurological problems (Leslie 2013: 150). This fatal effect is caused by the excessively strong bond between deuterium and carbon, which disorganizes a number of biochemical processes in the body (ibid.). The definition of water in terms of its composition, however, fails to distinguish water and heavy water, since both are H_2O. This problem is closely related to Kripke's (1980: 124) claim that gold essentially has the atomic number 79. Certainly, the property of having the atomic number 79 uniquely determines gold. But if we define elements solely in terms of their atomic number, it is not possible to distinguish protium and deuterium, since both have the atomic number 1. Kripke's claim seems to imply that water and heavy water are one and the same substance. It is unlikely, however, that we would make no distinction between a glass of water and a glass of heavy water in a restaurant, for example[9].

The point just made leads to another fundamental problem facing the KP-thesis. What motivates the distinction between water and heavy water is their differing macroscopic or relational properties; long-term consumption of heavy water causes serious damage or death. Putnam assumes that water and twater, while having completely different compositions, exhibit exactly the same macroscopic properties. Kripke (1980: 120, 124) imagines similar hypothetical cases about 'tiger' and 'gold'. Their assumptions, however, are grossly implausible. Grayling (1982, 1995: 76) calls into question Putnam's and Kripke's sheer dichotomy between the putative underlying structure of a natural kind and its superficial characteristics. Indeed, there is a consensus among philosophers of science that

---

9) Leslie (2013: 151) comments that if a philosopher stuck to the idea that "elements are identified by their atomic numbers, and compounds by the elements in them", an apt answer to that philosopher would be: "Well then, drink up!".

microscopic structures are not independent of macroscopic structures. Thus, Dupré (1981: 72) states that "[a]ll our scientific experience goes against the possibility of there being two substances that differed solely in having radically different molecular structures". Likewise, Needham (2011: 11) comments that "[i]f [Putnam's Twin Earth thought experiment] assumes that two substances are distinct at the microlevel and yet share all their macroproperties, so that they can't be distinguished in terms of macroproperties, then the scenario is wildly implausible", because "characteristic macroscopic properties like melting and boiling points, latent heats and specific heats are related to the microstructure". Indeed, Putnam (1990: 69) concedes that "differences in microstructure invariably (in the actual world) result in lawful behavior". This casts doubt on the priority of microstructure over macrostructure suggested by the KP-thesis. Brakel (1986: 291) claims that "in order to define or designate the referent of a mass term, we have to look for macroscopic sameness, not for underlying structure". Likewise, Needham (2000: 13) states that "microstructure does not play the leading role in individuating chemical kinds that recent discussions presuppose; rather, there is a complexity and variety at the microlevel which is unified only if seen in relation to single macroscopically distinguished kinds"[10]. It is rather macroscopic criteria that enable scientists to identify a substance, and only after the substance is thus identified do they set out to investigate its microstructure (Needham 2011: 16, Häggqvist and Wikforss 2020: 338). In this vein, Bursten (2014) proposes to individuate chemical substances according to their radioactivity, which is explained in terms of microstructure.

The putative coexistence of water and twater, namely twin-substances which are macroscopically identical but microscopically different, is incompatible with the known laws of nature (Fodor 1994: 38, Horst 1996: 244, Needham 2011: 11, Wikforss 2008: 179, n. 14, 2010: 75, 77-78, 2013: 257-258). As Wikforss (2013: 257) remarks, "there simply are no perfect twin-substances". Although, as we have seen in Chapter 1, Kripke (1980: 124) took gold and iron pyrites to be

---

10) Needham repeatedly stresses the same point:

As I say, so much has been clear since Perrin and Einstein's investigations into Brownian motion. What doesn't follow from this is that the details of the microstructure of any particular substance are reasonably well known, and certainly not that they are independent of macroscopic constraints or somehow determine the macroscopic features of substances or that substances are in some clear sense "nothing but" their microconstituents. (Needham 2011: 17)

twin-substances, Ben-Yami (2001: 161) points out that "iron pyrites has only a *faint* resemblance to gold" (see also Poncinie 1985: 419). Putnam (1975) offers other real-life candidates for such perfect twins, jadeite and nephrite. Jadeite and nephrite, Putnam suggests, are macroscopically identical, while their compositional structures are strikingly different:

> An interesting case is the case of jade. Although the Chinese do not recognize a difference, the term 'jade' applies to two minerals: jadeite and nephrite. Chemically, there is a marked difference. Jadeite is a combination of sodium and aluminum. Nephrite is made of calcium, magnesium, and iron. These two quite different microstructures produce the same unique textural qualities! (Putnam 1975: 160):

Putnam's chemical descriptions of the twin-substances are correct; jadeite is $NaAl(SiO3)_2$ and nephrite is $Ca_2(MgFe)_5Si_8O22(OH)_2$ (Leslie 2013: 134). But, as LaPorte (2004) points out, Putnam's macroscopic descriptions are misleading. Jade is of enormous importance for Chinese civilizations (Hacking 2007c: 271). Since ancient times, almost all Chinese jade, called 'yü' (玉) has been nephrite (LaPorte 2004: 94, Hacking 2007c: 271). When the Qianlong emperor annexed northern Burma in 1784 (Hacking 2007c: 271), as LaPorte (2004: 95) puts it, "jade met its XYZ", namely jadeite[11]. The emperor adored jadeite and the generic name 'jade' (yü) came to cover both nephrite and jadeite. Putnam's (1975: 160) statement that "the Chinese do not recognize a difference" is far from correct, because "the Chinese, who had carefully worked nephrite by hand for generations, could tell by its feel that it was a different material" (LaPorte 2004: 96). Jadeite is more slippery, harder and heavier than nephrite (Hacking 2007c: 270). Jadeite has a deep green color, while nephrite is creamy in color (ibid.). The differences in superficial properties are tied to the difference in composition. In 1863, Alexis Damour, a French scientist, discovered that jadeite and nephrite have totally different chemical compositions (LaPorte 2004: 95-96, Hacking 2007c: 271-271). It must be emphasized that Damour did not tell the Chinese that jadeite and nephrite were different stones. The Chinese were confident from the outset that they had encountered a new type of stone from Burma. As Wikforss (2013: 257, n. 35) makes clear, "jade

---

11) According to Hacking (2007c: 271), this is an exaggeration, because it is presumed that by the 17th century small amounts of jadeite were in circulation in China.

Chapter 5   Physical Externalism and Polysemy

is not an example of a perfect twin-substance, since there are observable differences between jadeite and nephrite".

Better candidates for twin-substances are provided by spin-isomers of hydrogen (Leslie 2013: 149). Molecular hydrogen (H_2) exists in two isomeric forms depending on whether its nuclear spins are parallel (orthohydrogen) or antiparallel (parahydrogen) (Tikhonov and Volkov 2002, Kravchuk et al. 2011: 319, Needham 2011: 11). These two isomers are known to have different macroscopic features pertaining to specific heat, boiling point, and so on (Tikhonov and Volkov 2002)[12]. Since water molecules contain hydrogen atoms, water molecules also have spin isomers, ortho-water and para-water, differing by the orientation of the nuclear spins of the hydrogen atoms (Kravchuk et al. 2011: 319). Although methods to separate orthohydrogen and parahydrogen were established in the first half of the twentieth century, it is far more difficult to separate ortho-water and para-water, and several techniques have been proposed (ibid.). This may provide a basis for a thought experiment similar to, but different from, Putnam's Twin Earth. Leslie (2013: 150) invites us to imagine two planets, Ortho-Earth and Para-Earth. The substance called 'water' on Ortho-Earth is ortho-water, while the substance called 'water' on Para-Earth is para-water. Accordingly, Ortho-Earthians' use of 'water' refers to ortho-water, while Para-Earthians' use of the same word form refers to para-water. In this situation, is it appropriate to say that 'water' has different meanings on the two planets? In other words, is it a mistake to call both ortho-water and para-water 'water'? In a sense, it is, because, as Tikhonov and Volkov (2002: 2363) remark, "[o]rtho and para water are expected to have notably different physical-chemical properties" and, as said earlier, attempts have been made to separate ortho-water and para-water. In another sense, it is not, since scientists usually treat water as a unique substance. Science does not give a definite answer to the question (Leslie 2013: 150).

Furthermore, Leslie's (2013) thought experiment reminds us that we use the word 'water' to refer to mixture of ortho-water and para-water, which differ in microstructure[13] . This strongly suggests that our act of ostension may not be

---

12) As Denbigh and Redhead (1989: 285) state, a mixture of orthohydrogen and parahydrogen increases the entropy of the system as much as a mixture of hydrogen and carbon dioxide. This phenomenon, known as 'entropy of mixing', is sometimes used to show that orthohydrogen and parahydrogen are different substances (Leslie 2013: 149). Hendry (2010: 932) counters this argument by saying that "entropy of mixing does not provide a criterion for the sameness and difference of substance".

305

sufficient for determining a unique substance defined by its microstructure. It seems that to ask whether our use of 'water' and the Ortho-Earthians' or Para-Earthians' uses of 'water' refer to the same substance is to ask the wrong question. In fact, as LaPorte (1996: 120) remarks, "the decision as to whether D_2O bears the relation *same microstructural kind* to the majority of what we called 'water' or whether it does not was optional". These considerations have led Putnam (1990) to qualify the view he expressed earlier in Putnam (1973, 1975) and explicitly depart from the KP-thesis (Ambrus 1999: 12, n. 17):

> For example, consider an ordinary sample of iron. By the standards of high school chemistry, it is "chemically pure". But is consists of different isotopes (these occur in fixed proportions – the same proportions – in all naturally occurring samples, by the way. Some philosophers who use isotopes as examples appear not to know this.) Any naturally occurring sample of iron (which is sufficiently free of impurities) will exhibit the same lawful behavior as any other (unless we go to a quantum-mechanical level of accuracy). But if we use a cyclotron or some other fancy gadget from atomic physics to prepare a sample of iron which is mono-isotopic, that sample will – if the tests are sensitive enough – behave slightly differently from a "natural" sample. Should we then say that a hunk of iron consisting of a single isotope and a hunk of natural iron (consisting of the various isotopes in their normal proportions) are two different substances or one? Indeed, two naturally occurring samples may have tiny variations in the proportions with which the isotopes occur, and perhaps this will result in a slight difference in their lawful behavior. Are they samples of different substances? Well, it may depend on our interests. (This is the sort of talk Kripke hates!) (Putnam 1990: 68)

To summarize, we cannot rely on the alleged hidden underlying structure to determine the meaning of a natural kind term. Contrary to Putnam's and Kripke's initial expectations, in most cases the physical environment does not cooperate with us to issue in the unique sameness relation that holds across possible worlds,

---

13) There is another sense in which water is a mixture. So-called pure water is known to usually consist of H_2O, D_2O and tritium, "with the first being the overwhelmingly dominant part" (Soames 2002: 286). One may use this fact to argue that ordinary samples of water are not pure. But this argument is hardly applicable to the mixture of ortho- and para-water, because it is quite arbitrary to restrict the use of the term 'pure water' to either of the two.

Chapter 5 Physical Externalism and Polysemy

or even within the actual world (Häggqvist and Wikforss 2018: 922). In short, what Weisberg (2006) refers to as the 'coordination principle' does not hold. Häggqvist and Wikforss (2018: 929) conclude:

> In conclusion, the Kripke-Putnam account of natural kind terms, which has dominated philosophy of language since the 1970s, is untenable. Although Kripke and Putnam were quite right to criticize traditional, definitionalist accounts of natural kind terms, and although they were right to stress the close interaction between semantics, metaphysics, and philosophy of science, the semantic paradigm that emerged, captured in the KP-thesis, cannot be sustained. Time is ripe to cut the cord with the legacy of Kripke and Putnam, and start afresh. (Häggqvist and Wikforss 2018: 929)

The KP-thesis seems scientifically uninformed, failing to unravel the metasemantic question of what makes 'water' refer to water as distinct from twater. Then, what guarantees that 'water' does not mean twater? It should now be clear that we are asking the wrong question. What should rather be asked is whether the semantic claim on which the metasemantic claim hinges is tenable. As Häggqvist and Wikforss (2015: 114) state, the claim that "'water' only has H_2O in its extension" is a "far from trivial" claim. Does the word 'water' really denote water as distinct from twater?

5.3.2 Physical Externalist Semantics vs. Linguistic Semantics
5.3.2.1 Relevance of Interests

According to physical externalist semantics, 'water' means water as distinct from twater. This view entails that it is erroneous to apply a natural kind term to several superficially similar but compositionally or structurally different substances. Thus, in this account, it is more than obvious that twater (XYZ) is no more water (H_2O) than iron pyrites (FeS_2) is gold (Au). However, physical externalist semantics does not comport with historical facts. In the eighteenth century, the Chinese accepted both jadeite ($NaAl(SiO3)_2$) and nephrite ($Ca_2(MgFe)_5Si_8O22(OH)_2$) as examples of jade, despite the remarkable differences between the two (LaPorte 2004: 96, Hacking 2007c: 271). Even though, so far, water has not met its XYZ, the historical facts about jade call into question Putnam's assumption that the term 'water' can never be applied to twater.

Following Putnam, Burge says that it is obvious that twater is no more water

307

than twin-alminium is alminium:

> I think it natural and obviously correct to say, with Putnam, that the stuff that runs in rivers and faucets on Twin-Earth is thus not water. I shall not argue for this view, because it is pretty obvious, pretty widely shared, and stronger than arguments that might be or have been brought to buttress it. (Burge 1982: 100/2007: 85)

> Anyone who wishes to resist our conclusions merely by claiming that XYZ is water will have to make parallel claims for aluminum, helium, and so forth. Such claims, I think, would be completely implausible. (Burge 1982: 119/2007: 85, n. 7)

Given that the Chinese did not hesitate to apply the term 'yü' to jadeite as well as to nephrite, Burge's analogy does not hold for the case of jade. It might be said that the Chinese were mistaken in applying the term 'yü' to the new stone from Burma. But recall that the Chinese were fully aware that nephrite and jadeite are both macroscopically and microscopically different stones. The recognition of the difference did not deter them from calling jadeite 'new jade'. While LaPorte (2004: 96) suggests that after 1784 there was a controversy in China whether or not the new jade from Burma was an authentic yü, Hacking (2007c: 273) is skeptical of this report, maintaining that "the Qianlong emperor (who ruled until 1796) loved the stuff, and the question of whether it was *yu* did not arise". What motivated the Chinese to treat both nephrite and jadeite in an equal fashion is, in Hacking's (2007c: 276) words, "aesthetics, ease of working into exquisite objects, and [...] money". This indicates that "interests trump metaphysics" (ibid.). The same point can be illustrated by diamond and graphite. These two substances, both of which are allotropes of carbon, are distinguished not by composition (C) but by economic significance (see also Poncinie 1985: 418).

As stated in Chapter 1, for Putnam, it is not an essential fact about water that it consists of hydrogen and oxygen:

> Importance is an interest-relative notion. Normally the "important" properties of a liquid or solid, etc., are the ones that are structurally important: the ones that specify what the liquid or solid, etc., is ultimately made out of – elementary particles, or hydrogen and oxygen, or earth, air, fire, water, or whatever

Chapter 5   Physical Externalism and Polysemy

– and how they are arranged or combined to produce the superficial characteristics. (Putnam 1975: 157)

As the hedge 'Normally' indicates, Putnam's (1975) view anticipates his later view
(Putnam 1990) that the identity of a substance depends on our interests. In this
respect, 'the KP-thesis' is a misleading label. For Kripke, the meaning of a natural
kind term is always determined by the essence of its reference. For Putnam, the
hidden underlying structure of a substance is only one of the factors which may be
relevant to the determination of the meaning of the corresponding natural kind
term. Since importance or relevance depends on our interests, as LaPorte (1996:
128) remarks, whether a newly encountered substance falls under the extension of
the natural kind term in question cannot be determined unless the need arises to
determine whether it does or not. In the same spirit, Hacking (2007c: 274) conjectures that, before 1784, the extension of the Chinese word 'yü' was undeter-
mined vis-à-vis jadeite. If there were allotropes of gold (AU) which were "far less
malleable and ductile" (Leslie 2013: 153), would we apply the word 'gold' to the
allotropes? It is not at all clear, Leslie (2013: 153) suggests, whether even Kripke
would continue to assert that "being composed of Au atoms is necessary and sufficient for falling under the manifest kind gold, despite lacking these economically
significant properties". As Hacking (2007c: 275) emphasizes, our practices of
naming are utterly contingent.

The same remark can be made for water. Hacking (2007c: 275) points out that
"[b]ecause of the sheer contingency we have no idea what we would say, let alone
should say, if a Twin-Earth were ever to be discovered". Likewise, Noonan (1984:
219) states that Putnam's assumption that 'water' has different meanings for Oscar
and Oscar$_2$ is doubtful especially if "even their most knowledgeable members possess no criteria by which they could judge samples of H_2O and samples of XYZ to
be distinct kinds of substance". Even if we know that water is H_2O, Putnam's
assumption is debatable. Thus, Steward (1990: 390) asks us to imagine that there is
a hypothetical planet where H_2O is a pink solid at normal temperatures and pres-
sures and that the opacity and high melting point of H_2O are caused by a previously unknown particle, proton-B, contained in the nuclei of hydrogen in place of
the normal proton. Would we call the pink solid 'water' without hesitation?
Steward (1990: 390) answers that "surely we would use different names for the
widely varying kinds of substance produced by the substitution of protons-B for
ordinary protons". This answer would be plausible if it turned out that on the

309

planet there was a liquid XYZ superficially similar to our water. In this case, we would be more likely to call the liquid XYZ 'water', refraining from applying the same word to the pink solid. LaPorte (1996: 128), on the contrary, answers that "we could go either way". Nevertheless, Steward and LaPorte agree that the compositional structure or microstructure does not fully determine whether the substance is water. As Wikforss (2013: 257) states, "in far removed worlds where the laws of nature are different and macro- and micro-level properties come apart, it will be indeterminate what to say: our use of these terms is simply not prepared for such cases", and "which way we go is a matter of decision, and is not laid down in the 'meaning' of the term". Nor can we expect scientists to answer the question, since scientists are only engaged in investigating what happens in the actual world (Putnam 1990: 71, Ambrus 1999: 7). As Steward (1990: 398) states, "it is entirely possible that we shall never know whether identity statements of the 'water = H_2O' variety are necessarily true, however much science progresses". This strongly argues against Kripke's claim that water is necessarily H_2O. These considerations finally led Putnam (1990: 69-70) to abandon the idea of metaphysical necessity.

Although Putnam (1990) thought that his rejection of metaphysical necessity would not affect the Twin Earth thought experiment, because "questions about worlds in which the *laws of nature can be different* were not on [his] mind" (Putnam, 1990: 69), Wikforss (2010: 77, 2013: 257-258) points out that the rejection of metaphysical necessity strips the Twin Earth thought experiment of its plausibility. On the one hand, Putnam (1990: 71) says that "we are not now talking about 'metaphysical possibility' but about *physical* possibility". As stated earlier, however, scientists agree that perfect twin-substances are physically impossible. On the other hand, Putnam (1973, 1975, 1990) distinguishes water from twater exclusively in terms of its compositional structure. But, now that water is known not to be necessarily H_2O, we must suppose that twater is not necessarily XYZ, either. If neither water nor twater is identified solely by its microstructures, there remains no compelling reason for claiming that Oscar's 'water' has a different extension, and hence a different meaning, from Oscar$_2$'s 'water'.

5.3.2.2 Linguistic Arguments for and against Essentialism

Based on experimental studies, Malt (1994: 66) claims that "the presence of H_2O, is necessary, but not sufficient, for a liquid to be considered water" and that "[i]f H_2O is believed to be present, the remaining factors may then determine whether the liquid will be considered water or a member of some other category".

Chapter 5   Physical Externalism and Polysemy

Among the factors relevant to the determination are the location, immediate source, function, and relative purity or composition of the substance (Malt 1994: 56). The physical externalist semantics unjustifiably privileges the last factor. For example, tea and coffee are not considered water despite the high amount of H_2O they contain. This has to do with the functional role which coffee and tea play in our daily life. We obtain coffee by adding to H_2O non-H_2O ingredients to differentiate it from other liquids served as beverages (ibid.: 66). This explains the fact that we reserve a special noun to denote coffee (ibid.). The mere presence of a high amount of H_2O is not sufficient for something to count as water, contrary to what physical externalist semantics suggests[14]. These findings are further supported by Kalish's (1995) experimental work on various kinds of terms. Chomsky (1995, 2000) makes the same point about 'water':

Substances reveal the same kinds of special mental design. Take the term "water", in the sense proposed by Hilary Putnam: as coextensive with "H_2O give or take certain impurities" (Putnam [1992], alluding to his 1975). Even in such a usage, with its questionable invocation of natural science, we find that whether something is water depends on special human interests and concerns, again in ways understood without relevant experience; the term "impurities" covers some difficult terrain. Suppose cup_1 is filled from the tap. It is a cup of water, but if a tea bag is dipped into it, that is no longer the case. It is now a cup of tea, something different. Suppose cup_2 is filled from a tap connected to a reservoir in which tea has been dumped (say, as a new kind of purifier). What is in cup_2 is water, not tea, even if a chemist could not distinguish it from the present contents of cup_1. The cups contain the same thing from one point of view, different things from another; but in either case cup_2 contains only water and cup_1 only tea. In cup_2, the tea is an "impurity" in Putnam's sense, in cup_1, it

---

14)   Braisby et al. (1996: 254) point out that, in order to argue definitively against physical externalist semantics, it is not sufficient to show that the extension of 'water' in the actual water is not circumscribed by the chemical composition of the substance denoted by the term. Since Kripke's essentialist claim is that water is H_2O in all possible worlds, we need to test speakers' intuitions about counterfactual situations. Braisby et al. (1996) test such intuitions and conclude that "natural kind terms are not employed in an essentialist manner" (ibid.: 272). In a similar vein, Häggqvist and Wikforss (2015) suggest that "the widely endorsed assumption that natural kind terms cannot be given a descriptivist semantics is nothing but armchair semantics" (ibid.: 131).

311

is not, and we do not have water at all [...] (Chomsky 1995: 22/2000: 127-128; see also Chomsky 2000: 189-190/2003: 281)

According to physical externalism, the meaning of 'water' is determined not by any mental representations, but by the nature of the physical environment itself. Malt's and Chomsky's arguments demonstrate that the meaning of 'water' partly depends on speakers' mental representations. As Chomsky suggests, if a tea bag is dipped into water, speakers no longer represent the liquid as water in their mind. Even though it is still H_2O, it is now construed as tea. But if it turns out that the tea bag is used as a purifier of water, speakers no longer represent the liquid as tea. Even though it is still filled with tea leaves, it is now construed as water. In Putnam's account, the stereotype of water, such as 'liquid which is colorless, transparent, tasteless, thirst-quenching, found in lakes, etc.' (Putnam 1975: 191), is insufficient to determine the extension of 'water', merely serving to identify a local paradigm of water. As Abbott (1997) makes clear, however, it is precisely this stereotype that distinguishes water from other liquids with a high percentage of H_2O:

[Chomsky's] (and Malt's) other main observation in this regard is that many substances, such as tea, clam juice, blood, and Windex, which are correctly believed to contain a high percentage of water, are nevertheless not called "water". None of these substances have the stereotypical properties of water and hence to that extent they would not fit the meaning of "water" under Putnam's approach. (Abbott 1997: 313)

Abbott herself is skeptical of Putnam's notion of stereotype (ibid.: 313) and proposes to account for the data observed by Malt (1994) and Chomsky (1995/2000) by appealing to the distinction between 'being water' and 'being called "water"'. Abbott (1997: 315) maintains that what categories something falls into is a different question from what you call it. The first question belongs to semantics while the second one belongs to pragmatics and hence has no direct bearing on the meaning of the term. This approach, Abbott suggests, salvages Kripke's claim that water = H_2O as far as the actual world is concerned. For Abbott, tea is water; it is just that tea is not called water. The meaning of 'water' is exhausted by its chemical definition, while the use of the term depends on "the other properties of the thing in question plus human interests and concerns which play no role in determining the extension of the term" (Abbott 1999: 145). The

312

Chapter 5   Physical Externalism and Polysemy

same reasoning holds for the use of 'tears' as opposed to 'water':

> If the same substance is called "tears" when it comes out of someone's eyes, but "water" when it is in a massive quantity lapping up against the coast of California, doesn't that mean that the property of source *is* forming part of the concept of "water" and the meaning of the word "water"? No. And here's why. The difference is not that one substance (e.g. the stuff coming out of your eyes) is not water and the other stuff is water. They are both water. The difference is only that one is *called* "water" and the other is not. And that only goes to show that we need to distinguish what something is from what it may be called on particular occasions. (Abbott 1997: 315, emphasis in the original)

LaPorte (1998) objects that Abbott's suggestion places too much a burden on pragmatics. Since babies, chickens and tomatoes consist mainly of H_2O, in Abbott's (1997) account, the sentences in (10a-c) are semantically perfect, their oddity being entirely attributed to pragmatic factors:

(10)   a. It is time to tend to "that crying water in the crib" (a baby).
      b. The time has come to cut off the head of that "clucking, messy water in the coop" (a chicken) and roast it.
      c. Pick the growing water (tomatoes) off the vines out back.
                                ((10a-c): LaPorte 1998: 453)

LaPorte (1998: 453) comments that "it seems incredible to suppose that an infant [...] instantiates the *water* kind". It is not clear at all whether Abbott's (1997) analysis serves other purposes than just saving Kripke's claim that water = H_2O. Although Abbott (1997: 316) suggests that her analysis is motivated by Gricean considerations (Grice 1989), the details of the putative Gricean account remain obscure. LaPorte (1998: 454) concludes that "[i]t seems much more likely [...] that the relevant organic objects do not belong to the extension of 'water'".

Abbott (1997: 147) concedes that (11a) sounds odd even if the telephone is 80 percent plastic, that (11b) is not a good way to refer to a 90 percent wooden door, and that it is difficult to ask someone to put the books on a 100 percent steel bookshelf by uttering (11c):

(11)   a. The plastic (the telephone) is ringing.

313

b. Someone shut that wood (the door).

c. Put the books on that steel (the bookshelf).

According to Abbott (1997: 147), however, the oddity of (11a-c) does not vindicate the semantic solution suggested by LaPorte (1998), because the telephone in (11a) is in the extension of 'plastic', the door in (11b) is in the extension of 'wood' and the bookshelf in (11c) is in the extension of 'steel'. Denying these facts is tantamount to denying that the telephone in (11a) consists mainly of plastic, for example. Abbott (1999: 147-148) insists that 'water' is no different. Babies, chickens and tomatoes fall in the extension of 'water'. Denying these facts is tantamount to denying that these objects contain a high proportion of H_2O. Abbott (1999: 145) stresses that the oddity of (10a-c) is pragmatic in character and that "[p]ragmatic reasons why we do not call babies, tomatoes and chickens 'water' are not far to seek". One of the reasons is externalist; ordinary speakers do not know that these things consist mainly of H_2O (ibid.). Another reason Abbott gives is that whether we call something 'water' or 'baby' usually makes a difference to our purposes (ibid.).

It is incorrect, however, to say that babies, chickens, tomatoes and tears are in the extension of 'water'. In essence, Abbott's argument runs as follows. What is commonly referred to as 'water' contains more or less impurities. Thus, even though seawater contains salt, it is still water. The extension of 'water' therefore consists of what contains a high proportion of H_2O. Now, babies, chickens, tomatoes and tears contain a high proportion of H_2O. It follows that babies, chickens, tomatoes and tears are in the extension of 'water', even though they are not called 'water'. The reason why we do not call them 'water' should be accounted for in purely pragmatic terms. The fallacy of this argument lies in the third step: the extension of 'water' consists of what contains a high proportion of H_2O. Since Abbott embraces Kripke's claim that water = H_2O, the extension of 'water' should be equated with that of 'H_2O'. But it is obvious that babies, chickens, tomatoes and tears are not in the extension of 'H_2O', because these objects contain other elements than hydrogen and oxygen.

One may worry that this implies that babies, chickens, tomatoes and tears do fall in the extension of 'water' if only Kripke's dubious claim that water = H_2O is overthrown. Indeed, the fact that seawater is water seems to suggest that water $\neq$ H_2O. Even if water $\neq$ H_2O, however, it does not follow that babies, chickens and tomatoes fall in the extension of 'water'. To substantiate Abbott's claim, both (12a)

Chapter 5   Physical Externalism and Polysemy

and (12b) must be true:

(12) a. Water is a substance with a high proportion of H_2O.
      b. A substance with a high proportion of H_2O is water.

But (12a) does not entail (12b). Whether one may endorse Kripke's claim that water = H_2O or only the weaker definition in (12a), it does not follow that babies, chickens and tomatoes are water, unless (12b) is independently motivated.

It might be said that if seawater is water, then tears are water, because, as Paul Bloom told Abbott, tears are perhaps made of exactly the same chemical composition as the Pacific Ocean (Abbott 1997: 315). Schematically, if both (13a) and (13b) are true, then (13c) seems to follow:

(13) a. Seawater is water.
      b. Tears are of exactly the same chemical composition as seawater.
      c. Tears are water.

Two remarks should be made about this reasoning. First, even if (13b) is true, being competent in English does not require knowing (13b), which made it possible for Paul Bloom to tell (13b) to Abbott, a competent speaker of English. This is reminiscent of the identity between the morning star and the evening star discussed in Chapter 4. In the same way that the discovery that the morning star = the evening star does not make 'the morning star' and 'the evening star' synonyms, the discovery of (13b) does not make 'seawater' and 'tears' synonyms. These two terms express different concepts to the extent that they construe the same substance in significantly different manners. Accordingly, we cannot attribute the difference between 'sea water' and 'tear' to pragmatic factors. This undermines Abbott's (1997, 1999) sheer dichotomy between semantic and pragmatics. Secondly, (13c) takes into consideration only one of the four dimensions which Malt (1994: 56) claims to be relevant for determining whether something is water, leaving out the other three dimensions, namely location, immediate source and function. Although seawater and tears may have almost the same chemical composition, they differ in location, source and function. This is the reason that those who accept both (13a) and (13b) may not accept (13c). This compromises Abbott's claim that tears are water. In sum, Abbott (1997, 1999) does not succeed in showing that babies, chickens, tomatoes and tears are water.

315

Steward (1990: 396) suggests that Kripke's argument is plagued with the same fallacy as Abbott's argument. To establish that water = H_2O, both (14a) and (14b) must be true:

(14) a. Water is H_2O.
    b. H_2O is water.

But no one has convincingly argued that (14b) is true. If being H_2O is equated with consisting mainly of H_2O, Abbott's statement in (12a) can be expressed by (14a). So far, so good. By the same reasoning, however, the falsity of (13b) is also reproduced as the falsity of (14b). That something consists (mainly) of H_2O does not make it water. Even though the pink solid which Steward (1990) asks us to imagine is H_2O, there are some speakers who hesitate to call the substance 'water'. Steward conjectures that the confusion between (14a) and (14b) underlies physical externalist semantics:

> Incidentally, I think the strangeness of the sound of this latter claim [= (14b)] is an indication that most of the time we tacitly read 'is' in place of the identity sign, and tacitly assume that the 'is' here is a simply predicative 'is' – perhaps one reason why it is usually thought that Twin-earth considerations and the like are sufficient to establish the identity claim. (Steward 1990: 396)

The conclusion to draw from the oddity of (12b) and (14b) is that 'H_2O' does not exhaust the meaning of 'water'. In other words, consisting (mainly) of H_2O is not sufficient for being water.

One may naturally ask whether consisting (mainly) of H_2O is necessary for being water. Abbott (1997: 135) explicitly sets aside this issue to focus on the sufficiency claim. Malt's (1994) claim is curiously hedged with 'strong', 'alone', 'highly', 'by itself' and so on:

> [...] this outcome would be inconsistent with the *strong* version of psychological essentialism. (Malt 1994: 57, my emphasis)

> [...] the proposed essential feature for water (a belief about H_2O) does not *alone* distinguish between water and non-water. (Malt 1994: 57, my emphasis)

Chapter 5 Physical Externalism and Polysemy

[…] a sense of "water" corresponding to pure H_2O is not *highly* available in this context. (Malt 1994: 60, my emphasis)

[…] belief in a particular essence, H_2O, does not *by itself* account for what liquids people consider to be water […] (Malt 1994: 65, my emphasis)

These hedges are necessary because "there may be a sense of 'water' in ordinary English that corresponds to the strong essentialist view, but it is not the only, and may be the less frequent, sense of the word" (Malt 1994: 64) and "[t]he modified version includes essentialist beliefs as a factor that influences category membership judgments and word use and may provide an important constraint on them" (ibid.: 67). While disputing the claim that H_2O is water, Malt (1994) seems to accept the claim that water is H_2O. It is important to realize, however, that accepting that water is H_2O is not tantamount to accepting that water is essentially H_2O. A person who believes that water is H_2O may regard a similar substance with different chemical composition as a kind of water when put in a context in which the chemical composition is unimportant. This is presumably part of the reason why Malt (1994: 67) states that "this modified version incorporates an important insight from Putnam's original analysis, but is much less true to the spirit of his approach".

The possible unimportance of microstructures is confirmed by psychological experiments. Thus, Tobia et al. (2020: 184) report that their findings "provide evidence against views that posit just *one* criterion involving deeper causal properties (e.g., H_2O), or *one* criterion involving a set of superficial properties (e.g., clear, potable, etc.), or even *one* set of criteria involving both kinds of properties (e.g., H_2O, clear, potable, etc.)". Rather, people employ two different criteria to categorize natural kinds. According to one criterion, twater is not water, whereas according to the other, twater is water (ibid.: 205). Haukioja et al. (2021) present experimental data suggesting that H_2O with a completely nonwatery appearance is categorized as not being water (ibid.: 397). This does not mean, however, that the chemical composition plays no significant role in the determination of the reference of 'water'. Haukioja et al.'s (2021) data also suggest that the judgment that twater is not water is the norm (ibid.: 397). In short, "neither a watery substance with a structure completely different from H_2O, nor a completely *non*-watery substance with structure H_2O, belong in the extension of 'water,' and similarly for other natural kind terms" (ibid.: 398). As Leslie (2013: 156) remarks, it is incorrect

317

to suppose that "manifest properties are *all* that matters", but it is also incorrect to say that manifest properties do not matter at all.

5.4 The Polysemy of 'water'[15]

5.4.1 Partial Semantic Representation of 'Water'

Putnam (1990: 69) states that "the layman's 'water' is not the chemically pure water of the scientist" and that "just what 'impurities' make something no longer water but something else (say, 'coffee') is not determined by scientific theory". This is not to say that the lay speaker's 'water' and the scientist's 'water' are mere homonyms, to the extent that "ordinary language and scientific language are interdependent" (ibid.). Both uses of 'water' embody one and the same lexical unit. This indicates that the word 'water' is polysemous rather than homonymous (Leslie 2013: 155), an idea initially proposed by Malt (1994). By making reference to Lakoff's (1987) cognitive linguistic conception of meaning, Malt (1994: 66-67) suggests that water constitutes a family resemblance category with no essential core.

Polysemy is one of the much discussed topics in cognitive linguistics. What motivates the cognitive linguistic approach to polysemy is the omnipresence and systematicity of polysemy stressed by Nunberg (1979) and more recently by Haber and Poesio (2023: 3-4). Carston (2021: 109-110) points out that "even new word coinages which start out as monosemous typically rapidly become polysemous (perhaps apart from some highly technical terms that remain within their circumscribed domain of use)". Accordingly, as Langacker (2008: 37) states, "[a] lexical item used with any frequency is almost invariably polysemous". To illustrate, the word 'window' means 'window glass' in (15a) and 'window opening' in (15b) (Nunberg 1979: 146):

(15) a. The <u>window</u> was broken. (= 'window glass')
      b. The <u>window</u> was boarded up. (= 'window opening')

Polysemy must be distinguished from homonymy, even though the two phenomena are often conflated in the literature (Quine 1960:§27, Sweetser 1990: Ch. 1, Taylor 2003: 107, Hawthorne and Lepore 2011: 470-471, Recanati 2017, Haber

---

15) Section 5.4 is partly based on Sakai (2016: Section 1).

Chapter 5 Physical Externalism and Polysemy

and Poesio 2023: 2, 4-5). Two words are homonymous when they happen to share the same phonological form without having similar meanings. For most speakers of English, the two senses of 'bank' observed in (16) are not similar to each other:

(16) John lives by a <u>bank</u>. (= 'financial institution' or 'side of a river')

This motivates linguists to posit two homonymous English words both spelled 'bank'. By contrast, the two senses of 'window' observed in (15) above are related to each other, making the word 'window' polysemous (Nunberg 1979, Lakoff and Brugman 1986, Lakoff 1987: 316, Langacker 1987: 162-166, 2006, 2008: 37, Ch. 8, Sweetser 1990, Taylor 2003, 2012, Tobia et al. 2020: 203, among others). The identity of a lexical item is guaranteed by the relatedness of the senses it exhibits. As Sweetser (1990: 9) states, "[a] word meaning is not necessarily a group of objectively 'same' events or entities; it is a group of events or entities which our cognitive system links in appropriate ways".

The intuitive difference between 'window' and 'bank' just mentioned relates to the possibility of anaphora. Anaphora tolerates the switching of the two senses of 'window', 'door', 'bottle' and 'book', as in (17), but not the switching of the two senses of 'bank' and 'bat' as in (18)[16]:

(17) a. The window was broken so many times that it had to be boarded up. (Nunberg 1979: 150)

    b. He opened the window and went through it. (Hawthorne and Lepore 2011: 472)

    c. We paint the door white and walk through it (cf. Chomsky 2000: 16)

    d. The baby finished the bottle and broke it. (cf. Chomsky 1995: 23, 2000: 128)

    e. The book that he is planning will weigh at least five pounds if he ever writes it (Chomsky 2000: 16)

(18) a. #He put some money in a bank and then swam to one. (Hawthorne and Lepore 2011: 472)

    b. #The bank cashes checks and slopes into the river. (Quilty-Dunn

---

16) (18b) may be considered an example of ellipsis, resulting from (i).

(i) The bank cashes checks and <u>the bank</u> slopes into the river.

But we can assume that ellipsis is nothing but zero-anaphora, as in (ii).

(ii) The bank$_i$ cashes checks and *pro$_i$* slopes into the river'.

319

2021: 163)

    c. #Mary bought a bat (to practice line drives) and so did Sue (to eat the mosquitoes in her garden). (Abbott 1997: 317)

The distinction between polysemy and homonymy is also illustrated by 'healthy' and 'light' (Hawthorne and Lepore 2011: 471):

(19) a. He is healthy and so is the food he prepares for his family.
      b. #After losing forty pounds, he is light and so is the color of his hair.

The acceptability of (19a) suggests that 'healthy' is a polysemous word, whereas the oddness of (19b) indicates that there are two homonymous words which happen to share the same word form 'light'. The anaphora test is not arbitrary, because the possibility of anaphora can be taken to show the coreference *de jure* of the two uses of the lexical item. Thus, the acceptability of (17a) indicates that the use of 'window' in the sense of 'window glass' is coreferential *de jure* with the use of 'window in the sense of 'window opening'. The coreference *de jure* of the two uses underwrites our intuition that we are dealing with a single lexical item spelled 'window'. The two uses of 'window' enable one to access the concept of *window* by highlighting different aspects of the entity denoted by the word.

    Putnam's (1990: 69) suggestion that the lay speaker's use of 'water' is not unrelated to the scientist's use of 'water' is supported by the linguistic data provided by Abbott (1997)[17]:

(20) a. Mary drank some water (it was pure) and so did Sue (yucky polluted stuff!). (Abbott 1997: 371)
      b. The water that the chemist discarded was later found in a puddle in the street. (Abbott 1997: 317)

The coreference *de jure* between the lay speaker's use of 'water' and the expert's use of the same term as observed in (20a-b) indicates that the two uses embody one and the same lexical unit 'water'. This is reminiscent of the difference between Adam's and the doctor's construals of *arthritis* discussed in Chapter 4. Lay

---

17) Abbott (1997, 1999) states that 'water' is vague rather than ambiguous. This difference is merely terminological.

Chapter 5 Physical Externalism and Polysemy

speakers and chemists construe the conceptual content expressed by the word 'water' in different fashions, but the divergence does not prevent their thinking and talking about the same topic, due to the deferential construal attached to lay uses of the term. When a speaker acquires the word 'water', she attaches to the word both individualistic construal and deferential construal. Her deferential construal of *water* is dependent on the chemists' individualistic construal of *water*. Lay speakers' deferential construal of *water* is one way to construe *water*, and the chemists' individualistic construal of *water* is another. This captures our intuition that, when Oscar conceptualizes water as a liquid which is colorless, transparent, tasteless, thirst-quenching, and found in lakes, while an expert conceptualizes it as H_2O, the difference resides in how much the two subjects know about water rather than what concept they attach to the word form 'water'.

Jylkkä et al. (2009: 43) argue against the polysemy of 'water, namely the view called 'hybrid externalism (HE)', which they spell out as in (21):

(21) a. Speakers believe that samples falling under natural kind concept C share some hidden, empirically discoverable, essence E.

b. The speakers hold that, in one (externalistic) sense, C applies to whatever possesses E.

c. The speakers hold that, in another (epistemic) sense, C applies to whatever fits the identificatory knowledge associated with C.

(Jylkkä et al. 2009: 42)

Hybrid externalism is different from both internalism and strict externalism. In order to make clear the difference between the three views, Jylkkä et al. consider the following scenario:

Imagine that a group of astronauts travel to the Moon and find a sample of a watery substance there. The sample fits all of the identificatory criteria associated with 'water', in particular, on close examination it turns out to be H_2O. One of the astronauts announces that 'there is water on the Moon'. Now, suppose that after the discovery of the sample on the Moon, all water on Earth turns out to have always been XYZ instead of H_2O, whereas the substance on the Moon was really H_2O. (Jylkkä et al. 2009: 42-43)

Internalism holds that the astronaut was right in saying that there was water on

321

the Moon, because the sample of the watery substance exhibited all the macroscopic properties of water. Strict externalism holds that the astronaut was absolutely wrong, because the chemical composition of the substance on the Moon is different from the chemical composition of our water, that is, the substance under consideration does not bear the relation $same_L$ to the local paradigms of water on Earth. Contrary to both internalism and strict externalism, hybrid externalism holds that "the astronaut was both right (in the epistemic sense) and wrong (in the externalistic sense)" (ibid.: 43). Jylkkä et al. design psychological experiments analogous to the Moon scenario just sketched to determine which of the three views is best placed to characterize lay speakers' natural kind concepts. The results obtained seem to vindicate strict externalism.

The trouble with Jylkkä et al.'s (2009) experiments is that the Moon scenario and the like almost inevitably evoke a scientific context. In general, the choice of the relevant sense depends on contexts in the broad sense of the term. Thus, put in the context 'the _ is broken', the word 'window' is liable to be interpreted as 'window glass' rather than 'window opening'. Language users tacitly choose the sense which is best suited to the given context. As discussed in Chapter 4, competent speakers have the ability to defer to experts for the correct meaning of the words they employ. To the extent that the Moon scenario and the like set a context for lay speakers to defer to scientists, Jylkkä et al.'s (2009) experiments fail to capture the polysemy of natural kind terms between the expert sense and the lay sense[18].

Kay (1983: 136) points out that the hedge 'technically speaking' is based on Putnam's notion of the division of linguistic labor, while 'loosely speaking' makes reference to the Fregean or purely internalist view of language:

(22) a. Technically speaking, a whale is a mammal. (Kay 1983: 134)
       b. Loosely speaking, a whale is a fish. (Kay 1983: 131)

As Sweetser (1990: 147) states, (22a) and (22b) reflect "two distinct (and

---

18) In a different context, Häggqvist and Wikforss (2020) make a similar point:

When the scientific context is stressed speakers pay more attention to underlying properties since they assume that is what matters to scientific classifications. (Häggqvist and Wikforss 2020: 341)

This, in turn, might be explained by the observation that people tend to assume that science is in the business of finding underlying essences, as suggested by studies of psychological essentialism. (Häggqvist and Wikforss 2020: 343, n. 12)

conflicting) folk theories of language use". By analogy, we can reasonably suppose that both (23a) and (23b) are true:

(23) a. Technically speaking, twater is not water.
      b. Loosely speaking, twater is water.

Indeed, Genone and Lombrozo's (2012) experimental work suggest that both descriptive and causal factors contribute to speakers' judgments of concept reference. The expert's use of 'water' is not the sole determiner of the reference of the term. This is confirmed by Haukioja et al.'s (2021) experiments, which suggest that "our natural kind concepts are associated with prototypes involving both appearance properties and (placeholders of) underlying properties that are not directly accessible, and of which we may even be ignorant" (ibid.: 400).

The view that 'water' is polysemous between an expert sense and a lay sense can independently be justified by Soames's (2002, 2006) argument. Soames observes that virtually all speakers of English accept (24a)-(24b) as true (ibid.: 638), while regarding (24c)-(24g) as false or bizarre (ibid.: 635, 636, 638):

(24) a. Water is H_2O. (Soames 2006: 635)
      b. Water is a liquid. (Soames 2006: 635)
      c. Water is a gas. (Soames 2006: 637)
      d. Water is frozen. (Soames 2006: 637)
      e. H_2O is a liquid. (Soames 2006: 636)
      f. H_2O is ice. (Soames 2002: 294)
      g. H_2O is water vapor. (Soames 2002: 194)

To make sense of these data, we must suppose, Soames (2002: 293, 2006: 638) claims, that 'water' is polysemous between the phase-neutral sense and the liquid sense. Although (24a) is true, 'water' and 'H_2O' have different lexical features, as illustrated by the naturalness of (24b) and the oddity of (24e-g). The naturalness of (24b) suggests that 'water' can specifically denote the liquid phase of H_2O, while the oddity of (24e-g) suggests that 'H_2O' only has a phase-neutral sense. The difference between 'water' and 'H_2O' is not pragmatic but semantic. If contextual factors were responsible for the ambiguity of 'water', the same factors should make 'H_2O' ambiguous, making (24e-g) acceptable. Moreover, it is not due to contextual sense narrowing that 'water' sometimes denote the liquid phase of H_2O. If the sense narrowing were governed by contexts, it would be possible for 'water' to denote the gas phase or solid phase of H_2O, depending on the context. But the sheer oddity of (24c)-(24d) as opposed to (24b) conflicts with the pragmatic analysis of the ambiguity of 'water'. Soames (2006: 638) remarks that 'water' is lexically ambiguous between the general phase-neutral sense and the restricted liquid sense in the same way that "'[c]at' is ambiguous between a reading on which it applies to all members of the cat family – tigers, lions, panthers, housecats, etc. – and a reading on which it applies only to housecats", as illustrated in (25):

(25) a. The zoo has many types of cats.
      b. Most cats are domesticated. ((25a-b): Soames 2006: 638)

Needham (2000) states that the phase-neutral use of 'water' was established when the notion of chemical composition was introduced into science:

> Although the phase-qualified sense of 'water' as liquid water seems to have been maintained from Aristotle until comparatively recently, it was definitely abandoned with the establishment of the law of constant proportions at the beginning of the eighteenth century. Water was then characterised in terms of its composition – the proportion of hydrogen to oxygen as indicated by its compositional formula, which eventually came to be written H_2O. (Needham 2000: 13-14)

It must be noted that the phase-specific sense of 'water' was "definitively abandoned" in scientific contexts, whereas it persists in daily uses of the term. As Leslie (2013: 155) states, even chemists employ 'water' to refer specifically to liquid water when they request a glass of water in restaurants. From a synchronic point of view, it is therefore safe to say that 'water' is polysemous (Leslie 2013: 155, Nichols et al. 2016, Tobia et al. 2020: 203-204)[19].

In cognitive linguistics, the relatedness of meaning exhibited by a polysemous word is commonly represented as a network, where the nodes correspond to the forms / senses, while the links between the nodes correspond to the relatedness felt between the forms / senses. The nuclear structure of the network is illustrated in Figure 5-1, where sense B is a metaphoric or metonymic extension of sense A, while C is a sense schematic for both A and B (Taylor 2003: 164-165).

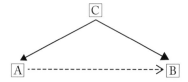

Figure 5-1: The Nuclear Structure of the Network Model (Taylor 2003: 165)

Although relations holding between two nodes may constitute an open-ended class and must be studied on a case-by-case basis, it is often assumed that nodes are linked by the 'referring function' (Nunberg 1979) or 'modulation' (Recanati 2017):

> [...] in language use, *senses multiply and diversify through modulation operations* [...]" (Recanati 2017: 394)

> Modulation covers processes of sense extension (loosening/broadening) and sense narrowing (enrichment) as well as semantic transfer (metonymy) and possibly other phenomena. (Recanati 2017: 379)

As an alternative to the criterial attribute model, where the meaning of a lexical item is viewed as a set of necessary and sufficient conditions for its use, the network model is designed to give an account of the fact that "the meanings of a commonly-used lexical item define a complex category, i.e. one that is not reducible to a single structure (node)" corresponding to sense C in Figure 5-1 (Langacker 1988: 135; see also Langacker 2008: 226).

Three remarks must be made about the network model of polysemy. First of all, as Lakoff and Brugman (1986) make clear, the network model is not designed

---

19) Nichols et al. (2016) do not draw a clear distinction between polysemy and homonymy, assimilating the lay and expert senses of 'water' to the two senses of 'bank':
> [...] there are two conventions that determine the reference of natural kind terms, much as there are two conventions that determine the reference of the word 'bank', though, as we will see, there are crucial differences between the ambiguity found in 'bank' and the one we think is operative in natural kind terms. (Nichols et al. 2016: 149)

This is probably a matter of terminology because elsewhere, they note the difference between natural kind terms and 'bank':
> Having said this, we do not mean to suggest that the ambiguity at issue is just like the straightforward lexical ambiguity of 'bank'. The meanings of 'bank' are semantically unrelated. (Nicholas et al. 2016: 162)

to recapitulate the historical change of the lexical item in question:

> Such polysemy chains are hypothesized to account for synchronic connections in the semantic knowledge of the user. [...] These chains exist statically to structure semantic information in the lexicon. We are not proposing them as parts of "semantic derivations", nor are we proposing them as recapitulations of historical change [...] (Lakoff and Brugman 1986: 451)

The network model purports to represent the speaker's knowledge of an expression usually independent of any historical facts about the expression. For instance, the network model does not address the question of whether or not the use of 'window' in (15a) is historically prior to that in (15b). The referring function or modulation operation can work in either direction[20].

Secondly, the network as a whole, and not a node therein, defines the expression in question. This fact entails that the meaning of the expression cannot be equated with any of its senses. As Recanati (2017: 397) puts it, "[n]o lexical meaning is a sense". In sentence (17d) above, for instance, the pronoun 'it' denotes a container, whereas its antecedent 'bottle' denotes what the container contains[21].

---

20) The referring function or modulation may underlie historical derivations. Thus, from a diachronic point of view, Ducrot (1980) claims that 'owe' is the original sense of the German verb 'danken' as observed in (i), which gave rise to its second sense 'thank', through the process which Benveniste (1958/1966) referred to as 'delocutivity':
(i) Paul dankt ihm das Leben.
     Paul owes him the life
     "Paul owes him his life."
In a nutshell, delocutivity derives the constative use of an expression from the performative use of a related expression. Fauconnier (1979), on the contrary, proposes synchronic processes called 'Incorporation' and 'Reduction', whereby constatives are turned into performatives. Fauconnier's proposal does not conflict with Ducrot's, since neither Incorporation nor Reduction is supposed to recapitulate historical changes. For more details, see Sakai (2019: Section 4). Possible divergences between a diachronic account and a synchronic account do not imply that meaning change has nothing to do with polysemy. Sweetser (1990: 9) points out that "[n]o historical shift of meaning can take place without an intervening stage of polysemy". Ducrot surely admits that the German 'danken' became polysemous when the relevant delocutivity took place.
21) Quilty-Dunn (2021) gives a similar example:
(i) Mary quickly drank her bottle of beer and then smashed it on the floor. (Quilty-Dunn 2021: 163)

Chapter 5   Physical Externalism and Polysemy

The possibility of anaphora suggests that 'bottle' is a polysemous word, with the two senses under consideration being linked by semantic transfer or metonymy (Nunberg 1979, Haber and Poesio 2023: 6-7), a type of referring function or modulation. Now, the network model of polysemy dictates that neither sense may be equated with the meaning of 'bottle'. It is rather the various senses, together with the links between them, that define its lexical meaning.

The network model presupposes what Recanati (2004: 140, 2017: 380, 394, 397) refers to as the 'Wrong Format view, according to which the lexical meaning of an expression is either too abstract and schematic or too rich to be a constituent of thought content. When interpreting an expression, we understand a particular sense, and not the lexical meaning, of the expression. Senses are basic and the notion of lexical meaning is an abstraction of such senses. Neither the lexical meaning of an expression nor its basic sense, if any, characterizes the knowledge of meaning possessed by competent speakers, the representation of each of its specific senses being required. This does not imply, however, that the various senses are stored separately in the mental lexicon; the relatedness of the senses is also represented over and above the nodes corresponding to those senses. In short, such words as 'window' or 'bottle' are neither monosemous nor homonymous (Recanati 2017: 393-394). Such is the gist of the network model, as Langacker (2006) expounds:

In general, a single structure is insufficient to describe the conventional knowledge of a basic linguistic element, such as a phoneme, lexical item, or grammatical construction. Usually such elements have an array of variant manifestations that cannot be fully predicted from either a prototype, representing the most typical variants, or a schema representing their abstracted commonality. The variants are thus described as the members of a category, which is complex in the sense that multiple structures are required for its full description. (Langacker 2006: 139-140)

The network model provides an anthesis to the assumption, which Langacker (1987: 29) refers to as the rule / list fallacy, to the effect that the existence of a general statement (rule) that subsumes particular statements (lists) enables one to do away with the latter statements. If, as Benveniste (1974: 227) suggests, modulation is the source of polysemy, it is not necessary to list conventional senses of a word, since it is, in principle, possible to derive, through modulation, all the senses

327

from the core meaning. Nevertheless, as Recanati points out, modulation is compatible with conventionalization:

A more balanced position such as Langacker's is needed to capture what is characteristic of polysemy: the two-sided aspect. One can reduce polysemy neither to modulation nor to convention, for it involves both. (Recanati 2017: 393-394; see also Haber and Poesio 2023: Section 3.3)

The two senses of 'window' observed in (15) are highly conventionalized. But this does not mean that the two senses are not linked by modulation. The fact that one sense is modulated into the other or vice versa ensures the identity of the word 'window', as opposed to 'bank', which corresponds to two distinct words whose senses are not linked by modulation.

The third point to be made about the network model is that there can be differences among individuals, due to the fact that "[m]odulation is optional and entirely a matter of 'speaker's meaning'", and that "there is nothing in the linguistic material that forces modulation to take place" (Recanati 2017: 380). The senses of a polysemous word are more or less conventionalized instances of modulation (Recanati 2017: 383; see also Benveniste 1974: 226-227), and the exact configurations of the networks depend on the speaker's linguistic experience:

[...] differently configured networks might very well give rise to linguistic judgments and behavior which are similar enough that discrepancies would seldom be detected. We can reasonably suppose that the network for a complex category differs somewhat from speaker to speaker depending on their individual linguistic experience. (Langacker 2006: 143)

Nunberg (1979: 177) goes so far as to say that "[i]n semantics, as opposed to phonology and syntax, the idealization to homogenous performance factor is intolerably unrealistic". Some speakers of English may consider the use of the word 'window' in (15a) to be more basic than that in (15b), and others may feel the other way round. There is no such thing as *the* network of senses which all competent speakers share for a given word. Accordingly, Langacker (2006, 2008) warns the linguist of the danger of giving too realist an interpretation to the network model:

The network model is inappropriate if pushed too far. In particular, it is wrong to "reify" the senses in a network by viewing them as well-delimited islands representing the only linguistic meanings a lexeme can assume. Such atomization of the field of meaning- or use-potential is artificial and leads to pseudo-problems, e.g., the problem of ascertaining which discrete sense a given use instantiates. (Langacker 2006: 144-145)

Bear in mind that the network model of complex categories is a metaphor. Like any metaphor, it is helpful in certain respects but potentially misleading in others, On the one hand, the network model is useful because it captures some essential properties of complex categories: that there are multiple variants, that these are related in certain ways, and that some are more central (or easily elicited) than others. On the other hand, the model proves misleading if the discreteness it implies is taken too seriously. It suggests that a category has an exact number of clearly distinct members, that it exhibits a unique configuration defined by a specific set of categorizing relationship, and that a target of categorization can always be assigned to a particular category member. Yet these entailments of the metaphor should not be ascribed to the actual phenomenon – if you look for a category in the brain, you will not find boxes linked by arrows. It may well be that the network metaphor has outlived its usefulness. At the very least, it should be counterbalanced with an alternative metaphor that emphasizes continuity rather than discreteness. (Langacker 2008: 227)

The network model is merely committed to the view that competent speakers of English can employ the word 'window' to refer to a window glass as well as a window opening and that they know that the two uses, conceptually related to each other, embody one and the same word 'window'. Speakers need not aware what is the input to modulation nor even the fact that they modulate senses in context. As Recanati (2017: 385) remarks, speakers' ability to modulate senses lies in the fact that they "exploit these modulation relations creatively in new contexts of use". This is sufficient to ensure communication success in normal contexts, because speakers' experiences about windows are similar (see also Chomsky 1995: Section 1/2000: Ch. 5).

With this in mind, we can represent a partial polysemy network of 'water' as in Figure 5-2[22] :

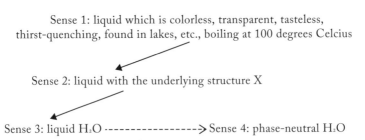

Figure 5-2: Partial Polysemy Network of 'Water'

Sense 1 is schematic in relation to sense 2, which is schematic in relation to sense 3. Sense 4, which is illustrated in the statements in (26), is an extension of sense 3:

(26) a. Ice is frozen water.
b. Water vapor is water in gaseous form. ((26a-b): Soames 2002: 292)

Sense 1 focuses on the functional role of water, while the other three focus on its chemical makeup (see also Bach 1987: 276, n. 9). The variable 'X' in sense 2 is a placeholder for the putative underlying structure of water which science is supposed to identify (cf. Haukioja 2015: 2148). We know today that the variable is filled with 'H$_2$O' as in sense 3. Since, as stated earlier, sense 4 emerged when science set out to investigate the chemical makeup of water (Needham 2000: 13-14), it presupposes sense 3, which in turn presupposes sense 2. Hence, the most remarkable gap lies between sense 1 and sense 2. This gap can plausibly be described in terms of what Recanati (1993: 243, 261, 2004:18, Ch. 2, 2017: 379) calls sense narrowing, specifization or (free pragmatic) enrichment, a species of modulation (Recanati 2010: 18, 22, 2017: 379; see also Haber and Poesio 2023: 13). The process of enrichment is illustrated in (27):

(27) a. After the accident, there was rabbit all over the highway.
c. He wears rabbit.
d. He eats rabbit. ((27a-c): Recanati 2004: 24)

The word 'rabbit' means *rabbit stuff* in (27a). This generic sense is converted into more specific senses in (27b) and (27c), in which the same word means *rabbit fur*

---

22) Figure 5-2 does not cover such uses of 'water' as illustrated by 'seawater' and 'heavy water'.

Chapter 5   Physical Externalism and Polysemy

and *rabbit meat*, respectively. Likewise, in (28), the generic concept *open* expressed by the verb 'opened' occurring in the second conjunct is enriched into the more specific concept *open with key* (Recanati 2004: 25):

(28) Mary took out her key and opened the door. (Recanati 2004: 23)

It is worth noting that pragmatic enrichment is a free process in the sense that it is not grammatically mandated (Recanati 2004: 18, 2010: 20, Pagin 2014: Section 2). Grammar is unable to rule out the possibility that (27b) means that the person in question wears rabbit stuff or rabbit meat or that (28) means that Mary opened the door by kicking it, after taking out and throwing away the key. An example of a non-free pragmatic process is saturation, whereby a specific value is assigned to an indexical expression like 'I', 'he' or 'today' (Kaplan 1989a, 1989b). Grammar forces us to identify the referent of 'he' in (27b); otherwise the sentence would fail to express any proposition or to have any truth condition.

Now, since senses 2 and 3 of 'water' are more specific than sense 1, we can assume that in some (but not all) contexts sense 1 is enriched into sense 2 or even into sense 3. Although the relation between sense 1 and senses 2–3 of 'water' may appear quite straightforward, it deserves a closer look. First of all, given that senses 2–3 are richer than sense 1, they have a smaller extension. Thus, the word 'water' used in sense 1 serves to differentiate water vis-à-vis orange juice, beer, wine, olive oil, hydrochloric acid, and so on. What Putnam's (1973, 1975) Twin Earth thought experiment revealed is that sense 1 is insufficient to exclude twater from the category of water, since twater is superficially indistinguishable from water (Stalnaker 1993: 306, Recanati 2000: 453). If we are to claim that twater is not water, we must appeal to the underlying structure of water as distinct from twater. This is where the scientific construal of water comes in. The word 'water' did not exhibit any division of labor before the rise of modern chemistry (Putnam 1975: 145). Homer arguably understood 'water' in sense 1 but not in senses 2–3 (Fodor 1998a: 155). For Homer as well as for us, *water* is a concept that may be characterized by the descriptions associated with sense 1. Lewis (1994: 424) points out that another description relevant to 'water' is that water is a natural kind. This description is one which, unlike us, Homer probably lacked. As Wikforss (2005: 81, 2013: 248) makes clear, the statement that something is a natural kind entails that "the term applies to a kind which is such that there is an underlying property that explains and holds together the observable properties of the cluster"[23] (Wikforss 2013:

331

248). Senses 2-3 of 'water' presuppose the notion of natural kind to which modern science gave rise. Understanding that 'water' is a natural kind term entails construing water to have some (possibly unknown) underlying properties explaining its surface lawful behavior.

Now we have two competing ways to access the concept of *water*. Sense 1 focuses on functional or superficial properties of water, while senses 2–3 refer to its hidden underlying structure. Due to the dual characterization of water, as Lewis (1994: 424) states, "we are in a state of semantic indecision about whether [twater] deserves the name 'water'". As we have seen in Chapter 1, although Putnam (1973, 1975) says that twater is not water, there are many people who do not share Putnam's intuition and think that twater is a kind of water. Thus, Chomsky (2000/2003) remarks:

> If, for example, Mary believes that there is water on Mars, and something is discovered there that she regards as water although it has the internal constitution of heavy water or XYZ, there is no general answer as to whether her belief is right or wrong. (Chomsky 2000: 199/2003: 281)

The controversy stems from whether 'water' should be defined in terms of sense 1 or sense 2 or 3. If one opts for sense 1, twater is included in the extension of the term, whereas if one opts for sense 2 or 3, twater is taken to be a substance completely different from water. Insofar as water has no twin-substance, the decision has no bearing upon the actual use of 'water'. This explains why most linguists dismiss Putnam's thought experiment as irrelevant to linguistics. By contrast, philosophers tend to go with senses 2–3:

> [Putnam's] conclusion, to repeat, is based on the intuition that, although the samples on twin Earth are macroscopically like samples of water, they do not, strictly speaking, count as samples of water because they are not composed of H_2O. (Bealer 1987: 296)

> *Without these intuitions Putnam would have no argument.* (Bealer 1987: 302)

---

23) Putnam (1970: 187) defines natural kinds as "classes whose normal distinguishing characteristics are 'held together' or even explained by deep-lying mechanisms".

In fact, a number of philosophers of biology and chemistry have argued that biological and chemical kinds do not have such essences, yet these arguments – particularly in the case of chemistry – have not been assimilated by philosophers more generally. The reason for this poor assimilation is, I suggest, that the Kripke/Putnam view *is just so intuitive.* (Leslie 2013: 109, emphasis in the original)

As remarked earlier, there are also experimental studies which support philosophers' intuition about Twin Earth (e.g. Jykklä et al. 2009). Linguistic theories must therefore account for the fact that so many people give priority to senses 2–3 over sense 1.

5.4.2 Meaning Change and Theory Change

It is important to realize that despite the difference in extension, senses 2–3 and sense 1 construe the same concept of *water* in distinct ways. Recall that the two uses of 'window' in (15a-b) above have different extensions, since window glasses are not window openings. This difference in extension does not prevent the two uses from expressing one and the same conceptual content, as illustrated by the coreference *de jure* in (17a-b). These uses provide two different ways to access the concept of *window* by highlighting different aspects of the entity denoted by the term. Similarly, sense 1 and senses 2–3 of 'water' provide different ways to construe the concept of *water* by highlighting different aspects of the substance.

What is apparently problematic with the polysemy analysis is that adding senses 2 and 3 to the polysemy network of 'water' inevitably leads to a meaning change (cf. LaPorte 2004: 93). Putnam (1973: 702-703, 1975: 142, 1990: 60) emphasizes that the discovery that water is H_2O did not change the meaning of 'water' (see also Abbott 1989: 273)[24] and that it merely affected the theory about water. In canonical cases of meaning change, the new sense of the relevant word is not viewed as more correct than its original sense. For example, it is known that the English word 'bead' (Middle English 'bede'), originally signifying 'prayers', came to signify 'ball of a rosary' (Stern 1931: 352-354, Taylor 2012: 251-252). This process can hardly be described as one whereby the word 'bead' came to be used

---

24) In a similar vein, Putnam (1992: 386) states that "the *meaning* of the word 'elm' does not change when an expert uses it (the expert just knows more about elms, he doesn't employ a word with a different meaning)".

more correctly. As discussed in Section 1.3.4, if the discovery that water is H_2O were assimilated to canonical cases of meaning change, it would be difficult to accommodate the fact that (29a) is more natural than (29b):

(29) a. Before 1750, people did not know that water was H_2O.
     b. Before the 13th century, people did not know that beads were small balls on a rosary.

Likewise, while both (30a) and (30b) make sense, (31b) is decisively odd in comparison to (31a):

(30) a. Before 1750, people were as competent with the use of 'water' as we are.
     b. Before 1750, people were less competent with the use of 'water' than we are.
(31) a. Before the 13th century, people were as competent with the use of 'bead' as we are.
     b. Before the 13th century, people were less competent with the use of 'bead' than we are.

We need to distinguish meaning changes which are equivalent to theory changes from meaning changes which are not.

The key to understanding that the addition of senses 2–3 to the meaning of 'water' amounts to a theory change is that the relation between senses 2–3 and sense 1 is not factual but normative. Sense 1 corresponds to the lay construal of *water*, while senses 2–3 correspond to the expert construal of *water*. As discussed in Chapter 4, competent speakers attach to a cluster word a deferential construal, which enables the speakers to refer to experts' individualistic construal of the concept expressed by the word. Before the rise of modern chemistry, 'water' was arguably a nominal kind word on a par with 'mud', 'fire' 'chair', and so forth. When chemists set out to investigate the composition of water, the word became a genuine cluster word, giving rise to sense 2. At this stage, some competent speakers came to feel that sense 1 displayed an incomplete understanding of the concept expressed by 'water' and, as a result, got ready to defer to experts for the correct sense of the term. Via the deferential construal attached to the term, lay speakers were able to roughly keep track of what experts took to be water, ensuring that lay

334

Chapter 5   Physical Externalism and Polysemy

people and experts continued to think and talk about the same substance. This underlies speakers' intuition that sense 2 is a more correct sense of 'water' than sense 1.

This is in sharp contrast with the case of 'bead'. Stern (1931: 352-354) describes the process of meaning change which the word 'bead' ('bede') underwent. In the Middle Ages, prayers were counted by means of the balls of a rosary. If, pointing to a man, someone uttered (32a), the utterance meant the same as (32b):

(32) a. He is counting (or telling) his beads. (Stern 1931: 352)
      b. He is counting his prayers. (Stern 1931: 352)
      c. He is counting the balls of his prayers. (Stern 1931: 353)

By being frequently used to describe a man telling his prayers, the sentence in (32a) got associated with the meaning expressed by (32c). This process was unintentional (Stern 1931: 353). It is possible that when 'beads' developed its second sense, almost no one was in a position to compare it with its original sense, leaving no room for the competing senses to correspond to distinct construals of the same object. The question of which was the correct sense of the word simply did not arise. Even if the utterer of (32a) had managed to observe the process of meaning change, she would have thought that her intention was misunderstood and that the new sense was incorrect. Furthermore, the extension of the word 'bead' changed so radically that the two uses were not coreferential *de jure* and that the original sense even became obsolete. From the synchronic perspective, it is not legitimate to suppose that 'bead' is polysemous between *prayer* and *ball of a rosary*. In no stage of the meaning change is the notion of semantic deference relevant to speakers' uses of the word.

The absence of deference is also observed in many words which are synchronically polysemous. No one would consider the uses of 'rabbit' in (27b-c) to be more correct than its use in (27a). Similarly, when Sweetser (1990) states that the two senses of the verb 'discern', namely 'to catch sight of' and 'to mentally realize' (ibid.: 38), embody "highly motivated [metaphorical] links between parallel or *analogous* areas of physical and internal sensation" (ibid.: 45), she does not mean that the metaphorical sense, 'to mentally realize', is the correct sense of the verb[25]. To be sure, semantic shifts are not random, whimsical, or irregular (ibid.: 21, 47), but are

---

25) 'Discern' derives from the Latin 'dis-' ('apart') + 'cernere' ('separate') (Sweetser 1990: 32).

335

motivated by "a pervasive metaphorical structuring of our internal mental world in terms of our physical world" (ibid.: 145). What Sweetser means by 'motivated', however, reduces to, in Jackman's (2005) words, 'pragmatically motivated' (as opposed to 'epistemically motivated'). Sweetser (1990: 3) states that "it is possible to crosslinguistically examine meaning changes and to observe what senses frequently historically give rise to what later senses". Historical linguistics shows little interest in the question what senses *should* give rise to what later senses. As Jackman (2005) remarks, meaning changes studied in historical linguistics are not epistemically motivated:

> In the historical linguists' pragmatically motivated cases, linguistic change is epistemically unmotivated, and the change may be from a pattern of usage that is perfectly consistent as it is. There was, for instance, nothing inconsistent in the older use of 'meat' to mean *food* more generically, and the term's current restriction to animal flesh did not follow from any sort of "epistemic" progress. (Jackman 2005: 371)

Historical linguistics explains, but does not justify, semantic shifts (Jackman 2005: 370). All historical changes may be pragmatically motivated, but only some of them are epistemically motivated. A meaning change is epistemically motivated just in case the original sense of the relevant term is felt to betray an incomplete understanding of the concept expressed by the term and, hence, lay speakers defer to experts for the putative correct sense of the term. Epistemically motivated semantic shifts are interpreted as aiming at an improvement of the usage of the word in question (ibid.: 371). When an epistemologically motivated change takes place, as Jackman states, "there is a sense in which the new usage could be seen as already there 'implicitly'" (ibid.). In this respect, the addition of senses 2-3 to the meaning of 'water' is epistemically motivated. When the word 'water' underwent semantic shifts, people came to feel that they should have construed water as H_2O from the outset. This is the reason that the meaning change of 'water' amounts to a theory change about water.

The foregoing argument may at first sight appear to assimilate the 'water' case with the 'arthritis' case discussed in Chapter 4. Adam, who thinks that he has arthritis in his thigh, displays an incomplete understanding of *arthritis*. Still, via the deferential construal he attaches to the word 'arthritis', he can access the same conceptual content of *arthritis* as the experts in his community. Similarly, Oscar, who is chemically ignorant, displays an incomplete understanding of *water*. Still, via the deferential construal he attaches to the word 'water', he can access the same conceptual content of *water* as the experts in his community. In this account, physical externalism is deemed a special case of social externalism.

Nevertheless, there is an important difference between the two cases. In the 'arthritis' case, Adam's construal of *arthritis* does not correspond to any community concept of *arthritis*. In the 'water' case, on the contrary, Oscar's construal of *water* corresponds to the concept of *water* which has long been rooted in the community. Before 1750, water was for everyone a liquid which is colorless, transparent, tasteless, thirst-quenching, found in lakes, etc., and boils and freezes at certain temperature. To be fully competent with the use of 'water' it was sufficient to understand sense 1 of 'water'. Importantly, sense 1 persists though the meaning change which took place in the second half of the eighteenth century. There is thus a sense in which, even now, normal competence with 'water' merely requires knowledge of sense 1. As Goosens (1977: 150) puts it, "a knowledge of the meaning of [natural kind] terms provide very little linguistic competence", if the word 'meaning' is understood in the metaphysical sense advertised by Putnam (1973, 1975) and Kripke (1980).

This is presumably what Burge (1986a: 708-709/2007: 264) has in mind when he ascribes "incomplete linguistic understanding" to Adam and "ignorance of expert knowledge" to Oscar. Even though Oscar is totally ignorant of chemistry, he can nevertheless be taken to have a complete grasp of the meaning of 'water' and the concept of *water*. This explains why there are speakers who do not give priority to senses 2–3 over sense 1. Chomsky (2000/2003) explicitly refuses to include sense 3 into the meaning of the English word 'water':

The arguments (for "water") are based on the assumption that water is H_2O. To assess the status of this statement we have to know to what language it belongs. Not English, which has no word "H_2O." Not chemistry, which has no word "water" (though chemists use the word informally). We could propose that chemistry and English belong to some "superlanguage," but it remains to explain what this means (see Bromberger [1997]). (Chomsky 2000: 189/2003: 281)

Such variation in speakers' intuitions lend support to Wikforss's (2005: 81, 2010: 75) and Häggqvist and Wikforss's (2015, 2018, 2020) claim that the meaning of a natural kind term consists of a cluster of descriptions:

> [The cluster theory] implies that whether a sample falls in the extension of the term depends on whether it fits the weighted majority of the associated descriptions. The cluster theory is not committed to "superficialism", to the idea that only observable properties belong to the cluster of descriptions. This means that both macro- and micro- level properties may matter, and that the intuitions about twin cases depends [sic.] on how individual speakers weigh these properties. (Häggqvist and Wikforss 2020: 338)

In the 'arthritis' case, on the contrary, the question whether tharthritis, a hypothetical rheumatoid ailment that may strike one's thigh, is a kind of arthritis does not arise, insofar as the community defines arthritis as an inflammation which only afflicts the joints[26].

5.5 Cognitive Linguistics and Physical Externalist Intuition

5.5.1 Quintessentialism

There is yet another fundamental difference between the 'arthritis' case and the 'water' case. As stated in Section 5.1, social externalism rests upon the fact that other people know better about the extension of the relevant word, whereas physical externalism can be established even when no one is aware of the nature of the environment. As stated in Section 5.2, physical externalism holds that the meaning of 'water' is determined not by conventions, but by the nature of the physical environment. Since even experts can be ignorant of the nature of the physical environment, deference to experts may prove vacuous, failing to determine the correct extension of the term in question. In Liu's words (2002: 391), "the social environment *misrepresents* the physical environment". In fact, before 1750, no one associated the meaning of 'water' with the concepts of *hydrogen* and *oxygen*. Nevertheless, physical externalism holds that the Earthian word 'water' has always meant water as distinct from twater (Crane 1991: 3). The meaning of 'water' is independent of

---

26) If someone doubts the correctness of the definition agreed upon by community members, she thereby assumes that arthritis has the essence possibly unknown to humans and that the true meaning of 'arthritis' is determined by the nature of arthritis itself, not by any mental representations. This scenario embodies physical externalism and has nothing to do with social externalism.

Chapter 5   Physical Externalism and Polysemy

any construal which language users, including experts, associate with the term. Thus construed, physical externalism obviously conflicts with the cognitive linguistic thesis that meaning is conceptualization. While this thesis enables us to ascribe the concept of *arthritis* to Adam, it prohibits us from crediting Oscar with the concept of *water*, insofar as none of his fellow community members possesses the concept of *hydrogen* or the concept of *oxygen*, both of which are indispensable for *water*. Liu (2002: 392) states that, when the social environment misrepresents the physical environment without anyone noticing, "one has to decide whether mental content is determined *primarily* in accordance with the physical environment, or with the social environment". The cognitive linguist must opt for the social environment. After all, Oscar has no ability to construe water as H_2O if hydrogen and oxygen are unknown to humans.

Then, what makes physical externalism so attractive and intuitive (Leslie 2013: 109)? As we have seen in Section 1.3, physical externalism holds that Oscar's thought corresponding to (33) is true if and only if there is water (H_2O) within twenty miles, whereas Oscar₂'s thought corresponding to (33) is true if and only if there is twater (XYZ) within twenty miles:

(33) There is some water within twenty miles, I hope. (Burge 1982: 101/2007: 86)

In this account, as Jykklä et al. (2009) expound, Oscar's and Oscar₂'s thoughts are different, even though they are intrinsically identical and their fellow community members are as ignorant of chemistry as they are:

In particular, externalism implies that natural kind terms apply in virtue of these deep properties even when we don't know what they are. For instance, even if we didn't know that the stuff we call 'water' actually consists of H_2O, according to externalism our term 'water' would nevertheless apply solely to H_2O. That is, even if nobody in our language community could distinguish H_2O from some superficially identical substance that differed in deep structure from H_2O (e.g., Putnam's XYZ), our term 'water' would still have only H_2O in its extension. We would undoubtedly *categorize* XYZ as 'water' if we ever met any, but according to externalism that would be a mistake – XYZ does not possess the deep structure of the substance we actually call 'water'. (Jykklä et al. 2009: 38)

339

In my view, there are three factors which motivate philosophers to ascribe different beliefs to Oscar and Oscar₂. First of all, as Leslie (2013: 129, 131) makes clear, behind the physical externalist intuition are quintessentialist beliefs (ibid.: 109ff) based on "an early-developing and deep-rooted bias to see the world in a particular way" (ibid.: 158). As surveyed by Malt (1994: 42-43), a number of psychological experiments suggest that "people *believe* there are essences shared by sets of things, and this belief plays a role in determining what things will be accepted as members of a category and called by the category name" (ibid.: 42, emphasis in the original)[27]. We are naïve essentialists inclined to believe, as Leslie (2013: 109, 124-125, 131, 144) state, that natural kinds are defined by the scientifically discovered or discoverable necessary and sufficient conditions, namely, their essences, independently of our recognition of the world. This mindset is largely independent of cultural backgrounds (ibid.: 115, 117) and in place at least by age 4 (ibid.: 109). Guided by this mindset, philosophers have assumed that the presence of H_2O is decisive for something to count as water and hence that twater is excluded from the extension of 'water'.

However, quitessentialism on its own is unable to justify the ascription of a

---

27) The same point has been made by a number of researchers:

> The use of a natural kind term carries with it the presumption of a shared common nature, even if we do not yet know what this nature is. (Schwartz 1978: 566)

> Whatever the problems that burden the notion of natural kind, the presumption that the world contains such kinds is unquestionably a very deeply ingrained presumption, so deeply ingrained, in fact, as to suggest that it not only springs from our native cognitive endowment, but that it does so in a way that shapes how we learn about the world, think about it, cope with it, and talk about it. (Bromberger 1997: 154)

> People's naïve intuition that certain categories have essences is called naive essentialism or psychological essentialism (Medin & Ortony, 1989). This proposal does not entail that people actually know what the essences are. For instance, to be an essentialist about water does not require that you know the internal properties that make something water (presumably being H_2O), just that you believe some such properties exist. Hence an essentialist should be able to entertain the possibility that something might resemble water but not actually be water (because it lacks the essence) or not resemble water but be water nonetheless (because it has the essence). It is possible that people were essentialists about water before the development of modern science; in fact, the belief that certain entities have essences might be what motivates scientific inquiry in the first place. (Bloom 2000: 152)

belief involving H_2O to Oscar (Leslie 2013: 144). As discussed in 5.3.1, it makes little sense to talk about the essence of water, if by 'the essence of water' one means something that unambiguously determines a unique kind of water. Science is not engaged in discovering such essences of chemical substances and biological species. This certainly undermines the physical externalist metasemantics. But one can think at the same time that the fate of such metasemantics has no bearing upon cognitive semantics. As stated in Section 3.3, veracity is not the primary concern of the cognitive linguistic approach to language and thought. That fictive motion is not real does not discourage cognitive linguists from studying the cognitive apparatus that allows speakers to construe static states of affairs as something dynamic. The purpose of cognitive linguistics is not to justify but to explain our language use. Accordingly, the primary concern of cognitive linguistics is not essence, that is, how the world is, but how we construe the world (see also Medin 1989: 1477).

Langacker repeatedly emphasizes that cognitive linguistics seeks for psychologically plausible accounts of linguistic phenomena (Langacker 2008: 3, 7-8, 10-11, 13-16). Although it is doubtful whether there are such things as natural kinds defined in terms of their metaphysical essences (Bromberger 1997: 154, Hacking 2007b, Leslie 2013, among others), our beliefs are inescapably based on the presumption of a shared common nature (Bromberger 1997: 154). If our cognition is partially characterized by quintessentialism or psychological essentialism (Medin 1989, Gelman and Wellman 1991, Bloom 2000: 151-154, Haukioja 2015: 2148, 2151), it should constitute a subject matter of cognitive linguistics. It is more than likely that cognitive linguists are intrigued by Gelman and Hirschfeld's (1999) remark:

One of the reasons the notion of essence is interesting is that it is remarkably pervasive despite its conflicts with reality. It has been pervasive across time (discussed at least over the past 2,400 years), across radically different philosophical traditions (e.g., embraced by both Plato and Locke), and across cultures. However, biologists insist that biological species do not truly have essences (Sober 1994; Mayr 1982), and certainly other essentialized categories such as race lack biological coherence (Hirschfeld 1996). Still, despite the fact that essentialism may yield little insight about the nature of the world, it promises to yield insights on how the human mind construes reality [...]
(Gelman and Hirschfeld 1999: 405)

In a similar vein, Medin and Ortony (1989: 183) state that cognitive psychology explores not metaphysical reality but psychological reality. If, as Gelman and Wellman (1991: 242) put it, quitessentialism is "a viable psychological phenomenon", it is no surprise that philosophers are inclined to ascribe a belief involving H_2O to ignorant speakers. Even though the belief that water is H_2O does not constitute metaphysical reality, it may nevertheless be part of psychological reality for Oscar and his fellow community members.

Quintessentialism or psychological essentialism is not enough, however, to explain the belief ascription in question, because, unlike us, Oscar and his fellow community members are not committed to quintessentialism about water. For them, water is nothing but a liquid which is colorless, transparent, tasteless, thirst-quenching, found in lakes, etc., and that boils at 100 degrees Celcius. Something more is needed.

5.5.2 Deference to Future Usage

As discussed in Section 4.4.3, the deferential construal lay speakers attach to the word 'arthritis' serves to connect them to more competent speakers in the community, enabling lay users of 'arthritis', despite the poverty of their individualistic construal, to express the concept of *arthritis* rather than idiosyncratic concepts. Lay speakers' deferential construal of *arthritis* is one way to construe *arthritis*, and experts' individualistic construal of *arthritis* is another. Now, we know that our linguistic practice spreads over space and time. Past and present uses of a word are coreferential *de jure* as long as their past and present forms and meanings are recognizably similar. Thus, there is a clear sense in which Old English 'wæter' and Modern English 'water' instantiate one and the same word. If it is legitimate to suppose that past speakers are in the same linguistic community as present speakers, it is in principle possible for past speakers to defer to present experts for the correct meaning of a word. When past speakers defer to present experts, there occurs what Putnam (1975) refers to as division of linguistic labor across time:

> [...] "water" on Earth and on Twin Earth in 1750 - does not involve division of linguistic labor, or at least does not involve it in the same way the examples of "aluminum" and "elm" do. There were not (in our story, anyway) any "experts" on water on Earth in 1750, nor any experts on "water" on Twin Earth. (The example can be construed as involving division of labor *across time*, however. I

Chapter 5   Physical Externalism and Polysemy

shall not develop this method of treating the example here.) (Putnam 1975: 146, emphasis in the original)

Even if the deferential construal associated with a word does not guarantee that some people in the linguistic community know, at the moment of the tokening of the word, the correct meaning of the word, speakers can expect that someday there will be someone to whom they will hopefully be able to defer (De Brabanter and Leclercq 2023: Section 1.2).

This view, known as temporal externalism, is elaborated by Jackman (1999, 2005). Temporal externalism holds that meaning and mental content are dependent for their individuation on subsequent uses of the relevant terms. The idea behind the proposal is that "[w]e typically see our predecessors, our successors, and ourselves as part of a continuous process of using, and discovering the correct extension of, the same terms" (Jackman 1999: 161). Jackman describes how the meaning of the term 'Grant's zebra' depends on its subsequent uses:

> [...] the term 'Grant's zebra' was introduced around 1820 for a type of zebra native to Kenya. A few years later, the term 'Chapman's zebra' was introduced for a morphologically distinct type of zebra found in present-day Zimbabwe. Later still it was discovered that the two types of zebra interbred near the Zambezi river and that, morphologically, one gradually faded into the other. Grant's and Chapman's zebras both turned out to be a races of the species *Equus burchilli* (one race of which, the quagga, is arguably not a type of zebra at all). [...] it is merely a *historical accident* that the term has the extension it does. If the taxonomists had investigated the area around the Zambezi river *before* they hit deepest Zimbabwe, they probably would have 'discovered' that Grant's zebra could be found through most of East Africa, gradually changing into a different subspecies as it drifted south. In such a case, 'Grant's zebra' would have picked out the entire species, not just the race found in Kenya. Such cases suggest that, when we interpret the past use of other speakers (and even ourselves), we help ourselves to subsequent specifications which were not determined by the facts available at or before the time of utterance. (Indeed, the specifications may even take place after the speaker's death.) (Jackman 1999: 159-160)

Temporal externalism implies that two speakers who are molecule-for-molecule

343

identical may nevertheless mean different things by the same word form, if the subsequent uses of the word form specify its meanings differently. Suppose that in 1750, Oscar and his fellow community members meant by 'water' a liquid which is colorless, transparent, tasteless, thirst-quenching, found in lakes, etc., and boils at 100 degrees Celcius. In the actual world, their successors have discovered that water is H_2O. According to temporal externalism, this discovery would enable one to think that by 'water', Oscar and his fellow community members meant a liquid H_2O. Now, suppose that, in a hypothetical world, Oscar's subsequent generations have found out that water is XYZ. This discovery would have led us to think that by 'water', Oscar and his fellow community members meant a liquid XYZ. If temporal externalism underlies our thinking, we would, in interpreting (33) above, be inclined to ascribe a belief involving H_2O to Oscar. If past speakers were to meet present speakers, they would recognize that their word 'water' was the same as present speakers' and that they were talking about the same thing denoted by the word (Jackman 1999: 161). If by 'water' present speakers mean H_2O, it must be the case that past speakers also meant H_2O, provided that both speakers think and talk about the same substance.

Brown (2000) insists that temporal externalism fails to take into consideration speakers' intention to use words in specific manners. If speakers in 1820 intended to apply the term 'Grant's zebra' to zebras of a particular morphological type, subsequent information about interbreeding is unable to alter the meaning of the term. If the subsequent generations were to employ the term to cover the whole species of *Equus burchilli*, the speakers in 1820 would have thought (if still alive) that the meaning of the term has changed. If, on the contrary, speakers in 1820 intended to apply the term 'Grant's zebra' to species of zebras that can interbreed with each other, subsequent information about morphological variations of zebras would be irrelevant to the meaning of the term. If the subsequent generations were to employ the term to refer only to zebras of a particular morphology, the speakers in 1820 would have thought that the meaning of the term has changed (Brown 2000: 183). Similarly, if by 'water', Oscar intended to mean a liquid with certain macroscopic features, subsequent information about the hidden underlying structure of water is simply irrelevant to the meaning of the word as employed by Oscar. In that case, we should rather say that the word 'water' underwent a semantic shift. Brown (2000: 187) claims that "we do not defer to future linguistic practice for the correct explication of our terms and concepts".

Brown's claim is certainly right about such cases as 'bead' and 'discern' mentioned earlier. If speakers of Old English were to observe the current usage of 'bead', they might not even realize that 'bead' was cognate with their word 'ġebed'[28]. Even if someone told them that it was, they would think not that subsequent speakers had identified the correct meaning of the word 'ġebed', but that its original meaning had been lost. Brown's objection, however, overlooks the fact that diachronic divisions of linguistic labor are not independent of synchronic divisions of linguistic labor. As suggested earlier, combined with the obvious assumption that our linguistic practice extends over time, the notion of synchronic division of linguistic labor implies the existence of diachronic divisions of linguistic labor. Generally speaking, a term is subject to a diachronic division of linguistic labor if and only if it is subject to a synchronic division of linguistic labor. As stated in Section 5.2, the division of linguistic labor presupposes the division of non-linguistic labor carried out by scientists. To the extent that it is unlikely that the meaning of 'bead' can be determined by science, it can hardly be subject to any synchronic division of linguistic labor. If this reasoning is correct, the hypothetical reactions of the speakers of Old English described above pose no problem for temporal externalism. There is no justifying the semantic shift which 'bead' underwent, because it is merely pragmatically motivated, and not epistemically motivated in Jackman's (2005: 367) sense. Deference to future usage makes sense only when we are dealing with words whose meanings are expected to be uncovered by science.

Jackman (2005: 372) states that "if we acquire information about future usage that reflects changes produced by epistemic factors, it would come not from a theory produced by linguists, but rather from one produced by people studying those aspects of the world relevant to the terms in question". Semantic shifts based on scientific discoveries are deemed epistemically motivated, rather than (merely) pragmatically motivated. The discovery that water is H_2O provides evidence that the definition of 'water' in terms of the superficial features of the substance denoted by the term is insufficient or even erroneous, urging lay speakers to revise the meaning of the term so that it coheres with the scientific discovery. In the eighteenth century, scientists did not change the meaning of 'water' (cf. Quine 1960: §12). Rather, they felt as if humans had long been ignorant of the true meaning of the term. Jackman imagines a similar scenario about 'protein':

---

28) https://en.wiktionary.org/wiki/gebed#Old_English
   Last accessed: 29/01/2024

For instance, if I could see into the future and discovered that a certain substance that scientists now call a 'protein' was no longer classified as a 'protein' by scientists three years from now, I would probably take it as evidence that that substance wasn't really a protein, and that current claims that it was must be false. It would be more plausible to think that biochemists had discovered something new about proteins (or the substance in question) than it would be to think that the scientific community would change what it meant by the term over the next three years. (Jackman 2005: 370)

Of course, as stated earlier, this intuition is not shared by everyone. There is a sense in which the meaning of 'water' remains the same before and after the discovery of the chemical composition of water. Nevertheless, we need the notion of deference to future usage to account for some linguistic data. In Section 1.3.4, we have seen a hypothetical situation described by Marconi (1997: 84), in which a modern chemist points out to Archimedes that some of the samples he believes to be gold, or χρῡσός (khrūsós), are not really gold. If Archimedes did not defer to this future usage, his response would be something like (34):

(34) Ah, but that's according to *your* notion of gold; according to *my* criteria, they are indeed gold! (Marconi 1997: 84)

This is certainly a possible response (cf. Jackman 2005: 373). But it is also conceivable that Archimedes accepts the correction, especially if he thinks that the chemist has superior knowledge of gold than he does. Jackman (2005) points out that Brown's (2000) argument leaves out our disposition to defer to future usage:

In short, Brown's claim that we would not defer to future usage seems to rely on understanding linguistic change as produced exclusively by pragmatic factors, and thus ignores the fact that we often have good reasons for changing how we use our terms, and that (like other sorts of externalism) TE [= temporal externalism] relies on this epistemic aspect of our evolving linguistic practice. (Jackman 2005: 373)

If Oscar and his fellows were to defer to future usage and come across future scientists, they would think that the meaning of their word 'water' should be revised

Chapter 5   Physical Externalism and Polysemy

in accordance with the chemical findings.

Temporal externalism, however, is still insufficient to give a full account of philosophers' ascription of a thought about H_2O to Oscar in (33). Jackman (2005) is clear that temporal externalism deals exclusively with epistemically driven linguistic changes and sets aside merely pragmatically motivated linguistic changes. Since epistemically motivated meanings are regarded as (more) correct meanings, adherence to epistemically motivated meanings is normative rather than factual. If a scientist tells you that water is H_2O, you *should* mean H_2O by the use of 'water'. But that you should mean H_2O does not entail that you *actually* mean H_2O. Bealer (1987: 289) remarks that "[i]n being interested in such things as the nature of mind, intelligence, the virtues, and life, philosophers do not want to know what those things just happen to be, but rather what those things *must* be" (emphasis in the original). In this sense, temporal externalism is a canonical philosophical (as opposed to linguistic) thesis. What we are after is the reason why, in (33), Oscar can be assumed to *actually* mean H_2O by his use of the word 'water'. All that temporal externalism tells us is that Oscar *should* have meant H_2O.

The temporal externalist might respond that, if Oscar were to come across a present scientist and were told that water was H_2O, he would actually mean H_2O by 'water'. In this account, Oscar's disposition to actually revise his use of the term is sufficient to credit him with the concept of H_2O. This response is unsatisfactory for two reasons. Firstly, as remarked by Putnam (1973: 705, 1975: 145), before 1750, people were not disposed to defer to experts for the correct use of 'water', because there were no experts of water in the first place. This contrasts with present speakers, who know that experts know more about chemical substances. This recognition is reflected in the deferential construal they attach to the word 'water', which enables them to think and talk about water despite their possible ignorance of chemistry. Before 1750, people had no such deferential construal of 'water'. Secondly, even if we can assume that Oscar was somehow disposed to revise his use of 'water', we can assume with equal validity that Oscar was disposed to apply 'water' to twater as well. After all, if he were to be transported to Twin Earth, he would have no hesitation to call twater 'water'. If Oscar's disposition justified the ascription of a certain thought to him, we would have to credit him with two contradicting thoughts; by 'water' Oscar means simultaneously a substance with composition H_2O and a substance encompassing H_2O and XYZ. Deference to future usage certainly reinforces our inclination to ascribe a belief involving H_2O to Oscar in (33), but something is still wanting.

347

5.5.3 Coherence Raising

What is crucial for determining the thought content expressed by (33) is the fact that we actually know that water is H_2O. As stated earlier, sense 3 in Figure 5-2 has a richer intension and a narrower extension than sense 1. Even if Oscar merely attaches sense 1 to the word 'water', we, who know that water is H_2O, tend to enrich sense 1 into sense 3 through the process of free pragmatic enrichment. Since, as mentioned above, pragmatic enrichment is not a grammatically mandated process, the sentence in (33) can express a complete proposition even if we do not enrich sense 1. It makes perfect sense to hope that there is a liquid which is colorless, transparent, tasteless, thirst-quenching, found in lakes, etc., and that boils at 100 degrees Celcius within twenty miles. If grammar does not mandate that any pragmatic enrichment take place, what motivates its application?

According to Pagin (2014), pragmatic enrichment is triggered by our disposition to raise the degree of coherence between background content and new content added to the discourse (ibid.: 69, 86)[29]. Pagin assumes five degrees of coherence illustrated in (35):

> (35) Scale of coherence strength (Pagin 2014: 70)
> 0) Vacuity
> 1) Contiguity type relations
> 2) Resemblance type relations
> 3) Possibility type relations
> 4) Necessity type relations

Pragmatic enrichment is applied in accordance with the principle outlined in (36):

> (36) Principle of Pragmatic Enrichment (Pagin 2014: 76)
> (Free) pragmatic enrichments strengthen the coherence between background content and new content to the highest available degree.

The zero degree of coherence is illustrated by (37), in which there is no intui-

---

29) Pagin would not regard (27b-c) above as cases of pragmatic enrichment. There is nothing incoherent in the statement that a person wears rabbit stuff or rabbit meat. It is just that the statement is implausible. Pagin (2014: 176) assumes that "[a] potential enrichment is *available* only if it satisfies requirements of *plausibility* and *simplicity*". For Pagin, plausibility is a precondition for pragmatic enrichment to take place.

Chapter 5   Physical Externalism and Polysemy

tive connection between the first and second sentences:

> (37) John broke his leg. I like plums. (Knott and Dale 1994: 39, Pagin 2014: 70)

We do not utter (37) unless there is special reason to do so. We normally aim to achieve at least the first level of coherence.

The first level of coherence is realized in contiguity-type relations, in which "the new content is in some salient respect *close to* the back ground content" (Pagin 2014: 70), as in (38):

> (38) The table is covered with books. A cat is lying on the sofa. (Pagin 2014: 70)

In (38), the sofa mentioned in the second sentence is taken to be in the same room as the table mentioned in the first sentence. By searching for the first degree of coherence, "we do get new information about the same object or objects that were known from the background content, or about objects closely related in space and time" (Pagin 2014: 73).

The second level of coherence is illustrated by (39):

> (39) Yesterday, my brother bought a car, and my sister went to Greece with her family. (Pagin 2014: 73)

The two events reported in (39) are close in time, satisfying a contiguity-type relation. In addition, we normally read into the sentence that the two events resemble each other in that both are examples of "expensive private consumption" (Pagin 2014: 74).

The third degree of coherence is realized in possibility-type relations in which "the new content represents a fact, state or event that has been *prepared* or *made possible* by what is represented in the background" (Pagin 2014: 71). In (40), the first sentence is naturally interpreted as describing an event which enabled George W. Bush to give his speech:

> (40) A flashy-looking campaign bus arrived in Iowa. Soon afterwards George W. Bush gave his first speech of the primary season. (Kehler 2002: 14,

349

Pagin 2014: 71)

Finally, the fourth degree of coherence is typically achieved when "the new content represents a state or event that in some respects a *consequence* of, or *necessitated by*, what is represented in the background content" (Pagin 2014: 72). In (41), John's facing the library building is normally interpreted as a consequence of his turning left:

(41) John turned left. He was facing the library building. (Pagin 2014: 72)

Note that pragmatic enrichment, or modulation in general, is a sub-personal process which is not consciously available (Recanati 193: 247-251, 2004, 14, 17, Pagin 2014: 95)[30]. In normal situations, the interpreter does not consciously compare the input sense of an expression and its enriched sense. The disposition to search for a higher degree of coherence is a built-in feature of the interpreter's linguistic competence, where no normative factors are at play[31]. The sentence in (38), for example, is automatically interpreted as concerning a table and a sofa found close to each other. There is usually no intermediate stage at which the table and the sofa are represented separately in the interpreter's mind. The sub-personal character of pragmatic enrichment is also illustrated by the sentence in (42):

---

30) In this respect, modulation and saturation constitute a natural class. Recanati (1993: 260-266, 2004: 13-14, 20-22) calls modulation and saturation 'primary pragmatic processes', contrasting them with (intuitive) truth-conditional content and pragmatic implicature, which are consciously available. Implicature-generation belongs to secondary pragmatic processes.

31) This may remind some readers of the principle in (i) assumed in Relevance Theory:
   (i) Human cognition tends to be geared to the maximisation of relevance. (Sperber and Wilson 1995: 260)
   However, Pagin (2014: 88-92) points out that the principle in (i) may deliver different results from the search for a higher degree of coherence. The pronoun 'He' in (ii) is usually read as anaphoric on 'A' in the first sentence, as illustrated in (iii):
   (ii) A walks in the park. He whistles. (Pagin 2014: 90)
   (iii) A walks in the park. A whistles.
   This is an example of a contiguity level of coherence. But the principle in (i) predicts that (ii) is interpreted either as in (iii) or as in (iv), because "we gain exactly as great an increase in knowledge from learning that A whistles as from learning that B whistles" (Pagin 2014: 91):
   (iv) A walks in the park. B whistles.
   For the same reason, it is unclear whether Relevance Theory can accommodate the physical externalist intuition that in (33) Oscar thinks about H_2O rather than XYZ.

(42) The temperature has risen to a dangerous level. (Pagin 2014: 83)

This sentence is normally interpreted as 'the temperature has risen from a non-dangerous to a dangerously high level' (ibid.). But the meaning of (42) allows for the possibility that the level was even more dangerous before the rising (ibid.: 84). This possibility is ruled out because we unwittingly interpret (42) as instantiating the necessity level coherence, resulting in the interpretation that the danger is a consequence of the rising (ibid.). This provides evidence that the interpreter of a sentence normally makes no comparison between the unenriched interpretation of the sentence and its enriched interpretation.

The principle in (36) is also at work when we interpret Oscar's utterance in (33) as meaning that Oscar hopes that there is H_2O within twenty miles. This interpretation instantiates the first level of coherence, because we know that Oscar lives on Earth, where there is a plenty of liquid H_2O. Since a watery liquid is found both on Earth and on Twin Earth, Oscar's utterance of (33) can also be interpreted as concerning twater, a watery liquid located on a planet remote from Earth, provided that Oscar merely attaches sense 1 to the word form 'water'. However, all other things being equal, it is more coherent to refer to a substance close to where Oscar, the utterer, is located[32]. By enriching sense 1 into sense 3, we can ensure that there is a contiguity relation between Oscar and a liquid to which he refers as 'water'. Philosophers' ascription of a thought involving H_2O to Oscar is motivated by their strong inclination to strengthen the coherence between the content of Oscar's utterance and the context in which the utterance is made. This view is reinforced by the fact that, if uttered on Twin Earth, the same sentence in (33) tends to be interpreted as concerning XYZ rather than H_2O, as illustrated by Liu's (2002) remark:

> Let us briefly go back to the case of Oscar's being transported to Twin Earth in his sleep. If his thought upon waking up (that is, before he has any linguistic contact with Twin-Earthians) is a different thought from *what he would be*

---

32) Pagin (2014: 91-92) makes a similar point about (i):

   (i)   Sara left Australia for England. She loves *the sandy beaches*. (Pagin 2014: 91)

   Pagin (2014: 92) remarks that "[w]e at any rate reach Contiguity level coherence by enriching into *the beaches of England*, since it is more coherent to refer to beaches close to Sara's location at the time of utterance, i.e. after the move".

351

thinking if he were still on Earth, then the change is brought about by his direct rapport with (the essence of) the object itself. There is no *mediation* through *the linguistic community* – whether it is represented by what the majority thinks about the macroproperties, or by what the experts say about the essence of the stuff. (Liu 2002: 394)

It might be said that Liu does not talk about pragmatic enrichment at all. But recall that pragmatic enrichment occurs without the interpreter noticing. Liu's reasoning implicitly presupposes Pagin's (2014) principle spelled out in (36) above. The interpreter's disposition to search for a higher degree of coherence is enough for her to interpret the sentence in (33) uttered on Earth as concerning H_2O and the same sentence as uttered on Twin Earth as concerning XYZ. By enriching sense 1, which Oscar attaches to 'water', into sense 3, of which he is ignorant, the interpreter can achieve a higher degree of discourse coherence. Since, aside from the zero degree of coherence, contiguity relations provide the lowest degree of coherence, the enrichment of sense 1 into sense 3 is most readily available at the lowest cost.

It must be noticed, however, that the enrichment of sense 1 into sense 3 comes at the price of lowering another kind of coherence. For, by ascribing a thought involving H_2O to Oscar, we are forced to say that Oscar thinks about H_2O while not possessing the concept of *hydrogen* or *oxygen* or having any contact with those who possess these concepts, contrary to the Groundedness Thesis articulated in Section 5.2. In this view, it is not Oscar's belief about water but the interpreter's belief about water that makes (33) a thought about H_2O. While cognitive linguistics identifies meaning with conceptualization, the present account identifies Oscar's meaning with the interpreter's conceptualization. If we give priority to the internal coherence of Oscar's thought, we should rather say that by 'water' Oscar only means a liquid which is colorless, transparent, tasteless, thirst-quenching, found in lakes, etc., and that boils at 100 degrees Celcius. This belief ascription, perfectly compatible with internalism, fails to vindicate physical externalism.

Pagin discusses similar cases where two competing considerations yield an ambiguity in interpretation. Consider (43):

(43) Mary embarrassed John, and Betty made fun of him. (Pagin 2014: 81)

(43) receives two interpretations. On one interpretation, (43) instantiates a

Chapter 5   Physical Externalism and Polysemy

resemblance-type scenario in which two unfortunate events happened to John (ibid.: 81). On the other interpretation, the event described in the second conjunct is a consequence of the event described in the first conjunct, satisfying a necessity-type relation. The first interpretation is more readily available, because the negative connotations which the first and second conjuncts convey are implied by the lexical meanings of the verbs 'to embarrass' and 'to make fun of'. The second interpretation, on the other hand, exhibits a higher degree of coherence than the first, as indicated by the scale of coherence strength in (35) above. Pagin (2014: 81) states that (43) is ambiguous because "the greater availability of the first reading (no enrichment is needed) is balanced by the higher degree of coherence of the second". We have a similar situation in the Twin Earth thought experiment, where two competing motivations for discourse coherence deliver two competing intuitions. If we give greater significance to Oscar's internal coherence, Oscar is credited with a concept including both water and twater in its extension. If we put more emphasis on the contiguity level of coherence, physical externalism ensues.

To summarize, quintessentialism and deference to future usage prepare Oscar's latent thought involving H_2O but not XYZ. Due to the interpreter's disposition to achieve a higher degree of discourse coherence, this thought is actually ascribed to Oscar, making physical externalism an apparently viable option. This, I submit, is the final piece of the puzzle.

Epilogue

I will be brief. Human cognition is biased toward both the internalist conception of linguistic meaning and the externalist conception of natural kinds. The first bias has made the word 'arthritis' unfamiliar to linguistic semantics, while the second bias has made the word 'water' one of the most debated terms in philosophy. Neither bias is rooted in reality.

Social externalism coheres with cognitive linguistics. That a speaker has an incomplete understanding of a concept entails that she is competent with the concept, which in turn entails that she associates a deferential construal with the word that expresses the concept. Even if you do not know that the morning star is the evening star, you can think about the morning star, because your deferential construal of the term 'the morning star' has the same conceptual content as the astronomers' individualistic construals of the term. It is hard to imagine how this view conflicts with the cognitive linguistic thesis that we have the ability to conceive the same situation in more than one way. What nevertheless makes social externalism somewhat unpalatable is our pre-theoretical inclination to define a speaker's thought exclusively in terms of her intrinsic properties. Henry Jackman writes:

> [...] if the scenarios associated with social externalism are presented in a way that a commitment to social externalism is made clear, people often become resistant to ordinary "social" ascriptions [...] People have a strong inclination to think that they must have the same mental states as their atom-for-atom duplicates, and they will often diverge from their ordinary ascriptions if they become aware that such accounts conflict with this intuition. (Jackman 2005: 368)

The meaning of a statement is partly dependent on its subsequent usage. At the time of writing, Jackman evidently did not intend his statement to indicate that social externalism was unpalatable to cognitive linguists. But I now construe it as implying that cognitive linguists do not recognize that their notion of construal presupposes the social externalist notion of incomplete understanding. Cognitive linguists are biased toward the internalist conception of linguistic meaning.

Physical externalism, by contrast, is incompatible not only with cognitive linguistics, but also with biology, chemistry and the philosophy of science. Nevertheless, the physical externalist intuition can be accommodated by the cognitive linguistic apparatus. Firstly, our quintessentialist bias, though often erroneous, leads us to believe that the microscopic properties of water are more fundamental to the characterization of the nature of the substance than its macroscopic properties. Secondly, deference to future usage invites us to believe that we are better placed to define the substance than past speakers and, hence, that past speakers should trust and accept our beliefs about the world. Finally, our strong inclination to raise the degree of discourse coherence turns 'should' into 'actually' and the contiguity of water into the indexicality of 'water'. The resulting picture seems to suggest that the word 'water' has always meant water to the exclusion of any superficially similar or even identical substances.

I have said relatively little in this book, despite its unusual length. It cannot be denied at this moment that the little the book says may turn out to be an unfortunate example of what Boyd (2013: 211) refers to as "pathologically defective inference patterns":

> [...] one cannot understand the literatures – one cannot see what inferential connections are being taken for granted – unless one engages with these pathologically defective inference patterns. They are malignant. (Boyd 2013: 211)

For better or for worse, temporal externalism holds that we are not fully aware of what kinds of things are relevant to the individuation of what we mean (Jackman 2005: 374). Hoping that "things get (epistemically and semantically) better" (Boyd 2013: 215), I defer to my present and future readers for what I mean by what I have said in this book.

356

References

Abbott, Barbara (1989) "Nondescriptionality and Natural Kind Terms", *Linguistics and Philosophy* 12: 269-291.

Abbott, Barbara (1997) "A Note on the Nature of 'Water'", *Mind* 422: 311-319.

Abbott, Barbara (1999) "Water = H₂O", *Mind* 429: 145-148.

Ambrus, Valer (1999) "Is Putnam's Causal Theory of Meaning Compatible with Internal Realism?", *Journal for General Philosophy of Science / Zeitschrift für allgemeine Wissenschaftstheorie* 30: 1-16.

Antony, Louise M. and Norbert Hornstein (eds.) *Chomsky and his Critics*, Oxford: Blackwell.

Armstrong, Sharon Lee, Lila R. Gleitman and Henry Gleitman (1983) "What Some Concepts Might Not Be", *Cognition* 13: 263-308.

Austin, John L. (1962/1975) *How to Do Things with Words*, Cambridge, MA: Harvard University Press.

Austin, John L. (1962) *Sense and Sensibilia*, Reconstructed from the manuscript notes by G.J. Warnock, Oxford: Clarendon Press.

Aydene, Murat (1997) "Has Fodor Really Changed His Mind on Narrow Content?", *Mind & Language* 12: 422-458.

Bach, Kent (1987) *Thought and Reference*, Oxford: Clarendon Press.

Baghramian, Maria (ed.) (2013) *Reading Putnam*, London: Routledge.

Barber, Alex (2003) "Introduction", in A. Barber (ed.), pp. 1-43.

Barber, Alex (ed.) (2003) *Epistemology of Language*, Oxford: Oxford University Press.

Barcan Marcus, Ruth (1961) "Modalities and Intensional Languages", *Synthese* 13: 303-322.

Bar-Hillel, Yehoshua (1954) "Indexical Expressions", *Mind* 63: 359-379.

Bealer, George (1987) "The Philosophical Limits of Scientific Essentialism", *Philosophical Perspectives* 1: 289-365.

Beaney, Michael (ed.) (1997) *The Frege Reader*, Oxford: Blackwell.

Beebee, Helen and Nigel Sabbarton-Leary (eds.) (2010) *The Semantics and Metaphysics of Natural Kinds*, New York: Routledge.

Bell, David (1984) "Reference and Sense: An Epitome", *Philosophical Quarterly* 34: 369-372.

Benveniste, Émile (1956/1966) « La nature des pronoms », in *For Roman Jakobson*, Den Hague: Mouton, reprinted in Benveniste 1966, 251-257. [The page number cited is of the reprinted.]

Benveniste, Émile (1958/1966) « Les verbes délocutifs », reprinted in Benveniste (1966), pp. 277-285. [The page number cited is of the reprinted.]

Benveniste, Émile (1966) *Problèmes de linguistique générale I*, Paris: Gallimard.

Benveniste, Émile (1974) *Problèmes de linguistique générale II*, Paris: Gallimard.

Ben-Yami, Hanoch (2001) "The Semantics of Kind Terms", *Philosophical Studies* 102: 155-184.

Bezuidenhout, Anne L. (1997) "The Communication of *De Re* Thoughts", *Noûs* 31: 197-225.

Bilgrami, Akeel (1992) *Belief and Meaning*, Cambridge: Basil Blackwell.

Bird, Alexander (2009) "Are Natural Kinds Reducible?", in A. Hieke and H. Leitbag (eds.), *Reduction-Abstraction-Analysis: Proceedings of the 31st International Ludwig Wittgenstein-symposium in Kirchberg, 2008*, Frankfurt: Ontos, pp. 127-136.

Bird, Alexander and Emma Tobin (2023) "Natural Kinds", *The Stanford Encyclopedia of Philosophy* (Spring 2023 Edition), Edward N. Zalta & Uri Nodelman (eds.), URL = <https://plato.stanford.edu/archives/spr2023/entries/natural-kinds/>.

Biro, John and Petr Kotatko (eds.) (1995) *Frege: Sense and Reference One Hundred Years Later*, Dordrecht: Springer Science + Business Media.

Blakemore, Diane (2002) *Relevance and Linguistic Meaning: The Semantics and Pragmatics of Discourse Markers*, Cambridge: Cambridge University Press.

Bloom, Paul (2000) *How Children Learn the Meanings of Words*, Cambridge, MA: MIT Press.

Bloomfield, Leonard (1933) *Language*, London: George Allen.

Boghossian, Paul A. (1992) "Externalism and Inference", *Philosophical Issues* 2: 11-28.

Boghossian, Paul A. (1994) "Transparency and Mental Content", *Philosophical Perspectives* 8: 33-50.

Bolinger, Dwight (1965) "The Atomization of Meaning", *Language* 41: 555-573.

Bonardi, Paolo (2019) "Manifest Validity and Beyond: An Inquiry into the Nature of Coordination and the Identity of Guises and Propositional Attitude States", *Linguistics and Philosophy* 42: 475-515.

Boyd, Richard (2013) "Semantic Externalism and Knowing our own Minds: Ignoring Twin-Earth and Doing Naturalistic Philosophy", *Theoria* 79: 204-228.

Braddon-Mitchell, David (2004) "Masters of our Meanings", *Philosophical Studies* 118: 133-152.

Braddon-Mitchell, David and John Fitzpatrick (1990) "Explanation and the Language of Thought", *Synthese* 83: 3-29.

Braisby Nick, Bradley Franks and James Hampton (1996) "Essentialism, Word Use, and Concepts", *Cognition* 59: 247-274.

Brakel, Jaap van (1986) "The Chemistry of Substances and the Philosophy of Mass Terms", *Synthese* 69: 291-324.

Braun, David and Jennifer Saul (2002) "Simple Sentences, Substitutions, and Mistaken Evaluation", *Philosophical Studies* 111: 1-41.

Bromberger, Sylvain (1997) "Natural Kinds and Questions", *Poznań Studies in the Philosophy of the Science and the Humanities* 51: 149-163.

Brown, Curtis (2022) "Narrow Mental Content", *The Stanford Encyclopedia of Philosophy* (Summer 2022 Edition), Edward N. Zalta (ed.), URL = <https://plato.stanford.edu/archives/sum2022/entries/content-narrow/>.

Brown, Jessica (2000) "Against Temporal Externalism", *Analysis* 60: 178–88.

Brown, Jessica. (2003) "Externalism and the Fregean Tradition", in A. Barber (ed.), pp. 431-458.

Brown, Jessica (2004) *Anti-Individualism and Knowledge*, Cambridge, MA: MIT Press.

Burge, Tyler (1977) "Belief *De Re*", *Journal of Philosophy* 74: 338-362.

Burge, Tyler (1978) "Belief and Synonymy", *Journal of Philosophy* 75: 119-138.

Burge, Tyler (1979a/2007) "Individualism and the Mental", *Midwest Studies in Philosophy* 4: 73-121, reprinted in Burge (2007), pp. 100-150.

Burge, Tyler (1979b/2005) "Sinning Against Frege", *Philosophical Review* 88: 398-432, reprinted in Burge (2005), pp. 213-239.

Burge, Tyler (1982/2007) "Other Bodies", A. Woodfield (ed.), *Thought and Object*, Oxford: Oxford University Press, pp. 97-120, reprinted in Burge (2007), pp. 82-99.

Burge, Tyler (1986a/2007) "Intellectual Norms and the Foundations of Mind", *Journal of Philosophy* 83: 697-720, reprinted in Burge (2007), pp. 254-274.

Burge, Tyler (1986b/2007) "Individualism and Psychology", *Philosophical Review* 95: 3-45, reprinted in Burge (2007), pp. 221-253.

Burge, Tyler (1988) "Individualism and Self-Knowledge", *Journal of Philosophy* 85: 649-663.

Burge, Tyler (1989/2007) "Wherein Is Language Social?", Alexander L. George (ed.), *Reflections on Chomsky*, Basil: Blackwell, pp. 175-191, reprinted in Burge (2007), pp. 275-290.

Burge, Tyler (1990/2005) "Frege on Sense and Linguistic Meaning", in David Bell and Neil Cooper (eds.), *The Analytic Tradition*, Oxford: Blackwell, pp. 30-60, reprinted in Burge (2005), pp. 242-269.

Burge, Tyler (1993/2007) "Concepts, Definitions, and Meaning", *Metaphilosophy* 24: 309-327, reprinted in Burge (2007), pp. 291-306.

Burge, Tyler (2005) *Truth, Thought, Reason: Essays on Frege*, Oxford: Oxford University Press.

Burge, Tyler (2007) *Foundations of Mind*, Oxford: Oxford University Press.

Burge, Tyler (2012) "Living Wages of 'SINN'", *Journal of Philosophy* 109: 40-84.

Burge, Tyler (2013) "Some Remarks on 'Externalism', in Baghramian (ed.), pp. 263-271.

Burgess, Alexis and Brett Sherman (eds.) (2014) *Metasemantics: New Essays on the Foundations of Meaning*, Oxford: Oxford University Press.

Bursten, Julia R. (2014) "Microstructure Without Essentialism", *Philosophy of Science* 81: 633– 653.

Carston, Robyn (2002) *Thoughts and Utterances: The Pragmatics of Explicit Communication*, Oxford: Blackwell.

Carston, Robyn (2021) "Polysemy: Pragmatics and Sense Conventions", *Mind & Language* 36: 108-133.

Chalmers, David J. (1996) *The Unconscious Mind: In Search of a Fundamental Theory*, Oxford: Oxford University Press.

Chalmers, David J. (2006) "The Foundations of Two-Dimensional Semantics", in Manuel García-Carpintero and Josep Macià (eds.), pp. 55-140.

Chalmers, David J. (2012) *Constructing the World*, Oxford: Oxford University Press.

Chomsky, Noam (1955) "Logical Syntax and Semantics: Their Linguistic Relevance", *Language* 31: 36-45.

Chomsky, Noam (1957) *Syntactic Structures,* The Hague: Mouton.

Chomsky, Noam (1959) "Verbal behavior. By B. F. SKINNER. (The Century Psychology Series.) Pp. viii, 478. New York: Appleton-Century-Crofts, Inc., 1957.", *Language* 35: 26-58.

Chomsky, Noam (1965) *Aspects of the Theory of Syntax*, Cambridge, MA: MIT Press.

Chomsky, Noam (1975) *Logical Structure of Linguistic Theory*, New York: Springer.

Chomsky, Noam (1986) *Knowledge of Language: Its Nature, Origin, and Use*, New York: Praeger.

Chomsky, Noam (1995) "Language and Nature", *Mind* 104: 1-61.

Chomsky, Noam (2000) *New Horizons in the Study of Language and Mind*, Cambridge: Cambridge University Press.

Chomsky, Noam (2003a) "Replies", in Antony and Hornstein (eds.), pp. 287-295.

Chomsky, Noam (2003b) "Internalist Explorations", in Martin Hahn and Bjørn Ramberg (eds.), *Reflections and Replies: Essays on the Philosophy of Tyler Burge*, Cambridge, MA: MIT Press, pp. 259-288.

Cohen, Jonathan (2000) "Analyticity and Katz's New Intensionalism: Or, if You Sever Sense from Reference, Analyticity is Cheap but Useless", *Philosophy and Phenomenological Research* 61: 115-135.

Cohnitz, Daniel and Jussi Haukioja (2013) "Meta-Externalism vs Meta-Internalism in the Study of Reference", *Australasian Journal of Philosophy* 91: 475-500.

Crane, Tim (1991) "All the Difference in the World", *Philosophical Quarterly* 41: 1-25.

Davidson, Donald (1987) "Knowing One's Own Mind", *Proceedings and Addresses of the American Philosophical Association*, 60: 441-458.

De Brabanter, Philippe, Neftalí Villanueva Fernández, David Nicolas and Isidora Stojanovic (2005) "Deferential Utterances", https://hal.science/ijn_00000575

De Brabanter, Philippe, David Nicolas, Isidora Stojanovic and Neftali Villanueva (2007) "Les usages déférentiels", in A. Bouvier and B. Conein (eds.), *L'épistémologie sociale: Une théorie sociale de la connaissance*, Paris: Editions de l'Ecole des Hautes Etudes en Sciences Sociales, collection Raisons pratiques 17, pp. 139-162.

De Brabanter, Philippe and Bruno Leclercq (2019) "Proposition d'une enquête empirique sur les intuitions « externalistes » des locuteurs à travers le mode de déférence sémantique", *Travaux du Cercle Belge de Linguistique-Studies van de Belgische Kring voor Linguïstiek* 13: 1-17. https://difusion.ulb.ac.be/vufind/Record/ULB-DIPOT:oai:dipot.ulb.ac.be:2013/285669/ Holdings

De Brabanter, Philippe and Bruno Leclercq (2023) "From Semantic Deference to Semantic Externalism to Metasemantic Disagreement", *Topoi*. https://doi.org/10.1007/s11245-023-09906-5

Denbigh, K. G. and M. L. G. Redhead (1989) "Gibbs' Paradox and Non-Uniform Convergence", *Synthese* 81: 283-312.

Deutsch, Harry (1993) "Semantics for Natural Kind Terms", *Canadian Journal of Philosophy* 23: 389-411.

Devitt, Michael and Kim Sterelny (1999) *Language and Reality: An Introduction to the Philosophy of Language, Second Edition*, Cambridge, MA: MIT Press.

Donnellan, Keith (1962) "Necessity and Criteria", *Journal of Philosophy* 59: 647-658.

Donnellan, Keith (1973) "Substances as Individuals", *Journal of Philosophy* 70: 711-712.

Donnellan, Keith (1974) "Speaking of Nothing", *Philosophical Review* 83: 3-31.

Donnellan, Keith S. (1983/2012) "Kripke and Putnam on Natural Kind Terms", in C. Ginet and S. Shoemaker (eds.), *Knowledge and Mind*, Oxford: Oxford University Press, pp. 84-104, reprinted in J. Almog and P. Leonardi (eds.), *Essays on Reference, Language, and Mind*, Oxford: Oxford University Press, pp. 178-203. [The page number cited is of the reprinted.]

Donnellan, Keith (1993) "There Is a Word for That Kind of Thing: An Investigation of Two Thought Experiments", *Philosophical Perspective* 7: 155-171.

Ducrot, Oswald (1972) *Dire et ne pas dire: Principe de sémantique linguistique*, Paris: Hermann.

Ducrot, Oswald (1980) « Analyses pragmatiques », *Communication* 32: 11-60.

Dummett, Michael (1973) *Frege: Philosophy of Language*, London: Duckworth.

Dummett, Michael (1978) *Truth and Other Enigmas*, Cambridge, MA: Harvard University Press.

Dummett, Michael (1991) *Frege and Other Philosophers*, Oxford: Clarendon Press.

Dupré, John (1981) "Natural Kinds and Biological Taxa", *Philosophical Review* 90: 66-90.

Dupré, John (1993) *The Disorder of Things: Metaphysical Foundations of the Disunity of Science*, Cambridge, MA: Harvard University Press.

Dupré, John (2004) "Review of Joseph LaPorte, *Natural Kinds and Conceptual Change*", *Notre Dame Philosophical Reviews* 2004 (6).

Edelstein Sidney M. (1948) "Priestley Settles the Water Controversy", *Chymia* 1: 123-137.

Egan, Frances (1995) "Computation and Content", *Philosophical Review* 104: 181-203.

Elugardo, Reinaldo (1993) "Burge on Content", *Philosophy and Phenomenological Research* 53: 367-384.

Evans, Gareth (1982) *The Varieties of Reference*, Oxford: Oxford University Press.

Falvey, Kevin and Joseph Owens (1994) "Externalism, Self-Knowledge, and Skepticism", *Philosophical Review* 103: 107-137.

Farkas, Katalin (2003) "What is Externalism?", *Philosophical Studies* 112: 187-208.

Farkas, Katalin (2006) "Semantic Internalism and Externalism", in E. Lepore and B. C. Smith (eds.), *The Oxford Handbook of Philosophy of Language*, Oxford: Oxford University Press, pp. 323-340.

Fauconnier, Gilles (1979) « Comment contrôler la vérité ? », *Acte de la recherche en sciences sociales* 25: 3-22.

Fauconnier, Gilles (1985/1994) *Mental Spaces*, Cambridge, MA: MIT Press, 1985, Cambridge: Cambridge University Press, 1994.

Fauconnier, Gilles (1997) *Mappings in Thought and Language*, Cambridge: Cambridge University Press.

Fillmore, Charles J. (1982a) "Frame Semantics", in Linguistic Society of Korea (ed.), *Linguistics in the Morning Calm*, Seoul: Hanshin, pp. 111-137.

Fillmore, Charles J. (1982b) "Towards a Descriptive Framework for Spatial Deixis", in R. J. Jarvella and W. Klein (eds.), *Speech, Place, and Action: Studies in Deixis and Related Topics*, Chichester: John Wiley, pp. 31-59.

Fine, Kit (2007) *Semantic Relationism*, Oxford: Blackwell.

Fodor, Jerry A. (1975) *The Language of Thought*, New York: Thomas Y. Crowell.

Fodor, Jerry A. (1980) "Methodological Solipsism Considered as a Research Strategy in Cognitive Psychology", *The Behavioral and Brain Sciences* 3: 63-109.

Fodor, Jerry A. (1987) *Psychosemantics: The Problem of Meaning in the Philosophy of Mind*, Cambridge, MA: MIT Press.

Fodor, Jerry A. (1994) *The Elm and the Expert*, Cambridge, MA: MIT Press.

Fodor, Jerry A. (1998a) *Concepts: Where Cognitive Science Went Wrong*, Oxford: Oxford University Press.

Fodor, Jerry (1998b) "There Are No Recognitional Concepts; Not Even RED", *Philosophical Issues* 9: 1-14.

Fodor, Jerry (2006) "What Is Universally Quantified and Necessary and A Posteriori and Flies South in the Winter?", *Proceedings and Addresses of the American Philosophical Association* 80: 11–24.

Frege, Gottlob (1892a/1997) "Über Sinn und Bedeutung", *Zeitschrift für Philosophische Kritik*, 100, pp. 25-50, G. Frege "On *Sinn* and *Bedeutung*", in Beaney (ed.) (1997), pp. 151-171.

Frege, Gottlob (1892b/1997) "Über Begriff und Gegenstand", *Vierteljahresschrift für wissenschaftliche Philosophie* 16: 192-205, G. Frege "On Concept and Object", in Beaney (ed.) (1997), pp. 181-193.

Frege, Gottlob (1918-1919a/1956) "Der Gedanke: Eine logische Untersuchung", *Beiträge zur Philosophie des deutschen Idealismus* 1: 58-77, G. Frege (1956) "The Thought: A Logical Inquiry", *Mind* 65: 289-311.

Frege, Gottlob (1918-1919b/1997) "Die Verneinung: Eine logische Untersuchung", *Beiträge zur Philosophie des deutschen Idealismus* 1: 143-157, G. Frege. (1997) "Negation", in Beaney (ed.) (1997), pp. 346-361.

Frege, Gottlob (1969/1979) *Nachgelassene Schriften und wissenschaftlicher Briefwechsel*, vol. 1, Hamburg: Felix Meiner, G. Frege (1979) *Posthumous Writings*, Oxford: Basil Blackwell.

García-Carpintero, Manuel and Josep Macià (eds.) (2006) *Two-Dimensional Semantics*, Oxford: Oxford University Press.

Garrett, B. T. (1983) "Grayling on Internal Structure", *Analysis* 43: 78-80.

Gasparri, Luca and Diego Marconi (2021) "Word Meaning", *The Stanford Encyclopedia of Philosophy* (Spring 2021 Edition), Edward N. Zalta (ed.), URL = <https://plato.stanford.edu/archives/spr2021/entries/word-meaning/>.

Geelen, Jeremy (2011) *Quine versus Kripke on the Metaphysics of Modality: An Examination and Defence of Quine's Position*, Ph.D Thesis, University of Ottawa.

Gelman, Susan A. and Lawrence A. Hirschfeld (1999) "How Biological Is Essentialism?", in D. L.

Medin and S. Atran (eds.), *Folkbiology*, Cambridge, MA: MIT Press.

Gelman, Susan A. and Henry M. Wellman (1991) "Insides and Essences: Early Understand Nonobvious", *Cognition* 38: 213-244.

Genone, James and Tania Lombrozo (2012) "Concept Possession, Experimental Semantics, and Hybrid Theories of Reference", *Philosophical Psychology* 25: 717-742.

Ghiselin, Michael T. (1987) "Species Concepts, Individuality, and Objectivity", *Biology and Philosophy* 2: 127-43.

Gilliéron, Jules and Mario Roques (1912) *Études de géographie linguistique*, Paris: Champion.

Goldberg, Sanford (2008) "Must Differences in Cognitive Value Be Transparent?", *Erkenntnis* 69: 165-187.

Goldberg, Sanford C. (2015) "Introduction", in Goldberg (ed.), pp. 1-15.

Goldberg, Sanford C. (ed.) (2015) *Externalism, Self-Knowledge, and Skepticism New Essays*, Cambridge: Cambridge University Press.

Goodman, Nelson (1949) "On Likeness of Meaning", *Analysis* 10: 1-7.

Goosens, William K. (1977) "Underlying Trait Terms", in Schwartz (ed.), pp. 133-154.

Grabarczyk, Paweł (2016) "How 'Meaning' Became 'Narrow Content'", *Studies in Logic, Grammar and Rhetoric* 46(59): 155-171.

Grayling, A. C. (1982) "Internal Structure and Essence", *Analysis* 42: 139-140.

Grayling, A. C. (1995) "Concept-Reference and Kinds", in Biro and Kotatko (eds.), pp. 75-93.

Greenberg, Mark (2014) "Trouble for Content I", in Burgess and Sherman (eds.), pp. 147-168.

Grice, Paul (1957/1989) "Meaning", *Philosophical Review* 66: 377-388, reprinted in Grice (1989), pp. 213-223.

Grice, Paul (1989) *Studies in the Way of Words*, Cambridge, MA: Harvard University Press.

Grice, H. P and P. F. Strawson (1956) "In Defense of a Dogma", *Philosophical Review* 65: 141-158.

Haber, Janosch and Massimo Poesio (2023) "Polysemy – Evidence from Linguistics, Behavioural Science and Contextualized Language Models", *Computational Linguistics*: 1-67.

Hacking, Ian (1993) "Working in a New World: The Taxonomic Solution", in P. Horwich (ed.), *World Changes: Thomas Kuhn and the Nature of Science*, Cambridge, MA: MIT Press, pp. 275-310.

Hacking, Ian (2007a) "Putnam's Theory of Natural Kinds and Their Names Is Not the Same as Kripke's", *Principia* 11: 1-24.

Hacking, Ian (2007b) "Natural Kinds: Rosy Dawn, Scholastic Twilight", *Royal Institute of Philosophy Supplement* 61: 203-239.

Hacking, Ian (2007c) "The Contingencies of Ambiguity", *Analysis* 67: 269–77.

Häggqvist, Sören and Åsa Wikforss (2015) "Experimental Semantics: The Case of Natural Kind Terms", in J. Haukioja (ed.), *Advances in Experimental Philosophy of Language*, London: Bloomsbury, pp. 109-138.

Häggqvist, Sören and Åsa Wikforss (2018) "Natural Kinds and Natural Kind Terms", *British*

Journal for the Philosophy of Science 69: 911-933.

Häggqvist, Sören and Åsa Wikforss (2020) "The Need for Descriptivism", in S. Biggs and H. Geirsson (eds.), *The Routledge Handbook of Linguistic Reference*, London: Routledge, pp. 335-344.

Haiman, John (1980) "Dictionaries and Encyclopedias", *Lingua* 50: 329-357.

Hale, Bob (1997) "Modality", in B. Hale and C. Wright (eds.) *A Companion to the Philosophy of Language*, Oxford: Blackwell, pp. 487-514.

Hampton, James A. (2006) "Concepts as Prototypes", *The Psychology of Learning and Motivation* 46: 79-113.

Hampton, James A. (2015) "Categories, Prototypes and Exemplars", N. Riemer (ed.), *The Routledge Handbook of Semantics*, London: Routledge, pp. 125-141.

Hanna, Robert (1998) "A Kantian Critique of Scientific Essentialism", *Philosophy and Phenomenological Research* 58: 497-528.

Harris, Randy Allen (1993) *The Linguistics Wars*, New York: Oxford University Press.

Haukioja, Jussi (2015) "On Deriving Essentialism from the Theory of Reference", *Philosophical Studies* 172: 2141-2151.

Haukioja, Jussi (2017) "Semantic Externalism and Semantic Internalism", in B. Hale, C. Wright, and A. Miller (eds.), *A Companion to the Philosophy of Language*, Second Edition, Malden, MA: Wiley-Blackwell, pp. 865-880.

Haukioja, Jussi, Mons Nyquist and Jussi Jylkkä (2021) "Reports from Twin Earth: Both Deep Structure and Appearance Determine the Reference of Natural Kind Terms", *Mind & Language* 36: 377-403.

Hawthorne, John and Earnest Lepore (2011) "On Words", *Journal of Philosophy* 108: 447-485.

Hayes, Patrick J. (1979) "The Naive Physics Manifesto", in D. Michie (ed.), *Expert Systems in the Micro-electronic Age*, Edinburgh: Edinburgh University Press, pp. 242-270.

Heck, Richard G. (1995) "The Sense of Communication", *Mind* 104: 79-106.

Heck, Richard G. (2002) "Do Demonstratives Have Senses?", *Philosophers Imprint* 2: 1-33.

Heck, Richard G. (2012) "Solving Frege's Puzzle", *Journal of Philosophy* 109: 132-174.

Hendry, Robin Findlay (2010) "Entropy and Chemical Substance", *Philosophy of Science* 77: 921-932.

Higginbotham, James (1998a) "Conceptual Competence", *Philosophical Issues* 9: 149-162.

Higginbotham, James (1998b) "On Knowing One's Own Language", in C. Wright, B. C. Smith and C. Macdonald (eds.), *Knowing Our Own Minds*, Oxford: Clarendon Press, pp. 429-441.

Hirschfeld, Lawrence A. (1996) *Race in the Making*, Cambridge, MA: MIT Press.

Horst, Steven (1996) "Review of *The Elm and the Expert*. BY JERRY FODOR", *Philosophical Quarterly* 46: 243-246.

Hull, David L. (1965) "The Effect of Essentialism on Taxonomy: Two Thousand Years of Stasis", *British Journal for the Philosophy of Science* 15: 314-26 and 16: 1-18.

Hunter, David (2001) "Knowledge and Understanding", *Mind & Language* 16: 542-546.

Hunter, David (2003) "Gabriel Segal, *A Slim Book About Narrow Content* (MIT Press, 2000), 177 pp.", *Noûs* 37: 724-745.

Ishiguro, Hidé (1990) *Leibniz's Philosophy of Logic and Language*, Second edition, Cambridge: Cambridge University Press.

Jackendoff, Ray (1989) "What is a Concept, that a Person May Grasp It?", *Mind & Language* 4: 68-102.

Jackendoff, Ray (2002) *Foundations of Language: Brain, Meaning, Grammar, Evolution*, Oxford: Oxford University Press.

Jackman, Henry (1999) "We Live Forwards but Understand Backwards: Linguistic Practices and Future Behaviour", *Pacific Philosophical Quarterly* 80: 157-177.

Jackman, Henry (2005) "Temporal Externalism, Deference, and our Ordinary Linguistic Practice", *Pacific Philosophical Quarterly* 86: 365-380.

Jackson, Frank (1998a) "Reference and Description Revisited", *Philosophical Perspectives* 12: 201-218.

Jackson, Frank (1998b) *From Ethics to Metaphysics: A Defense of Conceptual Analysis*, Oxford: Oxford University Press.

Jykklä, Jussi, Henry Railo and Jussi Haukioja (2009) "Psychological Essentialism and Semantic Externalism: Evidence for Externalism in Lay Speakers' Language Use", *Philosophical Psychology* 22: 37-60.

Kalish, Charles W. (1995) "Essentialism and Graded Membership in Animal and Artifact Categories", *Memory and Cognition* 23: 335-353.

Kamp, Hans (1985) "Context, Thought and Communication", *Proceedings of the Aristotelian Society* 85: 239-261.

Kaplan, David (1989a) "Demonstratives", in J. Almog, J. Perry, and H. Wettstein (eds.), *Themes from Kaplan*, Oxford: Oxford University Press, pp. 481-563.

Kaplan, David (1989b) "Afterthoughts", in J. Almog, J. Perry, and H. Wettstein (eds.), *Themes from Kaplan*, Oxford: Oxford University Press, 565-614.

Kaplan, David (1990) "Words", *Proceedings of the Aristotelian Society*, Supplementary Volumes 64: 93-119.

Kaplan, David (2011) "Words on Words", *Journal of Philosophy* 108: 504-529.

Katz, Jerrold J. (1972) *Semantic Theory*, New York: Harper & Row.

Katz, Jerrold J. (1978) "The Theory of Semantic Representation", *Erkenntnis* 13: 63-109.

Katz, Jerrold J. (1997) "Analyticity, Necessity, and the Epistemology of Semantics", *Philosophy and Phenomenological Research* 57: 1-28.

Katz, Jerrold J. and Jerry A. Fodor (1963) "The Structure of a Semantic Theory", *Language* 39: 170-210.

Kaufman, Arnold S. (1953) "The Analytic and the Synthetic: A Tenable 'Dualism'", *Philosophical Review* 62: 421-426.

Kay, Paul (1983) "Linguistic Competence and Folk Theories of Language: Two English Hedges",

BLS 9: 128-137.

Kehler, Andrew (2002) *Coherence, Reference, and the Theory of Grammar*, Stanford: CSLI Publications.

Keil, Frank C. (1989) *Concept, Kinds and Cognitive Development*, Cambridge, MA: MIT Press.

Khalidi, Muhammad Ali (1998) "Natural Kinds and Crosscutting Categories", *Journal of Philosophy* 95: 33-50.

Kimbrough, Scott (1998) "Anti-Individualism and Fregeanism", *Philosophical Quarterly* 48: 470-482.

Knott, Alistair and Robert Dale (1994) "Using Linguistic Phenomena to Motivate a Set of Coherence Relations", *Discourse Processes* 18: 35-62.

Komorjai, László (2006) "Sense and Understanding", *Logique et Analyse* 49: 137-167.

Kravchuk, T., M. Reznikov, P. Tichonov, N. Avidor, Y. Meir, A. Bekkerman and G. Alexandrowicz (2011) "Magnetically Focused Molecular Beam of Ortho-Water", *Science* 331: 319-321.

Kripke, Saul A. (1971/1993) "Identity and Necessity", in M. K. Munitz (ed.), *Identity and Individuation*, New York: New York University Press, pp. 135-64, reprinted in A. W. Moore (ed.), *Meaning and Reference*, New York: Oxford University Press, pp. 162-191. [The page number cited is of the reprinted.]

Kripke, Saul A. (1980) *Naming and Necessity*, Cambridge, MA: Harvard University Press.

Labov, William (1973) "The Boundaries of Words and Meanings", in R. W. Bailey and C-J. N. Shuy (eds.), *New Ways of Analysing Variation in English*, Washinton, DC: Georgetown University Press, pp. 340-373.

Lakoff, Georges (1976[1963]) "Toward a Generative Semantics", in J. D. McCawley (ed.), *Syntax and Semantics 7: Notes from the Linguistic Underground*, New York: Academic Press, pp. 43-61.

Lakoff, George (1973) "Hedges: A Study in Meaning Criteria and the Logic of Fuzzy Concepts", *Journal of Philosophical Logic* 2: 458-508.

Lakoff, George (1987) *Women, Fire, and Dangerous Things: What Categories Reveal about the Mind*, University of Chicago Press.

Lakoff, George and Claudia Brugman (1986) "Argument Forms in Lexical Semantics", *BLS* 12: 442-454.

Lakoff, Robin (1973) "Language and Woman's Place", *Language in Society* 2: 45-80.

Lakoff, Robin (1975) *Language and Woman's Place*, New York: Harper and Row.

Langacker, Ronald W. (1976) "Semantic Representations and the Linguistic Relativity Hypothesis", *Foundations of Language* 14: 307-357.

Langacker, Ronald W. (1987) *Foundations of Cognitive Grammar, vol. 1: Theoretical Prerequisites*. Stanford: Stanford University Press.

Langacker, Ronald W. (1988) "A Usage-Based Model", in B. Rudzka-Ostyn (ed.), *Topics in Cognitive Linguistics*, Amsterdam: John Benjamins, pp. 127-161.

Langacker, Ronald W. (2006) "On the Continuous Debate about Discreteness", *Cognitive Linguistics* 17: 107-151.

Langacker, Ronald W. (2008) *Cognitive Grammar: A Basic Introduction*, Oxford University Press, Oxford.

LaPorte, Joseph (1996) "Chemical Kind Term Reference and the Discovery of Essence", *Noûs* 30: 112-132

LaPorte, Joseph (1997) "Essential Membership", *Philosophy of Science* 64: 96-112.

LaPorte, Joseph (1998) "Living Water", *Mind* 426: 451-455.

LaPorte, Joseph (2004) *Natural Kinds and Conceptual Change*, Cambridge: Cambridge University Press.

Leslie, Sarah-Jane (2013) "Essence and Natural Kinds: When Science Meets Preschooler Intuition", in T. Szabó Gendler and J. Hawthorne (eds.), *Oxford Studies in Epistemology*, Volume 4, Oxford: Oxford University Press, pp. 108-65.

Levinson, Stephen (2000) *Presumptive Meaning: The Theory of Generalized Conversational Implicature*, Cambridge, MA: MIT Press.

Lewis, David (1970) "General Semantics", *Synthese* 22: 18-67.

Lewis, David (1994) "Reduction of Mind", in S. Guttenplan (ed.), *A Companion to the Philosophy of Mind*, Oxford: Blackwell, pp. 412-430.

Linsky, Bernard (1977) "Putnam on the Meaning of Natural Kind Terms", *Canadian Journal of Philosophy* 7: 819-828.

Liu, Jeeloo (2002) "Physical Externalism and Social Externalism: Are they Really Compatible?", *Journal of Philosophical Research* 27: 381-404.

Loar, Brian (1976) "The Semantics of Singular Terms", *Philosophical Studies* 30: 353-377.

Loar, Brian (1988/2017) "Social Content and Psychological Content", in R. H. Grimm and D. D. Merrill (eds.), *Contents of Thought*, Tucson: University of Arizona Press, pp. 99-110, reprinted in Katalin Balog and Stephanie Beardman (eds.), *Consciousness and Meaning: Selected Essays*, Oxford: Oxford University Press, pp. 153-164.

Löhr, Guido (2020) "Concepts and Categorization: Do Philosophers and Psychologists Theorize About Different Things?", *Synthese* 197: 2171-2191.

Locke, John (1690) *An Essay Concerning Human Understanding*, The Pennsylvania State University, 1999.
http://www.philotextes.info/spip/IMG/pdf/essay_concerning_human_understanding.pdf

Ludlow, Peter (2003a) "Referential Semantics for I-languages?", in Antony and Hornstein (eds.), pp. 140-163.

Ludlow, Peter (2003b) "Externalism, Logical Form and Linguistic Intentions", in Barber (ed.), pp. 399-414.

Lyons, John (1977) *Semantics*, Vol 2, Cambridge: Cambridge University Press.

Malt, Barbara (1994) "Water Is Not H_2O", *Cognitive Psychology* 27: 41-70.

Marconi, Diego (1997) *Lexical Competence*, Cambridge, MA: MIT Press.

Margolis, Eric (1994) "A Reassessment of the Shift from the Classical Theory of Concepts to Prototype Theory", *Cognition* 51: 73-89.

Mates, Benson (1951) "Analytic Sentences", *Philosophical Review* 60: 525-534.

Mayr, Ernst (1982) *The Growth of Biological Thought*, Cambridge, MA: Harvard University Press.

Mayr, Ernst (1988) *Toward a New Philosophy of Biology: Observations of an Evolutionist*, Cambridge, MA: Belknap Press of Harvard University Press.

Mayr, Ernst (1991) *One Long Argument: Charles Darwin and the Genesis of Modern Evolutionary Thought*, Cambridge, MA: Harvard University Press.

McDowell, John (1992) "Putnam on Mind and Meaning", *Philosophical Topics* 20: 35-48.

McGeer, Victoria (1994) *"Belief and Meaning.* by Akeel Bilgrami", *Journal of Philosophy* 91: 430-439.

McGinn, Colin (1977) "Charity, Interpretation, and Belief", *Journal of Philosophy* 74: 521-535.

McKay, Thomas and Cindy Stern (1979) "Natural Kind Terms and Standards of Membership", *Linguistics and Philosophy* 3: 27-34.

Medin, Douglas L. (1989) "Concepts and Conceptual Structure", *American Psychologist* 44: 1469-1481.

Medin, Douglas and Andrew Ortony (1989) "Psychological Essentialism", in S. Vosniadou and A. Ortony (eds.), *Similarity and Analogical Reasoning*, New York: Cambridge University Press, pp. 179-195.

Mellor, D. H. (1977) "Natural Kinds", *British Journal for the Philosophy of Science* 28: 299-312.

Mill, John Stuart (1843) *System of Logic*, London: Parker.

Millikan, Ruth G. (1993) *White Queen Psychology and Other Essays for Alice*, Cambridge, MA: MIT Press.

Millikan, Ruth Garrett (1997) "Images of Identity: In Search of Modes of Presentation", *Mind* 106: 499-519.

Minsky, Marvin (1974) "A Framework for Representing Knowledge", *MIT AI Laboratory Memo 306*.

McCulloch, Gregory (1995) *The Mind and its World*, London and New York: Routledge.

Naess, Arne (1957) "Synonymy as Revealed by Intuition", *Philosophical Review* 66: 87-93.

Needham, Paul (2000) "What Is Water?", *Analysis* 60: 13-21.

Needham, Paul (2002) "The Discovery that Water is H_2O", *International Studies in the Philosophy of Science* 16: 205-226.

Needham, Paul (2007) "Macroscopic Mixtures", *Journal of Philosophy* 104: 26-52.

Needham, Paul (2011) "Microessentialism: What is the Argument?", *Noûs* 45: 1-21.

Nelson, Michael (2023) "Propositional Attitude Reports", *The Stanford Encyclopedia of Philosophy* (Spring 2023 Edition), Edward N. Zalta & Uri Nodelman (eds.), URL = <https://plato.stanford.edu/archives/spr2023/entries/prop-attitude-reports/>.

Newman, Anthony E. (2005) "Two Grades of Internalism (Pass and Fail)", *Philosophical Studies* 122: 153-169.

Nichols, Shaun, N., Ángel Pinillos and Ron Mallon (2016) "Ambiguous Reference", *Mind* 125: 145-175.

Noonan, Harold (1984) "Fregean Thoughts", *The Philosophical Quarterly* 34: 205-224.

Nuccetelli, Susana (ed.) (2003) *New Essays on Semantic Externalism and Self-Knowledge*, Cambridge, MA: MIT Press.

Nunberg, Geoffrey (1979) "The Non-Uniqueness of Semantic Solution: Polysemy", *Linguistics and Philosophy* 3: 143-184.

O'Brien, Stephen J. (1987) "The Ancestry of the Giant Panda", *Scientific American* 257: 102-107.

Okasha, Samir (2002) "Darwinian Metaphysics: Species and the Question of Essentialism", *Synthese* 131: 191-213.

Onofri, Andrea (2016) "Two Constraints on a Theory of Concepts", *Dialectica* 70: 3-27.

Osherson, Daniel N. and Edward E. Smith (1981) "On the Adequacy of Prototype Theory as a Theory of Concepts", *Cognition* 9: 35-58.

Owens, Joseph (1992) "Psychophysical Supervenience: Its Epistemological Foundation", *Synthese* 90: 89-117.

Pagin, Peter (2014) "Pragmatic Enrichment as Coherence Raising", *Philosophical Studies* 168: 59-100.

Papineau, David (1996) "Discussion of Christopher Peacocke's *A Study of Concepts*", *Philosophy and Phenomenological Research* 56: 425-432.

Peacocke, Christopher (1992) *A Study of Concepts*, Cambridge, MA: MIT Press.

Perry, John (1988/1993) "Cognitive Significance and New Theories of Reference", *Noûs* 22: 1-18, reprinted in Perry (1993), pp. 227-247.

Perry, John (1993) *The Problem of the Essential Indexical and Other Essays*, Oxford University Press, Oxford.

Pinillos, N. Ángel (2011) "Coreference and Meaning", *Philosophical Studies* 154: 301-324.

Place, U. T. (1956) "Is Consciousness a Brain Process?", *British Journal of Psychology* 47: 44-50.

Pollock, Joey (2015) "Social Externalism and the Problem of Communication", *Philosophical Studies* 172: 3229-3251.

Poncinie, Lawrence (1985) "Meaning Change for Natural Kind Terms", *Noûs* 19: 415-427.

Porter, George (1975) "Joseph Priestley and his Contemporaries", *Journal of General Education* 27: 91-100.

Prinz, Jesse J. (2002) *Furnishing the Mind: Concepts and their Perceptual Basis*, Cambridge, MA: MIT Press.

Putnam, Hilary (1954) "Synonymity, and the Analysis of Belief Sentences", *Analysis* 14: 114-122.

Putnam, Hilary (1962a) "The Analytic and the Synthetic", *Minnesota Studies in the Philosophy of Science* 3: 358-397.

Putnam, Hilary (1962b) "It Ain't Necessarily So", *Journal of Philosophy* 59: 658-671.

Putnam, Hilary (1962c/1975) "Dreaming and Depth Grammar", in R.J. Butler (ed.), *Analytical Philosophy First Series*, Oxford: Blackwell, reprinted in H. Putnam, *Mind, Language and Reality, Philosophical Papers*, volume 2, pp. 304-324. Cambridge: Cambridge University Press. [The page number cited is of the reprinted.]

Putnam, Hilary (1970) "Is Semantics Possible?", *Metaphilosophy* 1: 187-201.

Putnam, Hilary (1973) "Meaning and Reference", *Journal of Philosophy* 70: 699-711.

Putnam, Hilary (1974) "Comment on Wilfred Sellers", *Synthese* 27: 445-455.

Putnam, Hilary (1975) "The Meaning of 'Meaning'", *Minnesota Studies in the Philosophy of Science* 7: 131-193.

Putnam, Hilary (1983) "Two Dogmas Revisited", in H. Putnam, *Realism and Reason*, Cambridge: Cambridge University Press, pp. 87-97.

Putnam, Hilary (1990) "Is Water Necessarily H_2O?", in J. Conant (ed.), *Realism with a Human Face*, Cambridge, Mass.: Harvard University Press, p. 54-79.

Putnam, Hilary (1992) "Replies", *Philosophical Topics* 20: 347-408.

Putnam, Hilary (2013) "Comments on Tyler Burge's "Some Remarks on 'Externalisms' " ", in Baghramian (ed.), pp. 272-274.

Quilty-Dunn, Jake (2021) "Polysemy and Thought: Toward a Generative Theory of Concepts", *Mind & Language* 36: 158-185.

Quine, Willard V. (1943) "Notes on Existence and Necessity", *Journal of Philosophy* 40: 113-127.

Quine, W.V. (1951) "Main Trends in Recent Philosophy: Two Dogmas of Empiricism", *Philosophical Review* 60: 20-43.

Quine, Willard Van Orman (1960) *Word and Object*, Cambridge, MA: MIT Press.

Recanati, François (1993) *Direct Reference*, Oxford: Blackwell.

Recanati, François (1995) "The Communication of First Person Thoughts", in Biro and Kotatko (eds.), pp. 95-102.

Recanati, François (1997) "Can We Believe What We Do Not Understand?", *Mind & Language* 12: 84-100.

Recanati, François (2000) "Deferential Concept: A Response to Woodfield", *Mind & Language* 15: 452-464.

Recanati, François (2001) "Open Quotation", *Mind* 110: 637-687.

Recanati, François (2006) "Indexical Concepts and Compositionality", in M. García-Carpintero and J. Macià (eds.), pp. 249-257.

Recanati, François (2008) *Philosophie du langage (et de l'esprit)*, Paris: Gallimard.

Recanati, François (2004) *Literal Meaning*, Cambridge: Cambridge University Press.

Recanati, François (2010) *Truth-Conditional Pragmatics*, Oxford: Oxford University Press.

Recanati, François (2016) *Mental Files in Flux*, Oxford: Oxford University Press.

Recanati, François (2017) "Contextualism and Polysemy", *Dialectica* 71: 379-397.

Rescorla, Michael (2019) "The Language of Thought Hypothesis", *The Stanford Encyclopedia of Philosophy* (Summer 2019 Edition), Edward N. Zalta (ed.), URL = <https://plato.stanford.edu/archives/sum2019/entries/language-thought/>.

Rey, Georges (1983) "Concepts and Stereotypes", *Cognition* 15: 237-262.

Rey, Georges (1985) "Concepts and Conceptions: A Reply to Smith, Medin and Rips", *Cognition* 19: 297-303.

Rey, Georges (1992) "Semantic Externalism and Conceptual Competence", *Proceedings of the Aristotelian Society* 92: 315-333.

Rey, Georges (2003) "Intentional Content and a Chomskyan Linguistics", in Barber (ed.), pp. 140-186.

Rey, Georges (2022) "The Analytic/Synthetic Distinction", *The Stanford Encyclopedia of Philosophy* (Summer 2022 Edition), Edward N. Zalta (ed.), URL = <https://plato.stanford.edu/archives/sum2022/entries/analytic-synthetic/>.

Robertson Ishii, Teresa and Philip Atkins (2020) "Essential vs. Accidental Properties", *The Stanford Encyclopedia of Philosophy* (Winter 2020 Edition), Edward N. Zalta (ed.), URL = <https://plato.stanford.edu/archives/win2020/entries/essential-accidental/>.

Rosch, Eleanor (1973) "Natural Categories", *Cognitive Psychology* 4: 32-50.

Rosch, Eleanor (1975) "Cognitive Representations of Semantic Categories", *Journal of Experimental Psychology: General* 104: 192-233.

Rosch, Eleanor (1977) "Human Categorization", in N. Warren (ed.), *Studies in Cross-Cultral Psychology*, Volume 1, London: Academic Press, pp. 1-49.

Rosch, Eleanor (1978) "Principles of Categorization", in E. Rosch and B. B. Lloyd (eds.), *Cognition and Categorization*, Hillsdale, N.J.: Erlbaum, pp. 27-47.

Rosch, Eleanor and Carolyn B. Mervis (1975) "Family Resemblances: Studies in the Internal Structure of Categories", *Cognitive Psychology* 7: 573-605.

Rosch, Eleanor, Carolyn B. Mervis, Wayne D. Gray, David M. Johnson, and Penny Boyes-Braem (1976) "Basic Objects in Natural Categories", *Cognitive Psychology* 8: 382-439.

Rowlands, Mark, Joe Lau, and Max Deutsch (2020) "Externalism About the Mind", *The Stanford Encyclopedia of Philosophy* (Winter 2020 Edition), Edward N. Zalta (ed.), URL = <https://plato.stanford.edu/archives/win2020/entries/content-externalism/>.

Saeed, John I. (2016) *Semantics, Fourth Edition*, Malden, MA: Wiley Blackwell.

Sainsbury, Mark (1990/1996/2002) "Concepts Without Boundaries", Inaugural lecture delivered at King's College London, 1990, reprinted in R. Keefe and P. Smith (eds.), *Vagueness: A Reader*, Cambridge, MA: MIT Press, 1996, pp. 251-264, and in Sainsbury (2003), pp. 71-84.

Sainsbury, Mark (2002) *Departing from Frege: Essays in the Philosophy of Language*, London: Routledge.

Sainsbury, Mark and Michael Tye (2011) "An Originalist Theory of Concepts", *Proceedings of the Aristotelian Society, Supplementary* Volume 85: 101-124.

Sainsbury, Mark and Michael Tye (2012) *Seven Puzzles of Thought and How to Solve them: An Originalist Theory of Concepts*, Oxford: Oxford University Press.

Sakai, Tomohiro (2016) "Realism and Anti-Realism of Polysemy", *Tokyo University Linguistic Papers (TULIP)* 37: 239-259.

Sakai, Tomohiro (2017) "On Frege's *Sinn* and Langacker's *Construal*: A Preliminary Survey of Their Compatibility", *Tokyo University Linguistic Papers (TULIP)* 38: 247-270.

Sakai, Tomohiro (2018) "Singular Thought in Non-Singular Propositions: A Cognitive Linguistic

Perspective", *Tokyo University Linguistic Papers* (*TULIP*) 40: 211-227.

Sakai, Tomohiro (2019) "Between Performatives and Constatives: Construal in Speech Acts", *Tokyo University Linguistic Papers* (*TULIP*) 41: 259-277.

Sakai, Tomohiro (2022a) "Toward an Internalist Construal of Semantic Externalism", in V. Hélène and M. Lammert (eds.), *A Crosslinguistic Perspective on Clear and Approximate Categorization*, New Castle upon Tyne: Cambridge Scholars Publishing, pp. 23-50.

Sakai, Tomohiro (2022b) "Incomplete Understanding Without Analyticity: Prototype Semantics and Social Externalism", *Tokyo University Linguistic Papers* (*TULIP*) 44: e102-e132.

Sakai, Tomohiro (2023a) "What Externalism Is Not (Necessarily)", *Tokyo University Linguistic Papers* (*TULIP*) 45: 181-201.

Sakai, Tomohiro (2023b) "Ontological Change Caused by Negation: The Case of Identity Statements", in M. Roitman (ed.), *Negatives and Meaning: Social Setting and Pragmatic Effects: Using Negatives in Political Discourse, Social Media and Oral Interaction*, Stockholm: Stockholm University Press, pp. 239–268. https://doi.org/10.16993/bcd

Salmon, Nathan (1981) *Reference and Essence*, Princeton: The Princeton University Press.

Salmon, Nathan (1986) *Frege's Puzzle*, Cambridge, MA: MIT Press.

Sarich, Vincent M. (1973) "The Giant Panda is a Bear", *Nature* 245: 218-220, https://doi.org/10.1038/245218a0

Sawyer, Sarah (2003) "Conceptual Errors and Social Externalism", *Philosophical Quarterly* 53: 265-273.

Schiffer, Stephen (1978) "The Basis of Reference", *Erkenntnis* 13: 171-206.

Schroeter, Laura (2008) "Why Be an Anti-Individualist?", *Philosophy and Phenomenological Research* 77: 105-141.

Schroeter, Laura and Schroeter François (2016) "Semantic Deference and Semantic Coordination", *American Philosophical Quarterly* 53: 193-210.

Schwartz, Stephen P. (1977) "Introduction", in Schwartz (ed.), pp. 13-41.

Schwartz, Stephen P. (ed.) (1977) *Naming, Necessity, and Natural Kinds*, Ithaca and London: Cornell University Press.

Schwartz, Stephen P. (1978) "Putnam on Artifacts", *Philosophical Review* 87: 566-574.

Segal, Gabriel M. A. (2000) *A Slim Book About Narrow Content*, Cambridge MA: MIT Press.

Segal, Gabriel (2003) "Ignorance of Meaning", in Barber (ed.), pp. 415-430.

Skinner, B. F. (1948/1957) *Verbal Behavior*, William James Lectures, Harvard University, 1948, New York: Appleton-Century-Crofts, Inc., 1957.

Soames, Scott (2002) *Beyond Rigidity: The Unfinished Semantic Agenda of* Naming and Necessity, Oxford: Oxford University Press.

Soames, Scott (2006) "Is H_2O a Liquid, or Water a Gas?", *Philosophy and Phenomenological Research* 72: 635-639.

Sober, Eliot (1994) *From a Biological Point of View*, Cambridge: Cambridge University Press.

Sperber, Dan and Deirdre Wilson (1995) *Relevance: Communication and Cognition, Second Edition*, Oxford: Blackwell.

Stalnaker, Robert (1993) "Twin Earth Revisited", *Proceedings of the Aristotelian Society* 93: 297-311.

Stalnaker, Robert (1997) "Reference and Necessity", in B. Hale and C. Wright (eds.), *A Companion to the Philosophy of Language*, Oxford: Blackwell, pp. 534–554.

Stanley, Jason (1999) "Understanding, Context-relativity, and the Description Theory", *Analysis* 59: 14-18.

Sterelny, Kim and Paul Griffiths (1999) *Sex and Death*, Chicago: University of Chicago Press.

Stern, Gustaf (1931) *Meaning and the Change of Meaning*, Bloomington: Indiana University Press.

Steward, Helen (1990) "Identity Statements and the Necessarily a Posteriori", *Journal of Philosophy* 87: 385-398.

Stich, Stephen P. (1978) "Autonomous Psychology and the Belief-Desire Thesis", *Monist* 61: 573-591.

Stich, Stephen (1992) "What Is a Theory of Mental Representation?", *Mind* 101: 243-261.

Stojnić, Una (2022) "Just Words: Intentions, Tolerance and Lexical Selection", *Philosophy and Phenomenological Research* 105: 3-17.
https://doi.org/10.1111/phpr.12781

Strawson, P. F. (1974/2004) *Subject and Predicate in Logic and Grammar*, London: Methuen.1974, London: Routledge, 2004.

Sweetser, Eve (1990) *From Etymology to Pragmatics*, Cambridge: Cambridge University Press.

Talmy, Leonard (1983) "How Language Structures Space", in H. L. Pick, Jr. and L. P. Acredolo (eds.), *Spatial Orientation: Theory, Research, and Application*, New York: Plenum, pp. 225-282.

Talmy, Leonard (1996/2000) "Fictive Motion in Language and 'Ception'", in P. Bloom, M. A. Peterson, L. Nadel and M. F. Garett (eds.), *Language and Space*, Cambridge, MA: MIT Press, pp. 211-276, reprinted in Talmy (2000), pp. 99-175. [The page number cited is of the reprinted.]

Talmy, Leonard (2000) *Toward a Cognitive Semantics*, Vol. 1, Cambridge, MA: MIT Press.

Taylor, John (2002) *Cognitive Grammar*, Oxford University Press.

Taylor, John R. (2003) *Linguistic Categorization, Third edition*, Oxford: Oxford University Press, 1974.

Taylor, John R. (2012) *The Mental Corpus: How Language is Represented in the Mind*, Oxford: Oxford University Press.

Tikhonov, Vladimir I. and Alexander A. Volkov (2002) "Separation of Water into Its Ortho and Para Isomers", *Science* 296: 2363.

Tobia, Kevin P., George E. Newman and Joshua Knobe (2020) "Water Is and Is Not H_2O", *Mind & Language* 35: 183-208.
https://doi.org/10.1111/mila.12234

Tobin, Emma (2010) "Crosscutting Natural Kinds and the Hierarchy Thesis", in Beebee and

Sabbartn-Leary (eds.), pp. 179-191.

Tomasello, Michael (2003) *Constructing a Language: A Usage-Based Theory of Language Acquisition*, Cambridge, MA: Harvard University Press.

Unger, Peter (1982) "Toward a Psychology of Common Sense", *American Philosophical Quarterly* 19: 117-129.

Unger, Peter (1983) "The Causal Theory of Reference", *Philosophical Studies* 43: 1-45.

Valente, Matheus (2019) "Communicating and Disagreeing with Distinct Concepts: A Defense of Semantic Internalism", *Theoria* 85: 312-336.

Weisberg, Michael (2006) "Water is Not H_2O", in D. Baird, E. Scerri and L. McIntyre (eds.), *Philosophy of Chemistry: Synthesis of a New Discipline*, New York: Springer, pp. 337-345.

Weiskopf, Daniel Aaron (2009) "The Plurality of Concepts", *Synthese* 169: 145-173.

White, Morton G. (1950) "The Analytic and the Synthetic: An Untenable Dualism", in S. Hook (ed.), *John Dewey: Philosopher of Science and Freedom*. New York: The Dial Press, pp. 316-330.

White, Stephen L. (1982) "Partial Character and the Language of Thought", *Pacific Philosophical Quarterly* 63: 347-365.

Wiggins, David (1995) "Putnam's Doctrine of Natural Kind Words and Frege's Doctrines of Sense, Reference and Extension: Can they Cohere?", in Biro and Kotatko (eds.), pp. 59-74.

Wikforss, Åsa Maria (2001) "Social Externalism and Conceptual Errors", *Philosophical Quarterly* 51: 217-231.

Wikforss, Åsa Maria (2004) "Externalism and Incomplete Understanding", *Philosophical Quarterly* 54: 287-294.

Wikforss, Åsa Maria (2005) "Naming Natural Kinds", *Synthese* 145: 65-87.

Wikforss, Åsa (2006) "Content Externalism and Fregean Sense", in T. Marvan (ed.), *What Determines Content?: The Internalism/Externalism Dispute*, New Castle Upon Tyne: Cambridge Scholar Publishing, pp. 163-179.

Wikforss, Åsa (2008) "Semantic Externalism and Psychological Externalism", *Philosophy Compass* 3: 158-181.

Wikforss, Åsa (2010) "Are Natural Kind Terms Special?", in Beebee and Sabbartn-Leary (eds.), pp. 64-83.

Wikforss, Åsa (2013) "Bachelors, Energy, Cats and Water: Putnam on Kinds and Kind Terms", *Theoria* 79: 242-261.

Wikforss, Åsa (2014) "Incomplete Understanding of Concepts", *The Oxford Handbook of Topics in Philosophy*, Oxford: Oxford University Press. https://doi.org/10.1093/oxfordhb/9780199935314.013.49

Wikforss, Åsa (2015) "Insignificance of Transparency", in Goldberg (ed.), pp. 142-164. https://doi.org/10.1017/CBO9781107478152.009

Williamson, Timothy (2007) *The Philosophy of Philosophy*, Oxford: Blackwell.

Wilson, Robert A. (2003) "Individualism", in S. P. Stich and T. A. Warfield (eds.), *The Blackwell Guide to Philosophy of Mind*, Basil: Blackwell, pp. 256-287.

Woodfield, Andrew (2000) "Reference and Deference", *Mind & Language* 15: 433-451.

Ziem, Alexander (2008) *Sprache und Wissen: Frames und Sprachliches Wissen – Kognitive Aspekte der Semantischen Kompetenz*, Berlin: Walter de Gruyter GmbH & Co.

Index (item)

absolutely indexical   42, 52
accuracy conditions   245
acid   256, 297, 331
active   172-174, 339
actuality-dependent   43
allophones   228, 229
allotropes   300, 308, 309
alminium   308
American structuralism   2
analytic   1, 44, 50, 80, 87, 93-99, 101-105,
    108-114, 117, 127, 128, 130, 132, 149,
    184, 194, 198-200, 202, 212
anaphora   319, 320, 327
a posteriori   44, 101, 102
a priori   6, 44, 45, 50, 101, 102, 104, 109,
    113, 138, 153, 167, 170, 175, 184, 185,
    188
arsenic   295, 296
artifacts   87, 93, 111, 112, 127, 198
atomic number   45, 46, 293, 302

baby   32, 313, 314, 319
Bachelor   1, 13, 101
bank   34, 130, 235, 319, 325, 328
baptism   291, 294
base   2, 135, 158, 256, 297
basic level categories   294, 295
basic level objects   294, 295
bat   122-124, 129, 320
bead   74, 333-335, 344, 345
beetle   295
behavioral psychology   2
being called "water"   312
being water   51, 74, 186, 312, 316, 317
biological species   280, 299, 341
biological taxon   295, 298

boiling point   300, 301, 303, 305
bond angle   301
book   16, 60, 105, 124, 163, 196, 269, 313,
    314, 319, 349, 356
bookshelf   313, 314
bottle   72, 319, 326, 327
boundaryless categories   139
boundaryless concepts   132
bowls   132
broad contents   42, 67, 214, 223
broadening   325

carbon   48, 300, 302, 305, 308
Cartesian   76
cats   44, 109, 113, 203
change in theory   149
chemical kinds   299, 303, 333
chemical properties   302, 305
chemical substance   40, 51, 303, 341, 347
chicken   118, 313-315
Clark Kent   188, 242, 243, 245, 246, 260,
    261
cluster words   105, 107, 108, 112-114, 117,
    201, 212, 254, 263
coffee   145, 311, 318
Cognitive Difference Principle   157
cognitive domains   160
cognitive psychology   119, 342
cognitive synonymy   100, 101, 175
cognitive value   151-154, 157, 158, 162,
    169, 175, 242
communicative intention   257, 258
composition   122, 300-302, 304, 308, 311,
    315, 317, 322, 324, 334, 346, 347
compositional   121, 122, 144, 301, 304, 310
compositional formula   299-301, 324

conception of a concept   142
conceptual competence   140, 148, 152, 192, 200, 201, 213, 254, 256, 257
conceptual content   143, 145, 146, 150, 151, 153, 160, 161, 164, 171, 187-189, 191, 192, 203-205, 207, 209, 212, 213, 215, 226, 227, 230, 234, 243, 244, 246, 255, 256, 258-260, 264, 265, 268, 277, 278, 285, 289, 321, 333, 336, 337, 355
conceptual fragmentation   165, 183, 264
constitutive authority of intentions   229
construal   3, 13, 14, 37, 45, 59, 60, 71, 84, 85, 102, 128, 143-148, 150-153, 160-163, 165, 168, 170-172, 174, 175, 178-180, 183, 184, 187, 189, 191-194, 203, 204, 207-209, 211-213, 215, 221, 224-227, 229-235, 237, 239, 240, 242-246, 255, 256, 259, 260, 264-266, 268, 274, 277, 278, 285, 289, 320, 331, 334, 335, 337, 339, 356
Consumerist Semantics   256
contiguity of water   356
contiguity type relations   348
conventional implicature   19
conventionality of construal   160, 225
conventionalization   207, 328
conventional meaning   84, 91-93, 151, 152, 219, 250
coreference de jure   224, 225, 229, 261, 268, 269, 320, 333
coreferential de facto   226, 260
coreferential de jure   224, 246, 255, 260, 265, 268, 269, 278, 284, 320, 335, 342
criterial attribute model   325
crosscutting categories   295, 296
crystal structures   300
cups   132, 311

dative   173
de dicto   241

default deference   257, 259
Deference to future usage   345, 347
deferential concept   250, 256, 257, 259, 261, 262, 265, 268
deferential construal   263-265, 267, 269, 271, 272, 274, 278, 280, 284, 285, 321, 334, 336, 337, 342, 343, 347, 355
degree of coherence   348-350, 352, 353
deliberate deference   257-259
delocutivity   326
demonstrative   15, 165, 218, 219, 262
De re   241
descriptive content   240, 241, 291
descriptive semantics   10, 290
descriptivism   12, 24, 161
deuterium   301, 302
diachronic divisions of linguistic labor   345
diamond   300, 308
different forms - different construals   230
differential dubitability test   157, 183
dimethyl ether   300
directly referential   241, 253, 259-261
direct reference   42, 241, 264
discern   121, 122, 142, 155, 170, 177, 255, 289, 335, 344
discourse coherence   277, 352, 353, 356
Distinctness of Concepts   163, 164
distinguisher   12, 13
division of linguistic labor across time   342
division of non-linguistic labor   286, 345
DNA   297, 298
dogs   110
door   313, 314, 319, 331

E-concepts   70, 71
E-language   5, 70
ellipsis   319
elor   100
Émile Ajar   242, 243, 245
empty natural kind terms   68, 69

enlightened speakers   242, 244, 245
enrichment   325, 330, 348, 352, 353
entropy of mixing   305
epistemically motivated   336, 345, 347
epistemic givenness of meaningfulness   170
epistemic givenness of meaning identity and
   difference   170
epistemic givenness of univocity   170
epistemology   27, 137-139, 158, 171
ethyl alcohol   300
etymology   205, 206
extension   11, 12, 14, 24-27, 31, 33, 35-41,
   43, 45-47, 54-59, 68, 74, 81, 89-92, 107,
   115, 117, 119, 123, 125, 128, 130-132,
   138, 144, 153, 155, 171, 204, 214, 246,
   271, 279, 282, 283, 286, 292, 294, 298,
   299, 307, 309-314, 317, 324, 330-333,
   335, 338-340, 343, 348, 353

failure of communication   221, 225, 226
family resemblance   318
fictive motion   147, 289, 341
first-person pronoun   220
fleas   296
Foundational Externalism (FE)   27
foundational semantics   10
frame semantics   195, 196
Fregean Constraint (FC)   157, 244
Fregean sense   26, 35, 36, 45, 59, 75, 160,
   163, 168, 217, 218, 267
Frege case   135, 136, 161, 167, 180, 214,
   215, 221-223, 244
Frege's Constraint   157, 158, 163-171, 174-
   180, 182, 183, 185, 203, 204, 206-208,
   212, 221, 223, 225, 226, 272-274
Frege's principle   157
Frege's test   157

gas phase   301, 324
general terms   16, 56, 143, 164, 185, 193

genetic code   293, 297, 298
gold   26, 32, 43-46, 54-56, 72, 141, 196,
   200, 247, 283, 291-293, 302-304, 307,
   309, 346
grammatical constructions   171, 180
graphite   300, 308
grasping a sense   16, 160, 179
Groundedness Thesis   285, 352

healthy   320
heat   283, 293, 303, 305
heavy water   301, 302, 330, 332
hedge   118, 122, 123, 137, 139, 196, 309,
   317, 322
hidden underlying structure   292, 293, 298,
   306, 309, 332, 344
historical change   326, 336
historical linguistics   336
homonymic collision   228
homonymy   227, 235, 318, 320, 325
hybrid externalism (HE)   321
hydrogen   33, 46-48, 280, 288, 289, 299,
   301, 302, 305, 308, 309, 314, 324, 338,
   339, 352
Hypothesis of External Definitions   140,
   262

ICMs   196
I-concepts   70, 71, 73
idealized cognitive models   196
idea (*Vorstellung*)   16, 20, 160
identity of a concept   139, 168, 211, 265,
   269, 282
idiomaticity   116
I-language   4, 5, 58, 61, 62, 70, 73, 248
I-meaning   67
implementing mechanism   135, 136, 215
incommensurability   50
incomplete understanding   34, 80, 83-89,
   91, 94, 95, 97, 108, 113, 114, 117, 124-

128, 131-133, 135-137, 139, 141, 142,
151, 153, 165-168, 182, 189, 190, 192,
194, 198-200, 204, 208, 212, 213, 252,
253, 267, 268, 270, 278, 280, 281, 334,
336, 337, 355, 356
incomplete understanding in the communal
sense   152, 192, 213
incomplete understanding in the
metaphysical sense   152, 192, 204, 213
indexical   26, 40-43, 52, 90, 218, 219, 250,
252, 253, 259, 271, 331
indexicality of 'water'   356
individualistic construal   211, 263-266,
269-272, 274, 278, 284, 285, 321, 334,
342, 355
inheritance   122
insects   124, 296
intension   11-14, 23, 24, 26, 27, 31, 35, 39,
47, 59, 81, 89, 117, 125, 128, 147, 286,
287, 348
intentional content   67, 135, 136, 214
intentional state   71, 135, 136, 215
Interpretation Principle   249, 256
intrinsic property   298
introspective knowledge of comparative
content   167
Intuitive Criterion of Difference for
thoughts   157, 169
ion   301
iron pyrites   45, 54, 55, 283, 303, 304, 307
irrationality   168, 182, 203, 212, 273
'is' of composition   186, 187
'is' of definition   186, 187
isomer   300, 301, 305
isotope   301, 302, 306

jade   304, 307, 308
jadeite   304, 305, 307-309

knowledge of synonymy   184

KP-thesis   281, 290, 298-300, 302, 303,
306, 307, 309
Kripke/Putnam essentialism   281, 299

landmark   172
language of thought   234
Latin   205, 227, 228, 335
lawful behavior   303, 306, 332
law of constant proportion   300, 324
lemon   108, 111, 114, 193, 200, 280, 293,
297, 298
lexical identity   228
lexical meaning   326, 327, 353
liberal criteria for possession of concepts
182, 183, 192, 213
light   18, 76, 87, 151, 152, 297, 301, 302,
320
linguistic competence   27, 152, 170, 179-
181, 186, 261, 337, 350
linguistic form   3, 100, 215, 216, 218, 224,
226, 228, 231
linguistic meaning   13, 40, 67, 83, 87, 167,
171, 178, 179, 218, 231, 250, 329, 355,
356
linguistic modes of presentation   178
liquid phase   301, 323
local paradigm   26, 37, 42, 45, 92, 290-292,
294, 298, 312, 322
locus of meaning   51
logical forms   233, 238, 239
loosening   325
LOT   234

meaning change   74, 326, 333-337
meaning-giving characterization   190
meaning-giving normative characterization
127
meat   144, 331, 336, 348
mechanism   2, 32, 36, 128, 215, 231, 252,
266, 332

melting point   300, 309
Mentalese   234-239, 249, 251, 256
mental file   187, 269
mentalism   2, 3, 36
mental lexicon   38, 257, 264-266, 278, 327
mental representation   13, 23, 61, 70, 71,
    213, 235, 250, 253, 282, 288, 312, 338
meta-internalism   255
meta-internalists   254
metaphor   18, 75, 120, 148, 274, 324, 329
(metaphysical) necessity   44, 49
metaphysical reality   342
metaphysics   27, 137-139, 142, 307, 308
metasemantics of natural kind terms   290,
    291, 294, 297
methodological solipsism   76
metonymy   325, 327
microessentialism   40, 299
Microraptor   203
microstructure   40, 49, 59, 92, 283, 288,
    300, 301, 303-306, 310, 317
Middle English   333
mode of presentation   14, 156, 157, 160,
    168, 171, 178, 208, 217, 219, 221, 224-
    226, 231, 233-235, 238-241, 244, 253,
    254, 259
moderate differences of construal   225
modulation   325-330, 350
monosemous   318, 327
mother   107, 108, 184, 200, 201, 234, 236,
    237
mugs   132

Naïve Conception of Communication   220
naive essentialism   340
narrow content   67-71, 161
natural kind term   26, 27, 32, 37, 39-46, 48,
    52, 94, 112, 152, 200, 256, 280, 282-
    287, 290, 293, 294, 299, 306, 307, 309,
    311, 317, 322, 325, 332, 338-340

necessity type relations   348
nephrite   304, 305, 307, 308
network model   325-329
neutron   301, 302
nominal essence   112, 292, 293
Nominal kind terms   112, 113
nominative   173
nonrigid designator   291
nontaxonomic scientific kind   296
normative characterization   127, 281, 282

oblique contexts   162
observable properties   331, 338
odd number   131, 133, 139
Old English   342, 345
Old Norse   205
one-criterion word   105-108, 112, 113, 115,
    193, 194, 196, 198, 251, 254
opaqueness of sameness of content (OSC)
    167
optimal account   140, 141, 262
orangutan   81, 82, 201, 202
ordinary language   57, 295, 318
orthohydrogen   305
ortho-water   305
ostension   290, 291, 294, 295, 299, 305
ostensive definition   42, 290
oxygen   33, 46-48, 280, 288, 289, 299, 301,
    308, 314, 324, 338, 339, 352

parahydrogen   305
parasites   296, 297
para-water   305, 306
passive   172-174
Pencils   111, 198
phase-neutral sense   323, 324
phase-specific sense   324
philosophy of science   277, 289, 290, 307,
    356
phlogiston   3, 68, 287, 288

380

phonology   5, 6, 62, 235, 237, 328
plastic   313, 314
poetic coloring   177, 178
poison   296
Polysemy   318
Pope   195-197
Possibility type relations   348
possible world   37, 43, 44, 49-51, 96, 291-293, 299, 306, 311
pragmatically motivated   336, 345, 347
pragmatic enrichment   331, 348, 350, 352
pragmatics   6, 7, 16, 19, 20, 62, 153, 312, 313, 315
presupposition (*Voraussetzung*)   16, 21
principle of compositionality   154
Principle of Pragmatic Enrichment   348
procedural meaning   19
pronoun   15, 40, 326, 350
proper name   15, 22, 37, 44, 45, 56, 155, 158, 159, 162, 173, 185, 218, 221, 244, 287, 291, 293
propositional attitude   28, 32, 156, 225, 233, 279
protein   57, 139, 345, 346
protium   301, 302
Proto-Indo-European   205, 206
proton   301, 309
prototype   70, 79, 80, 87, 118-122, 124, 127, 130-133, 137-139, 148, 150, 194, 196, 197, 323, 327
psychological essentialism   316, 322, 340-342
psychological experiments   317, 322, 340
Psychological Externalism (PE)   30
psychological modes of presentation   178, 224
psychological reality   342
Publicity (PUB)   34, 244
pure indexicals   40, 41
pure indexicals   40

qua problem   294, 295
quasi-quoting   249, 251, 257
quintessentialism   342
quotation marks   100, 101, 249-251, 253

rabbit   330, 331, 335, 348
radical differences of construal   225
radical internalism   55-57
rationality   73, 82, 158, 167, 168, 170, 175, 177, 182, 203, 206, 207
real definition   151
real essence   292, 293
real kind   296, 297
reference (*Bedeutung*)   16
referring function   325-327
relational properties   298, 302
relation same   74, 75, 292, 299, 306, 322
relations of repetition   228
Relevance Theory   350
representational pluralism   243
represented as being the same   222, 223
represented as the same   222, 223
resemblance type relations   348
rigid designation   43, 46, 49, 51
rigid designator   44, 47, 291, 293, 294, 299
Romain Gary   242, 243
rule / list fallacy   327

same form - different construals   230
sameness relation   33, 290-293, 297, 298, 306
saturation   331, 350
scientific language   318
seawater   314, 315, 330
semantic competence   170, 171, 175, 176, 178-180, 183, 189, 192, 193, 203, 206, 208, 287
semantic deference   247-249, 255-257, 259, 261, 268, 271, 278, 285, 286, 335

381

semantic marker   12, 13

semantic rationality   170, 184, 204, 206, 207, 236

semantic shift   335, 336, 344, 345

semantic transfer   325, 327

sense extension   325

sense narrowing   323-325, 330

sense (*Sinn*)   16, 153, 171

singular proposition   239-242

singular term   15, 16, 22, 156, 160, 161, 164, 171, 185, 187

solid phase   324

source language   271, 272, 278

speakers   243

speakers' intention   344

speakers' intuition   180, 181, 200, 205, 206, 311, 335, 337

specification   330

speech act   62, 257

spelling variants   228, 229

spin-isomers   305

steel   313, 314

stereotype   26, 37-40, 45, 56, 116, 117, 148, 196, 200, 201, 232, 284-286, 293, 312

Strawson-model   188

structural description   299

structural formulae   300

subjectification   148

subjective motions   147

sulphur   296

Superman   187, 242-246, 260, 261

synchronic divisions of linguistic labor   345

syntacticocentrism   8

syntactic structures   233, 235-237

syntax   5-7, 9, 61-63, 71, 116, 181, 234-236, 328

synthetic   80, 94-96, 98, 102, 104, 105, 114, 117, 127

taxonomic hierarchy   295-297

tea   311, 312

tears   313-315

telephone   313, 314

temporal externalism   343-347, 356

theory change   120, 334, 336

third realm   23, 52, 75

tiger   32, 38, 39, 44, 45, 48, 49, 56, 57, 92, 117, 193, 200-202, 270, 280, 293-295, 298, 299, 302, 324

tomato   139, 313-315

tone (*Beleuchtung, Färbung*)   16, 18, 171

trajector   148, 172

Transparency of Difference   167

Transparency of Sameness   167

transparency of sameness of content   167, 206

tritium   301, 306

truth-condition   30, 150, 159, 160, 186

truth-conditional content   143, 145, 259, 350

truth-conditional equivalence   158, 178, 180, 204, 207

truth-conditional meaning   19, 143, 171

truth-related notions   56, 60, 61, 63-65, 99, 138

Twin case   135-137, 167, 211

twin-substances   45, 303-305, 310

two-dimensional semantics   161, 165

underlying property   331

unenlightened speakers   242-246

vagueness   131

vantage points   179, 180, 207

vases   132

veracity of construals   146

Verification Principle   138

vixen   105-107, 115, 193, 194, 227, 273

water argument   293

Index（item）

whales   44, 109
wide content   67, 70
window   318-320, 322, 326-329, 333
wood   314
Wrong Format view   327

Index (person name)

Abbott   11, 14, 27, 38, 45, 56-58, 109, 111, 280, 282, 283, 295, 312-316, 320, 333

Ambrus   50, 109, 291, 306, 310

Armstrong   131, 139

Atkins   43

Austin   6, 18, 176, 197, 257

Aydene   29, 67, 68, 161, 247, 256

Bach   41, 58, 100, 330

Barber   33, 55, 58

Bar-Hillel   26, 40

Bealer   332, 347

Bell   14, 159

Benveniste   40, 326-328

Berzelius   300

Bezuidenhout   219, 243, 267

Bilgrami   38, 65, 67, 71, 76, 82, 214, 254, 255

Bird   12, 114-116, 124, 129, 150, 203, 299

Blakemore   19, 178

Bloom   93, 199, 244, 245, 315, 340, 341

Bloomfield   2, 3, 5, 7, 36, 47, 227, 228

Boghossian   41, 55, 167, 175, 205

Bonardi   187

Boyd   73, 129, 151, 170, 252, 294, 356

Braddon-Mitchell   41, 59, 161, 235, 236, 256

Braisby   311

Brakel   303

Braun   242, 245

Bromberger   26, 155, 186, 282, 283, 294, 337, 340, 341

Brown   1, 11, 24, 25, 28, 41, 54, 68, 157, 165, 167, 168, 182, 204, 206, 208, 212, 303, 344-346

Brugman   319, 325, 326

Burge   1, 5, 6, 11, 14, 15, 19, 22-25, 27-36, 40-42, 48, 51-53, 55, 58, 59, 62, 66, 67, 73, 75, 76, 79-85, 87-91, 94-98, 100, 104, 112, 113, 125-130, 136, 137, 140-142, 148-153, 157, 162, 164, 168-172, 175, 177-180, 182, 185-187, 190, 192-194, 199-202, 204, 208, 211-213, 218, 240, 249, 251-253, 255, 260, 262, 267, 268, 272, 279, 281, 282, 287, 295, 307, 308, 337, 339

Burgess   10, 290

Bursten   303

Carston   19, 20, 178, 318

Cavendish   33, 288

Chalmers   1, 42, 161, 163, 203, 247

Chomsky   1, 3-8, 11, 56-58, 61, 62, 67, 70, 73, 102, 174, 180, 181, 186, 248, 249, 311, 312, 319, 329, 332, 337

Cohen   99

Cohnitz   33, 36, 254, 255

Crane   29, 62, 67, 76, 338

Dale   349

Dalton   97, 151, 152

Davidson   53, 264

De Brabanter   23, 30, 41, 170, 247, 248, 252, 257-259, 262, 266, 269, 271, 285, 343

Denbigh   305

Deutsch   44, 55

Devitt   1, 287, 294

Donnellan   26, 42, 45, 46, 73, 109, 110, 159, 201

Ducrot   15, 16, 19, 21, 22, 326

Dummett   15, 16, 18-20, 52, 153, 155, 167,

169, 173, 180, 252
Dupré 38, 112, 169, 252, 282, 290, 292, 293, 295, 297, 298, 303

Edelstein 288, 289
Egan 42
Elugardo 29, 53, 87, 92, 182
Evans 15, 16, 156, 157, 169, 175, 177, 233

Falvey 165-167, 205, 206, 212, 273
Farkas 25, 28, 29, 36, 41, 189
Fauconnier 6, 8, 10, 60, 148, 289, 326
Feyerabend 50
Fillmore 194-196
Fine 222, 223
Fitzpatrick 235, 236
Fodor 1, 8-13, 33, 39, 47, 58, 62, 67, 68, 102, 105, 117, 121, 122, 135, 136, 207, 211, 214, 215, 219, 225, 231, 233-239, 247, 256, 257, 261, 283, 285, 287, 288, 303, 331
Frege 14-24, 46, 52, 56, 57, 59, 64, 65, 75, 99, 141, 142, 153-165, 168-179, 183, 187, 203, 206-208, 215-221, 224, 231, 234, 237, 262

Garrett 298
Gasparri 26, 47, 286
Geelen 291
Gelman 289, 341, 342
Genone 323
Ghiselin 297
Gilliéron 227, 228
Goldberg 157, 167
Goodman 90
Goosens 27, 38, 39, 109, 270, 337
Grabarczyk 14, 24, 29, 41, 67, 68, 70, 135
Grayling 267, 302
Greenberg 72, 80, 82, 83, 248, 256, 264, 266, 268, 285

Grice 19, 102, 104, 178, 257, 313
Griffiths 297

Haber 227, 318, 327, 328, 330
Hacking 37, 38, 46, 48, 49, 51, 56, 257, 281, 296, 298, 304, 307-309, 341
Häggqvist 10, 36, 37, 48, 281, 290, 294, 295, 299, 303, 307, 311, 322, 337, 338
Haiman 98, 117
Hale 104
Hampton 114-116, 124, 131, 139, 203
Hanna 44-46, 50, 293
Harris 2, 3, 7
Haukioja 1, 10, 11, 30, 32, 33, 36, 43, 45, 48, 54, 55, 72, 254, 255, 280, 317, 323, 330, 341
Hawthorne 100, 227, 229, 318-320
Hayes 70
Heck 14, 135, 156, 176, 220, 221, 234, 242, 243, 260
Heim 11
Hendry 305
Higginbotham 57, 71, 140-143, 181, 262
Hirschfeld 289, 341
Horst 68, 303
Hull 1, 297, 298
Hunter 29, 36, 53, 54, 58, 69, 249, 267, 287

Ishiguro 145, 146

Jackendoff 8, 70, 71, 73, 146
Jackman 264, 286, 336, 343-347, 355, 356
Jackson 41, 42, 44, 95
Jylkkä 321, 322

Kalish 311
Kamp 229, 241
Kant 45, 96
Kaplan 40, 52, 100, 161, 219, 228, 229, 232, 233, 250, 256, 290, 331

Katz   1, 8-14, 21, 28, 59, 60, 65, 99, 110,
   173, 184, 237
Kaufman   98, 102
Kehler   349
Keil   39, 70, 104, 105, 112, 131
Khalidi   296, 297
Kimbrough   24, 141, 149-151, 157, 182,
   183, 190, 192, 202, 208, 212, 213, 273
Knott   349
Komorjai   23, 158
Kratzer   11
Kravchuk   305
Kripke   14, 22, 25, 26, 37, 38, 40, 44-46,
   48-51, 55, 56, 92, 101, 138, 152, 185,
   280, 281, 283, 291, 293, 294, 297-299,
   302, 303, 306, 307, 309-316, 333, 337
Kuhn   50

Lakoff, G.   107, 108, 118, 122, 123
Lakoff, R.   107
Langacker   8-11, 16, 19, 37, 57, 60, 61, 63,
   65-67, 69, 73, 75-77, 79, 83, 117, 119,
   124, 128-132, 138, 143-148, 150, s152,
   153, 160, 161, 163, 165, 168, 171, 172,
   179, 180, 187, 192, 207, 211, 214, 215,
   224, 225, 230, 232, 234, 237, 257, 265,
   266, 278, 289, 318, 319, 325, 327-329,
   341
LaPorte   59, 286, 298, 300, 301, 304, 306-
   310, 313, 314, 333
Lavoisier   287
Leclercq   23, 30, 41, 285, 343
Leibniz   145, 146
Lepore   100, 227, 229, 318-320
Leslie   281, 283, 289, 290, 294, 295, 298,
   299, 301, 302, 304, 305, 309, 317, 318,
   324, 333, 339-341
Levinson   198
Lewis   11, 59, 61, 331, 332
Linnaeus   295

Linsky   39, 42, 43, 280
Liu   28, 29, 35, 42, 92, 194, 212, 255, 279-
   284, 286, 338, 339, 351, 352
Loar   35, 130, 211, 214, 218
Locke   112, 292, 293, 341
Löhr   120, 121, 197
Lombrozo   323
Ludlow   5-7, 61, 238, 239, 243
Lyons   205, 227

Malt   282, 283, 310-312, 315-318, 340
Marconi   26, 47, 72, 247, 270, 286, 289,
   346
Marcus, Barcan   294
Margolis   70, 138
Mates   47, 48, 96, 98-100, 102, 105
Mayr   297, 341
McCulloch   14, 23, 25, 38, 49, 59
McDowell   27-29, 70
McGeer   32, 214
McGinn   28
McKay   285, 294
Medin   340-342
Mellor   14, 45, 46, 58, 59
Mill   11, 296, 297
Millikan   22-24, 41, 168-170, 175, 188,
   189, 205, 218, 228, 229, 252
Minsky   195, 196

Naess   100, 105
Needham   39, 40, 51, 299-301, 303, 305,
   324, 330
Nelson   241
Newman   55
Nicholas   325
Nichols   324, 325
Noonan   28, 31, 33, 156, 309
Nuccetelli   29, 53, 75
Nunberg   318, 319, 325, 327, 328

Index (person name)

O'Brien 286
Okasha 297-299
Onofri 27, 34, 35, 135, 157, 244
Osherson 121
Owens 29, 76, 165-167, 205, 206, 212, 273

Pagin 331, 348-353
Papineau 142, 143, 163, 170
Peacocke 70, 120, 124, 131, 132, 142, 170, 194, 213
Perry 241, 242
Pinillos 223, 224
Place 186, 187, 190
Poesio 227, 318, 319, 327, 328, 330
Pollock 35, 219, 221, 226, 245, 267
Poncinie 11, 37, 39, 286, 304, 308
Porter 288
Priestley 288
Prinz 67, 121, 124, 135, 214
Putnam 7, 10, 12, 22-30, 32, 33, 35, 37-53, 55-60, 65, 66, 70, 71, 73-76, 79, 89, 92-95, 97, 98, 101-111, 113-117, 120, 125, 138, 141, 148, 149, 152, 186, 189, 193, 194, 196, 198, 200, 201, 203, 204, 212, 246-249, 251, 254, 255, 257, 262, 270, 271, 279-284, 286-294, 297-299, 302-312, 317, 318, 320, 322, 331-333, 337, 339, 342, 343, 347

Quilty-Dunn 319, 326
Quine 1, 12, 50, 55, 56, 80, 87, 95, 96, 98-106, 113, 127, 139, 169, 185, 194, 206, 252, 271, 274, 275, 298, 318, 345

Recanati 39, 40, 121-123, 157, 159, 160, 169, 170, 178, 187, 203, 219-221, 224, 240, 241, 243, 244, 249-259, 261, 262, 267-269, 285, 318, 325-331, 350
Redhead 305
Rescorla 234, 235, 238

Rey 12, 27, 62, 67, 69, 76, 100, 101, 104, 117, 118, 131, 133, 137-141, 165, 200, 262, 265, 293, 294
Robertson Ishii 43
Roques 227, 228
Rosch 118, 119, 294, 295
Rowlands 32, 52-54, 76

Saeed 83, 247
Sainsbury 14, 26-30, 41, 45, 69, 72, 82, 90, 95, 131, 132, 136, 138, 139, 154, 161-164, 166, 208, 228, 229, 287, 298
Sakai 1, 11, 24, 30, 36, 55, 79, 153, 165, 176, 239, 242, 246, 318, 326
Salmon 14, 41, 42, 44, 153
Sarich 286
Saul 242, 245
Sawyer 87-91, 113, 127, 199, 200, 281
Schiffer 157
Schroeter 31, 32, 41, 42, 52, 53, 72, 79, 90, 130, 157, 187, 223, 248, 266, 269, 270, 285
Schwartz 11, 26, 44, 45, 93, 109, 111-113, 127, 185, 198, 200, 286, 291, 340
Segal 11, 25, 26, 29, 33, 54-58, 68, 84, 120, 248, 267, 272-275
Sherman 10, 290
Skinner 3, 4
Smith 121, 218, 224, 225, 237
Soames 37, 44, 45, 301, 302, 306, 323, 324, 330
Sober 341
Sperber 350
Stalnaker 10, 28, 331
Stanley 170, 252, 261, 286, 287, 290
Sterelney 1, 287, 294
Stern 74, 285, 294, 333, 335
Steward 293, 309, 310, 316
Stich 25, 29, 62, 117
Stojnić 100, 229

387

Strawson   102, 104, 187, 188
Sweetser   8, 318, 319, 322, 326, 335, 336

Talmy   116, 147, 289
Taylor   74, 100, 110, 116-118, 122-124,
     132, 148, 194-197, 200, 201, 205, 206,
     227, 228, 235, 264, 265, 295, 318, 319,
     324, 325, 333
Tikhonov   305
Tobia   317, 319, 324
Tobin   12, 295
Tomasello   73
Tye   14, 26-30, 41, 45, 69, 72, 82, 90, 95,
     131, 136, 138, 154, 161-164, 166, 208,
     228, 229, 287

Unger   66, 67, 109

Valente   1, 11, 50, 82, 83, 85, 105, 193, 202,
     219, 244, 264-266, 270, 271
Volkov   305

Weisberg   307
Weiskopf   121, 243
Wellman   341, 342
White   96, 98, 99, 104, 254, 271, 284, 285
Wiggins   15, 42, 94, 169, 252, 261
Wikforss   10, 24, 27, 30, 36, 37, 41, 42, 45,
     46, 48-50, 55, 58, 80, 82, 84-87, 89-92,
     94-96, 98, 104, 106, 107, 125-127, 137,
     140, 149, 151, 152, 157, 164, 165, 167,
     168, 170, 182, 183, 185, 190-192, 199,
     200, 202, 204, 207, 208, 212, 213, 252,
     253, 264, 267, 268, 281, 283, 290, 291,
     294, 295, 299, 303, 304, 307, 310, 311,
     322, 331, 337, 338
Williamson   106, 107, 195
Wilson   5, 350
Woodfield   28, 170, 249, 251-257, 262, 263

Ziem   230-232

Author's Profile

Tomohiro Sakai is Professor of linguistics at the Faculty of Letters, Arts and Sciences at Waseda University in Japan, where he has been since 2014, after working as an assistant professor at Atomi University for three years. He received a Ph.D in Arts and Sciences from the University of Tokyo in 2003 and a Ph.D in Linguistics from the University of Paris VIII in 2004. He held a French Government Scholarship from 2001 to 2002 and was a research fellow of the Japan Society for the Promotion of Science from 2006 to 2009. His research interests include syntax, semantics, pragmatics, cognitive linguistics and philosophy of language and mind.

早稲田大学学術叢書 60

Semantic Externalism and Cognitive Linguistics

2024年9月20日　初版第1刷発行

著　者……………酒 井　智 宏
発行者……………須 賀　晃 一
発行所……………株式会社 早稲田大学出版部
　　　　　　　　〒169-0051　東京都新宿区西早稲田 1-9-12
　　　　　　　　TEL03-3203-1551　　https://www.waseda-up.co.jp
校正協力…………株式会社クリムゾン インタラクティブ ジャパン
本文組版…………株式会社ステラ
装　丁……………笠井亞子
印刷・製本………精文堂印刷株式会社

©Tomohiro Sakai 2024 Printed in Japan　　ISBN978-4-657-24701-8
無断転載を禁じます。落丁・乱丁本はお取替えいたします。

刊行のことば

　1913（大正2）年、早稲田大学創立30周年記念祝典において、大隈重信は早稲田大学教旨を宣言し、そのなかで、「早稲田大学は学問の独立を本旨と為すを以て　之が自由討究を主とし　常に独創の研鑽に力め以て　世界の学問に裨補せん事を期す」と謳っています。

　古代ギリシアにおいて、自然や社会に対する人間の働きかけを「実践（プラクシス）」と称し、抽象的な思弁としての「理論（テオリア）」と対比させていました。本学の気鋭の研究者が創造する新しい研究成果については、「よい実践（エウプラクシス）」につながり、世界の学問に貢献するものであってほしいと願わずにはいられません。

　出版とは、人間の叡智と情操の結実を世界に広め、また後世に残す事業であります。大学は、研究活動とその教授を通して社会に寄与することを使命としてきました。したがって、大学の行う出版事業とは大学の存在意義の表出であるといっても過言ではありません。これまでの「早稲田大学モノグラフ」「早稲田大学学術叢書」の2種類の学術研究書シリーズを「早稲田大学エウプラクシス叢書」「早稲田大学学術叢書」の2種類として再編成し、研究の成果を広く世に問うことを期しています。

　このうち、「早稲田大学学術叢書」は、アカデミック・ステイタスの維持・向上のための良質な学術研究書として刊行するものです。近年の学問の進歩はその速度を速め、専門性の深化に意義があることは言うまでもありませんが、一方で、複数の学問領域の研究成果や手法が横断的にかつ有機的に手を組んだときに、時代を画するような研究成果が出現することもあります。本叢書は、個人の研究成果のみならず、学問領域を異にする研究者による共同研究の成果を社会に還元する研究書でもあります。

　創立150周年に向け、世界的水準の研究・教育環境を整え、独創的研究の創出を推進している本学において、こうした研鑽の結果が学問の発展につながるとすれば、これにすぐる幸いはありません。

2016年11月

早稲田大学